ALSO BY GAVIN EDWARDS

Kindness and Wonder:
Why Mister Rogers Matters Now More Than Ever

The World According to Tom Hanks:
The Life, the Obsessions, the Good Deeds of
America's Most Decent Guy

The Beautiful Book of Exquisite Corpses:
A Creative Game of Limitless Possibilities (editor)

The Tao of Bill Murray:
Real-Life Stories of Joy, Enlightenment,
and Party Crashing

Can I Say: Living Large, Cheating Death,
and Drums Drums Drums
(with Travis Barker)

Last Night at the Viper Room:
River Phoenix and the Hollywood He Left Behind

VJ: The Unplugged Adventures of MTV's First Wave
(with Nina Blackwood, Mark Goodman,
Alan Hunter, and Martha Quinn)

Is Tiny Dancer Really Elton's Little John?:
Music's Most Enduring Mysteries, Myths,
and Rumors Revealed

'Scuse Me While I Kiss This Guy:
And Other Misheard Lyrics

BAD MOTHERFUCKER

The Life and Movies of Samuel L. Jackson, the Coolest Man in Hollywood

Gavin Edwards

hachette BOOKS

NEW YORK

Hachette Books
Hachette Book Group
1290 Avenue of the Americas
New York, NY 10104
HachetteBooks.com
Twitter.com/HachetteBooks
Instagram.com/HachetteBooks

First Edition: October 2021

Published by Hachette Books, an imprint of Perseus Books, LLC, a subsidiary of Hachette Book Group, Inc. The Hachette Books name and logo is a trademark of the Hachette Book Group.

The Hachette Speakers Bureau provides a wide range of authors for speaking events.

To find out more, go to www.hachettespeakersbureau.com or call (866) 376-6591.

The publisher is not responsible for websites (or their content) that are not owned by the publisher.

Print book interior design by Six Red Marbles

Library of Congress Control Number: 2021943801

ISBNs: 9780306924323 (hardcover); 9780306924309 (ebook)

Printed in the United States of America

LSC-C

Printing 1, 2021

For Jeff Jackson (no relation)

Contents

INTRODUCTION Worth of the Cool   1

  1   Half a Piece of Candy   11

  2   Desk Lamp (with Bulb)   21

  3   Little Cooked Onions   33

  4   Bill Cosby's Sweaters   41

  5   The Films of Samuel L. Jackson, 1977–1988   54

  6   Emergency Cord   65

  7   The Films of Samuel L. Jackson, 1989–1991   73

  8   Brown Envelope   88

  9   The Films of Samuel L. Jackson, 1992–1994   99

10   Two Lights and Some Batteries   119

11   The Films of Samuel L. Jackson, 1995–1998   130

12   Engraved Handle   150

13   The Films of Samuel L. Jackson, 1999–2001   158

14   Berry Popsicles   169

15   The Films of Samuel L. Jackson, 2002–2004   175

16   Rental Clubs   189

17   The Films of Samuel L. Jackson, 2005–2007   194

18   Eye Patch   209

19   The Films of Samuel L. Jackson, 2008–2011   218

20   Hot Poker   238

21   The Films of Samuel L. Jackson, 2012–2015   244

22   French Braid   264

23   The Films of Samuel L. Jackson, 2016–2018   270

24   Alligator Loafers   281

25   The Films of Samuel L. Jackson, 2019–2021   289

26   Greenhouse Roof   302

Acknowledgments   304

Look-at-Me Business   307

Sources   313

Index   341

say 'cool' all the time," Samuel L. Jackson told me. Jackson believed that "cool" was his second-most-used word but conceded that he didn't always wield it precisely, offering examples such as "Oh, yeah, that's cool" or "Oh, that would be very cool" or just "Cool." The most frequently uttered word in his vocabulary? You can probably guess it, but more on those four syllables soon.

"Hot," "hip," and "cool" have different meanings, even if they're sometimes used interchangeably on magazine covers. "Hot" delineates what is desirable in this moment: the new trend, the sex symbol, the consumer object so perfectly crafted that it unites the sins of lust and avarice. "Hip" is the state of enlightenment that leads to understanding the hidden architecture of square society. But "cool"? Cool is hip put into action; cool is necessary to make something hot. Cool is a way of life.

They're all social constructs, but while "hot" is evanescent and "hip" is malleable, "cool" is the value that endures. When you're cool enough, you're unruffled by the gyrations of popular culture, even as they spin faster and faster. And if you're really cool? Then you're Samuel L. Jackson.

What makes Jackson cool? To better understand the man, consider him playing a supporting role that's not among his best-loved or most-quoted: John "Ray" Arnold, the harried administrator in *Jurassic Park* who chain-smokes his way through the crisis when the power fails and the genetically engineered dinosaurs escape from their cages.

"I never feel like he's going to run up against somebody that he doesn't have the guts to confront," Hollywood screenwriter Matthew Aldrich said of Jackson. "But it's the fearlessness that comes from experience, as opposed to bravado, which is the opposite. I think back to *Jurassic Park*, where this whole movie he's got this hangdog look and always has this cigarette limply hanging from his mouth. I don't know how, but you can tell that somehow he has been here and done that already: this is like the third time he's worked at a park with dinosaurs, and he knows every way this is going to screw up."

Cool is calm in the face of a crisis. Cool is also the way you walk, the way you wear your hat, and the way you don't care what other people think of your life choices. Cool is a mask that you wear out in the world; if you put it on just right, it becomes your face.

And so Samuel L. Jackson has brought his personal cool to dozens of movie roles: gangsters and secret agents; superheroes and supervillains; Jedi and DJs; hit men, con men, and G-men. He's starred in *Hard Eight*, *The Hateful Eight*, and *1408*. He's acted in over 140 feature films in his career: more than Bill Murray and Tom Hanks put together. Because of his popularity, his relentless work ethic, and his willingness to play supporting roles in films big and small, he's achieved the largest cumulative box office of any movie star ever: as of 2021, over $8.1 billion in the USA and $19.4 billion worldwide. Asked about the record, Jackson will point out that most of that money "didn't end up in my pocket." But the residuals don't hurt: "I get paid all day, every day," he said. "Which is almost too much for a sensitive artist."

Jackson's a first-rate actor with a wider range than most people realize, but he doesn't appear in all those movies because he's a chameleon who disappears into each role with a new accent, barely recognizable as himself. He gets cast because he's cool: audiences not only enjoy spending time with him, they feel comfortable when he's onscreen, knowing that the movie's in good hands.

If cool is a mask that we wear in public, then what does it mean to be an actor known for playing cool roles? It means that the mask fits more naturally every time you put it on, and that it leaves an impression on your face. It means that people remember how you looked the last time you wore it—and are ready to believe that it isn't actually a mask at all.

Consider Lester Young (1909–1959), a jazz saxophonist who played in the Kansas City style. He's best known as a sideman to Count Basie and Billie Holiday, but one of the coolest people on the planet once told me a secret: Young's "Back to the Land," if played daily, could be a balm for the soul. (It's true.)

All jazzmen circa 1943 lived outside the cultural mainstream, but even in that demimonde, Young was an unusual figure. In an era not rich with gender ambiguity, he grew his hair long, gestured in a way people found effeminate, and routinely called other men "lady." Although his most famous nickname was "Prez," the other musicians in Basie's band called him "Miss Thing." Was Young gay? When asked, he said, "I never even auditioned!"

Young was a brilliant musician (arguably Holiday's greatest collaborator) and a pioneer gender bender, but his greatest legacy may be linguistic. Musician John Lewis said, "He was a living, walking poet. He was so quiet that when he talked, each sentence came out like a little explosion." Among Young's idiosyncratic slang terms: "Johnny Deathbed" for a sick person, "deep sea diver" for a particularly adept bass player, and most lastingly, "cool," in the modern sense of chilled-out hipness. (The word previously had negative connotations in American slang: Hemingway's 1939 short story "Night Before Battle," for example, included the dialogue "I'd like to cool you, you rummy fake Santa Claus.")

When there's no written record, it can be difficult to pinpoint who coined a particular slang term—if you want to fall into a rabbit hole sometime, try to figure out the earliest usage of "mullet" and whether Mike D of the Beastie Boys invented the term for the haircut or just popularized it—but a multitude of musicians who knew Young gave him the credit for "cool." One of the coolest cats ever gave us the vocabulary we needed to describe him and his impact.

To see the oral tradition of "cool" in action, think of Samuel L. Jackson teaching a young woman how to be cool. You may remember the moment: it happened in a Los Angeles diner, and he gave the lesson totally unfazed by the fact that she had a gun aimed at him most of the time. But as he told one of the two small-time stickup artists collecting people's wallets, "I hate to shatter your ego, but this ain't the first time I've had a gun pointed at me." As ever, Jackson had the fearlessness that comes with experience.

After he deposited his wallet in the bag held by Tim Roth, but before he gave a close reading of scripture, Jackson took charge of the situation, disarming Roth and jabbing his own gun into Roth's neck. The woman—Amanda Plummer—understandably freaked out, pointed her own gun at Jackson, and threatened to kill him.

"We're all going to be like three little Fonzies here," Jackson told her. "And what's Fonzie like?"

She fell silent, twitching, overwhelmed by the standoff.

"Come on, Yolanda, what's Fonzie like?" he shouted.

"Cool?" she offered hesitantly, desperate to get the answer right.

"What?"

"Cool," she said, a hair more confidently.

"Correctamundo!"

The lessons of cool, as learned in the Hawthorne Grill in the final scene of *Pulp Fiction*: Stay calm in an emergency. Apply your overarching philosophy to the smaller moments of your existence. Walk in the footsteps of your cool predecessors.

The Fonz was cool, even if it was cool as distilled through a 1970s sitcom: Henry Winkler played Arthur "Fonzie" Fonzarelli with such tough-guy élan that even later-season misadventures (most famously, Fonzie on water skis and in a leather jacket, jumping over a shark) diminished the show rather than the character.

Some other members of the Cool Hall of Fame: Questlove. Keith Richards. Nina Simone. Prince. Robert Mitchum. Patti Smith. Frida Kahlo. Leonard Cohen. Poly Styrene. Serena Williams. Alan Turing. Richard Pryor. Calvin (the tiger king, not the sixteenth-century theologian). Toshiro Mifune. There are many more; you will have your own nominations.

Impeccably cool pop star Harry Styles watched *Pulp Fiction* for the first time when he was just thirteen years old: "probably too young," he admitted. He imprinted on Jackson playing Jules Winnfield and wanting to follow the master, "saved up money from my paper route to buy a 'Bad Motherfucker' wallet. Just a stupid white kid in the English countryside with that wallet."

"Cool," like so many of humanity's bedrock inventions, really started in Africa. The concept of coolness—often associated with water, chalk, and any other substance that renders you so fresh and so clean— extends across many African languages. In Yoruba, "enun tutu" means "cool mouth," while in Kikuyu, "kanua kohoro" means "cool tongue": both describe the power of keeping silent instead of running your fool mouth.

"This is the mask of mind itself," art historian Robert Farris Thompson wrote of these idioms and how they shaped behavior. Thompson distilled this West African definition of cool: "The ability to be nonchalant at the right moment, to reveal no emotion in situations where excitement and sentimentality are acceptable—in other words, to act as though one's mind were in a different world."

The idea of emotional reserve is found in non-African cultures: you may be familiar with French sangfroid or the British pride in keeping a stiff upper lip. What distinguished the African version of stoicism was that coolness was an important posture not just in times of stress, but during celebrations and dances. It took real talent to look casual during those exuberant, expressive moments: that's why we marvel at movie actors who retain their cool, even while engaged in absurd exercises in make-believe, such as interacting with computer-generated extraterrestrials in front of a bright green screen.

Actor Hugh Laurie once told me that the quality of detached cool was why Cary Grant might have been the greatest of all twentieth-century film stars: "He always looked aware of the fact that he was in a film. He was amused by his predicament: not the predicament of his character but the predicament of Cary Grant in a film."

Or as Thompson put it, describing unruffled detachment in the African context: "Manifest within this philosophy of the cool is the belief that the purer, the cooler a person becomes, the more ancestral he becomes. In other words, mastery of self enables a person to transcend time and elude preoccupation."

In a cloud of cigarette smoke, jazz musicians were the modern American architects of the attitude that Lester Young gave the name of cool—with beatnik writers following right behind them. In 1957, Miles Davis released the album *Birth of the Cool*, collecting recordings he made with musicians who included saxophonist Gerry Mulligan and drummer Max Roach, responding to the heated invention of bebop by opening the doors to the chill-out room. That same year, Jack Kerouac published *On the Road*, an autobiographical novel composed on a single roll of paper that inspired a generation to head out on the New Jersey Turnpike to look for America.

In his autobiography, Davis acknowledged the inspiration of white bandleader Claude Thornhill on those sessions, but took pains to strip any white influences out of his story: "We were trying to sound like Claude Thornhill, but he had gotten his shit from Duke Ellington and Fletcher Henderson." Given that the music of Ellington and Henderson blended jazz and African music with European symphonic traditions, this isn't as pure a through line as Davis touted. While coolness is sometimes just code for Blackness, cool in the United States doesn't exist without a variety of racial influences mingling in a complex legacy.

Also in 1957, Central High School in Little Rock was integrated by nine African American teenagers. (The governor of Arkansas sent out the Arkansas National Guard to stop the teens from entering the school; President Dwight Eisenhower responded by federalizing the Arkansas National Guard and ordering them to protect the students.) The Little

Rock Nine walked to school through a jeering white mob, serene and self-possessed, maintaining their cool in the face of mortal danger. One of them, Minnijean Brown-Trickey, later said, "What bothered them was that we were as arrogant as they were."

In Chattanooga, Tennessee, four hundred miles east of Little Rock, 1957 marked the ninth birthday of Samuel L. Jackson, also living in a segregated world. The older he got, the more white people he knew, but when he was a child, almost everyone he met was Black. Growing up under segregation didn't make Jackson angry: it forged his steely cool. But as an adult, he became enraged by the voices of conservative politicians, inheritors to the traditions of his childhood oppressors. "They're the same fucking guys," he said. "And when I hear their voices, I hear the same voices. Those twangs where they didn't specifically call you 'nigger,' they said 'nigra.' 'The nigras.' There was no doubt about where they stood—that you were never going to be their equal and, if possible, they were going to make sure you never had as much shit as they had."

Miles Davis began his autobiography by writing, "The greatest feeling I ever had in my life—with my clothes on—was when I first heard Diz and Bird together." The year was 1944; Dizzy Gillespie and Charlie Parker were playing together in Billy Eckstine's band, inventing the bop sound every night. Parker (aka Bird) became an icon of cool for both his visionary genius and his dissolute lifestyle: shooting up heroin, pissing in phone booths, pawning his horn right before a gig so he could score and then getting brilliant sounds out of a last-minute substitute, such as a child's plastic saxophone. When Parker died, just thirty-four years old, the coroner estimated his age as somewhere between fifty and sixty years old.

Gillespie, on the other hand, lived to age seventy-five, married to the same woman for over fifty years. Although he had an impeccably cool CV, having been an innovator both of bebop and Afro-Cuban jazz, he didn't feel the compulsion to burn himself out like his partner. In his New Jersey home, the icebox held a stash of nonalcoholic beer; asked about his abstemious nature, Gillespie used to joke, "I was always afraid of needles." He knew that his cool wasn't built on self-destruction.

While Samuel L. Jackson cultivated a hellacious addiction to freebasing cocaine, he ultimately chose Dizzy's path instead of Bird's: getting clean after he turned forty, he then proceeded not just to stick around for a few more decades but to do his best work. When he wasn't on a movie set, he didn't show up at hot clubs or in tabloid photographs: he played golf and binge-watched *Law & Order*. "Most people would be surprised at how boring my life actually is," he confessed. But when he was working, he transformed into an international movie star—and he seemed to be working all the time, often making five or six movies in a year.

Growing up, Jackson played a variety of brass and woodwind instruments. He fantasized about being a jazz musician—a dream that ended abruptly in eleventh grade when he discovered that he wasn't a good musical improviser. But he had already absorbed the jazzman code of cool, and it turned out that Jackson did just fine working from a script.

Jazz scholar Gary Giddins wrote of Gillespie, "At the time he turned sixty, Gillespie said he had once thought that playing the trumpet would get easier over time, but that it got harder—not because his lip was showing wear, but because he had exhausted so many ideas that he used to explore. He could spell himself with comedy and other diversions, but in the heat of improvisation, he was saved only by the truth." Similarly, Jackson made so many movies that his cadences and crescendos became familiar—but if he lost some of his ability to surprise audiences, his accumulated body of work revealed his true, coolest self.

Jackson had something else in common with Gillespie: musicality. Gillespie's chosen instrument was the trumpet, specifically a horn with a bell bent at a forty-five-degree angle. Jackson's instrument was his own voice, especially as he applied it to obscenity. When Jackson cursed, it was a tone poem built around the two iambic feet in one compound noun that he said was the word in the English language he deployed most often: *motherfucker.*

"I use 'motherfucker' at least eight times a paragraph," Jackson told me. "I refer to everything as a motherfucker. I say, 'Oh this shit was a motherfucker' or 'Do you know what that motherfucker was like?' or 'Well, you know, the motherfucking thing.' That's my perfect noun/pronoun/expletive/everything."

Rolling around in Jackson's mouth, the profane becomes sacred. Not just punctuation, not just emphasis, but the raw material for verbal solos that can sing with rage or swing with awe at the enormity of the universe. To help us better understand the work of a master artist, when writing about each of his movies, I've tabulated every one of his curses. In the "Films of Samuel L. Jackson" chapters, look for the census under the heading "Expletives not deleted" for the count of each *fuck, asshole,* and *shitfire*—and yes, *motherfucker.*

Many of us still pepper our speech with "cool" (or if you're a sitcom character like Jake on *Brooklyn Nine-Nine* or Abed on *Community,* perhaps the "cool cool cool" triple-lutz variation). But we live in an era where cool feels like a cultural value as outmoded as chivalry or courtly love. In an anxious, sweaty time, we suffer from the dearth of the cool.

That's not because corporations suddenly began employing "cool" as a marketing strategy: there have always been cool products and accessories that consumers can acquire as easily as Snoopy slips into a "Joe Cool" sweatshirt. Shortly after the end of World War II, the Fox Bros. tailors in Chicago advertised their "leopard skin jacket as worn by Dizzy Gillespie": mail-order cool for the low price of $2.50.

Celebrity endorsements go as far back as the notion of celebrities—the British royal family has long issued royal warrants of appointment to businesses that it frequents—but maybe reached their pinnacle with the 1980s rock-'n'-roller cola wars, when Michael Jackson, David Bowie, Tina Turner, and Madonna all lent their cool to the multinational conglomerate PepsiCo. In the twenty-first century, however, those without cool—who George Clinton personified on Parliament-Funkadelic albums as Sir Nose d'Voidoffunk—learned how to fake the funk. Gesturing in the direction of cool proved to be enough in many situations and made it look as if cool had been reduced to a collection of gestures.

The modern world exists most purely on social media: on Twitter and Instagram and Facebook, it seems like everyone is marketing themselves, each individual trying to sell themselves like a two-liter bottle of Crystal Pepsi. Ironically, everyone's thirsty but nobody's buying. Social media is built on our shared vocabulary of cool, translated by advertising agencies and then quoted once again by the general population, telling anyone who will listen how groovy their lives are.

A fundamental component of cool is being unconcerned what other people think of you. That's what lets people lead revolutions and pull off improbable gowns on Oscar night. That's part of why politics and cool often don't blend well—nobody would mistake C-SPAN's live feed of the Senate floor for MTV's red carpet at the Video Music Awards. And the disengaged stance of the hipster isn't very effective in the world of public affairs; "Whatever, man" doesn't scale up well.

It turns out that cool is a more important value for the citizens of a healthy society than it is for its political leaders. And although cool seems out of phase right now, it's still essential as a counterweight to the prevailing trends of emotional clickbait and brazen spon-con hucksterism. Cool can help you spin the world on a different axis, and it can make your corner of it a better place while you're trying to enact miracles of gravity. And the patron saint of twenty-first-century cool? Samuel motherfucking Jackson.

"I'm comfortable in the skin I'm in," Jackson said. "For so long I was uncomfortable being who I was. I did drugs, drank, and did all that other shit to kind of keep the world off me, keep myself from feeling the stuff I was feeling. I was insecure, worrying about my stutter, about not having a job, about not being as rich or successful as the next guy. Those things don't bother me anymore. I've been fortunate enough to play some characters people perceive in a certain way. That's rubbed off on me, so people attribute those character traits to me."

Jackson added, "I don't know where the 'King of Cool' moniker came from or how it evolved. But it had a lot to do with *Pulp Fiction* and how even-keeled Jules was. He was such a professional. Minimum movement, he doesn't get distracted—he's a straight-line guy and people found that cool."

Jackson knew there was a huge gulf between himself and Jules: his reaction in a situation where two parties were pointing guns at each other would probably involve high-pitched screaming. But his steady devotion to his own work not only constructed images of cool for other people to emulate and quote, it made the man himself cool.

"It was no burden to be cool," Jackson said. "I just present myself as I am."

BLACK SNAKE MOAN

Years later, he would say that the "L" stood for "Lucky." But on December 21, 1948, he was not yet able to make his own reality with the force of his will and his imagination, and so he was born in Washington, D.C., as Samuel Leroy Jackson.

His mother, Elizabeth Harriett Montgomery Jackson, twenty-five years old, had moved to the nation's capital from Tennessee during World War II: she and her sister Frances had been recruited by the U.S. Navy for jobs as clerks and typists. His father, Roy Henry Jackson, just nineteen years old, was on duty as a private in the Army (he would later fight in the Korean War).

In Jackson's memory, his mother was always walking fast, striding through life. As a child, he needed to hang on to her skirt if he wanted to keep up with her. He had no childhood memories of his father: Roy visited his son only once before abandoning the family.

His parents split up before Sam's first birthday; Elizabeth brought her son home to her parents' house in Chattanooga, Tennessee. Loath to give up a great job—she would eventually receive a Recognition of Service Award from the Bureau of Navy Personnel—she left young Sam to be raised by her mother and father, Pearl and Edgar Montgomery, and returned to D.C., making the six-hundred-mile trip to Chattanooga at irregular intervals.

"My grandfather was my best friend," Jackson said. Edgar worked at a hotel, running an elevator. In the evenings, he was a maintenance man, cleaning three different offices in a one-block area. Pearl also had a full-time job, as domestic help. The young boy absorbed a simple but crucial life lesson: adults woke up in the morning and they went to work. Sometimes Edgar would bring Sam along on his janitorial rounds. The young boy would help empty the wastebaskets, and when Edgar used the buffer, the heavy-duty machine that polished the floors, he would let his grandson ride on top of it.

The family lived at 310½ Lookout Street, in a Black neighborhood in a segregated southern city. The neighborhood was poor, but the Montgomerys were working class. "I was never hungry and I was never ragged," Jackson said. Nearby were two (white) houses of prostitution and three different houses selling moonshine liquor, which customers could purchase by the shot, the half pint, or the half gallon. "There'd be bullets flying occasionally, the occasional knife fight, there were drunks passing through the neighborhood—but there were all these old people that took care of us." Any neighbor who spotted young Sam getting into trouble would inevitably tell his grandparents about it. When Sam came home, corporal punishment awaited—often, that meant getting whipped with a switch. He'd know he was in trouble the moment he walked through the door, because his grandparents would be calling him Samuel, not Sam.

The Montgomery house was small but nevertheless had a front room, off-limits to Sam except when company came to visit: it had the good rugs, the starched curtains, and the three-tier tables with little figurines. There were a lot of hungry kids in the neighborhood, so Pearl was constantly baking. At 310½ Lookout Street, the cookie jar was never empty; any kid who visited the house would get fed.

"I grew up with segregation in the South," Jackson said. "But my world was full." If his grandmother took him downtown, she had to teach him the boundaries of legalized racism, such as the separate water fountains for white people and colored people. Almost everybody Jackson saw was Black, with a few exceptions, such as the white kids on a school bus that would pass through his neighborhood, who would "unscrew the lightbulbs from inside and throw them at us, yelling 'Nigger!'"

There was one white family in the neighborhood, generally looked down on as "P.W.T.": "Poor White Trash." But although their house had no running water and so they would bathe only when it rained, the white family always called Jackson "nigger boy" and his grandmother "Miss Nigger"—always "Miss," as if it were "a term of respect," Jackson remembered. When his grandfather went to work, Jackson noticed, twenty-year-old white guys would call him Ed or Edgar, and his grandfather would always call them Mister. The white men would rub Sam's head—and he'd look them straight in the eye. At first he did that because he didn't know that he wasn't supposed to; later on, he did it just to discomfit them.

"My grandfather was this old guy, very dignified, but he never looked 'em in the eye. He'd look at me like, 'Turn your head down! Don't look the white men in the eye 'cause they'll think you being uppity or arrogant.'" Jackson recognized later that his grandfather was just trying to teach him survival skills. "It was very dangerous being a Black man in the era when he grew up," he said.

One day when Sam was five, he was sitting on the front porch of the family home and he whistled at a white girl walking by. His grandparents feared for his life: "Everybody was out of the house, snatching me up, hitting me. Because I could have been killed for that."

Jackson remembered his childhood fondly, because it was full of love, but he was fully aware that it was walled in by segregation. "You had to learn how to live in a society where your life was devalued," he said. "My family would point out this or that person as a Klansman or a grand wizard and tell me who specifically those men had killed and gotten away with it just because they'd said that Black person was doing this or that. You could not look suspicious, because when people can accuse you of anything, there's nothing you can say. They'd tell me not to get in a car with this or that policeman, saying, 'I don't care what happens, you run and run till you get here, and then we'll deal with it here.'"

If somebody in the family got sick, they wouldn't necessarily go to the doctor or the hospital—"we figured they weren't going to see us anyway," Jackson said. Instead, the Montgomerys would call on the woman known as "the root lady," who would come over, smear your body with herbal ointments ("very stinky stuff"), and chant.

Jackson loved listening to the radio, sitting on the porch with his grandfather in the evenings: serials like *The Shadow* and *Sergeant Preston of the Yukon* and the popular if perniciously stereotypical comedy *Amos 'n' Andy*, firing his imagination and teaching him how voices can create their own worlds. And sometimes his grandfather told him ghost stories with local flavor: a school bus had turned over nearby, and if you went to the scene of the tragedy at a certain time of night, you could hear the squealing of old tires and the panicked screams of children.

The precocious Jackson learned to read at an early age, around two or three. When he was alone in his room, he would sometimes stand in front of his mirror, acting out the stories that thrilled him, pretending to be the characters in his favorite books. He said, "I was acting for myself before I ever did it for anybody else."

For every five comic books, he was required to read something more substantial. "We were always told we had to be five, ten times smarter; had to act differently because we were representing not just ourselves, but the race, when we went out. People in the community had expectations, and you respected the people who had those expectations. You didn't resent the teacher, the preachers. You didn't resent the police, even."

His aunt Edna Montgomery, who received a performing arts degree at the historically Black university North Carolina A&T, was also living at 310½ Lookout Street; she had returned to Chattanooga to teach the fourth grade. Before Jackson officially enrolled in school, she would sometimes bring him to her classroom and sit him at the back. If one of her students didn't know the answer to one of her questions, she would call on her young nephew, who invariably did know. Then, at lunchtime, Jackson would have to defend himself physically against the older kids who were angry they had been shown up by a preschooler.

Aunt Edna also made Sam join the dance classes that she taught, both tap and modern; the modern dance classes featured the kids doing unusual neck movements to the music of Yma Sumac, the Peruvian soprano with a five-octave range. Twice a year, Aunt Edna was responsible for putting on a pageant: the audience was the members of the school board and other white Chattanooga panjandrums, "to see how the young Negroes were advancing." The children would recite poems, sing and dance, and wear costumes. Aunt Edna never had enough boys available, so over the years, Sam was drafted against his will to play Humpty Dumpty, a Chinese man with a pigtail, and the Sugar Plum Fairy in the *Nutcracker Suite*. "I was always crying when she dragged me out of the house," he said.

On Sundays, Jackson had to wear his best clothes and go to Sunday school. Sometimes the Sunday school teacher would suddenly announce that she wanted everyone to recite a Bible verse. Because "Jesus wept" and John 3:16 would always be claimed before Jackson got his turn, he memorized an unusual passage that he knew nobody else would say, John 3:8: "The wind bloweth where it listeth and thou hearest the sound thereof, but can't tell whither it goeth or whither it cometh, for so is everyone born of the spirit."

Jackson's favorite day of the week was Saturday: he would spend the entire day at the movies, leaving 310½ Lookout Street around nine a.m. and getting home around ten p.m. Chattanooga had two movie theaters for Black audiences, the Liberty and the Grand, and at either one he could take in a full program of newsreels, cartoons, serials, and double features: movies ranging from *Francis the Talking Mule* to *Creature from the Black Lagoon* to westerns starring Gene Autry or Roy Rogers or Lash LaRue. One of his favorites was *The Crimson Pirate*, starring Burt Lancaster.

On days when he wasn't at the movies, he reenacted the onscreen adventures that enthralled him, having epic pirate adventures with other neighborhood kids, or sometimes staging fight scenes on nearby Civil War battlefields: they would substitute bicycles for horses, roll down hills, and give everyone their own theme song. "But there was a time of day when I needed to stop and go read my book," Jackson said. "Go into my head world. I didn't want to run and jump and hear them make noise anymore."

He liked being an only child, enjoyed his own company, savored the feeling that it was him against the world. "And I was a selfish child," he said. If he was instructed to share a piece of candy, he would throw his half away: "If I couldn't eat the whole thing, I didn't get any satisfaction out of it." He learned to be alone, entertaining himself for hours on end, and "not to have separation anxiety. I would see my mother maybe two times a year. She'd leave, and there was nothing I could do about it. I learned to accept it. If a person leaves me, I immediately forget them. I don't dwell on people who leave."

Jackson did have a stutter—one that became so bad that he barely uttered a word through the entire fourth grade. The thoughts racing through his mind were colorful and nuanced, but he couldn't get them out of his head. He was passing all his tests and his sympathetic teachers knew he could read, so they let him stay silent. Aunt Edna took him to a speech therapist, but Jackson said that the library was even more helpful: he found some books on breathing exercises and taught himself how to avoid the worst effects of the stutter. And as his vocabulary increased, he could navigate around words that were impossible to say on a particular day. (The stutter never went away entirely: even as an adult, he said, "There are still days when I have my n-n-n days or r-r-r days. I try to find another word." He noted that James Earl Jones and Bruce Willis each had a childhood stutter. Having to concentrate intensely on something that most people take for granted—the simple act of saying a sentence—can give actors unusually powerful speaking voices as they grow older.)

When Jackson was in the fifth grade, his mother, Elizabeth, moved back to Chattanooga, into her parents' house and back into Sam's life. She found work at a clothing store called Young Ages, just across the state line in Rossville, Georgia. (Chattanooga hugs the southern border of Tennessee.) Jackson said that his mother's job as a buyer kept his closet well-stocked: "She always worked at sample shows with the owners, so she always came back home with all this stuff that people were going to be wearing next season, so I never looked like anybody else. But she dressed me very Ivy League, so I wore a lot of Ivy League clothes, so I didn't get to dress in the hip clothes that everybody else was wearing, so I was kind of square, but well-dressed." That meant sweater vests, corduroys, "herringbones, and patches on the elbows, and oxford shoes and button-down shirts with monograms, that kind of shit."

310½ Lookout Street was more crowded than ever, and always seemed to be full of women. When his mother had friends over, entertaining in the front room, sometimes they would summon Sam to demonstrate the latest dances, like the Twist or the Jerk. The older ladies would watch with avid curiosity, saying that they'd throw out their backs if they even tried to duplicate his moves. He would get not only applause but loose change: "The ladies would give you quarters, dimes, whatever."

Jackson grew even closer with his grandfather. "We took the heat in the house, because it was a house full of women," he said. And he watched how Edgar handled conflict with Pearl. "He told me not to talk back!" Jackson said. "There's only one way to have an argument—and that's if two people are having it."

Elizabeth wanted Sam to participate in traditionally male activities: she made sure that her son played Little League baseball. "She sent me out of the house," he said. "She always made sure I was doing *guy* stuff."

Jackie Robinson had broken the color line in Major League Baseball the year before Jackson was born, but Chattanooga Little League, like everything else in Tennessee, was divided between Black and white. "Segregation was just a way of life," Jackson said. "It was nothing to worry about." He was sometimes puzzled by the odder manifestations of racism: he wondered why when he went to the movies, Sidney Poitier's character always seemed to die. But segregation seemed like an immutable reality, and so not worth railing against.

Then, when Sam was in sixth grade, his grandmother took him and his cousin Wanda on a train trip across the country to Los Angeles to visit his aunt. In California, for the first time, Jackson saw white people and Black people together. "What's happening here? What is this?" the stunned boy thought. Thousands of miles away from home, he had a revelation: not only could the world operate with new rules, some parts of it already did.

Every summer, Jackson would go to a different world of his own:

his grandfather's sister's farm, in rural Georgia. "All her kids and me running up and down dirt roads, feeling all that freedom," he remembered. He saw his grandfather's brothers doing backbreaking work in the fields, moving slowly and efficiently. He saw how they had very strict moral guidelines but would drink on weekends. He saw cows and chickens doing what came naturally. And soon enough, he was doing it too.

"There was a family of girls who lived through the woods from us, and we all used to meet at this creek and swim naked," he said. "I was about 10 or 11. I think two of the girls were about 14, 15, so that's when it happened. Girls were interesting to me, period. They could be fat, skinny, tall, short, ugly, beautiful—as long as they were willing to do that thing."

Back in Chattanooga, everybody in the Black community seemed to know each other: "There were only two Black schools," he said. Many of Jackson's teachers had previously taught his mother, and her brothers and sisters. They knew he was expected to go to college, and so when other kids were learning to diagram sentences, he was allowed to go to the other side of the room and read *Beowulf* and Shakespeare.

Jackson didn't hang out in the street with other kids; when his friends started making plans that were going to end up with people getting in trouble, he'd head home. He knew the one cardinal rule: don't embarrass his family. If somehow he ended up in jail, he was pretty sure they would come visit him, but they wouldn't do anything to get him out.

On the afternoon of February 1, 1960, four freshmen at North Carolina A&T State University (Aunt Edna's alma mater) walked into the Woolworth's department store in Greensboro, North Carolina. They bought a few sundries—toothpaste, a hairbrush—and then sat down at the store's lunch counter and asked to be served. The facilities were segregated: white people were allowed to sit at the counter, while Black people were supposed to buy their food only from the "stand-up counter." By sitting at the counter, the quartet were facing arrest; they were risking physical assault, maybe even death; they were reclaiming their dignity from a racist system that had tried to strip it from them every day. One of them, Franklin McCain, said years later, "Almost instantaneously, after sitting down on a simple, dumb stool, I felt so relieved. I felt so clean, and I felt as though I had gained a little bit of my manhood by that simple act."

Refusing to serve them, the store closed early instead, and the four young men returned to campus to tell their fellow students what had happened. More protesters came to Woolworth's every day: three days later, there were hundreds of them. The movement inspired similar sit-ins in dozens of other segregated cities—including Chattanooga. On February 19, Black students from Howard High School began peacefully sitting in at the lunch counters of the variety stores in Chattanooga's downtown. The movement grew until five days later, there were thousands of people, Black and white, milling around in the streets downtown. Chattanooga's mayor, P. R. "Rudy" Olgiati, ordered the streets cleared, and the fire department turned its hoses on the crowd: shamefully, the first southern city to assault civil rights protesters in that fashion, but not the last.

The demonstrations continued in Chattanooga until August, when all the city's lunch counters were integrated; three years later, all public facilities in the city were integrated. The sit-in movement had similar success across the South—and was an important milestone toward segregation being struck down nationally by the Civil Rights Act of 1964. They also directly led to the formation of the Student Nonviolent Coordinating Committee; the SNCC became a central national organization for college students fighting for civil rights.

Jackson, just eleven years old, took part in the sit-ins but didn't tell anyone in his family he was doing so. "I would participate, sit at the lunch counter," he said. "And when the police would show up, I would just run!"

When Jackson got to seventh grade, he had some classmates who were seventeen or eighteen: they were, essentially, grown men, but they had just gotten out of reform school and were still on a junior-high academic level. "They used to take our money or you had to do their homework for them," Jackson said. But to his surprise, they looked out for him if he was getting hassled on the street in his neighborhood: "Sam from Lookout Street? Yeah, I know him. I know his mama. Leave him alone."

As Jackson saw it, "my job was to go to school and bring home good grades. I was on the honor roll, I swam, ran, and did my homework. I didn't stay out late. I was more concerned about the consequences I'd face at home than I was about peer pressure."

When he reached Riverside High School, Jackson was still bookish, but he sometimes stayed out late enough on Saturday nights that he looked conspicuously red-eyed when the family went to Sunday services at the Wiley Memorial United Methodist Church. "We drank beer like soda," he said. His mother made it clear that he wasn't allowed to miss church; the compromise was that he wore sunglasses.

Like generations of overachieving high school kids before and after him, Sam filled up his time with extracurricular activities. He joined the model United Nations. He played trumpet, flute, and French horn in the marching band; he knew he had great style on the field when the band performed, but he also knew it wasn't the coolest activity. He swam competitively and ran hurdles on the track team. "I definitely didn't have the hot chicks," he complained. "I was popular because I was funny." But he was, nevertheless, popular enough to be elected senior class president.

When he talked about growing up under segregation, Jackson often tried to shrug it off, emphasizing the happy aspects of his childhood and minimizing how it affected him. But "I had anger in me," he conceded. "It came from growing up suppressed in a segregated society. All those childhood years of 'whites only' places and kids passing you on the bus, yelling 'Nigger!' There was nothing I could do about it then. I couldn't even say some of the things that made me angry—it would have gotten me killed. But I had a dream of my own. I was determined to get out and make my family proud."

Jackson's family wanted him to have a "productive" career: basically, that meant being a doctor, a lawyer, or maybe a teacher. Chattanooga didn't have a Black pediatrician, so his mother hoped he would fill that gap. Jackson, meanwhile, wanted to get as far away from Tennessee as he could. He was a candidate for the Naval Academy at Annapolis, and he also applied to UCLA, Cal Berkeley, and the University of Hawaii. "I had read too many books about the world, and I wanted to see it," he said.

When his mother found out he had signed up for a berth on a merchant marine ship, she made Jackson's decision for him. "My mother had it in her mind that I was going to Morehouse College in Atlanta," he said, "and that's where I went."

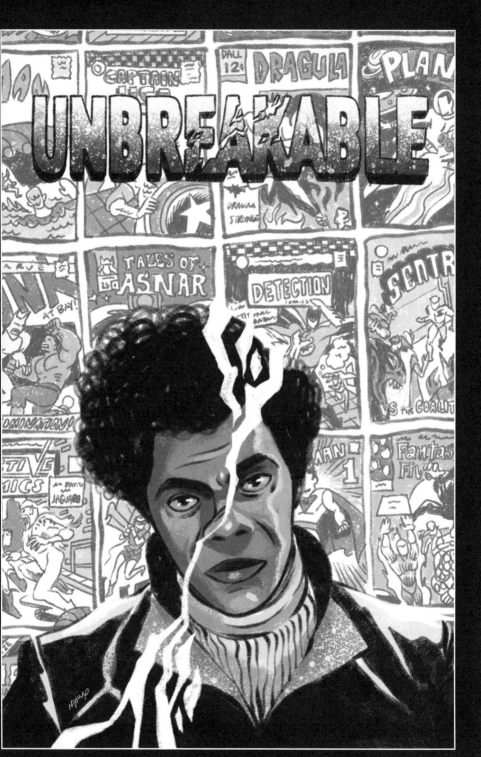

Nicole Goux.

Self-mastery, symmetrical character, high ideals and purposes are regarded as the chief end of education." So read the *Morehouse College Bulletin*, the handbook issued to all students arriving on campus in the fall of 1966. It laid out the college's lofty ideals: "The character of the work done and the increasing efficiency of every department insure the highest and most lasting results in the lives of the students and those among who they will labor."

Morehouse, an all-male college in Atlanta founded two years after the Civil War, was one of the most prestigious of the nation's historically Black colleges and universities. The school carefully guarded the reputation of its graduates, approximately 225 a year, whom they called Morehouse men; its most famous alumnus was Dr. Martin Luther King Jr. "We were told that we were in the top tenth of the Black race that was going to lead everybody out of the darkness into the light," Samuel L. Jackson remembered. "At that time something like seventy-five percent of all the [Black] doctors in America were Morehouse men. Morehouse men were publishers, editors, they were the leaders of the race."

That dream of a respectable future was why Elizabeth pushed Sam to attend Morehouse, and why Edgar and Pearl were willing to mortgage 310½ Lookout Street to pay the necessary fees: in the 1966–1967 academic year, Morehouse cost a minimum of $1,430 for tuition, room, board, and laundry. (Adjusted for inflation, that would be the equivalent of $11,545 in 2021.) "Each student will supply his own linens, blankets and desk lamp (with bulb)," warned the *Bulletin*.

On Sunday, September 11, 1966, Morehouse freshmen were allowed to move into their dormitories starting at eight a.m. Jackson's mother dropped him off—with linens, blankets, and desk lamp—and drove back home, secure in the belief that in the arms of Morehouse, he would be safe from temptation. She was wrong. "I went wild," Jackson said.

As soon as his mother was gone, Jackson left the Morehouse campus, bought a quart of beer, and walked up the street to a basketball court he had spotted. He asked who was up next and spent the rest of the day in the projects. (University Homes, right next to the Morehouse campus, was the first housing project in the United States for Black families built with federal funds.) "I balled with them, hung out with them that night," Jackson said. His new friends had no idea he was a Morehouse student and assumed he had just moved into their neighborhood.

Jackson was back on campus for the first day of freshman orientation, which tried to instill Morehouse's ideals and to intimidate the new arrivals with the school's rigors. The students were given the traditional speech where they were told to look to their left, and then to look to their right: one of those people (spoiler alert!) won't be here next year.

Jackson arrived at Morehouse planning to major in marine biology; he wanted to be an oceanographer, because of watching *Sea Hunt* on TV (the adventure series starring Lloyd Bridges as an underwater diver), not to mention being a huge fan of the classic submarine yarn *20,000 Leagues Under the Sea* (the Jules Verne novel more than the 1954 Disney film). He dreamed of being the Black Jacques Cousteau—despite growing up more than three hundred miles from the nearest ocean.

"For the first time, I was on my own. I did all the things I didn't do in high school: got drunk, stayed up all night playing cards, had lots of girlfriends," Jackson said. (Morehouse was a men's college, but its sister school, the historically Black women's school Spelman College, was right across the street.) "Still, I went to class and maintained a B average."

And Jackson kept going back to the projects to play basketball with his friends in the hood, who called him Slim. "I was there every day, and a long time most of the days," he said. Having been admitted to the ebony tower, he felt more comfortable standing outside it, with the townies—or as they were known around campus, "the block boys." Jackson described them fondly: "The reprobates who stood on the corner. They smoked weed, they drank wine, they drank beer, they talked shit. A lot. That was us."

The block boys thought that Morehouse students were stuck up, or in the slang of the day, "saditty." (The modern equivalent would be "bougie.") Jackson agreed with them: he saw how his fellow students not only thought they were superior to the locals, they had that belief reinforced by the school's administration. "They ignored those people who lived in the community—they invaded these people's community and felt they were there to run it." So when the block boys said hello to the Morehouse men, they often wouldn't get a response. "And that would be cause for a beating," Jackson said. "Or they would run 'em back to campus. Mainly because they wouldn't speak."

Sometimes the block boys would rob Morehouse students, which didn't bother Jackson. "Ninety percent of the time, they were correct in that the person they were taking stuff from could afford to have it taken. And they were people with petit-bourgeois ideas who needed a lesson like that in reality."

One time, however, their victim was somebody Jackson knew from school. He looked Jackson in the eyes, but before Jackson could say anything, somebody hit the student: the block boys relieved the student of his valuables and they all left. "As a result of that, I ended up in the dean's office," Jackson said. "Because the guy did recognize me, he did report the robbery, and did say that I was with them. As a consequence of that, I was put on probation a few times, because I refused to identify the people who did it."

Jackson ran with the block boys for six months before they found out he went to Morehouse: they spotted him at a dance where Jackson showed up wearing Morehouse gear. "Slim, you actually go to college?" one of them asked, dumbfounded. Jackson admitted that he did—and so, in a very small way, he improved town-gown relations. "It actually changed their image of the Morehouse guys and they didn't beat them up so often."

Jackson found his own ways to participate in Morehouse life: he became a cheerleader. He discovered that the job had perks, like getting to audition and select the female cheerleaders from Spelman. "I got to travel to other historically Black colleges; I was hanging out with the basketball and football teams, meeting girls." He laughed fondly at the memory. "It wasn't about school spirit."

Some of the students in Morehouse's freshman class, maybe eight of them, stood out: a few years older, more intense, more intimidating. Many of them wore their hair in Afros and had necklaces of braided rope; all of them took their classes more seriously than the average freshman. They were Vietnam veterans, going to college on the G.I. Bill. One night, Jackson and his friends were staying up late, drinking and being rowdy—pissing off some of those vets, who were trying to study.

As Jackson remembered the late-night conversation, the vets came in and lectured them: "You guys need to study, pay attention, and get serious! There's a *war* going on. We just came from it."

"What fucking war?"

"Vietnam."

"Where's that?"

"Let's get the map."

"There's no place called Vietnam on this map!"

"Right there: Indochina. That's Vietnam. We're in a war over there. My friends are dying there—your relatives are going to be dying there."

It didn't take long for that prediction to come true. One of Jackson's cousins in Georgia—they had spent every summer together, running down dirt roads and getting into trouble—had joined the Army around the same time Jackson went to college. "Sure enough, a month and a half later, my cousin was killed in Vietnam," Jackson said. "That really woke me up."

The more Jackson read about Vietnam, the more his convictions against the war hardened. He was careful to get good enough grades that he would be able to stay in school—but everything else about his life was up for grabs. For many people, college is based on identity as much as academics: away from home, you have the freedom to experiment with how you present yourself to the world and figure out what type of person you want to be as an adult. Jackson had always been a complicated guy with a repertory company of personalities inside him, and had lived in a house with four adults watching over him. Now he was finding out that he could be a different person, or even a whole bunch of different people, from block boy to cheerleader to anti-war protester. (He also discovered that having a variety of social circles gave him access to a wider range of women: "Like every sport has its own set of groupies, those circles have their own groupies.")

He switched his major to architecture and changed the way he dressed, dropping the herringbone wardrobe. "I became a hippie. Bell-bottom jeans with patches on 'em, leather fringe vests and you know, wild T-shirts and tie-dye and all that stuff."

In a sign of the times, he took an English class with a professor who, during a class discussion of Ken Kesey's *One Flew Over the Cuckoo's Nest*, encouraged the students to use hallucinogenics: "You guys have some great ideas, maybe you should try this."

Jackson didn't need any encouragement. He did every drug he could get his hands on during his college years, including acid, weed, and even heroin during a period when nothing else was available: "We actually thought that the government took all the marijuana off the streets. There was no marijuana. There was very little acid. The only thing that you could get, and get in quantity, was heroin, and that's what we got." Jackson and his friends snorted it for a while, and then figured they might as well shoot up. "I was a weekend tippler," he said. "I didn't want to do it on a regular basis. I understood the dangers."

Understanding the dangers didn't stop him from overdosing on heroin. Jackson had an out-of-body experience where he saw his friends saving his life: "It's like I'm floating above the room, and I look down and there I am, and there's some guy pounding me in my chest, and somebody else is trying to hold me up, walk me around, and I'm just watching all this shit. It's a fucked-up feeling." But not fucked-up enough to get him to stop right away, apparently: Jackson had two more near-death experiences before he swore off heroin. "My third OD was the end of my run with heroin. I didn't want to die doing drugs, and I saw that. I was smart enough to recognize that and stop."

"You don't think of an event being an historic event in the moment the event's taking place," Jackson said. And you especially don't think of it being an historic event when you're watching the movie *John Goldfarb, Please Come Home!*—a Cold War satire starring Peter Ustinov that somehow ends with Shirley MacLaine scoring the winning touchdown against the Notre Dame football team. But on the evening of April 4, 1968, a Thursday night in the spring semester of his sophomore year, that's exactly where Jackson was: at campus movie night, watching what he judged to be "one of the worst movies ever made."

Jackson knew that Dr. Martin Luther King Jr. had been shot in Memphis and rushed to the hospital; the cashier at the liquor store told him the news when Jackson bought a quart of beer to drink during the movie. However, he wasn't expecting the movie to be interrupted. Somebody came into the theater to make an announcement: "Dr. King is dead. We need to do something." Everyone filed out and milled around in the streets, grieving, trying to make sense of senseless events.

Jackson felt like he was in a fog. Looking at his fellow students, he could see that many of them looked just as numb as he felt. And then, "sure enough, someone threw a brick through a store window, and I was standing there, thinking, 'This is not what we should be doing.'" When Jackson went back to his dorm to check on his roommate, he wasn't there: "He was already in the streets with a whole bunch of other people, tearing up and burning up our neighborhood."

King was in Memphis because he had come to lend support to the city's striking sanitation workers. A few days later, Robert Culp and Bill Cosby paid for the plane fare for any Morehouse and Spelman students who wanted to go to Memphis to march with the sanitation workers, so that King's work would not end with his death. (Culp and Cosby were the stars of the then-current TV show *I Spy*, a secret-agent adventure series that was groundbreaking because of its interracial lead actors.) Jackson flew to Memphis with a group of Morehouse and Spelman students. "We all thought it was probably going to be something physical, even though the National Guard was there," Jackson said. "Culp and Cosby were trying to give us instructions on how to carry ourselves and enact King's dream of being nonviolent." The march proved to be peaceful; the students flew back that night. "We were glad there was something we could do other than burn, loot, and destroy our own neighborhood."

King's funeral was the next morning, on Tuesday, April 9: after a private service at the Ebenezer Baptist Church, where King had been senior pastor, the body was carried to Morehouse on a farm wagon pulled by two mules, in a procession observed by over one hundred thousand people. The school needed volunteers to help visitors find their way around campus, so Jackson put on a suit and served as an usher. The funeral itself was an overwhelming blur of grief, although he was impressed by gospel singer Mahalia Jackson, who sang King's favorite gospel song, "Precious Lord, Take My Hand."

Jackson said, "I was angry about the assassination, but I wasn't shocked by it. I knew that change was going to take something different: not sit-ins, not peaceful coexistence." His family understood his growing militancy—they were just worried that he was going to get himself killed expressing it. On a visit back home to Chattanooga, Jackson was sitting on the porch of 310½ Lookout Street when a white man came calling: Mr. Venable. "From the time I was an infant, my grandmother had been buying all these bullshit life-insurance and burial policies," Jackson said, "and every week this insurance guy, Mr. Venable, came to collect his nickel premiums."

This time, when Mr. Venable walked up to the house and said, "Hi, Sam, is Pearl here?" something snapped inside Jackson, and he said what he had never been able to verbalize as a child when he saw, again and again, how young white office workers condescended to his grandfather.

"Motherfucker, why are you calling my grandmother, a woman three times your age, Pearl?" Jackson demanded. He was cursing and yelling at maximum volume, so overcome with rage that he was babbling. Hearing the commotion, his grandmother came out on the porch and grabbed him by the hair.

"What the hell is wrong with you?" she demanded.

Jackson wasn't sorry for the outburst: from his point of view, it was the first time that Mr. Venable had to consider the notion that he might have been wrong. Mr. Venable apologized, but after he left, Pearl laid into her grandson: "She still thought that he was going to call somebody and have me hanged."

English 353, as listed in the *Morehouse College Bulletin*: "ELEMENTARY PUBLIC SPEAKING. A course in the fundamentals of speech preparation and speaking." Back at Morehouse, Jackson, who still sometimes struggled with his stutter, thought that a public-speaking class might reduce its severity. The class helped, although not as much as an independent discovery Jackson made: he could almost always avoid stuttering by using the word "motherfucker."

Even more important than the class itself was an offer made by the professor: a Morehouse-Spelman production of *The Threepenny Opera* (the Brecht-Weill musical famous for the song "Mack the Knife") needed more actors. Anyone in the class who joined the cast would get extra credit. Jackson couldn't really sing, but it turned out that he "could act like I could sing." He was cast in the supporting role of Ready-Money Matt. As soon as Jackson walked into the theater, something clicked: he knew that he had found the place he should have been all along. Possibly influencing this sense of belonging was that his first rehearsal doubled as a photo shoot for the play, so the women in the cast were dressed in bustiers and garter belts. Since six of the nine men in the cast were gay, it didn't take Jackson long to figure out how that tilted the odds in his favor with the women in lingerie. Soon there was a brand-new thrill: "on opening night, you get that applause. I guess it's like a rush. Wow!"

Nobody believed that *The Threepenny Opera* marked the theatrical debut of a world-shaking thespian talent, not even Jackson himself. "I was horrible," he conceded. He was aware of the contempt he inspired in the undergraduate women who formed the core of the Spelman theater program (Morehouse had no drama department of its own—Morehouse men who wanted to major in drama had to go across the street to Spelman). One of those theater majors said her initial response to the sight of Jackson in rehearsal was, "What's cheerleader boy doing on my stage?" She did concede that he had his virtues: "He was very, very fine." Her name was LaTanya Richardson, and Jackson had noticed her too: the first time he spotted her was the tumultuous week after King was assassinated, when they were both on the same plane flight to Memphis, heading for the march with the sanitation workers. Richardson thought that Jackson looked just like Linc Hayes, the character played by Clarence Williams III in the TV show *The Mod Squad*: "this huge Afro, little bitty round sunglasses, and long sideburns."

Jackson noted that there were certain parts of that style he never adopted: he was too tall to wear platform shoes, for example. "And I didn't have a medallion," he emphasized. "Those were cheesy."

Jackson was still experimenting with different identities in different social contexts, but there was one role he wasn't interested in: the traditional Morehouse man. "Morehouse was breeding politically correct negroes," Jackson said. "They were creating the next Martin Luther Kings. They didn't say that because, really, they didn't want you to be that active politically, and they were more proud of the fact that he was a preacher than that he was a civil-rights leader. That was their trip: they was into making docile negroes."

"SOMEBODY'S WATCHING EVERYTHING YOU DO," said a flyer distributed on the Morehouse campus in the spring of 1969. Over the image of a clenched fist, the sheet had typed thoughts such as "Is the slogan 'Power to Black people' or 'Power to some Black people...and not most'?" and "Pretty soon the rhetoric of blackness will degenerate into expositions and arguments of my mama is blacker than your mama" and "Either the tension is subsiding or the lull before the storm is here." Most ominous was the section that read "Little House, little House, how strong are you? Somebody's trying to huff and puff and blow the little House down. If made of sticks and straw the little House can't stand. Little House, little House, how strong are you?" The flyer was signed, "I remain sincerely and always: God (p.s. you'd better wipe that damn silly grin off your face!!)"

In that atmosphere of threats and consciousness-raising and black comedy, Jackson joined a group of Morehouse undergraduates called Concerned Students, who wanted to petition the Morehouse board of trustees to remake the college. Their four principal demands: a Black studies program; improved community involvement with the housing projects adjacent to the Morehouse campus; people of color forming a majority of the voting members of the board of trustees; and for the six Black colleges in the Atlanta area to consolidate as one larger institution, with a focus on Black studies, to be known as Martin Luther King University.

When the Concerned Students tried to discuss their issues with the board of trustees, they were rebuffed—so they went outside Harkness Hall, the stately brick administration building where the board was meeting, and gathered up the chains that inhibited pedestrians from walking on the grass lawns. "We had read about the lock-ins on other campuses," Jackson said. With some padlocks purchased at a local hardware store, they chained the doors to Harkness Hall shut, locking themselves in with the trustees.

The standoff lasted for twenty-nine hours. Students painted revolutionary slogans on campus sidewalks and buildings, including "M. L. King University Now." Some Spelman students wanted to join the protest, so they found a ladder and climbed in through a second-floor window. Those women included LaTanya Richardson: "Wherever somebody was speaking about revolution and change, I showed up for it."

Concerned Students made sure that they fed the trustees and took care of them. About six hours into the standoff, when trustee Martin Luther King Sr. (not just the father of MLK Jr., but a minister and civil rights leader in his own right) complained of chest pains, they allowed the seventy-year-old to leave via that second-story ladder. "We let him out of there so we wouldn't be accused of murder," Jackson said.

The hostage situation ended when the trustees made various concessions (which the Morehouse administration later repudiated). Charles Merrill, the chairman of the board of trustees, signed an agreement granting the protesters amnesty, promising that they would not be punished for participating in the protest. As soon as the semester ended, however, dean of students Samuel J. Tucker, heading the Morehouse Advisory Committee, sent registered letters to various Morehouse students—including Samuel L. Jackson—summoning them back to campus for a hearing.

"It has been reported to the Advisory Committee that you were among the individuals who participated in [the] lock-in," Tucker wrote. "During the lock-in the following illegal actions were committed; forcible confinement and detention of Board members and student representatives; forcible seizure and occupation of the administration building; and unauthorized use of office supplies, unauthorized use of office telephone for long distance calls, and damage to school property." The timing—after the student body had gone home for the summer and couldn't protest any discipline—wasn't an accident.

The Advisory Committee peremptorily expelled Jackson. He recalled his freshman orientation, when they had told students to look to the left and then the right, and warned them that one of the three of them would not be there the following year. "Finally I was that person who was not there the next year," he realized.

Jackson couldn't, or wouldn't, go home to Chattanooga; 310½ Lookout Street was full of disappointment and broken promises. He stayed in Atlanta, sleeping in a house rented by the SNCC, which had its national headquarters near the Morehouse campus, in a cramped second-floor office above a beauty parlor. Jackson spent his summer doing volunteer work for the SNCC at the Rap Brown Center: "We fed kids in the morning and did field trips," he said. Leaving Morehouse had only pushed him further into political activism. "I wasn't one of those people that was gonna walk around and get spit on and get slapped and not fight back," Jackson said.

Jackson was spending time with Stokely Carmichael and H. Rap Brown, each of whom served as chairman of the SNCC (succeeding John Lewis), leading the organization as it made the transition from the Freedom Riders to the Black Panthers. "I was never a Black Panther," Jackson clarified. "But the fact that you were alive during that period in America, you had to either be part of the problem or part of the solution. We chose to be part of the solution."

Jackson became part of what he termed "the radical faction" of SNCC. He was instrumental in a scheme to steal the credit cards of white people and then to use them to buy guns, building a stockpile of armaments for the conflict that seemed imminent: not just a race war, but young versus old, rebels versus the establishment. The stakes seemed much larger than who got to sit on the Morehouse board of trustees. "All of a sudden, I felt I had a voice," he said. "I was somebody. I could make a difference."

Radical conspiracies didn't come without risk; some of Jackson's friends died in mysterious car explosions. But Jackson's life as a revolutionary ended abruptly on the day when his mother showed up in Atlanta and told him that she was taking him to lunch.

He got in her car, but instead she drove him to the airport. On the way, she told him that two FBI agents had knocked on the door of 310½ Lookout Street and told her that they had her son under surveillance, and that if he didn't get out of Atlanta, he would probably be dead within a year. She handed him a plane ticket to Los Angeles and instructed him: "Get on this plane. Do not get off. I'll talk to you when you get to your aunt's in L.A."

Ali Fitzgerald.

n Los Angeles, Samuel L. Jackson put his politics away. Just nineteen years old, he moved in with his aunt and got a job as a social worker, in the county bureau of public assistance. He was still smoking weed and dropping acid—but, he said, "I learned how to take care of myself a little better."

By this time, Jackson fancied himself quite the operator with women. He had figured out his essential seduction techniques: "That bedroom look: eye contact that lets a woman know 'I'm really with you and I love you.' The soft voice that goes along with it. And my ability to unhook a bra with one hand."

Something took Jackson by surprise in California—he fell in love. The object of his desire was an older woman, in her thirties. They had a passionate relationship, but it ended with his first adult heartbreak. "At a certain point, she told me she loved me but she had needs I couldn't meet," Jackson said. "I couldn't afford her."

He didn't take the news well. He'd drive by her house just to see if her car was parked there. Sometimes, he would park and gaze at her windows, hoping to catch a glimpse of her, wanting to knock on her door but knowing what a terrible mistake it would be. In a rainstorm, he hid behind a palm tree while his car radio played the hit songs of 1970. James Taylor crooned "I always thought that I'd see you again," but somehow the lyrics of "Fire and Rain" didn't assuage Jackson. With the buffer of some decades, Jackson could judge his youthful lovelorn behavior: "It was pathetic."

Jackson stayed in Los Angeles for almost two years, long enough to get a reality check and to consider how privileged his life had been. "I learned that I wanted to be back in school and not in the real world, working," he said.

He also didn't want to be in Vietnam, but when the first draft lottery happened at the end of 1969—the random drawing of birthdays that determined the order in which young American men would be drafted for the Vietnam war—Jackson had an uncomfortably low number (70 out of 366). That provided an additional incentive for him to return to school: he could benefit from a student deferment again.

Morehouse readmitted Jackson after his mother threatened to sue the school. He returned for the spring semester of 1971 and found that the school had quietly implemented many of the changes that Concerned Students had agitated for: the Martin Luther King University consortium remained a dream, but there was now a meaningful Black studies program.

Returning to campus, Jackson had one more epiphany, an unexpected one: "I found out that I wanted to be an actor." He changed his major one last time, to drama. To make that happen, he went across the street to the Spelman campus, to talk to Dr. Baldwin Burroughs, the dean of the theater department there. While Dr. Burroughs spoke with Jackson, laying out the expectations for the major, the dean was looking out the window, with his back turned. That's when a female student crept into his office: LaTanya Richardson. She and Jackson locked eyes for a moment and she put a finger to her lips. She slipped an overdue assignment—a production book for a play she was working on—onto a pile of similar books on Dr. Burroughs's desk and silently backed out of the office.

As soon as she was gone, Dr. Burroughs turned around, took her production book, marked it with a big red F, and threw it back on the pile. "He saw her reflection in the window," Jackson said.

That night, Jackson went to the theater, reporting for his first rehearsal as a drama major. Richardson, as usual, was backstage. They had their first conversation, but not for long—she had to leave for a recording session, doing some backup vocals for the Commodores.

Jackson threw himself into the drama major, doing as many plays as possible. When he was a freshman, he had been taken aback by the Vietnam veterans and their seriousness of purpose: now he was acting like one of them. He was at Morehouse for a reason, and that reason was theater. He did as many productions as he could with the Morehouse Spelman Players, but he also joined a student troupe called the Black Image Theater Company.

Black Image was a funhouse-mirror version of the pageants that Jackson had done with Aunt Edna as a child: Black students doing variety shows for the edification of white audiences. There was a fundamental difference, however: the Black Image actors referred to their productions as "Hate Whitey Theater."

The cast members would run out and shout, "Die, whitey! Die, whitey, so Black folks can take over!" The performance would include dancing, drumming, recitations of consciousness-raising poetry by

Amiri Baraka (then known as LeRoi Jones), and performances by a singing group in the style of the Supremes—here called the Supremacists. Their shows began as guerrilla street theater but soon drew a wider audience than expected. "People were paying us to do this stuff," Jackson marveled. "We were going to Tulane and Florida State and all sorts of big white schools and they were like, 'Yes, yes, denigrate us! Denigrate us, do it!'"

Jackson got used to performing under the influence of drugs and booze; it was not only tolerated in the drama department, but encouraged. "If you're going to do it, do it like the great ones," Dr. Burroughs told his students. They knew what that meant: "The great ones got blind," Jackson said. "So we started out in the morning drinking wine or bourbon and got to an eight o'clock class and then all afternoon we worked in the shop, building sets while drinking more and smoking a joint, and by the time 7:30 rehearsal rolled around we were stoned. But because we rehearsed stoned, we knew the lines so we could perform stoned."

When Jackson returned to Morehouse, he intended to marry a girl he had known before he left, a Spelman student named Lucene Moore. But two weeks after he got back together with Lucene, he had his first real conversation with LaTanya Richardson, who he had been noticing in the periphery of his world for years: on the plane to Memphis, coming in the second-floor window of Harkness Hall, sneaking her homework into the dean's office. "We started talking and boom! I knew she was the person for me," Jackson said. "From then on, we were always together."

Richardson, born October 21, 1949 (one year younger than Jackson), grew up in Atlanta, a fact she took pride in, even calling the city by the nickname "the Mecca of the South." When she was a child, her family home was a hub of the civil rights movement: on Sunday afternoons, after church services, local ministers would drop in for fried chicken and potato salad before meeting to discuss the next steps in the struggle. Growing up, Richardson thought she was going to be a doctor—but when she saw the musical *Camelot*, she fell in love with the theater. (Being part of King Arthur's court seemed impractical.) "When you think about what acting actually is, it's a very unnatural thing to do as a vocation," she said. "It needs to be somewhere inside you."

Richardson, who started acting when she was fifteen, made sure that she attended the Atlanta performances of great actors on tour, such as Ruby Dee, Cicely Tyson, and Geraldine Page—not to mention the Negro Ensemble Company. In the movies, she loved Bette Davis: "It's horrible to say, but she's why I started smoking!" But the essential, inspirational influence: Diahann Carroll in the TV series *Julia*, the groundbreaking sitcom that ran from 1968 to 1971 in which Carroll played a nurse and a widowed single mother. Carroll "made everything seem possible," Richardson said. "I was always emboldened by the idea that I was going to succeed."

After Jackson graduated from Morehouse in 1972, his life continued much like before; he and Richardson stayed in Atlanta and did as many plays as they possibly could. They moved into a small apartment building on Seventh Street in downtown Atlanta: the rent was cheap, but the rooms were large, and there were wooden floors and fireplaces. The other five units in the building were also occupied by actors, mostly friends of Jackson and Richardson. "It was like living in a little bohemian community," said one of those neighbors, Albert Cooper. "We hung out, talked, read books, made families."

One acting job for both Jackson and Richardson: children's improvisational drama, as sponsored by the Academy Theatre (the first integrated theater in the South). For a show called "Something in a Box," the five-member cast would visit elementary schools, bringing along one piece of scenery: a refrigerator box that had been painted with various backgrounds. After asking the children to write down their fears on slips of paper, the performers would pick two or three slips and act the fears out, helping the children to conquer them. "We would also get the kid who wrote down that fear," Jackson said, and give the child "a product called Dr Woolapowers Placating Placebo."

Every six weeks, there seemed to be another play opening that featured Jackson, or Richardson, or both. "I know what it's like to stand there and trade lines with Sam Jackson for an hour and something," said Cooper. "He is a powerhouse of an actor—he makes you raise your game." But as well-regarded as Jackson was in the Atlanta theater scene, Richardson was held in even higher esteem. The couple aspired to be the Black version of Elizabeth Taylor and Richard Burton. "Sam and Tanya set the tone for quality acting and quality theater," Cooper said. And when Jackson wasn't onstage, he was in the audience, where he also made his presence known: at a performance of Melvin Van Peebles's play *Ain't Supposed to Die a Natural Death*, Cooper said, Jackson "was standing up, screaming, and pumping his fist."

Atlanta was home to multiple Black theater companies, most notably the People's Survival Theater. Some of them featured a mélange of poetry and dance and drums, but the Jackson/Richardson cohort was more interested in traditional plays (which could include musicals, although the men drew the line at wearing leotards). When they heard of an Atlanta impresario looking for a new Black theater company he could present, the result was the Just Us Theater Company, whose founders included Richardson, Jackson, Cooper, and Bill Nunn.

One particularly memorable Jackson performance was in *Purlie*, the musical based on Ossie Davis's play *Purlie Victorious*—he played the lead role of a fast-talking preacher in the segregated South. (Cleavon Little won a Tony in 1970 for originating the role on Broadway.) Jackson had learned to carry a tune adequately and wasn't afraid to belt out songs like "Newfangled Preacher Man." "It's important to me that people hear the lyrics," Jackson said. "I always considered myself an Ethel Merman-type singer."

As the 1960s moved further into the past, Jackson progressed from his life as a hippie, trying new things—even learning to box at his local YMCA. He put away the Jimi Hendrix headbands and the "Free Angela Davis" T-shirt. "In the seventies I went Edwardian," he said. "Slim-cut clothes, double-breasted jackets with big lapels."

Atlanta in the 1970s was not the hub of film production that it later became, but some productions shot there—including *That Old Sweet Song*, a made-for-TV movie about a Detroit family on a southern vacation, starring Cicely Tyson. Cooper and Jackson scored some work as stand-ins; they were thrilled to be on a real movie set, watching the professionals, and noted the precision with which the production ran. "It's scheduled down to the minute," Cooper marveled.

Another movie, *Together for Days*, was made in Atlanta for just $600,000. It was a blaxploitation movie about an interracial romance, notable mostly because of what various participants did later on: the female lead, Lois Chiles, went on to be a Bond girl (Holly Goodhead in *Moonraker*). The director, Michael Schultz, made *Cooley High*, *The Last Dragon*, and four Richard Pryor movies. And Stan, the eleventh-billed role in the cast, was played by one Samuel L. Jackson.

With terrible reviews and no distribution deal, the movie was barely released in 1972, sneaking into a few theaters; it was later renamed *Black Cream*, with no greater success. (Tagline on the poster: "A brother's struggle for identity!") It never came out on video and hasn't been seen in decades; "Don't go looking for it," Jackson warned. The movie didn't make Jackson rich or famous, but it did gain him membership in the Screen Actors Guild—crucially, having a SAG card allows you to audition for a better class of projects.

More lucrative and much more widely seen was the commercial Jackson filmed for Krystal, the southern hamburger chain. After a woman in pigtails testifies that she once ate twelve Krystal burgers in a single sitting (not as gluttonous as it might sound: they're small, square sliders), but before the announcer assures you that Krystal is the one place in town where you can eat a lot of good food and still not spend a lot of money, Jackson, wearing a necktie, appears to explain the burgers' appeal: "Probably it's these little cooked onions."

Jackson had some local fame: he loved the thrill of strangers recognizing him from plays, even if they called him by his character's name, or people calling out "Probably it's these little cooked onions!" if they saw him on the street. "It was the best feeling in the world," he said. But he was having trouble getting noticed outside the 404 area code.

Roots, the acclaimed miniseries about the history of Alex Haley's African American family, from eighteenth-century Gambia through slavery and the U.S. Civil War, was a television landmark when it aired in January 1977. With eight generation-spanning episodes and dozens of juicy roles, it was practically a full-employment program for Black actors circa 1976—but not for Jackson. "I've been told that I wasn't African enough or not an exotic Negro," he complained. "What does that mean?"

Meanwhile, Richardson had appeared in a production of Gore Vidal's play *The Best Man*, about the backroom jockeying of presidential candidates at a political convention, starring E. G. Marshall. Joseph Papp, the producer who was founder of Shakespeare in the Park and the Public Theater in New York City, attended a performance while he was visiting Atlanta. Papp met Richardson backstage and told her, "You definitely need to be in New York. Come see me."

That was all the encouragement Richardson needed. Jackson consented: they weren't going to become the Black Elizabeth Taylor and Richard Burton by doing regional theater in Georgia. They paid their rent in Atlanta through October 1976 and drove north, arriving in New York City on October 31. Some friends on Barrow Street, in the West Village, had invited the couple to stay with them for a while.

Their first impression of New York wasn't what they expected: "We pulled into the Village at night and everyone on the street looked really bizarre," Jackson said. The streets of the city were filled with samba bands and drag queens and enormous puppets. "What we didn't realize was that it was Halloween and we were in the middle of a parade," Jackson said. "I saw a nun crossing the street with a guy in a diaper. And the nun turned around and had a big green beard. I said, 'I guess we've arrived.' "

CAN YOU DIG IT?

SAMUEL L. JACKSON
IS
SHAFT

Todd Radom.

LaTanya Richardson didn't waste time: the next day, she headed straight for Joseph Papp's office at the Public Theater. She told the receptionist, "Mr. Papp sent for me." The office staff just laughed: a producer being polite to an actress backstage was not the same thing as summoning her for a high-level meeting.

"In my country mind, that was what he had done!" Richardson said. "But it worked out. He put me in a play right away, Aishah Rahman's *Unfinished Women Cry in No Man's Land While a Bird Dies in a Gilded Cage*. Joseph Papp ended up as a great mentor to me." Richardson was soon getting steady work at the Public—and when Ntozake Shange's *For Colored Girls Who Have Considered Suicide/When the Rainbow Is Enuf* had a national tour produced by the Public, Richardson was one of the seven women in the ensemble. (Shange called her play a "choreopoem": it combined monologues with dancing.)

Left by himself in New York City, Samuel L. Jackson spent six months working as a security guard in an apartment building in midtown Manhattan. "I didn't have a gun," Jackson said of his post. "I had a nightstick—which I really didn't want either, because I didn't want to pose a threat to anyone." His job, as he saw it, was to be a reporter, not a hero. "If I saw something happening, I would call them on a walkie-talkie and tell them it was happening," he said. "Or probably, wait until it was over and then tell them what had happened."

Jackson worked the night shift from eleven p.m. to seven a.m.; that left him time to go to auditions during the day and perform in the evening. He tried to approach his career like an air-traffic controller: at all times, he wanted to be performing in one play, rehearsing for another, and auditioning for the next one. Many of the plays paid a pittance—on the order of $50 for a four-week run, which barely covered subway tokens—but his priority was to keep acting. "If my résumé says showcase after showcase, at least I'm not waiting tables. But if I did one showcase a year and I wait tables every night, I'm a waiter, not an actor."

While Richardson's rise seemed charmed, Jackson was still trying to suss out how to work the system. "I thought this was like every other job," he admitted. "You start in the mailroom and then you get higher and higher. So I thought, 'Okay, I'm doing theater, and eventually I'll get a commercial, and then I'll become a movie star.'" Unfortunately, he had no guidebook on how to make those things happen.

"There's always a time in any actor's life where you wonder if you're doing what you're supposed to be doing," Jackson said. "You're kind of doing some showcase somewhere and there's no job on the horizon, and ConEd's kind of beating at your door and you're dodging that guy, and your outgoing phone service is gone, you can only receive calls. You're waiting on the subway to pull in, so you can hear it come, so you jump the turnstile, and run down before the police see you. And you got seventy-five cents to go to Gray's Papaya and make your meal that day."

When he went home to visit his mother, her friends would give him advice: "Why don't you get on one of them soap operas?" they'd ask him. He refrained from telling them that he couldn't just fill out an application.

Fortunately, there was no shortage of plays to audition for. In 1965, writer Amiri Baraka founded the Black Arts Repertory Theater in Harlem: that's regarded as the beginning of the Black Arts Movement (essentially, the cultural expression of the Black Power movement). While some historians say the movement ended circa 1975—in other words, just before Jackson and Richardson arrived in New York—the city still had plenty of active African American theater companies, most of them focusing on work by Black playwrights. To name a few: The New Heritage Repertory Theatre. The New Federal Theater. The New Lafayette Theater. It wasn't a coincidence that so many had "New" in their name: they were wrestling with the racist traditions of American drama and trying to create a brand-new theatrical grammar.

In the summer of 1979, Richardson joined the cast of *Spell* #7, a new choreopoem by Shange: the characters telling their stories here were Black artists in a bar. After a workshop production, *Spell* #7 debuted at the Public Theater with a cast that included Richardson (taking the role played by Shange herself in the workshop) and Avery Brooks (the actor later famous as Captain Sisko on *Star Trek: Deep Space Nine*). When a company in London wanted to do a production of *Colored Girls*, Shange asked Brooks to direct it, so Papp gave him two weeks off from *Spell* #7. Jackson came on as Brooks's temporary replacement—but when Brooks stayed in London longer than expected, Papp fired him. That gave Jackson a much-needed job through the end of the run.

One of the show's dancers, Dyane Harvey-Salaam, had a duet with Brooks—she moved while he recited a poem—that she had to learn how to perform with a new partner, Jackson. "Sam's rhythms were different," she said. "Avery seemed to have a more urban interpretation of the language, whereas something about Sam's tones and southern accent made me move differently. I kept trying to figure out how to work with this new interpretation and finally it dawned on me: you have to breathe with him, silly rabbit! You have to open yourself up and let yourself hear Sam's inflections and Sam's feelings. At first, Sam was struggling with the dance stuff—even then, he was large and he embodied the character."

The show began with what the cast called "the Mammy Dance": a dance routine performed while wearing blackface masks with enormous red lips. Harvey-Salaam reflected, "Was the Mammy Dance the actual play that these actors did before they came to the bar? Possibly. Was it a dream? Possibly. Totally up for interpretation." Trading in minstrel-show stereotypes a century after the Civil War ended was powerful—but upsetting for audiences and performers alike.

Harvey-Salaam spent time in the Lincoln Center library, researching minstrelsy. "It was not only stereotypical mimicry, it was a form of a racism that was designed specifically to keep Black people controlled," she concluded. "Once I understood that Black people were stereotyping the white people who were stereotyping the Black people, I was no longer as embarrassed or ashamed."

Young actors suffer all sorts of indignities starting out in their profession; actors of color, doubly so. But even knowing that, Samuel L. Jackson couldn't have expected that so many of his acting jobs would require him to wear blackface: aside from the Mammy Dance, he appeared in minstrel garb in a public-television broadcast of the play *The Trial of the Moke*.

When Jackson joined the cast of *Spell #7*, he was thirty years old. "The American ideal is that everyone wants to make their first million dollars by the time they're thirty," Jackson said. "When I was thirty, I was in New York doing off-Broadway plays, maybe one TV job a year and a small part in a movie, thinking I should have been discovered by then." And if he had somehow gotten that million dollars? "One of my plans was to take all my friends to Brazil, and we'd lay on a beach with a kilo of coke and have all the fun we could possibly have and then go back to work."

If Jackson was performing in a play at night and had time to kill during the day, he would head to Times Square—the diseased heart of 1970s New York City, still many years away from being a gleaming center of international commerce. Jackson fondly remembered the "no-man's-land part of Times Square, with transvestite hookers and kung fu movie theaters." He knew at least four theaters where for the price of one ticket, he could see a triple bill of Hong Kong martial arts movies like *Five Deadly Venoms*, *One-Armed Swordsman*, and *Master of the Flying Guillotine*. "I would go to Times Square at eleven in the morning, buy a quart of beer, a nickel bag of weed, and see three movies for a dollar until it was time to go to the theater."

Many of Jackson's friends were also Black actors trying to make it in New York City—some of them future stars like Denzel Washington, Laurence Fishburne, Morgan Freeman, Wesley Snipes, and Alfre Woodard, some of them talented people who never broke through—taking any acting job available. "We worked off-Broadway, off-off-Broadway, nowhere near Broadway," Washington said. Jackson and Washington costarred in one production, *The Mighty Gents*, about the aging members of a gang in Newark; the show had a truck tour in all five boroughs of New York City, making impromptu stages on basketball courts and in public parks.

"We rode the train together, we walked from audition to audition, we went to each other's plays, we were an interactive community," Jackson said. When money was tight, which it almost always was, they would end up at the unemployment office together, which they nicknamed Club 25—or would pool their money for communal dinners so that nobody went hungry.

Sometimes there would be a casting call for a Black role that would seem to bring in every actor in town, Jackson remembered: "Everybody from age twenty to age fifty was called because they had no idea what kind of Black person they wanted for the role. That kind of let you know that they didn't have a clue as to who these people are." Conversely, if Jackson was auditioning for a role that he knew he wasn't going to get but that seemed tailor-made for the talents of a friend, he made sure to call that friend and let him know there was a job he'd be perfect for.

Jackson and Richardson had been together for most of a decade when she let him know that it was time to get married. More precisely, she told him that her grandfather's health was failing, and that before he died, he wanted to make sure that he got to walk her, the last of his grandchildren, down the aisle. She instructed Jackson, "You have to ask him if you may marry me. And then you have to ask me, will I marry you." They were wed on August 18, 1980. As Richardson saw her options, she could marry a rich boy or a smart boy: "I married the smart boy." (After their wedding, her chosen name for most of her professional credits remained LaTanya Richardson.)

The following year, the couple bought a four-story brownstone in Harlem, at 522 W. 143rd Street (on a block between Broadway and Amsterdam Avenue), paying $35,000. Jackson did much of the renovation himself, putting in many hours stripping the paint off walls and repainting them.

Waiting for paint to dry was a good exercise in patience, which proved necessary with Jackson's career—his star was rising, but very slowly. He booked his first role in a studio movie, *Ragtime*, directed by Milos Forman (most famous for *One Flew Over the Cuckoo's Nest*). His character had a number, not a name ("Gang Member No. 2"), but the production bought him a plane ticket to London to shoot his scenes: Jackson's first time in Europe. "That was a big, big experience, figuring out that the world wasn't what I thought it was," Jackson said. He had thought of Great Britain as monolithically white, and was amazed to discover the West Indian culture it contained. And the movie's cast included James Cagney, in his last movie role: Jackson used to have lunch with him every day, listening to stories of old Hollywood. "Stars don't come bigger, yet he would hang out and talk with us," an impressed Jackson said.

Jackson appeared at the Public Theater in an adaptation of Brecht's play *Mother Courage*, with a script by Shange, understudying Morgan Freeman, eleven years his senior, learning from the veteran actor onstage and off. After warning Jackson that he wouldn't be missing any performances, Freeman told him, "I don't know why you're working so hard, boy. You got it. Just don't quit." Jackson didn't, mounting up credits in town and at regional theaters: *Ohio Tip-Off*, at Baltimore Center Stage, was set in the locker room of a minor-league basketball team. *District Line*, at the Negro Ensemble Company (in New York), was about a group of taxicab drivers waiting for fares. *The New York Times* praised Jackson as "vibrant" in the role of "a fast-talking jive artist who wittily defends robbery as a form of sophisticated protest against economic injustice."

Jackson's longest-running stage production, however, was *A Soldier's Play* by Charles Fuller, which ran at the Negro Ensemble Company from November 1981 to January 1983, and then spent another year on a nationwide tour. The play, a murder mystery set at a Louisiana Army base in 1944, when the armed forces were still segregated, was a powerful examination of racism and how it festers. The cast of twelve men comprised nine Black actors, including Denzel Washington, and three white actors: one of the white performers, Steve Zeller, stumbled into his audition because the Negro Ensemble Company had its offices in the same building as the Actors Equity offices. "My agent said don't do it: You're going to be cast as a racist forever if you do this part," Zeller remembered. But he took the part, both because he thought it was a powerful play and because he needed the $350 a week.

"Sam is one of the brightest people I've ever run into," Zeller said. "Nothing got past him." Jackson played Private Louis Henson, whose dialogue whipsaws from crude jokes ("Cobb, the kinda women you find, it's a wonda your nuts ain't fell off—crabs? You probably got lice, ticks, bedbugs, fleas—tapeworms—") to bleak acknowledgments of American racism ("I just hope we get lucky enough to get shipped outta this hellhole to the War!").

Over a thousand performances, the cast fell into habits. Before shows, they'd play Trivial Pursuit in the dressing room and watch *Family Feud*. It emerged that Jackson and Zeller were the cast's biggest practical jokers. To look sweaty for a scene where the characters were supposed to have come directly from a baseball game, the actors would spray themselves with mist bottles offstage—unless Jackson and Zeller ambushed them with water pistols first.

The play won the Pulitzer and the cast was honored by backstage visits from the likes of Sidney Poitier and Peter O'Toole and Diana Ross, but what Zeller particularly remembered about those years was witnessing the racism his fellow actors faced offstage. After shows in New York, Zeller got in the habit of hailing taxis—otherwise they wouldn't stop for the Black members of the cast. When the show arrived in Seattle for a monthlong stand, Zeller rented a furnished apartment that seemed nicer than the hotel where the cast had been booked—but when Black actors went to the same building, they were turned away.

One visitor who talked his way backstage at the Theater Four on West 55th Street was a film student at NYU. He introduced himself to Jackson as a fellow Morehouse alumnus, and told Jackson he was going to be a filmmaker—and that when he started to make movies, he would love for Jackson to be in them. "I had my dream and he had his," Jackson said with a shrug. And while both dreams seemed destined to run up against "a surplus of reality," Jackson nevertheless remembered the young man's name: Spike Lee.

While *A Soldier's Play* was still on tour, Norman Jewison directed the film version—called *A Soldier's Story.* Jewison used only a few essential members of the original cast; the scuttlebutt among the actors was that the theatrical producers, not wanting to recast the stage production, discouraged him from hiring the whole ensemble. When *A Soldier's Story* was released, Adolph Caesar's work earned him an Oscar nomination; Denzel Washington's performance turned him into a movie star.

During the run of *A Soldier's Play*, Jackson and Richardson had a baby: Zoe Jackson, born on March 28, 1982. "The first few years of Zoe's life, one of us always had to not work so that somebody could be at home with her," Jackson said: with his extended run in *A Soldier's Story*, that was mostly Richardson for quite a while.

When Richardson realized she was effectively putting her career on hold in favor of Jackson's, and they weren't going to be the Black Taylor and Burton anytime soon, she said, "I cried like a banshee." But, she said, "I had to deal with my feelings. I wasn't going to be good with just nannies raising Zoe." Her mantra: "We'd vowed to be a revolutionary Black family." That was a double-edged phrase: it meant both that they came from a background of revolutionary politics and that not breaking their family up could be a revolutionary act in itself.

That stood in stark contrast to Jackson's own childhood: his father, Roy Jackson, had visited him once, when he was still an infant, and then abandoned his mother, Elizabeth. Roy's mother, however, had always stayed in touch with her grandson Sam, sending him birthday cards and Christmas cards, even though they had never met. So in late 1982, when his own daughter Zoe was about six months old, not even walking yet, Jackson decided it was time to meet his paternal grandmother. The national tour of *A Soldier's Play* had reached Topeka, Kansas, and she lived about an hour away, in Kansas City, Kansas.

When Samuel Jackson arrived at his grandmother's house, much to his surprise, Roy Jackson was also there: for the first time in his life, he had a conversation with his father. After a little while, Roy told Samuel, "I want to show you something. I want you to meet your sister."

Samuel objected—he was an only child. Roy told him that wasn't actually true: he had brothers and sisters in Philadelphia, among other places. But there was one particular sibling he wanted Samuel to meet.

"So we go to his house, maybe four blocks from my grandmother's house," Samuel said. "There's an elderly lady, a middle-aged lady, and a teenager there. And I'm thinking, *Well, maybe the teenager.* And then the teenager goes upstairs and comes down with a baby, who's younger than my daughter—*that's* my sister."

Whatever reaction Roy hoped for was not the reaction he got from his son: "Are you fucking out of your mind? What the fuck is wrong with you? Why are you still out here making babies?"

Roy told Samuel, "You can't talk to me that way. I'm your father."

Thirty-three years after their last visit, Samuel wasn't having any of it: "We're just two guys talking. We can't go to this father-son space."

The elderly lady asked Samuel how long it had been since he had seen his father: were they close?

He told her the truth: "This is only the second time I've seen this motherfucker in my life."

The elderly woman stared at her daughter, the middle-aged woman—who in turn stared at her daughter, the teenager, who looked about sixteen years old. The teenager just hung her head. Jackson felt sorry for all of them.

The capper: "And then when we leave, he wants to be pissed with me because I didn't lie for him!"

That was the last time they ever spoke. Six years later, Jackson got a call from a hospital in Kansas; Roy, an alcoholic, was dying from cirrhosis. "Your father is gravely ill," they said. "And we want to know if you want us to take drastic action to keep him alive."

He asked, "Are you calling to ask if I want you to put him on life support, or are you calling to see if I'm going to be responsible for his medical bill?" When they hemmed and hawed, Jackson told them, "He's got a sister in Kansas City—you should call her." And he hung up the phone. "I'm not going to make that decision," Jackson said. "I wasn't trying to be cold, but he wasn't my responsibility."

Even temporarily retired from the stage, Richardson retained a gift for drama, both as an art form and as an approach to personal dynamics. She bluntly informed her husband that his acting was bloodless. "You're smart," she told him. "You know the right facial expression. You know the vocal inflection. You know everything to do except how to feel it."

Understandably stung, Jackson told her that she had no filter—but as time went on, he conceded that she was right. "I was always watching people react to me rather than my being inside the character," he said. He was gifted enough to fool audiences, and even to fool himself, but the performances were all happening on the exterior of his soul.

More encouragingly, when Jackson felt like he was getting type-cast as a heavy, Richardson reminded him that some great actors, like James Cagney and Humphrey Bogart, had begun their career with a steady diet of bad guys. That made it easier for him to accept small roles on programs like *Spenser: For Hire* (the detective show starring Robert Urich and Avery Brooks). "Every year I went up to Boston to get beat up by Spenser and Hawk," Jackson said.

Jackson also got steady work in TV, if not on TV: for two and a half years, he served as Bill Cosby's stand-in on *The Cosby Show*. On Monday mornings, Jackson, along with the stand-ins for the rest of the cast, would watch America's favorite TV family rehearse the show, taking notes on the blocking and any other movements on the set. Then for the next two days, the stand-ins would walk through the episode, scripts in hand, so that the crew could make sure all the technical elements were working smoothly. "We were the junior Huxtables," he joked.

"I wore Bill's clothes over my clothes, because he's larger than I am, so that the lights would be correct and they could get that color palette down," Jackson said. "You learn how to work with three to four cameras. When they move them, and where to look, how to move. So I told myself I was learning how to do three-camera television."

Jackson honed his impression of Cosby and delivered his line readings of parental wisdom for the benefit of the stagehands, but he never tried to schmooze the star or jawbone his way into a guest spot. "I didn't impose myself on them," Jackson said. "I didn't want to be on the show, so I never tried that." (It's totally reasonable to have career aspirations other than appearing on *The Cosby Show*, but it seems odd, even self-defeating, to treat a job as a two-and-a-half-year seminar on the techniques of sitcom acting, and then not try to put the lessons into action.) The only time he ever appeared on camera for *The Cosby Show* was when the crew needed to film an exterior shot of some passersby on the sidewalk outside the Huxtables' home in Brooklyn Heights: metaphorically and literally, Jackson stayed outside.

While Jackson was wearing the sweaters of the stars, many of his friends had moved on to actual fame. Morgan Freeman was making movies; Denzel Washington joined the cast of *St. Elsewhere*. Alfre Wood-ard was nominated for an Oscar for her performance in the 1983 movie *Cross Creek*. "The opportunities were there," Jackson said. "But I was never prepared, because I was a little bit off, you know?" He told him-self that his time would come, since it had for so many people he knew.

Jackson's pal Albert Cooper was visiting New York when Jackson booked an appearance in the Eddie Murphy comedy *Coming to Amer-ica*, as a stickup man robbing a fast-food restaurant. "When Sam got that part where he played the guy with the shotgun, I was staying with him," Cooper said. "That was a day's worth of work—we were so excited about that. Sam got a day's worth of work!"

Another important day of work came in the summer of 1987 when Spike Lee followed through on his promise from years earlier and cast Jackson in his second feature film, *School Daze*. The movie was set at a thinly disguised version of Morehouse; in Jackson's scene, shot on the very first day of filming, he played Leeds, a belligerent local who hassles some students. Acting in the scene with him were friends of Jackson from various points of his life, including Cooper, Bill Nunn, and Laurence Fishburne. It was a trip back in time: not only was Jack-son returning to Atlanta to make a movie, he was playing the role of a block boy once again. The performance unlocked some of his old resentments about the high-handed attitude of Morehouse men, and he was protective of the character. Years later, when a radio interviewer referred to the character as a "hostile townie," Jackson bristled: it was a replay of Morehouse students dismissing their neighbors in the projects as an undesirable class of people, rather than individuals. "He had a name," Jackson interrupted. "L-E-E-D-S. Leeds."

Fishburne was the lead in *School Daze*, while Jackson was a day player. Fish was an old friend, so Jackson swallowed any resentment he felt at the respective arcs of their careers. But that detachment proved harder to sustain with another project later that year: *The Piano Les-son*, a play by August Wilson set in 1936 Pittsburgh (the fourth play in his ten-play sequence *The Pittsburgh Cycle*, about the African American experience, with each play representing a different decade in the twen-tieth century). Wilson had written the leading role of Boy Willie, who wants to sell his family's heirloom piano so he can buy the land where his ancestors were sharecroppers, specifically for Charles S. Dutton, who had won a Tony nomination for his work in an earlier Wilson play, *Ma Rainey's Black Bottom*. But Dutton had committed to shoot the movie *Crocodile Dundee II*, so there was an unusual compromise, to let the actor have both commerce and art: Jackson would play the role in the initial out-of-town production (at the Yale Rep theater in New Haven, Connecticut) but when *The Piano Lesson* moved to Broadway in early 1988, Dutton would take over the role and Jackson would serve as his understudy.

The two theater directors whom Jackson has named as especially influential on him are Douglas Turner Ward of the Negro Ensemble Company, who directed him in *A Soldier's Play*, and Lloyd Richards, who directed *The Piano Lesson*. Richards was the director of the Yale Drama School, and his pedagogy extended into his rehearsals, Jackson recalled. "They both taught me how to ask myself the right questions when I'm preparing to do a role or how to sit down and read a script and figure out who that person is: write an autobiography, give him a complete life from birth, family, educational background."

"You never know what's going to come out," Richards said of Jackson's fertile mind. "You were glad he thought of it, because you would have thought of it if you could have thought of it."

"August writes three-hour plays," Jackson said, and Boy Willie "talks for about two hours and ten minutes in a three hour play, so all you can do as an actor is grow."

Onstage at the Yale Rep, Jackson found himself at a new peak of performance. (Backstage, he would affectionately tease the young girls in the cast if he heard them practicing: "Y'all doing our lines?") It lasted only a few weeks: when the play relocated eighty miles south, to New York City, it was time for Jackson to step back. He still showed up at the theater every night as an understudy, but unless Dutton was gravely ill, he wouldn't be going onstage. "I was okay with it," Jackson said, "until it was time to do it."

Jackson would sit outside on the Walter Kerr Theatre's fire escape, listening to Dutton doing the role that he had originated, feeling the sour bile churning in his guts. "I rocked that play," Jackson said matter-of-factly. "Charles was great, but I was better."

He had never been resentful about losing out on a part previously—but he had never gotten demoted before. Jackson explained, "It's frustrating knowing that you've done something that was raved about critically, that you had to listen to every night backstage, and not just saying to yourself, 'I would have done that differently,' but hearing the audience response to it—because that's what theater is. It's that live give-and-take and knowing that you used to be out there doing that and the audience was responding to you."

Eight performances a week, Jackson "sat backstage, feeling sorry for myself." To take the edge off his bitter, self-pitying mood, he used cocaine more heavily. He snorted enough coke that he blew a hole through the septum in his nose (the cartilage separating the two nostrils), so he started smoking it instead. Every success the play had only fueled his resentment, and there were plenty of honors: the Drama Desk Award, the Pulitzer Prize, Tony Award nominations for the play and, painfully, for Dutton. "The mounting frustrations of knowing how well you did something, and not doing it and seeing someone else reap all the benefits of doing it kind of combined to make me a bit crazier than I probably normally would have been," Jackson admitted.

Jackson became an expert at getting high on a tight schedule. He would check in at the Walter Kerr before showtime, and then in the space of forty-five minutes, "I could go score, go by my house, cook it, get back on the train, and be back at the theater—nobody would miss me." He told himself that nobody at the theater noticed what he was doing, so he didn't need to make any efforts to cover up his escalating cocaine consumption. "That's how people saw me every day, so it was nothing unusual," he rationalized. They didn't see him first thing in the morning before he left home—that was the one time of day he was guaranteed to be sober.

THE
HITMAN'S
BODYGUARD

Nancy Chiu.

want to get up and act every day," Samuel L. Jackson said. "And there's a limited number of acting possibilities in everybody's lifetime. So I'm trying to maximize my shit."

This filmography (divided into eleven chapters) covers all of Samuel L. Jackson's acting work in movies fifty-five minutes or longer from 1977 to 2021, regardless of whether the movies debuted at the Cinerama Dome, on a television network, or on a streaming service. While once it seemed useful to differentiate between movies that were projected in theaters from 35mm prints and ones that made their way into our homes through other means, modern technology has made those distinctions mostly pointless. Our tally doesn't include Jackson's appearances in commercials, music videos, or episodic TV series, or his work in documentaries, either as a narrator or as a talking head. (And we went to press before the release of *The Protégé* and *Blazing Samurai*.) That still leaves us with 140 movies: consider Jackson's shit to be maximized.

Unless you are Samuel L. Jackson himself (hi, Sam), you probably haven't seen all these movies, so to help you navigate the ocean that is the man's filmography, I offer two ratings on a ten-point scale: an assessment of the movie itself and the "SLJ Factor." The SLJ Factor measures the entertainment value of Samuel L. Jackson in any given movie, factoring in the quality of his performance and the amount of his screen time (and acknowledging that sometimes he can rock a movie with just a cameo). Think of it as a numerical answer to the question "If I'm watching this movie primarily because I'm a fan of Samuel L. Jackson, how much will I enjoy it?"

My spoiler policy: I try not to give away a movie's surprises gratuitously, but I also don't worry about keeping every secret of a film that came out years ago. When bad movies have dumb plot twists, I get particularly loose-lipped.

Watching 140 Samuel L. Jackson movies in the space of a year, I witnessed Jackson giving the best part of himself: not just showing up and doing his job in masterpieces and turkeys alike, but injecting every role with intelligence and panache. In good times and bad, we can count on Jackson to illuminate the human condition and inspire our inner motherfucker.

The Displaced Person (1977)

Sulk

MOVIE: 4/10   SLJ FACTOR: 3/10   MINUTES UNTIL HE SHOWS UP: 2

It's not surprising that a public-television drama from 1977 was slow and talky by modern standards; it is surprising how relentlessly it used ethnic slurs. That isn't just a reflection of the casual racism in its setting, a Georgia farm right after World War II: xeno-phobia and a fear of miscegenation are what drive this thorny little tale. Mrs. McIntyre, the proprietor of the farm, takes on a Polish refugee family. At first she is delighted by the work ethic and mechanical aptitude of Mr. Guizac—qualities that rankle the other workers on the farm, Black and white alike. But when he tries to bring over a young blond female cousin, a concentration-camp survivor, to marry one of the Black laborers, she sours on him and reveals the limits of her Christian charity. She doesn't fire Guizac, but she stands by silently when a disgruntled worker lets a tractor crush him.

> *"I never felt no need to travel."*

The movie, clocking in around an hour, was presented on *The American Short Story* series: it's an adaptation of a Flannery O'Connor novella, with a script by Horton Foote, approached so reverently that it was filmed on O'Connor's family's farm. But while the original novella still has bite, this version feels toothless. The cast includes Irene Worth, John Houseman, and Robert Earl Jones (father of James); Samuel L. Jackson plays Sulk (the laborer getting set up with the Polish cousin), who is described by O'Connor as "a yellowish boy with a short woodchuck-like head pushed into a rounded felt hat." Jackson plays a servile support-ing character who doesn't seem to be disguising any greater intelli-gence, but he has one arresting moment, when Sulk shares in the moral responsibility of Mrs. McIntyre: when a disgruntled worker lets a trac-tor roll over Guizac and crush him, they stand by silently, and their faces tell you that they're horrified both by what's about to happen and by themselves.

The Trial of the Moke (1978)

Johnson Whittaker
MOVIE: 6/10   SLJ FACTOR: 4/10   MINUTES UNTIL HE SHOWS UP: 30

The Trial of the Moke tells the true story of Henry O. Flipper, the first Black graduate of West Point, running up against a racist commanding officer at Fort Davis in Texas in 1881 and then being framed and court-martialed. A stage play presented by the Milwaukee Repertory Company, it was filmed for public television; it had a shoestring budget and the play was unexceptional, but it got by on the strength of the underlying story. The uneven cast included compelling work in a supporting role by Alfre Woodard.

> *"Henry, you've got to stand up for me! There's no one else on my side!"*

Jackson plays Johnson Whittaker, another one of the first Black cadets to attend West Point. Whittaker appears in brief flashbacks in his dress uniform, first hopeful and luminously handsome, then despondent when he's being hounded out of West Point and Flipper won't vouch for him. And then, when Flipper is being railroaded, Whittaker and James Smith (another pioneering Black cadet) appear in top hats, tails, and blackface, apparitions speaking in minstrel-show dialect about Flipper's predicament. Their appearance is a gut punch, as it's meant to be: a vivid expression of the inescapable racism surrounding Flipper.

The Exterminator (1980)

Extra (uncredited)
MOVIE: 5/10   SLJ FACTOR: 1/10   MINUTES UNTIL HE SHOWS UP: 53

Samuel L. Jackson took pride in not working as an extra: when he was a stand-in for Robert Hooks on the 1976 TV movie *Just an Old Sweet Song*, he observed that in the caste system permeating a movie set, the extras reside at the bottom. They're not quite lepers, but nobody learns their names, they eat last, and sometimes they don't even have access to a bathroom. The one exception to his no-extra-work policy was this lurid exploitation movie, a surprise hit. As the lead actor, Robert Ginty, walks through Times Square, Jackson is visible for a few seconds behind him, wearing a hat and oversized sunglasses, holding a cigarette and a shopping bag—and then he's lost in the crowd.

Ginty, previously better known as a law student on *The Paper Chase*, seems miscast as a Vietnam vet who takes the law into his own hands after his best friend is savagely beaten by a New York City street gang. He's following in the mode of Clint Eastwood in the *Dirty Harry* series or Charles Bronson in *Death Wish*, indulging in the same vigilante fantasy that led Bernhard Goetz to shoot four teenagers on a New York City subway in 1984. The movie delivers the violent thrills of a mobster who gets lowered into a meat grinder and a purveyor of child rape who gets burned alive: torture with a righteous sheen. The bloody narrative hurtles along, but it finds time to pause for a Stan Getz concert in Battery Park, for a cop who carefully cooks a hot dog at his desk by running electrical current through it, and for us to see the protagonist's chosen reading material: Jean-Paul Sartre and the *New York Post*.

Ragtime (1981)

Gang Member No. 2
MOVIE: 6/10   SLJ FACTOR: 3/10   MINUTES UNTIL HE SHOWS UP: 86

Ragtime feels like an American history class taught by Mr. Forman, who was groovy but unorganized and so had to cram everything that happened in the twentieth century into the final week before summer vacation. It warms up with the "Trial of the Century," ripped from the actual headlines of 1907: the prosecution of

"Don't turn around and you won't get hurt."

Harry Thaw, the deranged millionaire husband of model Evelyn Nesbit, for the murder of famous architect Stanford White. Nesbit is played by Elizabeth McGovern, in an Oscar-nominated performance; in an unlikely bit of casting, novelist Norman Mailer plays White. The cast is filled with future stars, including Jeff Daniels, Debbie Allen, John Ratzenberger, and Fran Drescher—and on the other end of the career timeline, it features the final hurrah of James Cagney.

It doesn't always cohere; much of E. L. Doctorow's novel is reduced to period window dressing. In a role that seems like it was mostly left in the editing room, Mandy Patinkin shines as a Jewish silhouette artist who leaves the Lower East Side to become a successful film director. The center of the movie, we eventually learn, is Coalhouse Walker (a strong performance by Howard E. Rollins Jr.), an African American jazz pianist who gets hassled by some racist firemen in New Rochelle, a suburb of New York City. (Doctorow's inspiration for that character was Heinrich von Kleist's 1810 novella *Michael Kohlhaas*.) When Walker's car gets vandalized by the firemen and he can't get legal satisfaction, he embarks on a campaign of retribution, bombing firehouses and ultimately invading the swank Pierpont Morgan Library. Stubborn and proud, Walker refuses to back down, even though that costs him his family, his job, and ultimately his life.

Jackson plays a member of Walker's gang. He doesn't get many scenes, and his face is often covered with a baggy cloth hood. When we can see him, he makes for an imposing but extremely dapper Black revolutionary, accessorized with a vest, a bow tie, and a cigarette insouciantly dangling from his mouth. We don't know the specifics of the racial insults that have led him to join this terrorist campaign, but his eyes burn with righteousness.

Uncle Tom's Cabin (1987)

George
MOVIE: 4/10   SLJ FACTOR: 4/10   MINUTES UNTIL HE SHOWS UP: 0

Uncle Tom's Cabin sold more copies than any other novel in the nineteenth century; by effectively, if sentimentally, dramatizing the horrors of slavery, it fueled the abolitionist movement and arguably led to the Civil War. For some reason, this cable-TV movie adaptation was motivated less by a desire to educate a new generation about slavery's moral stain and more by a desire to rehabilitate the reputation of Harriet Beecher Stowe's 1852 book. Although this

> *"I am a free man, standing on God's green soil, and I claim my wife and my son as my own."*

was the first English-language movie version of *Uncle Tom's Cabin* with sound, the novel spawned countless stage adaptations in its heyday, many of them with blackface and minstrel-show stereotypes—some of them even pro-slavery. Those productions are how the phrase "Uncle Tom" got fixed in popular culture as a cringing, ingratiating slave who betrays other Black people.

The Uncle Tom played here by Avery Brooks is noble, proud, and moral; Brooks, the best thing about this movie, said that he based his performance on Josiah Henson, the fugitive slave whose autobiography inspired Stowe. Phylicia Rashad (of *The Cosby Show*) portrays Eliza, who flees with her young son after he is sold by the Kentucky farmer who owns them both. Eliza's famous crossing of the Ohio River, hopping from one ice floe to another, is reduced here to a more placid swim with a raft, because Rashad was pregnant during the shoot. On the other side, she is reunited with her husband George (Samuel L. Jackson), who leads his family north to the freedom that awaits them in Canada. George is little more than a stock role in a melodrama—the upright and brave husband—and Jackson's performance is stiff. He has one memorable scene, however, where he confronts the slave catchers pursuing them, even shooting one.

Director Stan Lathan contrasted his work here with the movie version of *The Color Purple* released two years earlier, where a white man (Steven Spielberg) adapted a novel by a Black woman (Alice Walker). Lathan said, "I liked the challenge this production presented: A Black man's interpretation of a white woman's interpretation of Black reality."

Magic Sticks (1987)

Straßenhändler ("Street Peddler")
MOVIE: 3/10   SLJ FACTOR: 4/10   MINUTES UNTIL HE SHOWS UP: 2

When they build the One-Joke Comedy Movie Hall of Fame, the 1980s wing will include specimens such as *Weekend at Bernie's* (the joke: it's funny when people pretend a corpse is still alive!) and *So Fine* (the joke: people go crazy when the hot fashion trend is jeans with see-through panels on the butt!). And the curatorial staff will give a prominent location to *Magic Sticks* (the joke: magical drumsticks produce a beat that make people lose control of their bodies, with movements somewhere between dance and rhythmic spasms!). The gimmick is only fitfully amusing, and the filmmakers don't seem to know what to do with it. Felix, the scarf-wearing percussionist who acquires the sticks, plays in a band, but the movie bogs down in a subplot where gangsters want to use his magical abilities to assist in criminal enterprises.

> *"Hier läuft ja nicht jeden Tag ein Drummer über den Weg."* ("It's not every day that a drummer passes this way.")

This West German production, filmed in New York City with an English-speaking cast, never reached theaters in the USA; the German-language dub did get a commercial release. George Kranz, starring as Felix, was a real-life German musician (best known for the club hit "Trommeltanz (Din Daa Daa)"), but the cast included at least three American actors who went on to bigger things: Samuel L. Jackson,

Lauren Tom (Amy in *Futurama*), and Jackson's pal Reginald VelJohnson (Sgt. Al Powell in *Die Hard*, or as Jackson put it, "that fat black cop that's outside talking to [Bruce Willis] anytime he's in the building").

As a guy selling detritus on a New York City sidewalk, Jackson kicks off the movie when Felix crashes his bike into a nearby taxicab. Checking out the miscellaneous junk, Felix offers to trade shoplifted yogurt and sardines for an LP and a flyswatter, but Jackson gives him the magical drumsticks. Having provided the inciting incident, Jackson disappears from the movie, never to be seen again. Jackson plays his brief scene winningly: he knows he's just a human plot device, but with a cheroot in his mouth and a savvy air, he makes for a charming one.

Eddie Murphy Raw (1987)

Eddie's Uncle
MOVIE: 5/10 SLJ FACTOR: 2/10 MINUTES UNTIL HE SHOWS UP: 0

Eddie Murphy, one of the biggest stars in the world, swaggers onstage in New York City, wearing a black-and-blue paisley leather suit, and does a masterful set of stand-up comedy. He does a lethal bit on Bill Cosby; he tells the story of getting into a fight at a nightclub (he blames

> *"That boy has got talent!"*

white guys getting belligerent after watching *Rocky* movies); he concludes with a brilliant impression of his drunken father, ineffectually laying down the law while misquoting Motown songs.

Murphy also is gleefully homophobic and totally toxic when it comes to gender relations, obsessed with the notion that a woman might be trying to trick him into marriage so she can then divorce him and take half his money, which launches him into an extended riff about wanting to find an African wife (a "crazy nekkid zebra bitch") unschooled in American ways. It's not surprising that he's hilarious even when he's spewing bile: what's more interesting is how fully he inhabits the shoes of his female characters, not just capturing their physical essence but having enough empathy to make them vivid. Even if he couldn't admit it, he knew life was complicated. (Years later, he would recant much of this material, saying that he was coping with an ugly breakup. "I was a young guy processing a broken heart, you know, kind of an asshole," he confessed.)

His take on Michael Jackson was incredibly prescient for 1987, by the way. Discussing how palatable Jackson was to white America,

Murphy says, "We don't know everything about Michael Jackson. He might be this bad motherfucker behind closed doors. He's a recluse. You know, behind closed doors he might be completely different."

Before Murphy comes onstage, we get footage of his limo and excited fans outside Madison Square Garden. And before *that*, we get a three-minute curtain-raising sketch, set in 1968, when Murphy was seven. Murphy's extended family gathers for Thanksgiving and the kids entertain the adults with an after-dinner talent show: one boy does a "shufflebutt" dance and one girl (a young Tatyana Ali, later of *Fresh Prince of Bel-Air* fame) sings a song. Young Eddie then tells a dirty joke about a lion and a monkey. The family is shocked, but one of Eddie's uncles—wearing a mod sweater, a white hat, and sunglasses—claps and laughs heartily. Jackson's job, playing that uncle, is to make his enthusiasm seem plausible—which he does, even selling the awkward dialogue "I love that doo-doo line!"

School Daze (1988)

Leeds

MOVIE: 7/10   **SLJ FACTOR:** 7/10   **MINUTES UNTIL HE SHOWS UP:** 66
EXPLETIVES NOT DELETED: bitch, motherfuckers, shit, fuck (x2)

Spike Lee's second feature film feels like the work of a director who's not sure he'll ever get to make another movie and wants to cram everything he can into this one, putting as much previously unrepresented Black life as possible up on the big screen. So this musical-comedy-drama about life at a historically Black college includes both a step show and "Straight & Nappy," a song about the sociopolitical significance of Black women's hair.

You can see Lee's passion, not least in the final sequence when the cast breaks the fourth wall, looking into the camera and imploring the audience to "wake up." You can see his low-budget inventiveness: instead of staging a football game, Lee keeps his camera on the fans in the stands. You can also see his weaknesses, especially

> *"We ain't your brothers. How come you college motherfuckers think y'all run everything?"*

in his treatment of female characters: when one fraternity brother (Giancarlo Esposito) orders his girlfriend (Tisha Campbell) to deflower a new pledge (Lee himself) and then cruelly breaks up with her, saying she failed a test of loyalty, it plays like a reflection of Lee's gender pathologies more than his characters'.

To fill a campus of disparate characters, Lee cast a whole generation of Black actors who were roughly college-age. Laurence Fishburne (then billed as "Larry") was twenty-seven, which stretched the age boundaries, but he gave a magnetic, star-making performance in the lead role of the campus activist Dap. Jackson, forty on the film's release, was too old to pass as a philosophy major, but he got a memorable scene as Leeds, a local who mocks and confronts Dap and his friends when the college kids visit a Kentucky Fried Chicken.

In the parking lot, Leeds spits out his resentment in an argument about identity and the class divide. The scene climaxes with him telling the students, "Y'all niggers—and you gonna be niggers forever. Just like us. Niggers."

Dap powerfully replies, "You're not niggers." As he walks away, a bell is heard on the soundtrack, maybe from a train or a streetcar. Lee observed of that sound cue, "It's like the round is over," and that's what the scene feels like. It's a verbal boxing match pitting Jackson against Fishburne: two Black actors, both up-and-coming, both heavyweights.

Coming to America (1988)

Hold-Up Man
MOVIE: 5/10   **SLJ FACTOR:** 5/10   **MINUTES UNTIL HE SHOWS UP:** 60
EXPLETIVES NOT DELETED: fucking, asshole, fuck (x2)

Only one year after *Raw*, Eddie Murphy flipped his offensive stand-up scenario where he found an African wife whom he could control ("Murphy Marries Bush Bitch," as he imagined the headline) and played a pampered African prince who visits the United States in search of self-reliance and an intelligent, independent bride. It's a sweet rom-com fairy tale, even if the humor leans too heavily on seeing Murphy (and his sidekick Arsenio Hall) in various disguises: Murphy plays not only the good-natured Prince Akeem, but an opinionated older barber, a white Jewish boxing fan who argues with that barber about Rocky Marciano, and an R&B singer (a discount-rack version of Rick James) who fronts the band Sexual Chocolate.

> *"Take the money out, all of it! Don't stall me, fat boy!"*

The cast is almost all African American and the nation of Zamunda (ruled over by James Earl Jones's monarch) is a wonderland seemingly undisturbed by colonialism, the most idyllic African kingdom in film until Wakanda in *Black Panther*, three decades later. Spike Lee, never reluctant to call other moviemakers out, deemed the movie "a serious move by Eddie Murphy to do a film by and about Black people."

In pursuit of the girl of his dreams, Prince Akeem gets a job working at a fast-food restaurant, a McDonald's knockoff called McDowell's. Halfway through the movie, an unkempt Jackson shows up to rob the joint, blasting a hole in the ceiling with a shotgun. Jackson's role in the movie is to bark orders until an unruffled Prince Akeem can defeat him with a mop handle. But although Jackson is intimidating, he also conveys the desperation of his nameless hood with just one line reading. When he impatiently mutters "come on" to himself, we see a man who knows that things are going to end poorly for him, even though he's the one holding the gun.

"I had a great time doing it, and I got paid," Jackson said. "But you have to inform the place with some kind of energy, and some kind of motivation, so you figure out *why* you're doing it. Why are you robbing this place? What desperate situation caused you to go into a place in broad daylight with a shotgun and rob somebody? Find a great motivation, and get in there, and do it. And use that energy to, hopefully, fire up the other people in the scene, and it'll be infectious. and the scene will have that kind of energy and that kind of dynamism, and people will remember it."

So what was his secret motivation in this scene? Jackson said he wasn't playing a junkie looking to buy drugs; in his head, the desperation stemmed from "a person back home, a girlfriend who's telling you, 'You're out the bills and food. You need this, you need that. And you either get it, or don't come back.' That was me."

Alixa Garcia.

S pike Lee's Summer Film Camp." That's what Samuel L. Jackson called the annual experience of working on Spike Lee's movies. At the time, Lee filmed his movies once a year, always in the summer, hiring mostly the same cast and crew for each one. "Spike was like our savior when we were all struggling actors in New York," Jackson said. "Every summer we knew we were going to go to Spike Lee's Summer Film Camp, and make enough money to get us through to Christmas."

Lee would recruit his cast some months before with rat-a-tat phone calls. According to Jackson, they would clock in under a minute and run along the lines of: "Sam! 'Sup? How 'bout the Knicks? *Do the Right Thing*, this summer!"

Lee preferred actors based in New York over those from L.A. "The actors from New York are more about work, which is the way it should be," he opined. "Give me actors like Bill Nunn and Sam Jackson any time." As it happened, Nunn had recently moved into the basement of Jackson's brownstone on W. 143rd Street. The friends nicknamed the subterranean apartment the Cave—and the Cave became party central. Jackson needed only to walk down a staircase to descend into his bad habits.

Lee's third feature film was *Do the Right Thing*, set on a single block in the neighborhood of Bedford-Stuyvesant in Brooklyn. Four months before the shooting started, Lee planned to cast Laurence Fishburne as Radio Raheem (a character with few lines, but an imposing presence with his boom box), Nunn as Mister Señor Love Daddy (the neighborhood's radio DJ), and Jackson as Buggin' Out, an excitable local. Then Fishburne dropped out. "Fish has decided that he no longer wants to play supporting roles after *School Daze*. He feels he's a leading man now," Lee wrote in his journal in April 1988. "Knowing that Fishburne won't be down with this film means it's time to juggle." He moved Nunn into the role of Radio Raheem, bumped up Jackson to the vacant spot behind the DJ's microphone, and shifted Giancarlo Esposito into the part of Buggin' Out.

The movie shot on location in Bed-Stuy; Lee hired the Fruit of Islam to clean out the local crack houses. Jackson said that the neighborhood's drug dealers held a grudge. When he wandered off the movie's set and went to a local store, the greeting was not "Probably it's these little cooked onions," but something closer to "You acting motherfuckers came in here and ruined our business, we're gonna fuck you up."

Jackson wouldn't back down. "There were some guys they could intimidate, but there were others of us that were like, 'You know, I just happen to be an actor, but I used to be the same kind of guy you are, so when you talk about fuckin' me up, you think I'm just gonna stand there and let you fuck me up? That's not gonna happen.'" Veteran actor Ossie Davis, also in the cast, defused more than one confrontation. "We were all pretty crazy during that time," Jackson said. "Ossie was sort of our balance."

Jackson spent most of the shoot inside the booth of FM 108 We Love Radio, isolated from the rest of the ensemble, appearing in the background of shots, watching wistfully through the window like a little kid who can't go out and play until he finishes his homework. Jackson always brought a book to the set: sometimes he'd kill time by reading, sometimes by taking a nap. "Half the time I'd be in there sleeping, because I'd been up pretty much the night before, fucked up, hanging out with my friends," he said.

When the movie wrapped, Jackson kept hustling, auditioning all over town, accepting any role he was offered. His technique: "I go to the audition, act my brains out, and get picked." Whenever he checked with his agent on the phone, Jackson would ritualistically ask, "Hollywood call today?" In their show-business catechism, the answer was always the same: No.

Jackson had racked up small parts in enough films that his friends nicknamed him "King of the Cameos." He was a master of making a big impression in a small amount of screen time, even if many of his parts were conceived as generic types—most obviously in the case of the 1989 movie *Sea of Love*, where his role was actually billed as "Black Guy." Jackson scoffed, "That was the character name. That's what it says in the credits: Black Guy."

On December 14, 1988, Jackson was riding the subway, just like he did most days. As he was getting off his train, exiting the middle door of the last car, he saw that a woman had dropped some of her possessions, so he stopped to help her pick them up. "Very un–New York–like of me," he noted. While he was leaning over, the subway doors closed on his ankle: most of his body was on the station's platform, but his right foot was trapped inside the subway car. That was annoying, but not a remarkable moment in the history of the New York City mass transit system. What happened next wasn't typical, however: the subway started moving out of the station, pulling Jackson along with the train. (The operator of the train was supposed to make a visual check at every station so nobody would get caught in the doors. "Dude said he didn't see me, even though I had on a red coat," Jackson complained.)

In the space of a few seconds, a lot happened. Jackson, yelling at the top of his lungs, did his best to keep up with the moving train, hopping on his left leg. The people inside the subway car tried to pull off his right shoe so he could squeeze his foot out of the door. Jackson frantically looked around for something to grab onto, but found nothing. Two transit cops ran after the train, shouting at the motorman. As the train accelerated, Jackson lost his balance and fell onto his back, getting dragged along the platform. (Fortunately, he was wearing a backpack, which protected him from a massive head injury.) As the subway entered the tunnel, Jackson resigned himself to his impending death and the knowledge that it was "going to be a sad Christmas." And then, just before he smashed into the wall by the tunnel, the train stopped. "A guy on crutches pulled the emergency cord," Jackson said.

When the train lurched to a halt, Jackson was lying on his back about a car and a half shy of the wall. He was lucky to be alive, but he was nevertheless hobbled: he suffered a complete tear of his ACL and a partial tear of his meniscus, plus lots of cartilage damage. After his right knee was surgically repaired, he spent ten months on crutches and a year and a half in physical rehab. For the rest of his life, he would have a couple of extra screws in his right leg.

Professionally, the injury took Jackson out of commission for months—there's not a lot of call for actors on crutches—but he still participated in the 1989 edition of Spike Lee's Summer Film Camp (also known as *Mo' Better Blues*). Jackson had to play his character, a thug looking to collect a gambling debt, with a conspicuous leg brace and cane. One day, a crew member told Jackson about a job she was doing on the side: the music video for Public Enemy's "911 Is a Joke." They hadn't found anybody to play Flavor Flav's dad in the video— could Jackson come to the Bronx that night? "I had no idea what it was—I just showed up," Jackson said. His job in the video was basically to stand in the background, wearing black sweats and holding a glass of wine in his hand, looking concerned about his wife, who needed an ambulance. With his trademark clock around his neck, Flavor Flav seized the foreground, rapping about the deficiencies of emergency services in Black neighborhoods and mugging for the camera. The video was an all-night shoot: off-camera, Jackson and Flav hung out together, drinking and smoking weed.

Once he healed, Jackson kept auditioning; Hollywood kept on not calling, while his peers kept landing major projects. "You feel like you're on the same level talentwise and you go to an audition and you know you rocked it, but you didn't get it, and you wonder why," Jackson said. "I would go to an audition and my eyes are a little too red or I smell like that beer I drank before I went to the audition, or whatever, and I didn't get the job."

The writer and film producer Nelson George ran into Jackson on 57th Street around this time; Jackson accosted him, trying to see if George could get him any work. "He was looking sketchy," George said. "I didn't really know at the time that he had a drug problem, but he didn't need to tell me. I could see: he looked feral. This was the height of the crack era in New York City. I was around a lot of people who were using, and Sam was in a dark place."

"I was a fucking drug addict and I was out of my mind a lot of the time, but I had a good reputation," Jackson insisted. "Showed up on time, knew my lines, hit my marks."

In the fall of 1989, LaTanya Richardson acted in a play at the Manhattan Theater Club called *The Talented Tenth*, a dramedy by Richard Wesley about the consciences of aging buppies. One person working on the play remembered spotting Jackson at the cast party: "In the multi-roomed pre-War uptown apartment of one of the cast members, he was sitting curled in a ball, in a dark room. Not a good time in his life, I suspect."

Richardson knew her husband had a problem, even if she didn't know the full extent of it: she referred to their brownstone on 143rd Street as the "Villa in Hell." Jackson was gone a lot of the time, and when he was around, he admitted, he was "always isolated, snappy, and irritable." He clung to the smallest gestures of respectability. Jackson never did drugs in front of Zoe, even when he took her to the park to play on the swings—and then he acted as if that were a major accomplishment.

"I paid my bills," Jackson said, somewhat defensively. "I didn't steal shit to sell out of my brownstone. I didn't steal my daughter's toys. I didn't steal my wife's money out of her purse. I could go to the ATM and get money for cocaine. I just kept spending money and finding people to get high with."

Jackson didn't think he was smoking crack, because he bought powdered cocaine and cooked it up himself: he enjoyed the hands-on rituals of drug preparation before getting high. "People who smoke crack buy rocks. I thought I was freebasing, but as it turns out, it's the same thing."

Jackson returned to the Yale Rep in March 1990, starring in the latest August Wilson play, *Two Trains Running*, set in a restaurant in a 1969 Pittsburgh neighborhood about to be overrun by gentrification. He played Wolf, a numbers runner, starring opposite Laurence Fishburne—but the play ran for only a month and a Broadway transfer was delayed.

In the early summer of 1990, Jackson spent the day at the bachelor party of a friend, writer-actor-director Ruben Santiago-Hudson (who had been part of the touring company for *A Soldier's Play*). All day long, Jackson celebrated his pal's impending wedding by guzzling tequila. Stumbling home that night, totally smashed, he thought, "I need some coke so I can even my shit out." With the wrongheaded certainty of the addict, he executed that plan: "I went by the spot, copped, went home, cooked the shit, and passed out before I had even smoked it, drunk. That's when my wife and daughter found me on the floor."

LaTanya and Zoe woke up the next morning to an undeniable problem: Sam was unconscious on the kitchen floor, still clutching his cocaine. Richardson made some phone calls and within twenty-four hours, Jackson was in a rehab center in upstate New York. "I threatened to leave him if he didn't see the rehab through," she said. "I knew I couldn't leave this boy I admired so much. But I resented him too. I hated it when he slurred his words. A wife hates to see her husband be weak."

Jackson spent twenty-eight days in rehab and loathed every single day. In group therapy, his fellow addicts kept messing with his head, and the counselors were in full-time tough-love mode, "which was not working for me." But he learned about how alcoholism runs in families, and he finally acknowledged his relentless need for excess. If there was a six-pack of beer, he could never have just one: he needed to drink them all. "I never thought I was an alcoholic; I just drank all my life," he said. "But I was a blackout drinker: I would wake up in places and not know how I got there."

He worried that he wouldn't be fun if he got sober; he worried that he wouldn't be able to perform without substances in his body. But he also recognized that he needed a change: "I figured that if I tried this other way for, you know, twenty-eight years and it hadn't worked, why not give this a try and see what happens?" And he learned to pray for the strength he needed to not drink or take drugs: "I found the humility I needed to get down on my knees."

The whole time Jackson was in rehab, he was making phone calls to Spike Lee, who was in preproduction for his next movie, *Jungle Fever*. There was a crucial supporting role that Jackson very much wanted to play: Gator Purify, a crack addict whose habit tears his family apart. "I've done all the research, so I know I'm gonna be good," Jackson assured Lee. "Just hold on."

Lee was, understandably, doubtful—and Jackson's counselors in rehab were dead-set against him taking the role. They thought that handling drug paraphernalia and discussing the joys of crack would inevitably trigger him and send him right back into his addiction. Jackson's counterargument: for eight weeks of work, he would be paid roughly $40,000. He told them, "I will never come back here, if only because I never want to see you again."

Less than two weeks after Jackson left rehab, he was working on *Jungle Fever*. Skinny and detoxing, he very much looked the part of a strung-out addict—so much so that his first day of shooting, when he went to the craft services table to get something to eat, security guards tried to chase him away, thinking that he was a local crackhead.

What Jackson brought to the role, beyond firsthand knowledge of what it was like to be high on cocaine, was the knowledge of how addicts alienate everyone around them. In his own life, he had made everyone in his house afraid to speak to him, and he had drained every ounce of money and goodwill from his own friendships. "The few friends that I used with, we were all kind of looking at each other strange too, because we were using each other up," he observed. Because Jackson made Gator funny and personable, it was easy to imagine the character before he was in the grips of his addiction, and to see the personal connections that he was exploiting.

The heart of the movie was Gator's relationships with his indulgent mother (Ruby Dee) and religious father (Ossie Davis). Gator dances for his mother to charm cash out of her—but late in the movie, when he dances for his father, it's confrontational, a menacing, shoulder-shaking shimmy. Jackson said, "I wanted him to look at me and actually see all the things in me that frightened him about himself as the good reverend doctor: the womanizer, the abuser, the self-righteous monster. That dance that I thought of at that moment was what I figured the personification of evil was for him."

Gator succeeds in provoking him—so well that his father shoots him. That scene was intensely cathartic for Jackson: "When my character died, it was almost like I was killing off that part of my life," he said. His death scene was the final scene Lee shot for the movie.

Once Jackson was clean, he realized how much he had been cutting himself off from his own talent: Gator was the best work he had ever done. He was finally able to move beyond the "bloodless" performances that Richardson had warned him about because he was no longer numbing his own emotions. Jackson said it was "like the petals were closed and, all of a sudden, the sun hit the flower and opened it up."

"STACKS WAS ALWAYS CRAZY"

GOODFELLAS
— A MARTIN SCORSESE PICTURE —

LINIERS—

WARNER BROS. PRESENTS

AN IRWIN WINKLER PRODUCTION A MARTIN SCORSESE PICTURE GOODFELLAS • ROBERT DE NIRO • RAY LIOTTA
JOE PESCI • LORRAINE BRACCO AND PAUL SORVINO NOT TO MENTION SAMUEL L. JACKSON PRODUCTION DESIGNER KRISTI ZEA
FILM EDITOR THELMA SCHOONMAKER ACE DIRECTOR OF PHOTOGRAPHY MICHAEL BALLHAUS A.S.C. EXECUTIVE PRODUCER BARBARA DE FINA
SCREENPLAY BY NICHOLAS PILEGGI & MARTIN SCORSESE PRODUCED BY IRWIN WINKLER DIRECTED BY MARTIN SCORSESE

Liniers.

Dead Man Out (1989)

Calvin Fredricks
MOVIE: 5/10   SLJ FACTOR: 7/10   MINUTES UNTIL HE SHOWS UP: 53

When we meet Calvin, the death row prisoner played by Samuel L. Jackson, he's minutes away from his execution. Stammering and sounding confused, he asks the prison guards for a little time to collect himself. Time is exactly what he doesn't have: they hoist him out of his cell and carry him toward the gas chamber. First he pleads for his life, and then he just asks for the dignity of being able to walk to his fate. But when he tries to stand up, his legs buckle underneath him.

> *"I know I gotta go, and I'm, I'm, I'm ready. I, I, I just need a minute, okay?"*

We leave Calvin shaking and sweating, strapped into the chair where he will die. It's an entire life in two minutes, and Jackson imbues it with drama and heartbreaking humanity.

The premise of this premium-cable-TV movie is an ethical dilemma: a psychiatrist (Danny Glover) treats a death row inmate (Rubén Blades) who appears to have been driven mad by his years of incarceration. So long as the inmate's mentally incapacitated, he can't be executed—so is it better to help him get well or to leave him alone? Glover, only two years older than Jackson, similarly achieved movie stardom in his 40s (via *Lethal Weapon*); he anchors *Dead Man Out* with a dignified, thoughtful performance. Most of the movie is taken up by the sessions between Glover and Blades; the rest of it seems to be devoted to the detailed procedures of prisoner transfers. When Jackson appears, about two-thirds of the way through the talky narrative, he viscerally reminds viewers of the life-and-death stakes, giving the movie exactly the tragic jolt that it needs.

Do the Right Thing (1989)

Mister Señor Love Daddy
MOVIE: 10/10   SLJ FACTOR: 7/10   MINUTES UNTIL HE SHOWS UP: 4
EXPLETIVES NOT DELETED: shit

Spike Lee's greatest joint, *Do the Right Thing*, was also the movie Barack and Michelle Obama saw on their first date. When they told Lee that, he responded, "Good thing you didn't choose *Driving Miss Daisy!*"

The movie tells the story of the hottest day of the summer on one Bed-Stuy block. "I knew I wanted the film to take place in one day," Spike Lee said. "And I wanted to reflect the racial climate of New York City at that time. The day would get longer and hotter, and things would escalate until they exploded." The movie teems with as much color and life and music as an MGM musical, which makes it all the more harrowing when it erupts in violence: New York City cops kill Radio Raheem (Bill Nunn) in a stranglehold; Mookie (Lee) throws a garbage can through the window of Sal's Pizzeria, and a crowd then burns it down; firemen turn their hoses on the crowd. In two hours, we see how fractured humanity can be, even in the space of one city block.

"My people, my people, what can I say? Say what I can. I saw it, but I didn't believe. I didn't believe it, what I saw. Are we gonna live together? Together, are we gonna live? This is your Mister Señor Love Daddy talking to you from We Love Radio 108 FM on your dial, and that's the triple truth, Ruth. Today's weather? Hot! Wake up!"

Before the murder and the riot, the movie wheels around the block, spending time with the family that owns Sal's (Danny Aiello, John Turturro, Richard Edson), Mookie's girlfriend (Rosie Perez), neighborhood youths (Giancarlo Esposito, Martin Lawrence), a local elderly woman (Ruby Dee), even the neighborhood drunk (Ossie Davis). The voice uniting all these disparate threads and characters? The local radio DJ played by Samuel L. Jackson, who plays love jams, gives a roll call of the giants of Black music, and can be seen behind a plate glass window sporting a colorful array of hats. He's also the movie's conscience, stepping outside the narrative when characters start spouting racial invective to shout "You need to cool that shit out!" He begins the movie by holding up an alarm clock to his microphone to tell his listeners "Wake up!"—a literal eight a.m.

message from a DJ, but also an echo of the plea for greater social awareness in *School Daze* and a bridge from that movie's final moments.

Sea of Love (1989)

Black Guy
MOVIE: 6/10   SLJ FACTOR: 4/10   MINUTES UNTIL HE SHOWS UP: 4
EXPLETIVES NOT DELETED: fuck

After an opening murder sequence, *Sea of Love* kicks off with a classic sting operation: dozens of New Yorkers with outstanding arrest warrants get invited to a breakfast with the Yankees. But when they show up, they find out that they're going to jail, not to the ball game. Samuel L. Jackson plays the last suspect to get into the room: tall and rangy, with a bright red T-shirt and matching cap, he looks more like a teenager than the middle-aged man that he was.

> *"Yo yo yo, fuck that. Give up the bad news, homeboy."*

Al Pacino plays the cop who promises the crowd both bad news and good news. Jackson hectors him, first for the bad news (the breakfast is actually hosted by the NYPD), then for the good news (everyone will get a slug of vodka with their orange juice before they get arrested). Jackson's role is small (and, let us again emphasize, credited as "Black Guy"), but he shows that he has the charisma and the confidence to go toe-to-toe with Pacino, one of the most intense actors in the business. Years later, director Harold Becker praised Jackson's work in the bit part and asked, "Who could have predicted that he would be the major star he is now?"

For its remaining 105 minutes, *Sea of Love* is a 1980s erotic thriller, centered on the hard body and uncertain motives of Ellen Barkin's character, but one with the heart of a 1970s drama. It's anchored by Pacino (a strong performance as an alcoholic detective looking for a serial killer—he falls for Barkin, even though she's a suspect), John Goodman (his genial partner), and screenwriter Richard Price, who like Jackson was forty years old but in the early days of a remarkable film career. Price already had an exceptional ear for dialogue, as in this succinct description of a shooting victim delivered by Goodman: "facedown taxpayer, back of the head in his own bed."

A Shock to the System (1990)

Ulysses
MOVIE: 5/10 **SLJ FACTOR: 2/10** **MINUTES UNTIL HE SHOWS UP: 5**

Michael Caine plays a New York City marketing executive, working in the sort of office where people hand over memos with "the results of the great Kentucky gelatin wars." Discontented with his domestic life in Connecticut and furious at being passed over for a promotion, he arranges for his wife and his new boss to meet with fatal accidents (electrocution and gas explosion, respectively).

> *"Play to win, baby. Play to win."*

This black comedy isn't sufficiently black-hearted or comedic enough, and it's larded with narration (inconsistently shifting from first person to third person) that betrays its origins as a well-mannered British novel—but it gets by on engaging performances from Elizabeth McGovern, Swoosie Kurtz, and especially Caine.

Samuel L. Jackson makes a fleeting appearance as a three-card monte dealer hustling the working people of New York on their morning commute. (McGovern declines to loan her roommate $20 to get in the game.) In an aloha shirt, a bucket hat, and eyeglasses, seemingly more focused on his cards than on his marks, Jackson carries himself like a librarian on vacation. He's there to make street-level New York City feel like a vulgar assault on the sensibilities of suburban commuters—but at least he seems like an individual rather than a stereotype.

Def by Temptation (1990)

Minister Garth
MOVIE: 3/10 **SLJ FACTOR: 4/10** **MINUTES UNTIL HE SHOWS UP: 10**

Def by Temptation was made on such a low budget that the film could have doubled its production values if the producers had checked under the couch cushions for loose change. It's historically important as a horror movie with an African American cast, however: there had been a long gap in Black horror after movies

> *"Blessed is the man that endureth temptation."*

such as *Blacula* (1972 camp classic, with a sequel, *Scream Blacula Scream*, the following year), *Ganja & Hess* (1973 experimental vampire horror, remade forty-one years later by Spike Lee), and *Sugar Hill* (1974 blaxploitation zombies).

The movie hints at issues of politics and media consumption—in a scene clearly inspired by David Cronenberg's *Videodrome*, a character gets swallowed up by his TV set and spat out in bloody pieces—but the central theme is AIDS. A beautiful succubus (Cynthia Bond), billed as the Temptress, seduces a series of men at an upscale cocktail bar and brings each of them home for a night of passion, followed quickly by a gruesome death.

Troma Films, famous for low-budget gore, acquired and released the movie, but horror junkies won't find much here to scare them. The best thing about *Def by Temptation* are the scenes featuring two brothers: K (Kadeem Hardison) is a suave young actor on the rise in New York City, while Joel (James Bond III, who also wrote and directed the movie) is a shy country boy uncertain about his future as an evangelical preacher. Their relationship feels relaxed and real—but only one of the brothers survives his encounter with the demonic Temptress.

Samuel L. Jackson, billed fourth, is onscreen for just a few minutes, playing the brothers' father, a North Carolina preacher who died in his own encounter with the Temptress. (The details are confusing but involve a black veil, a car crash, and a lot of blood.) Even in his fleeting scenes, Jackson is fierce and commanding from the pulpit: full marks to Bond for figuring out that Jackson is the man you hire when you want somebody in your movie to quote from scripture.

Betsy's Wedding (1990)

Taxi Dispatcher (Mickey)
MOVIE: 3/10   SLJ FACTOR: 1/10   MINUTES UNTIL HE SHOWS UP: 67

Alan Alda was such a big star because of the TV series *M*A*S*H* that studio executives green-lit him to direct four feature films, all of them competent but mild comedies. This one, the last, is about a Long Island contractor who

> *"Yo!"*

gets overwhelmed planning a lavish wedding for his daughter. It has a first-rate cast, including Molly Ringwald, Catherine O'Hara, Madeline Kahn, and Joe Pesci, all giving their professional best in one under-cooked scene after another. Early on, it seems like the movie's gimmick is going to be that Alda's character lives in a Walter Mitty fantasy world—when he throws a soda can in the trash, the New York Knicks show up to guard him—but that idea is quickly abandoned (or more likely, left on the cutting-room floor). Ultimately, the movie doesn't have much of a point of view beyond "it's fun to see Molly Ringwald wearing crazy outfits" (which is, in fact, true).

One subplot feels random but has some juice: the budding romance between Ally Sheedy, playing the bride's sister, employed as a cop, and Anthony LaPaglia, as a young mafioso, doing a sustained impression of Robert De Niro's performance in *The Godfather Part II*. When Alda and Pesci have dinner with LaPaglia and his powerful uncle (Burt Young), they end up getting shot at by rival gangsters. They flee to a mob-owned taxi garage run by a guy called Mickey (Samuel L. Jackson), who strides through the scene with a loping gait, relaxed and efficient in a crisis. Mickey puts each of the refugees in a separate cab, and ten seconds later he's gone, leaving us with only a memory of his cream-colored sweater and his bald spot.

Mo' Better Blues (1990)

Madlock
MOVIE: 6/10   **SLJ FACTOR:** 6/10   **MINUTES UNTIL HE SHOWS UP:** 73
EXPLETIVES NOT DELETED: fuck (x2), shit, fucking, bitch

Sometimes brilliant, more often frustrating, *Mo' Better Blues* is a baggy, self-indulgent film by Spike Lee about a young jazz trumpeter, Bleek Gilliam, who is equal parts talent and hubris. Denzel Washington is exceptional in the leading role; unfortunately, his Oscar-caliber work is side-by-side with some performances that would be more at home in a student film, such as the dueling love interests of Clarke (Cynda Williams) and Indigo (Joie Lee). And the Jewish nightclub owners Moe and Josh Flatbush (John and Nicholas Turturro) are played as greedy anti-Semitic stereotypes—not a good look for a filmmaker who worked so hard to shatter ethnic pigeonholing.

> *"We're not going to kill you. We don't believe in killing our brothers and sisters."*

Lee casts himself as Bleek's manager, Giant: a childhood friend with a gambling problem. When Giant owes his bookie (Rubén Blades) too much money, a couple of thugs show up, first to break his fingers—and later, when he's still in arrears, to pound him bloody in an alley. When Bleek tries to intercede, he gets beaten for his troubles, ending up in the hospital with injuries that leave him unable to play the trumpet at a professional level.

Samuel L. Jackson plays the role of one of the enforcers with a leg brace and a cane—he was still recovering from having been dragged nearly the length of a New York subway platform—which doesn't make him any less intimidating. His brutality has a veneer of bonhomie and racial solidarity; after breaking Giant's fingers, he offers to drop him off at a nearby hospital. But as he gleefully demonstrates the fragility of the human body, it becomes abundantly clear that his character loves his work.

Jackson also has an uncredited second role in the movie, audio only: he reprises the DJ character of Mister Señor Love Daddy from *Do the Right Thing*. Surprisingly, the scene where he comes on the radio, introducing Fontella Bass's "Rescue Me," is the same scene where he shows up as a smiling heavy. While this seems careless, it could be a decision by Lee that Jackson wasn't famous enough for the juxtaposition to seem jarring. (At the time, this was probably correct.) But it also plays as a comment on the duality of human nature, and how easily good vibes can conceal cruelty. Later, Jackson will shout "Wake up!" at Lee's battered, unconscious body, transforming his plea for greater consciousness from *Do the Right Thing* into a sadistic taunt.

The final six minutes of the movie, largely scored by John Coltrane's *A Love Supreme*, are a montage of Bleek and Indigo after he sheds his arrogance and gives up the trumpet: marriage, parenthood, domestic bliss in Brooklyn. That sequence feels like the reason Lee made the movie: if *Mo' Better Blues* is a metaphor for his own life as a driven artist, then it ends with a reminder to himself that there's a world beyond art. That seems preferable to the more cynical autobiographical moral, drawn from how Bleek gets his face bashed in: a rising artist can't afford to be loyal to old friends.

The Exorcist III (1990)

Dream Blind Man
MOVIE: 4/10   SLJ FACTOR: 1/10   MINUTES UNTIL HE SHOWS UP: 26

Savor this two-minute dream sequence, set in a train station populated by angels where a voice on the PA informs us of "the 12:18 to Elsewhere, now departing from track 11." As George C. Scott walks through the station, he sees dead friends, little people lugging around

> *"The living are dead."*

an enormous clock, the model Fabio (uncredited, making his film debut), a woman broadcasting "Earth, come in please," and New York

Knicks basketball star Patrick Ewing, credited as the Angel of Death and sporting enormous white wings, silently laying down tarot cards. Samuel L. Jackson is there too, for a few seconds, sitting in a chair, wearing a pink-and-green plaid jacket over pajamas. Jackson has dark glasses and a white cane, suggesting that he's blind; he speaks one line of dialogue, but it's overdubbed by somebody with a growly voice.

(Jackson's two primary memories from shooting this movie: 1. Getting bumped out of first class on the flight from New York to Wilmington, North Carolina, because Patrick Ewing took his seat. 2. Fabio making a spectacle of himself at their cheap hotel. "He was always in the lobby, standing under a fan with his hair blowing and his shirt open. Fabio!")

The dream is the invention of writer-director William Peter Blatty (who wrote and produced the original 1973 *Exorcist* film, not to mention the novel it was based on)—and it's one of this movie's most successful flourishes. Blatty also sets up a particularly clever jump scare (which I won't ruin for you) and gives Scott, playing a gruff police lieutenant investigating a series of lurid murders, some meaty, eccentric dialogue to sink his teeth into. (Scott took over the role of Kinderman from the late Lee J. Cobb, who played him in the original *Exorcist*.) Scott discusses *Macbeth*, complains about grammar, and gets a great monologue where he complains that he doesn't want to go home because there's a live carp swimming in his bathtub.

Unfortunately, long sections of this sequel (which ignores the events of the benighted *Exorcist II: The Heretic*) are overripe and incoherent. People are possessed by evil forces; bodies are decapitated, eviscerated, and exsanguinated; after a while, all the bloody drama becomes routine. Earth, come in, please.

Goodfellas (1990)

Stacks Edwards
MOVIE: 10/10   SLJ FACTOR: 6/10   MINUTES UNTIL HE SHOWS UP: 90
EXPLETIVES NOT DELETED: fuck (x2), shit

A good gangster movie shows us the violent embodiment of the American dream; a great gangster movie slices open that all-American body and displays the diseased organs within. A masterpiece like *Goodfellas* implicates everyone for their rapacious hearts and capitalist spleens:

"You didn't bring coffee?"

you, me, director Martin Scorsese, protagonist Henry Hill (Ray Liotta), small-time guitarist Stacks Edwards (Samuel L. Jackson).

Stacks is a member of the *Goodfellas* gallery of supporting criminals with names like Jimmy Two Times and Johnny Roastbeef, all of whom are vivid enough in their brief appearances that you'd happily watch a whole movie about any of them. When Stacks neglects to dispose of the getaway truck after the Lufthansa heist, he gets woken up in his apartment by Tommy (Joe Pesci). They banter with each other—"I thought you had one of your bitches in here." "Yeah, I did. Where the fuck is she?"—before Tommy pumps him full of bullets.

Stacks is one of a very few speaking roles for Black actors in this movie. The mobsters are intensely tribal: Henry Hill and Jimmy Conway (Robert De Niro) will never become made men, simply because of their Irish heritage. The racism of their world is at its most explicit in a scene at the Copacabana: when Tommy's date (Elizabeth Whitcraft) admires Sammy Davis Jr. in hedged language ("you can see how a white girl can fall for him"), Tommy browbeats her, declaring, "I just want to make sure I don't wind up kissing fucking Nat King Cole over here."

Shooting in neighborhoods with mob connections, Jackson remembered, "there would be guys hanging around the set who actually knew Stacks Edwards, my character, and gave me a lot of insight into who he was. They would kind of stash me in people's houses that I would use as my dressing room. I would spend a lot of time with these Italian families in Queens, eating dinner with them, watching TV, and hanging out."

As played by Jackson, Stacks makes himself at home in this bigoted world, utterly relaxed around stone killers and looking cool whether he's sauntering through a bar in a suede jacket or drowsily tumbling out of bed in patterned briefs. "Everybody loved Stacks," Henry says. His reward for his acceptance? A bullet through the back of his head and his blood spraying over his own mattress.

Jackson said that much of his role was improvised—even his death scene, where he and Pesci tried various approaches, all of which ended with his execution. "Marty [Scorsese] got concerned about the blood spatter and kept saying 'No, no. More, more!' So I took about eight showers that day while Marty kept upping the amount of blood and brains he wanted flying across the room."

The Return of Superfly (1990)

Nate Cabot

MOVIE: 2/10   **SLJ FACTOR:** 5/10   **MINUTES UNTIL HE SHOWS UP:** 18
EXPLETIVES NOT DELETED: shit (x3), fucking, bullshit, fuck (x3)

Is it a problem that this film is poorly lit? It looks cheap rather than moody, and the dim atmosphere makes it hard to follow the action. On the other hand, most of this movie's scenes are staged so ineptly, obscuring them seems like an act of kindness.

> *"Me and Priest go back to the golden age of hustling, when a dime was a dime and time was relative to the moment."*

Sig Shore produced the 1972 blaxploitation classic *Super Fly* and the following year's half-baked follow-up *Super Fly T.N.T.* before trying his hand at directing a sequel nearly two decades later. Original star Ron O'Neal was gone (replaced by Nathan Purdee), as were all members of the supporting cast; the only real continuity with the original was the score by the legendary Curtis Mayfield. Not coincidentally, the music is the best thing about this movie—and it's better appreciated in the dark!

The original *Super Fly* was about a Harlem drug dealer making one last big score before going straight and leaving town. Now he returns from Paris for no good reason and gets pulled into a war with a New York City drug lord. The muddled, borderline-incoherent screenplay squanders some talented performers, including Margaret Avery (Oscar-nominated for *The Color Purple*), but Samuel L. Jackson makes the most of his limited screen time—cut off abruptly when he gets executed with a pistol in his mouth.

Jackson plays a veteran drug dealer, now living in a middle-class home, wearing a bright yellow button-down shirt, cooking up crack over his kitchen stove like a suburban dad who takes particular pride in his French toast. Jackson can't turn the awkward dialogue into poetry, but he can make you feel something just from his body language: the bitter taste of nostalgia, filling his nostrils like acrid smoke, as he tries to figure out why his life used to be better.

Jungle Fever (1991)

Gator Purify
MOVIE: 8/10   **SLJ FACTOR:** 10/10   **MINUTES UNTIL HE SHOWS UP:** 21
EXPLETIVES NOT DELETED: motherfucker, shit (x12), bitch (x3), fuck (x6), motherfucking (x5), goddamn (x3), fucking (x3), bitches, bullshit, motherfuckers

When we first meet Gator, Samuel L. Jackson looks like a little boy playing dress-up, with a colorful sweater and tie and a Bulls cap, only scruffy and soiled. In his mother's kitchen, he munches on a chocolate bar instead of eating a real meal and does a shuffling dance like he's in a grade-school talent show. He also cajoles, wheedles, and tells a transparent lie about how he needs $100 for a job application. He's not actually a little boy: he's a grown man with an addiction to crack cocaine. As an addict, he reduces every one of his family relationships,

> *"Where do you think the motherfucking color TV is? It's right here—me and Viv smoking the fucking color TV."*

and even his parents' memories of his childhood, to money—because money converts into another hit of crack.

"Generally, when you saw Gator, he wasn't high," Jackson pointed out. "It was all about the manipulation of family members, or people he was close to, and pretending you're sorry about something you'd already done, so you could get what you needed. Consequently, Gator became this iconic character that most people got, that because during that time—this was in the midst of another opioid epidemic—everybody had a family member. You had a brother, an aunt, a husband, an uncle, cousin, somebody who came by your house and stole your shit, or broke your heart in some kind of way. I thought that was more important than just being a junkie."

Gator's tale, incredibly, is a subplot in *Jungle Fever*. The main story concerns his brother Flipper (Wesley Snipes), an architect who has an interracial love affair with his temp assistant Angie (Annabella Sciorra), upending his life in Harlem and hers in Bensonhurst. Director Spike Lee was being deliberately provocative about interracial relationships, starting with his movie's title, and too many scenes feel like he's parallel-parking his characters into scenarios that will let him make another ideological point about race relations. What saves him is that he hired excellent actors: Snipes and Sciorra portray their relationship with nuance and tenderness, belying the idea that they're only having a fling that's sexy because it's taboo.

What endures are Gator's scenes. The most tragic ones are with his parents (the great Ruby Dee and Ossie Davis), but the movie's tour-de-force sequence is a visit to an enormous crack house called the Taj Mahal, edited to Stevie Wonder's "Living for the City." Gator is there at "the Trump Tower of crack dens," getting high and squabbling with his addict girlfriend Viv (Halle Berry, making her film debut). Confronted by his brother, Gator tries charm and jokes but finally falls back on brutal honesty: "Just tell Mama her oldest son is a crackhead." Then he falls silent while Viv screams at him and scrabbles for another hit. He closes his eyes, trying to vanish into a cocaine haze, but he knows he can't escape his own life.

Johnny Suede (1991)

B-Bop
MOVIE: 4/10   SLJ FACTOR: 3/10   MINUTES UNTIL HE SHOWS UP: 39

Watch Brad Pitt learn to act! In his first leading film role, he plays Johnny Suede, an aspiring musician who wanders through his low-rent life with a humongous pompadour, a pair of black suede shoes, and a perpetually baffled expression. His musical taste stopped somewhere around the time Ricky Nelson's career peaked: "I'm not into now," he says.

> "I seen a cat cut in two once."

Everything in *Johnny Suede* feels vaguely portentous and meaningful, even though very little of it pays off. Tom DiCillo was the cinematographer for Jim Jarmusch's *Stranger Than Paradise*, and his directorial debut has the meandering low-life vibe of that film, crossed with some surreal flourishes on interlibrary loan from David Lynch. Nevertheless, the movie is more watchable than it has any right to be, partially because it's extremely well cast. Pitt, although untutored, is charismatic and vulnerable, obviously an A-list star in the making; Catherine Keener plays his girlfriend, who has refreshingly little time for his bullshit; Nick Cave makes a cameo as a dissolute rock star with bleached hair named Freak Storm.

Samuel L. Jackson appears as an intimidatingly cool musician named B-Bop, who plays stand-up bass in Johnny Suede's band. He's in full jazzbo attire: a gray pinstriped suit, accessorized with a goatee, a dangling cigarette, and a bright yellow beret. He tells a quick anecdote about seeing a human body get removed in two separate trash bags—and then the band plays a song called "Midtown," rehearsing in a warehouse so cold you can see their breath the whole time.

Soon after, Johnny Suede learns that B-Bop has left town for a three-month gig on a cruise ship. He's devastated—that means his band is breaking up—but he can't be any more disappointed than viewers who were hoping that B-Bop would have more than one scene.

Strictly Business (1991)

Monroe
MOVIE: 3/10   **SLJ FACTOR:** 5/10   **MINUTES UNTIL HE SHOWS UP:** 4
EXPLETIVES NOT DELETED: shit

A rom-com that's not especially romantic or comedic, *Strictly Business* tells the story of Waymon, a young buttoned-up buppie real estate investor (awkwardly played by the stiff Joseph C. Phillips) and his old friend Bobby (Tommy Davidson), a B-boy working in the mailroom of the same real estate firm. When Waymon falls hard for a gorgeous club promoter (Halle

> *"Johnson! You wouldn't happen to be just getting here at 9:15?"*

Berry), Bobby agrees to introduce them in return for a spot in the firm's executive training program: Waymon and Bobby teach each other to loosen up and straighten up, respectively.

The movie is largely predictable, but it has some virtues, including a Nelson George script with a good ear for slang, a musical performance by Jodeci, and some of the earliest screen performances by both Berry and Sam Rockwell. Samuel L. Jackson plays Monroe, Bobby's nemesis: his boss in the mailroom, which he rules like a petty tyrant with a gray Brillo haircut. Monroe knows that he's near the bottom of the firm's org chart; he saves an obsequious grin for any executive who shows up in his mailroom. To compensate, he zealously exerts every ounce of his meager power: just about every time he appears onscreen, he is either threatening to fire Bobby or actually terminating his employment. Monroe is a small-time middle-management villain, but Jackson plays him with gusto—both the character and the actor know what it takes to be the bad guy.

Dead and Alive: The Race for Gus Farace (1991)

Everett Hatcher

MOVIE: 6/10   **SLJ FACTOR:** 5/10   **MINUTES UNTIL HE SHOWS UP:** 1

Playing an undercover DEA agent, Samuel L. Jackson gets to hit a lot of different notes in a short amount of time: the loving father playing soccer with his kid, the professional law enforcement officer getting wired for a night on the job, the make-believe drug dealer acting tough with a potential supplier. But the only one that's memorable is his brief turn as a guy bewildered by Staten Island's traffic patterns, looking for the expressway that's right underneath the overpass where he's parked. That's where he gets shot fifteen minutes into the action, kicking off a pulpy feds-versus-gangsters plot.

> *"I don't know you from a hole in the wall, except for the fact some lowlife I met in the pen vouches for you."*

Based on a true crime story of 1989 and also known as *Mob Justice*, this TV movie centers on the small-time thug who killed Jackson's agent—played by a menacing Tony Danza, surprisingly effective as a coked-up killer. The law wants to bring him to trial, so they turn up the heat on New York City organized crime; the mob responds by putting out a contract on him so they can deliver his corpse and get back to business.

While the movie is often formulaic, it moves quickly, has style, and features a slew of classy New York character actors. At some moments, it even reaches for an elegiac tone: the crime bosses know that the glory days of the Mafia are behind them. That theme would be explored with greater depth and intelligence a few years later by *The Sopranos*; here it just gives some flavor to the froth.

There were still holes in Samuel L. Jackson's life, and even one in his body: he never repaired the fissure in his septum. He could put a match up his left nostril and pull it out of his right nostril. But he didn't keep that hole so he could perform unusual party tricks: he wanted the empty space to serve as a reminder of the damage he had inflicted on himself with cocaine.

Every day, Jackson made the decision not to drink or use drugs. He regularly attended Alcoholics Anonymous and Narcotics Anonymous meetings, but AA meetings bummed him out: he thought people mostly seemed unhappy that they couldn't drink. He did the twelve steps, but in his own way, which mostly ignored the eighth step. "I never made amends," he admitted. "I didn't need to go back and clean up everybody's life that I had fucked over."

Jackson tried to figure out who he was without drugs, and to be a better husband and father, with a family that he had neglected for so many years in favor of cocaine. And while he waited for *Jungle Fever* to hit theaters—it would be most of a year between the wrap party and opening night—he needed work. He auditioned for any job available, including a minuscule role in *My Cousin Vinny* where, by his count, the character said exactly seven words ("Mud. You got mud in your tires."). Jackson knew that not getting the part wasn't a reflection on his talents—with a role that small, there's no way to impress a casting director, so you just show up and hope you look like the person they imagined—but he really needed the work.

Jeff Stanzler, who wrote and directed the low-budget drama *Jumpin at the Boneyard* (financed by 20th Century Fox as a favor to Lawrence Kasdan), had never directed before. He'd also never heard of Jackson—but John Turturro, part of the *Jungle Fever* ensemble, told him how great Jackson was in it. "I had never put the name with the face, but then I got a reel," Stanzler said. Duly blown away by Jackson's performances in an array of films, Stanzler cast him in a small part as the head of a community center, paying $800 for a week's work.

When Stanzler called Jackson to offer him the role, the actor tried to play it cool, covering his phone's mouthpiece while he told LaTanya Richardson the news, but the director could hear them jumping up and down and celebrating: at that moment, $800 was a significant paycheck for the family. Jackson said, "Oh, I finally get to play a good guy": it felt unusual for him to play a selfless character who was not running afoul of the law in any way.

Jackson was scheduled for the first week of shooting, which meant that on Stanzler's first day as a professional director, he had to give notes to Jackson, Tim Roth, and Jeffrey Wright. When Stanzler gave Jackson some feedback that morning, the actor just stared at him—completely intimidating him. "He's about four hundred feet tall," Stanzler said with a laugh.

During the lunch break, Jackson stayed in the community center's gym, shooting free throws, and Stanzler hung out with him. "I remember he made seventeen free throws in a row," he said. While sinking basket after basket, Jackson told Stanzler about his near-death experience on the subway platform.

After lunch, they went back to work, and a nervous Stanzler found that Jackson was now completely congenial; together, they figured out how to make the scene work. "He wanted me to stand up to him, and then he was a teddy bear," Stanzler said. "I don't think it was a conscious thing, but he knows that he's one of the greatest actors on the planet—so if you're going to get in the ring with him, you better be able to take a punch and throw a punch."

In May 1991, Jackson ran into Lee, who was heading to France a few days later: *Jungle Fever* was debuting at the Cannes Film Festival and the buzz around the film was excellent.

"Probably gonna get an award at Cannes," Lee told him.

Jackson knew that they didn't give out awards for supporting actors at Cannes. "But I'd still love to go with you," he told Lee. "Are you gonna take me?"

The answer was no: Lee was bringing over an array of collaborators, including Wesley Snipes and Anthony Quinn and Stevie Wonder (who did the movie's score), but there was no budget to buy Jackson a plane ticket.

A week later, Jackson got a call with the news from France: while *Jungle Fever* had not received any major overall awards (*Barton Fink* won the Palme d'Or), the jury had been so impressed by Jackson's performance, it created a special award for Best Supporting Actor just to honor him. Jackson was ecstatic—and pissed that Lee hadn't brought him to Cannes. Lee accepted the award on Jackson's behalf, although it took him most of a year to deliver the hardware.

In June, when the movie was released in the USA, it did solidly at the box office and got favorable reviews—but the consensus was that Jackson's performance as Gator made him the movie's breakout star. Jackson was the subject of magazine and newspaper profiles, in which he was, at first, circumspect about how his own drug experiences had informed his performance. "I know people who were addicted," he told NPR, truthfully but misleadingly. "Commercial agents say I don't look like a responsible adult," he told *The New York Times*. "Look, other Black actors carry on about this and that. Me, I got a cat, a kid, and a car. I got bills," he told *New York* magazine, whose reporter took note of the *BORN TO ACT* bumper sticker on his jeep.

The gossip columnist Liz Smith wrote, "Who is America's most charismatic black actor—once we set aside Morgan Freeman, Danny Glover, Denzel Washington, and Sidney Poitier?" Which was both marginalizing and ludicrously precise, apparently ranking Jackson as America's fifth most charismatic Black actor exactly, but it was a huge improvement over being billed as "Black Guy" in *Sea of Love*.

And one day, Jackson checked in with his agent. As always, he asked, "Hollywood call today?"

This time, the answer was "Well, as a matter of fact, they did."

His agent sent him the script for *White Sands*, an overheated thriller set in New Mexico. When Jackson read it, he assumed that the producers were asking him to play Lennox, a shady criminal with connections to gunrunners. "When I read that name Lennox, it was like, oh, that must be the black character. Then they call me back and say no, you're Meeker, the FBI agent. What? I had to go back and read it again," Jackson said. (Lennox, it turned out, was played by Mickey Rourke.) Jackson liked the moral ambiguity of Meeker, and how the role would give him a chance to show off his range—but he especially liked that the movie paid $75,000.

Shooting at the same time was *Malcolm X*, Spike Lee's epic biography of the Black leader. Lee wanted Jackson to be in the movie, although he hadn't determined which part—he wanted Jackson to read for him first. Jackson found that insulting, and was also offended that he would be working for scale. He went to New Mexico.

"The reality is way bigger than the dream," Jackson said. For years, he had been imagining what it would be like to work on a big Hollywood movie as more than a day player, and now he found out exactly how many perks came with the job. "I got to New Mexico, and they had boarded me out. They said, 'You actually work a total of about ten days in this movie, but you got to be here for the whole seven weeks, because you're the cover set.' I was like, 'What the hell is that?' I had no idea what that was, because I hadn't been on enough movie sets. 'Okay, whenever you wake up, and it's not raining, you're off.' I went, 'Really? Get the fuck out of here.' 'Okay, here are the keys to your car.' My car? They gave me a Continental. 'And here are the keys to your house.' And they had this gorgeous three-level house in Santa Fe with a deck and heated floors and I was like *damn!* That's the kind of stuff that you can't even imagine when you're a young actor in New York and you're walking to the theater, catching the subway, and getting paid $150 a week. And your trailer is bigger and better than anything you've ever been in in your life. You've been in theater dressing rooms all your life—you get there, you've got a trailer. Not to mention, they gave me this brown envelope full of money. 'Okay, here's your per diem.' More than I used to make a month, they gave me in a week, to just hang out with! Stuff like that."

After *White Sands*, Jackson booked a supporting role in *Patriot Games*, a Harrison Ford thriller, and suddenly he was a working Hollywood actor. ("I don't have to worry about where my next job is coming from," he marveled. "I just have to worry about doing the work when it comes.") Meanwhile, two years after it premiered, *Two Trains Running* finally went to Broadway, another August Wilson play without Jackson in the role he had originated at the Yale Rep. This time, however, Jackson was too busy to dwell on it.

In 1992, Sam and LaTanya and Zoe packed up and relocated to Los Angeles—but not because of his own film career. Richardson had been cast in *Frannie's Turn*, a CBS sitcom starring Miriam Margolyes as a put-upon housewife and seamstress. The family rented a home in Encino, in the unfashionable San Fernando Valley, so Richardson would be close to Studio City, where the show filmed.

Once they had unpacked, Jackson explored L.A.: "I spent a lot of time going in and out of stores with somebody following me, thinking I'm going to steal something. Then someone would recognize me and say, 'I loved your movies,' and they'd leave me alone." Unfortunately, sometimes it would turn out that person actually thought Jackson was Laurence Fishburne. Jackson and Fishburne were friends and peers, but this was still insulting (and racist). "Even when we've been standing together, people have called him by my name and me by his," Jackson grumbled.

Frannie's Turn was the first series created by writer-producer Chuck Lorre (previously a writer on *Roseanne*). He would go on to make long-running hit series such as *Grace Under Fire* (112 episodes), *Two and a Half Men* (262 episodes), and *The Big Bang Theory* (279 episodes). *Frannie's Turn*, however, filmed just six episodes, of which only five aired. But since Jackson was booking work that filmed in L.A., such as *National Lampoon's Loaded Weapon 1*, the family decided to stay in the Pacific time zone for a while.

When Jackson auditioned for *Jurassic Park*, the screenplay adapting Michael Crichton's novel wasn't done yet, so director Steven Spielberg had him read from the book. After Jackson finished, Spielberg just told him, "Faster." So he did it again, faster. Spielberg's note the second time: "Faster." So Jackson picked up the pace even more. Spielberg's note the third time: "Faster." Jackson accelerated his way through the scene, but was disconcerted by the whole experience; he left the audition thinking, "Gee, I'm not sure if I got that part, or what that was all about."

In fact, he did get the part: John "Ray" Arnold, an overwhelmed administrator at Jurassic Park. On the set, he paid close attention to how Spielberg worked: "Steven had what I thought was a comic book, but it was really a shot list. And sometimes he'd even get behind the camera and operate. He was meticulously prepared. He's both a technical director and an actor's director, which is a rare combination."

Jackson also pursued roles he didn't get, including Ike Turner in *What's Love Got to Do with It*—Laurence Fishburne edged him out for that one. When Jackson auditioned for *Reservoir Dogs*, the debut film by Quentin Tarantino, he memorized a scene, and thought he'd be playing it opposite Tim Roth and Harvey Keitel. However, when he got to the audition, on a Sunday afternoon, he instead had to perform with two dudes who didn't know the lines and kept cracking up; he found himself overacting to compensate for their being so hapless. Jackson said, "I didn't realize it was Quentin, the director-writer, and Lawrence Bender, the producer, but I knew that the audition was not very good." He didn't get the part.

After making *Loaded Weapon* with Emilio Estevez and *Amos & Andrew* with Nicolas Cage, Jackson had to wait for the movies to come out so the Hollywood studios could figure out how bankable he was: was he a character actor or a marquee name? As an artist, he found that a difficult concept to bend his brain around, even if he understood it on a business level. His agent and his manager kept telling him that he needed to be patient now that he was a movie star, not hustling for any available job like he did in New York. But that was a lesson he didn't want to learn. If you mentioned over lunch that somebody was casting a western on the other side of town, he'd lunge at the opportunity: "Any brothers in it?"

Jackson's representatives also discouraged him from auditioning for roles, telling him that he had reached the point of his career where it was better to take a meeting with the director of a film. "I find that really bizarre," he complained. "I don't know what to say or what to do in those kinds of meetings. It's a lot easier for me to go in there and take the character that they have on this page and show them what I think of this character and just do it, do an audition. Then they know if they want to work with me or not, not if I can eat with a fork, or if I eat with my fingers or chew with my mouth closed. Some people are afraid to let their actors audition, and that's the one thing I'm not afraid of."

January 1992 marked the annual migration of Hollywood executives and agents to Park City, Utah, for the Sundance Film Festival. Three years earlier, Steven Soderbergh's debut film, *Sex, Lies and Videotape*, had premiered at Sundance; its acquisition by Miramax and subsequent mainstream success had transformed the festival. Once a modest gathering of cineastes in the snow, Sundance was now an annual indie-film feeding frenzy. Jackson attended because he had supporting roles in two movies that had screenings—*Jumpin at the Boneyard* and *Johnny Suede*—but while he was there, he went to see the premiere of *Reservoir Dogs*.

Famously, the movie's torture scene, where Michael Madsen's Mr. Blonde cuts off the ear of a cop, made dozens of audience members flee from the theater. (As it would at every subsequent festival screening of *Reservoir Dogs*. "I started counting the walkouts during the torture scene," Tarantino said. "Thirty-three was the largest.") After the credits rolled, Jackson walked up to Tarantino—he knew what the director looked like now—to shake his hand and congratulate him. "Hey, man, this was a really good movie," Jackson told him.

"Yeah yeah yeah, I remember you," Tarantino said. "How'd you like the guy who got your part?" (That was Randy Brooks, playing Detective Holdaway, who teaches Tim Roth's character how to go undercover.)

"Really? I think you would have had a better movie with me in it."

Tarantino, unfazed, told Jackson, "I'm actually writing something for you right now."

Jackson figured Tarantino was feeding him a Hollywood line so he could escape from the conversation. He went about his business, in Park City and then back home—and later that year he even got to say some of Tarantino's dialogue on camera, when he appeared in *True Romance* (written by Tarantino and directed by Tony Scott).

Jackson was half-right about Tarantino's level of sincerity: Tarantino was writing a screenplay for a movie called *Pulp Fiction* that he knew Jackson would be excellent for, but he visualized Michael Madsen and Laurence Fishburne in the lead roles of Vincent and Jules. Then Madsen was unavailable (he took a part in *Wyatt Earp*) and Fishburne turned down his role because it wasn't a solo lead, so Tarantino adjusted his conception of Vincent and Jules—less fearsome, more of a lethal comedy duo—and decided he wanted John Travolta and Jackson.

A year after that Sundance encounter, while Jackson was in Virginia, shooting the TV movie *Assault at West Point*, he received a package wrapped in brown paper: the screenplay for *Pulp Fiction*. It had an image of two gangsters printed on the front and there was a note attached: "If you show this to anybody, two guys from Jersey will come and break your legs." (Danny DeVito's company Jersey Films was producing the movie.)

Jackson read the script straight through, totally absorbed, and then wondered, "Is this as good as I just thought it was? Wait a minute. Start over." He read it again, loved it just as much, and immediately accepted the part of Jules. Or so he thought. When he was back briefly in Los Angeles before heading out to New York City to make the movie *Fresh* (produced, like *Pulp Fiction*, by Lawrence Bender) the *Pulp Fiction* brain trust called him in so they could hear what Jules would sound like. Jackson hadn't had the time to do his usual meticulous preparation, so he basically gave a cold reading of the script. They gave him a thumbs-up and he went to New York.

While Jackson was in New York, however, the actor Paul Calderón auditioned in L.A. for a smaller *Pulp Fiction* role. Since there weren't a lot of lines for Calderón to work with, Tarantino let him read the dialogue of Jules—and he killed it. Jackson began to hear murmurs that he might be losing the role he thought had been written expressly for him. He objected, "Wait, wait, wait, wait. Wait now. Nobody told me when I came in there to read that day that I was auditioning. They just said they wanted to hear." His agents got involved, lobbying Harvey Weinstein and Bob Weinstein at Miramax: the upshot was that Jackson would be given a chance to audition properly, going head to head with Calderón.

Tarantino and his collaborators referred to the Jules-off as "Sunday Bloody Sunday." Jackson flew back from New York the day before; on the plane, he did his customary background work with the script, thoroughly breaking it down, considering his motivations, his cadences, his relationships. But when he showed up for the audition on Sunday— "angry, pissed, tired"—nobody was around. Calderón had come in first and, once again, nailed it. The producers went to lunch, assuming that Jackson's audition was just a formality before they told Calderón he had the role.

When they returned, somebody started introducing Jackson to a line producer, who said, "Oh no no no no. You don't need to introduce me to this man. I love your work, Mr. Fishburne." Insulted and feeling like he had nothing to lose, Jackson entered the audition room in a full lather—and a hamburger in one hand and a milkshake in the other.

Richard Gladstein, the head of production at Miramax, recalled, "Me and Quentin and Lawrence were sitting on the couch, and he walked in and just started sipping that shake and biting that burger and looking at all of us. I was scared shitless. I thought that this guy was going to shoot a gun right through my head. His eyes were popping out of his head. And he just stole the part."

This time, Jackson wasn't reading with Tarantino and Bender: they had hired a young actor to do lines. Unfortunately, the actor kept losing his place in the script. "Dude, read the script," Jackson told him. "Just look at the page. You don't have to look at me." And then Jackson realized: he was rocking it so hard, the actor kept looking at him because he was fascinated by what he was doing. The room grew rapt as they worked their way through the screenplay, and utterly transfixed when Jackson did the movie's final diner scene.

Jackson left the audition and flew back to New York to continue working on *Fresh*. On Monday morning, Bender came by his trailer and told him the good news: he would play the philosophical hit man Jules Winnfield. Bender added, "We never really knew how this movie was supposed to end until we heard you read the speech." Calderón was the runner-up: as a consolation prize, he would play the small role of English Dan, the bartender at Marsellus Wallace's club.

In preproduction, Jackson came in for meetings on Jules's wardrobe and appearance, which included a fateful encounter with a Jheri-curl wig. "I had it in my mind that I wanted Sam to wear an Afro," Tarantino said. "I like Afros. If I was Black, I'd wear an Afro. And Sam was up for it. But the makeup woman who was getting the wigs I don't think knew the difference between an Afro and a Jheri-curl. It was there by mistake, and he put it on, and he looked so great, I can't tell you."

Jackson loved it: "All the gangbangers had Jheri-curls." He grew muttonchop sideburns to complete the look.

Before shooting began, Tarantino rehearsed the cast for the better part of a month on a soundstage in Culver City. "We rehearsed *Pulp Fiction* so thoroughly, it was incredible," Jackson said wistfully. Tape on the floor marked out the dimensions of the rooms and hallways and restaurants where they would be shooting. "We actually knew how many steps it was from the trunk of the car to the front door of the apartment building, to the front door of the building to the elevator, how wide the elevator was. So we never had to look down and we never had to count, we'd just do it."

Phil LaMarr, who played Marvin (the character whose head gets blown off in the back seat of the car) remembered rehearsing the apartment scene with Jackson, in which Jules and Vincent retrieve Marsellus Wallace's briefcase. "My scenes were mostly with Sam," LaMarr said. "John [Travolta] was there too, but they were Sam's scenes. I have to tell you, it's rare in your twenties that you realize the significance of a moment, but I did. I met Sam at a moment when he crossed over from remarkably respected character actor to movie star. I knew about Sam's career: I had actually seen him onstage at the Yale Rep, in the premiere of *The Piano Lesson*. He was heading towards fifty when we did the movie, but he was so at ease. He'd be sitting there, talking about something going on with his daughter, no bullshit at all, and then we'd step on the set. The guy I'd been talking to while he drank his coffee was gone. I looked across the room and there was somebody else's eyes. Where did he go?"

LaMarr said, "It's caught on camera. He's talking to Frank Whaley's character [Brett], and it's like the one line I have in that scene. He says, 'You swiped the briefcase, Brett.' I'm supposed to say 'It's over there,' and he turns and says, 'I don't remember asking you a goddamn thing.' And every time in rehearsal, he said that line to me and then he'd look back at Frank. We're rolling, doing the wide coverage, and he says,

'I don't remember asking you a goddamn thing'—and he *doesn't look away*. He starts talking to Frank's character, but he's still staring at me. I swear to God, I began to get physically afraid. 'Why's Sam still looking at me? Did I do something wrong? What's going on?' That is *exactly* the reaction you should have when a guy with a motherfucking gun decides to stare at you. The thing that blew my mind at the time was how he could make that transformation so effortlessly. I was thinking to myself, 'My God. Here is a man who has traveled the roads of himself and knows them so well, he can get from one point in his psyche to another instantly,' I was like, 'I've got to figure out how he does that. That's what I want to be when I grow up.'"

Lauren Purje.

Juice (1992)

Trip
MOVIE: 7/10   SLJ FACTOR: 6/10   MINUTES UNTIL HE SHOWS UP: 12
EXPLETIVES NOT DELETED: shit

Teenagers make their own worlds, as do movies. Good movies about teenagers invite you inside that double world: in *Juice*, that means hanging out with four best friends in Harlem as they cut high school, watch gangster movies, and eat eggs flavored with hot sauce and malt liquor. The tight-knit group self-destructs when they rob a convenience store, but not because of the cash they run away with—it's because of the handgun they use. That pistol becomes the wedge that splits their bond, an amplifier of toxic masculine pride, and repeatedly, an instrument of death.

> *"You done slid down a razor blade and landed in an alcohol river."*

    Juice had the raw energy of a first-time director (Ernest Dickerson) working on a minimal $3 million budget. It also had an insanely great hip-hop soundtrack (thank you, Hank Shocklee of the Bomb Squad) and in the two central roles, future stars making their acting debuts: Omar Epps (as Q, an aspiring DJ) and Tupac Shakur (as Bishop, a scowling loose cannon). Dickerson had been the cinematographer on a half-dozen Spike Lee movies, four of which featured Samuel L. Jackson, and so he cast Jackson here as Trip: a likable authority figure surrounded by youth, a character in the tradition of Doc in *West Side Story*. (He also cast LaTanya Richardson as the mother of Steel, Jermaine Hopkins's character.)

    Trip runs the local pool hall and video arcade, where candy bars are fifty-five cents and single "loosie" cigarettes are twenty-five cents. He rocks a variety of gold chains and an impressive orange velvet shirt, and although he's aware of what's going on with his teenage customers—with a flurry of cool hand gestures, he congratulates Q on making the cut for a DJ competition—he's mostly concerned with his own adult life. Whenever Trip appears, he's flirting with a woman or arguing with a friend played by the singer Oran "Juice" Jones, memorably making the point that "just because you pour syrup on shit don't make it pancakes."

In a few fleeting scenes, Jackson perfectly pitches his performance halfway between sympathy and self-interest. When the cops raid the pool hall in the middle of the day to round up truants, Trip shouts a warning so the kids can scatter. And when Q, whose life is in danger, needs to get a message to Bishop, Trip will do the job, for a price. Jackson's disgusted expression when he sees the paltry amount of money that Q presses into his palm isn't just a great comedic moment, it's the movie in microcosm: an accelerated education in the adult world and the price of making mistakes.

White Sands (1992)

Greg Meeker
MOVIE: 4/10 **SLJ FACTOR:** 6/10 **MINUTES UNTIL HE SHOWS UP:** 22
EXPLETIVES NOT DELETED: shit (x3), fuck (x3), fucking (x4), asshole, fucked, bitch, bullshit

When characters in a thriller make illogical decisions, you can accept it as people succumbing to their own venal natures (if the movie's well constructed) or bending to the demands of the genre (if it's not). When *every* character in a thriller lacks common sense, you wonder whether they're all suffering from brain injuries—or if the screenwriter's the one who got whacked in the head.

"Do you like snapshots, Ray? I love snapshots. Little frozen fragments of time."

Watching *White Sands*, you want everyone involved to enter the concussion protocol. The movie, about a small-town deputy sheriff in New Mexico (Willem Dafoe) who finds an apparent suicide alongside a suitcase filled with hundred-dollar bills, is stylishly filmed by director Roger Donaldson. However, when the deputy investigates the death by assuming the corpse's identity, the FBI, the CIA, and international arms smugglers all get involved; various parties double-cross and triple-cross each other and the plot gets as unpleasantly tangled as a hairball in a shower drain.

Most of the big names in the cast, like Dafoe and Mickey Rourke and Mary Elizabeth Mastrantonio, give solid but forgettable performances—but there are a few standouts in supporting roles. Maura Tierney, making her film debut, is intense and tearful as a bohemian fugitive. Veteran character actor M. Emmet Walsh throws his full weight into his scenes as a ribald coroner. And Samuel L. Jackson, playing an FBI agent who dresses like a stockbroker, is a self-described "respected senior minority agent who hasn't so much as a bugstain on his record." His corruption isn't the least bit surprising, which doesn't diminish the pleasure in watching Jackson's manipulative, commanding performance. Whether he's faking out internal affairs or delivering a monologue with a mouthful of blood, he always seems like he's amused by a private joke that nobody else in the movie knows.

Patriot Games (1992)

Robby
MOVIE: 5/10   **SLJ FACTOR: 3/10**   **MINUTES UNTIL HE SHOWS UP: 41**

Consider Jack Ryan and Robert Langdon, two of the most popular fictional characters of the last forty years. What do they have in common, other than being the stars of massively popular airport novels and being played in hit movies by A-list actors? (Tom Hanks took on Dan Brown's Langdon, while a variety of big names, including Alec Baldwin and Ben Affleck, have served their time as Tom Clancy's Ryan.) They are, fundamentally, explainers. Langdon is a "symbologist" at Harvard who reveals the messages hidden in masterpieces of art history. Ryan holds a variety of jobs (including, eventually, president of the United States), but he begins as a CIA data analyst, teasing out hidden meaning from reams of raw intelligence. These professions give readers the sensation that they can better understand our complicated world by plowing through a page-turner novel—and they make the characters convenient mouthpieces for exposition, and for the authors' own interpretations of the world.

> *"For service above and beyond the call of duty of a tourist, even a Marine, we recognize Professor John Patrick Ryan with the Order of the Purple Target, and hope that he will duck next time, lest he become part of history rather than a teacher of it."*

Patriot Games is a serviceable techno-thriller set in the era (before the Good Friday accords) when Irish separatists were go-to Hollywood bad guys; it's watchable mostly because Harrison Ford steps into the role of Jack Ryan. (He saves a member of the British royals from assassination, making him the target of a vengeful Irish militant played by Sean Bean.) The film's real claim on history, however, is that it appears to be the first movie where a modern-day crimefighter looks at a digitized picture (here, a satellite photo of an Irish terrorist training camp in North Africa (?!)) and demands, "Can you enhance that?" That's a fitting legacy for Clancy, who preferred military hardware over human relationships.

Samuel L. Jackson appears as Lt. Commander Robby Jackson, a colleague of Ryan's at the Annapolis Naval Academy; he gives Ryan a joke medal and shows up at his friend's dinner party. Jackson delivers his lines capably enough, and returns fire when Ryan's house is invaded by Irish terrorists, but doesn't leave much of an impression. Ultimately, the movie asks little more of him than that he stand up straight in a dress uniform.

Jumpin at the Boneyard (1992)

Mr. Simpson
MOVIE: 5/10   SLJ FACTOR: 6/10   MINUTES UNTIL HIS FIRST APPEARANCE: 42
EXPLETIVES NOT DELETED: shit

Empty city, empty lives, can't win. The brothers Danny and Manny (Alexis Arquette and Tim Roth), who haven't seen each other in three years, reunite because Danny tries to rob Manny's apartment. (Danny's a drug addict; Manny has issues with anger and violence.) This movie tells the story of their day together as they travel across the Bronx on a quest to see their

> *"I hope you're not standing there waiting for me to thank you."*

mother: the tone wavers between hard-bitten realism and melodrama, but the film gets by on the strength of the acting.

For much of the movie, the brothers trek through burnt-out urban streets without another soul in sight—an indication both of their emotional isolation and of the movie's low budget. When supporting players do appear, they take on an outsize importance, like other survivors in a postapocalyptic drama; the cast includes the excellent character actors Luis Guzmán and Jeffrey Wright. Nobody here is better, however, than Danitra Vance as Danny's crackhead girlfriend, displaying power and pathos that went untapped in her tenure on *Saturday Night Live*.

A humble community center is the Rivendell on the brothers' quest: a clean, well-lit sanctuary where a strung-out Danny can get a much-needed shower before they resume their journey. Samuel L. Jackson plays Jerry Simpson, who presides over the center like Elrond in a hoodie sweatshirt. Protective of his wards and unfazed by strangers needing help, he's a man with a caring soul who has learned to clothe his kindness with stern leadership. When he tells Manny "the only place the city has for people like your brother is Riker's Island," Jackson finds an emotional pitch that is neither callous nor bleeding-heart: he sees the inequities of the world but doesn't have time to lament them. Since a large portion of the movie is the main characters bemoaning their fates, he provides a bracing counterpoint just by striding through industrial beige hallways with confidence.

Fathers and Sons (1992)

Marshall
MOVIE: 3/10   **SLJ FACTOR:** 2/10   **MINUTES UNTIL HE SHOWS UP:** 15
EXPLETIVES NOT DELETED: fucked

Marketed as a thriller, *Fathers and Sons* is actually a domestic drama about a widower (Jeff Goldblum) and his teenage son (Rory Cochrane), who's still riding a bicycle but beginning to explore sex and drugs. (*Fathers and Sons*, unlike the Turgenev novel it borrowed its title from, has just one father and one son.) Their strained

> "Now look where all this integrity's got you."

relationship has well-played moments, and some of their voice-over monologues are poetic, but the movie is a dizzying patchwork of clashing storylines.

Michael Imperioli plays a hipster drug dealer who narrowly escapes a revenge killing. Famke Janssen makes her film debut as a wholesome love interest for Goldblum, met during a road race. Michael Disend lurks around as a serial killer who has also self-published a book of sci-fi mysticism that purports to teach its readers telepathy—in a crucial scene, much to the surprise of Goldblum and anybody watching the movie, the telepathy actually works. Rosanna Arquette, playing a coquettish fortune-teller working on the boardwalk of the Jersey shore, is completely superfluous to the story and seems to have wandered into the movie from an early Bruce Springsteen song.

Goldblum's character, Max Fish, is a film director who has left the cinematic world behind for a quieter life running a bookstore. Goldblum wisely underplays most of the melodramatic aspects of the script

(Max's anger issues, his drinking problem)—except for when he tearfully recounts how before his wife died of cancer, he abused her, even separating her shoulder. In a better movie, this could be a pivotal scene, exploring questions of moral responsibility and the path to making amends after committing unspeakable acts. Here, it's just another stop on the spinning wheel of subplots.

One of those subplots: Max is starring in a community theater adaptation of *Don Quixote*, a modern-dress version where he's led away at the end in a straitjacket. Joie Lee is the play's writer and director; Samuel L. Jackson plays her significant other, whom she's cast in the Sancho Panza role. Jackson appears in a few scenes, showing an easy rapport with Lee, and when the *Quixote* gang takes a break from rehearsal for some beer and bowling, we see him bowl a frame; even though he doesn't roll a strike, he showboats anyway.

Without much material to work with, Jackson creates a character he knew all too well from the Atlanta theater scene: an inexperienced actor who's stiff in rehearsal and better on opening night. Jackson gets the climactic line of *Quixote*—"Don't forget the quest"—and milks it with the solemnity of a small-time actor finally getting his big moment.

National Lampoon's Loaded Weapon 1 (1993)

Wes Luger

MOVIE: 4/10   **SLJ FACTOR:** 5/10   **MINUTES UNTIL HE SHOWS UP:** 6 (audio: novelty answering machine message), 7 (still photo: black-and-white picture with an Afro), 10 (in action onscreen)

EXPLETIVES NOT DELETED: shit

The Marx Brothers came before; the Wayans brothers came after. But in 1980, the Zucker-Abrahams-Zucker team invented a new style of film comedy with *Airplane!*: a parody crammed wall-to-wall with absurd jokes and sight gags, all bouncing off an imperviously deadpan lead actor. Their movies (which later included *Top Secret!* and the *Naked Gun* series) are closer to the rat-a-tat rhythms of vaudeville or Catskills stand-up than most other film comedy.

> "Hell, I breastfed until I was sixteen years old and I still don't understand women."

This movie, directed by Gene Quintano (best known for writing a couple of *Police Academy* sequels) is in that mode, except less funny. The project is handicapped from the start by being a parody of the *Lethal Weapon* buddy-cop series; the best targets for satire have some self-importance that needs deflating, but since the *Lethal Weapon* movies already had a healthy sense of humor about themselves, the parody falls flat.

The actors who did the best here were the ones with the least amount of screen time: they showed up for one day on the set, did a quick bit, and got out. And so this movie features guest appearances from a higher caliber of star than it deserves: Bruce Willis, Whoopi Goldberg, Phil Hartman, Denis Leary, and even (reprising their *CHiPs* characters) Erik Estrada and Larry Wilcox. (Future tabloid couple Denise Richards and Charlie Sheen both have scenes but didn't meet until years later.)

Emilio Estevez plays the Mel Gibson role of an unhinged gun-happy cop (less charming now than it seemed to many viewers in 1993), while Samuel L. Jackson stands in for Danny Glover as the by-the-book partner on the verge of retirement. Jackson's job is mostly to play straight man to the cascading absurdity around him. Now and then, however, he gets to do something deeply silly: the movie ends with Jackson and Estevez in a small car, thrashing around to Queen's "Bohemian Rhapsody" like they're in *Wayne's World*.

Amos & Andrew (1993)

Andrew Sterling
MOVIE: 3/10   SLJ FACTOR: 5/10   MINUTES UNTIL HE SHOWS UP: 1
EXPLETIVES NOT DELETED: goddamn

Andrew Sterling (played by Samuel L. Jackson) is a Pulitzer-winning playwright and cultural commentator who styles himself as "a loud, angry voice that's not afraid to speak the truth about white America." For some reason, *Amos & Andrew* establishes his credentials by putting his photo on the cover of *Forbes*, a glossy financial magazine not in the habit of featuring playwrights, regardless of their skin color. Sterling's recent Broadway hit,

> "Listen to me: I bought this house. I paid cash for it. I own it."

which we learn has been adapted into a feature film, is a good example of this movie's sense of humor: it's called *Yo Brother, Where Art Thou?*

That's not just a strained joke about race: it's a twist on *O Brother, Where Art Thou?*, the movie within-the-movie in Preston Sturges's 1941 film classic *Sullivan's Travels*. (You may know the title better from the 2000 movie by the Coen brothers, who were also paying tribute to Sturges.) Writer-director Max Frye (best known for the screenplays for

Something Wild [1986] and *Foxcatcher* [2014]) was aiming for a Sturgesian blend of smart comedy and social satire but fell short.

The story: Andrew Sterling buys a vacation home on a moneyed island off the Massachusetts coast. When some local Karens spot a Black man through a window, they assume he's a robber and call the local police—who escalate the situation and open fire on Andrew. The sheriff (Dabney Coleman) tries to cover up for his mistake by releasing a white man from jail, the small-time crook Amos Odell (Nicolas Cage), telling him that if he pretends to hold Sterling hostage, he will then be allowed to flee for the Canadian border. Events careen out of control when TV news crews show up, followed by an activist crowd of protesters led by a Black preacher (Giancarlo Esposito).

The tone of the whole project is off: the light slapstick doesn't match well with the horror of the police almost executing a man in his own home for the crime of being Black. An excellent satire with an acid heart could be made on racism and the police and liberal pieties, but it would need to be much sharper than this movie.

Jackson and Cage both give subdued performances (for them, anyway), but Jackson is fully believable as a firebrand intellectual with a luxury car. And as the movie pushes Amos together with Andrew, Jackson and Cage make their gradual appreciation of each other feel like a human relationship rather than an inevitable plot point.

Samuel L. Jackson almost passed on the movie because of its title. "I read the name *Amos & Andrew* and I said, 'I don't think so.'" He had grown up with *Amos 'n' Andy*, the massively popular comedy series rife with minstrel caricatures that ran on radio and television between 1928 and 1960. Having invoked that history with its provocative title, the movie then runs from it. The film has time for Amos to deliver a monologue about his childhood experience with sea monkeys; when Amos says "Amos and Andrew," however, Andrew bristles but won't explain why, saying only, "I'll spare you the history lesson."

Menace II Society (1993)

Tat Lawson
MOVIE: 8/10   SLJ FACTOR: 8/10   MINUTES UNTIL HE SHOWS UP: 5
EXPLETIVES NOT DELETED: bitch, fuck (x5), shit, motherfucker (x3)

Samuel L. Jackson had already portrayed a variety of criminals: some amiable, some desperate, some businesslike. But his short scene here as a small-time drug dealer unlocked a crucial aspect of his cinematic identity: the quick-to-anger badass, a Category 5 hurricane who can blow away any weaker men standing in his way (which is to say, all of them). We meet his character, Tat Lawson, in a 1970s flashback, lit in red, hosting a party in his Watts home and playing cards in his undershirt. When one of his guests, fearless after five years in jail, tells him that he'll pay off an old debt when he feels like it, punctuating his defiance with "suck my dick," Tat doesn't play it cool. He gets angry, he gets loud, and then he shoots him dead across the card table.

> *"Look here, man, now that you out the joint about two weeks, don't you think it's about time you gave me my money?"*

That ends Jackson's time onscreen: we jump to Watts in the 1990s and learn in voice-over that Tat was killed offscreen in a busted drug deal. But that brief prologue sets the tone for the rest of the movie: Tat's son Caine is the heir to violence so pervasive that when his grandfather asks if he cares whether he lives or dies, he doesn't know the answer. And when Caine is gunned down at the end of the movie, in a beef over his own child, it's clear that the bloody legacy will be passed down to another generation.

Black filmmakers making movies in the 1990s about crime-ridden neighborhoods felt pressures that white filmmakers making gangster movies mostly didn't: to represent the truth of urban violence without glorifying it, to provide a core of morality without making (as N.W.A rapper Eazy-E dismissed the movie *Boyz N the Hood*) "a Monday after-school special with cussin'." The brothers Albert and Allen Hughes, who directed this movie, found a tone that was neither nihilistic nor hopeful. *Menace II Society* was angry, smart, propulsive—and sometimes as terrifying as looking down the barrel of a gun held by a seething Samuel L. Jackson.

Jurassic Park (1993)

Arnold
MOVIE: 7/10   **SLJ FACTOR:** 5/10   **MINUTES UNTIL HE SHOWS UP:** 28 (audio: making a PA announcement), 40 (onscreen)
EXPLETIVES NOT DELETED: goddammit

The same year he released his harrowing Holocaust masterpiece *Schindler's List*, Steven Spielberg also unleashed what was then the highest-grossing film of all time, *Jurassic Park*. If ever a story was made for Spielberg in B.W.T.C.I.W.E.W. mode (that's "Blockbuster With The Characters In Wide-Eyed Wonder"), it was Michael Crichton's novel about a theme park featuring cloned dinosaurs.

Those dinosaurs, both mechanical and CGI, are the stars of the movie, but Spielberg also spent the money for a top-notch human cast. Standouts include Richard Attenborough as the avuncular

"Ladies and gentlemen, last shuttle leaving for the dock leaves in approximately five minutes. Drop what you're doing and leave now."

park owner, Wayne Knight as a traitorous computer expert, and Jeff Goldblum with an amazing, absurd performance as a leather-clad rockstar mathematician, posturing and pontificating like the whole movie's about him.

Jackson plays a harried park administrator, trying to figure out why all the systems are failing—"item 151 on today's glitch list"—and chain-smoking, usually with a cigarette dangling from his lips, sporting an absurd amount of unattended ash. Jackson said that Spielberg knew he had quit smoking before the movie: "He wanted to make sure I didn't go back, so he got me the worst-tasting fake cigarettes ever." (Jackson started smoking again anyway.)

His character, John "Ray" Arnold, has a bald spot, an off-the-rack necktie (which gets loosened as the tension mounts), and zero swagger. Jackson doesn't try to outdo the dinosaurs (or Goldblum), but he's low-key riveting nevertheless: not an action hero, not a tortured soul, just a smart guy who knows how to get things done.

Arnold gets chewed up by a velociraptor when he's heroically trying to flip the park's circuit breakers, but it doesn't happen on camera; all we see of him in his final appearance is his severed right arm, which falls onto Laura Dern. "I was actually supposed to go to Hawaii to shoot my death scene," Jackson said. "But there was a hurricane that destroyed all the sets. So I didn't get to go to Hawaii."

True Romance (1993)

Big Don
MOVIE: 8/10 **SLJ FACTOR:** 5/10 **MINUTES UNTIL HE SHOWS UP:** 19
EXPLETIVES NOT DELETED: motherfuckers, shit, motherfucker, motherfucking (x2)

Whipsawing between comedy and violence and everlasting love, *True Romance* is the surprisingly sweet story of a horny young couple who get married in Detroit and take off for Los Angeles with a suitcase full of stolen cocaine. Director Tony Scott gives the whole affair a professional sheen, but the movie belongs to screenwriter Quentin Tarantino, eager to entertain, full of surprises—and also full of his youthful tics and pathologies.

> *"Yeah, motherfucker, I eat everything. I eat the pussy, I eat the butt, I eat every motherfucking thing."*

Way too many of the characters have the same cadences and pop-culture obsessions, with dialogue such as "I always wanted to see what TV in other countries looks like." Christian Slater, playing a comic-book clerk, is transparently an idealized version of Tarantino the video store clerk, cool enough to win the love of Patricia Arquette's vivacious call girl (who seems to be as devoid of opinions as he is full of them). And Tarantino loves to throw racial hand grenades—like the scene where Dennis Hopper's character goads Christopher Walken's mob enforcer into killing him by delivering a monologue about how "Sicilians were spawned by niggers"—but doesn't much care where the shrapnel lands.

Tarantino's voice has become more familiar in the decades since *True Romance*'s release, heard in his own movies and echoed in dozens of others. But this movie is still full of delights, not least its top-notch cast. Walken and Hopper facing off is a heavyweight bout, but there's also an undercard of future superstars James Gandolfini and Brad Pitt: Gandolfini plays a gangster trying to worm some information out of Pitt's stoner. And Gary Oldman has an unforgettable turn as Drexl, a vicious white pimp with dreadlocks. He faces off against Samuel L. Jackson, who holds his own, albeit briefly. Jackson's low-level mobster brings Chinese takeout to a drug deal at a motel, shaking off the cold and declaring that "any nigger say he don't eat pussy's lying his ass off"—and approximately one minute later is shot dead by Drexl, not having realized that he was actually bringing Chinese food to an ambush.

Assault at West Point: The Court-Martial of Johnson Whittaker (1994)

Richard Greener

MOVIE: 4/10   SLJ FACTOR: 5/10   MINUTES UNTIL HE SHOWS UP: 7
EXPLETIVES NOT DELETED: shit (x2)

Johnson Whittaker, born into slavery in 1858 South Carolina, was one of the first Black cadets to attend West Point—where he faced constant hostility and racism, culminating in the night in 1880 when he was attacked by three fellow cadets in his room. After he was beaten, bound, and sliced up by a razor, West Point administrators accused him of faking the attack so he could avoid a philosophy exam. Whittaker was court-martialed and expelled.

> *"At the moment, the wind is behind you. When it changes, all the shit you've been writing's going to blow back in your face."*

His story, all too emblematic of American history, is important and dramatic. This movie, made for cable television, tells it in the most wooden fashion possible. The script is heavy on blunt exposition and cringey moments; the movie does better in the courtroom, where all the dialogue is drawn from transcripts of the court-martial. The production blew its acting budget on Sam Waterston, playing Whittaker's ineffective lawyer, and Samuel L. Jackson, playing Richard Greener, the first African American graduate of Harvard, helping with the defense. (Coincidentally, Jackson had played Whittaker himself sixteen years earlier—he was a supporting character in the 1978 broadcast of *The Trial of the Moke*.)

As Greener, Jackson sports some spectacular nineteenth-century facial hair and carries himself in public with upright rectitude and unflappable calm, even when dealing with bald bigotry. Although he spends most of the movie seething because Chamberlain is ignoring his legal counsel, their conflict is mostly subdued and minor-key. That may be historically accurate, but it doesn't make for very compelling viewing.

Assault at West Point feels like the sort of educational film that a junior-high social studies teacher might play in class on the morning after a late night, to avoid teaching while hungover. Remarkably, it had real-world impact: spurred by the movie, President Bill Clinton granted Whittaker his officer's commission (115 years late) and hailed him as a "pathfinder" in a White House ceremony.

Against the Wall (1994)

Jamaal
MOVIE: 8/10   **SLJ FACTOR:** 8/10   **MINUTES UNTIL HE SHOWS UP:** 4
EXPLETIVES NOT DELETED: motherfuckers, shit

The masterful director John Frankenheimer specialized in thrillers with a political bent, such as *The Manchurian Candidate*, which led him into actual politics, working on the 1968 presidential campaign of Robert F. Kennedy. "We were very, very close friends," Frankenheimer said of Kennedy. "He stayed with me and I drove him to the Ambassador Hotel the night he was shot. All his clothes were in my house—and I really had a nervous breakdown after that." After RFK's assassination, Frankenheimer dropped out of filmmaking for a while (studying cooking in France), and when he returned to movies, he stayed away from political themes for decades.

Against the Wall marked his return to politics—and to prison movies, which are inherently political, since

> *"We demand better food. We demand better medical facilities. We demand an end to censorship of inmate-attorney correspondence. We demand the right to worship how we please. We demand a rehab system that works. We demand Spanish-speaking officers for our Latino brothers."*

they're portraits of societies that (more obviously) suppress the underclass by force. (Frankenheimer's first success as a movie director was 1962's *Birdman of Alcatraz*.) Made for cable television, it was a dramatization of the 1971 riots at Attica Prison in upstate New York, when prisoners took over the institution for four days, taking hostages and demanding better living conditions. After a four-day standoff, the state ended negotiations and violently retook the prison. By the end, forty-three people were dead, including ten hostages—almost all of them from gunfire by New York State Police troopers.

This Emmy-winning movie stars Kyle MacLachlan and Samuel L. Jackson as fictionalized versions of real-life Attica figures. MacLachlan plays Michael Smith, who has recently cut his hair and taken a job as a corrections officer at "the factory," as locals call the prison. Following his father (Harry Dean Stanton) into the family business, he's quietly appalled by conditions at the institution. "We're all doing time here, tiger," another guard warns him. "The only difference is, we're doing ours on the installment plan."

Jackson plays Jamaal X, a principled Muslim prisoner who has been advocating for prisoners' rights. Jackson gives him intelligence, clipped diction, and steely dignity, even when he's being strip-searched. When the uprising begins, Jamaal becomes a leader of the inmates and tries to negotiate with the representatives of Governor Nelson Rockefeller.

Jamaal and David develop a cautious respect for each other, and when they realize there's about to be a bloodbath, they try to keep each other alive and promise that if one of them survives, he will contact the other's family. But a flickering moment of human connection doesn't make this a feel-good movie: it's a claustrophobic, unflinching look at the American penal system hurtling toward tragedy.

Hail Caesar (1994)

Mailman

MOVIE: 1/10   SLJ FACTOR: 3/10   MINUTES UNTIL HE SHOWS UP: 5

Things that Julius Caesar inspired but can't be held personally responsible for: the anchovy-based salad, the casino in Vegas, and this toothache of a movie. Anthony Michael Hall, having filled out to hockey-player proportions after a successful teenage run as the adorable twerp of the Brat Pack, starred as Julius Caesar MacGruder, an aspiring rock star.

> *"I could have been a doctor, but no, I had to take drugs in college!"*

For unfathomable reasons, Hall also directed the movie, keeping the camera in focus and the pace reasonably brisk but failing to find a single laugh across its ninety-seven minutes. The plot, for what it's worth: Julius bets the plutocrat father of his girlfriend that he can prove himself by earning $100,000 in six months, and then goes to work in the father's pencil-eraser factory, which is actually a front for the manufacture of plastic explosives. The screenplay claims to be based on a short story by Mark Twain (which one isn't clear), but like Caesar, Twain should remain blameless.

All the unfunny shenanigans are motivated by Julius's infatuation with his rich girlfriend—but since she's hostile and contemptuous of him, it's hard to care. (The beautiful bassist in his band quietly pines for him but will have to wait until the end of the movie to get her ass squeezed by Julius.) He's not an antihero or a charming stoner baffled by the world—he's just a rude idiot doofus with bleached hair.

(His band, surprisingly, isn't terrible.) To make this character appealing would take a significantly more winning performer than Hall.

Robert Downey Jr. and Samuel L. Jackson both showed up for small supporting roles; each actor decided that since the script was thin, the only way to survive a day of shooting was to bring as much attitude to their scenes as possible. So Downey Jr. goes full coked-up motormouth as a mailroom employee impersonating the president of a record company. Jackson plays a postal worker who gets attacked by Julius's dog (and then quits, going to work for the water department, only to get attacked by the same dog again). Jackson can't sell the sight gag when the front door topples on him, but he does bop down the sidewalk in shorts, walking with as much attitude as John Travolta strutting with a can of paint at the beginning of *Saturday Night Fever*—that's fun to watch, for at least a few seconds.

Hall was Downey's close friend and the godfather of his son. What was Jackson's excuse?

Fresh (1994)

Sam

MOVIE: 8/10   **SLJ FACTOR:** 8/10   **MINUTES UNTIL HE SHOWS UP:** 28
EXPLETIVES NOT DELETED: shit (x4), bullshit, bitch, motherfucker, goddamn

By 1994, a coming-of-age story set in the projects was no longer that, well, fresh. And so this low-budget drama was largely overlooked by moviegoers—but it was a multifaceted gem. "I really wanted to tell a story about someone that I felt would be the weakest possible character possible and force them to deal with a situation all by themselves," said writer-director Boaz Yakin. "And obviously the weakest person in society is a child."

Michael, nicknamed Fresh, is just twelve years old, but he's already

> *"All those grandmasters and Europeans with their subsidies and whatnot to sit on their asses and play all day? They ain't living in the world. Put the clock on 'em. Put the heat on their backs, they break down. Put 'em in the park, fishing for dollars, and they break."*

working as a courier and a pusher for two different drug lords in inner-city Brooklyn. He's hardened enough to watch acts of horrible violence while snacking on a chocolate bar, but he's fundamentally an emotionally vulnerable kid who's adopted stoicism as a survival strategy. The movie's biggest problem is that it features a slew of kids (playing Michael's cousins and classmates) and the quality of their acting is erratic—but Sean Nelson delivers a complex, moving performance in the lead role.

Fresh has two father figures, played by Giancarlo Esposito and Samuel L. Jackson, neither of whom could be considered a positive role model. Esteban (a strong performance by Esposito) is a sinewy heroin dealer who seems genuinely fond of Fresh and wants to groom him as his protégé but also relishes how smack lets him keep Fresh's older sister in his sexual thrall. Sam (Jackson) is Fresh's actual father, an alcoholic chess genius living in a trailer and hustling speed-chess games in Washington Square Park to get a few bucks so he can buy beer. Fresh isn't supposed to visit him, but he takes the subway into Manhattan to get chess lessons from him.

Jackson does remarkable work rendering a man who is brilliant, resentful, brusque—and completely oblivious to his son's emotional needs. During one game, he barks, "Where you at? If your mind is somewhere else, pick your ass up, take it over there, and keep it company. I'm not having my time wasted by some half-ass fishcake opponent today." What he doesn't know, because he doesn't ask, is that Fresh has just seen two kids senselessly gunned down on a basketball court, including the girl he had a crush on. Sam teaches his son chess because he thinks that's all he knows. In the movie's cleverest gambit, however, when Fresh takes his father's chessboard strategy and applies it to real life, he finds that it can get him and his sister out of the projects—but not without great cost.

The New Age (1994)

Dale Deveaux
MOVIE: 6/10   SLJ FACTOR: 8/10   MINUTES UNTIL HE SHOWS UP: 89
EXPLETIVES NOT DELETED: fucking

Michael Tolkin, best known for the screenplay for *The Player*, wrote and directed this film, another satire of the rich and vacuous upper crust of Los Angeles. A married couple (Peter Weller and Judy Davis) skate on the matte-black surface of life, experimenting with drum circles, self-actualized orgies, and a passive-aggressive separation where they stay in the same house but take lovers. When their careers (agent, graphic designer) founder, they open an upscale clothing boutique called, unsubtly, Hipocracy. Sometimes *The New Age* skillfully captures two privileged people flailing around, trying to make sense of their world; other times, it just flails along with them.

Their lives are overpopulated with venal gurus and selfish father figures; when they finally run out of money, Samuel L. Jackson shows up as the most flawed role model of all, the guy running a shady telemarketing firm peddling a phony sweepstakes to small-business owners. Looking sharp in a mustard-colored suit, he exhorts his new recruits to hit the phones and swindle whoever answers. Jackson gives the movie a welcome jolt of energy—and with his exuberantly amoral performance, a glimpse into a world where he used his charisma for evil rather than good.

> *"You have to visualize yourself in that little pet store, in that little yoga store, in that little flower shop. You have to see yourself making friends with them, talking with them, stroking them, so confident of yourself and the lie you're telling that you get radioactive—you start to glow! Why? So they'll do what you want them to do. And what is it you want them to do? You want Mom and Pop America to reach down in their pockets, pull out their wallets, and read you the number off their credit card."*

Pulp Fiction (1994)

Jules Winnfield
MOVIE: 10/10 SLJ FACTOR: 10/10 MINUTES UNTIL HE SHOWS UP: 7
EXPLETIVES NOT DELETED: fucking (x26), goddamn (x9), fucked (x3), bitch (x10), shit (x42), fuck (x15), motherfucking (x7), motherfucker (x18), fucked-up, motherfuckers (x2)

The first time you see *Pulp Fiction*, the looping, overlapping narratives can feel clever, even thrilling, but ultimately a gimmick—a postmodern trick akin to changing the radio station from "Misirlou" to "Jungle Boogie" during the opening credits. However, rewatching reveals

> *"Check out the big brain on Brett!"*

how the structure supports the movie's themes: writer-director Quentin Tarantino doesn't just elegantly dovetail separate storylines, he dramatizes how each character lives in a larger world and plays a supporting role in somebody else's downfall or redemption. That's a lesson they all need to understand as they profanely grope their way toward a state of grace.

"*Pulp Fiction* works in a series of couples," Tarantino observed. "Everybody's a couple all the fucking way through. It starts off with Tim Roth and Amanda Plummer, then it goes to Sam Jackson and John Travolta, then John Travolta and Uma Thurman, then it goes to Bruce Willis and the cab driver [Angela Jones], then it's Bruce Willis and Maria de Medeiros—and then for a moment after he leaves her, he's the only character in the movie. He's viewed completely alone. Then he makes a bond with this other character [played by Ving Rhames] and they become a team. It's only when they become a team that they can do anything. Circumstances make them a couple."

Of all these partnerships, the most memorable is Jules (Samuel L. Jackson) and Vincent (John Travolta), as gangsters bantering about hash bars and cheeseburgers and *Green Acres*. They so enjoy each other's company that when it's time to go kill some people, Jules has to remind Vincent, "Let's get into character." And even though Vincent's spent the last several years in Amsterdam, he knows that when Jules starts reciting Ezekiel 25:17, it's time to pull out his gun.

When it came time for the Oscars, Miramax pushed Travolta for Best Actor and Jackson for Best Supporting Actor, for reasons of show-business politics. Their screen time is basically equivalent, however: while Travolta has a whole sequence with Thurman, Jackson is the dominant personality in two scenes they share (the apartment scene and the diner scene). The way you can tell Jackson's playing a leading role: he has the movie's defining dramatic arc, as the character who witnesses a miracle and resolves to leave the criminal life. The movie's climax is when he thinks about the biblical passage he's been reciting for years as a prelude to violence—and realizes that he himself is the tyranny of evil men. "But I'm trying, Ringo," he says, with unwavering force even more persuasive than the loaded gun in his hand. "I'm trying real hard to be the shepherd."

"That was the hardest part of the film," Jackson said, "to be able to take a speech that you used to create mayhem to discover a sense of peace, and still have that menace in it. Because he's still at a crossroads. Even though he's made up his mind not to do this anymore, there are little things that could trigger him right back into that space he was trying to escape."

In Tarantino's original screenplay, there was a scene in the diner where Jules, a bad motherfucker in a Krazy Kat T-shirt, ended the standoff by shooting Pumpkin and Honey Bunny—and then opened his eyes, because that was a vision of what he was capable of, not the life he wanted to lead. The greatness of Jackson's performance is that he can reconcile all the conflicts in Jules's soul; doing that, he holds together the entire movie.

Jackson thought Jules was the moral center of *Pulp Fiction* "because he carried himself like a professional." That perspective, it turns out, tells us just as much about what values Jackson considers to be important in his own life. Others might say it was because Jules was the movie's Shakespearean fool—getting the funniest lines empowered him to tell the greatest truths—or because he acknowledged the presence of the divine when he felt the hand of God spare him from a point-blank barrage of bullets.

Asked why the bullets didn't hit Jules, Jackson said, "Deus ex machina. And that motherfucker wasn't that good a shot."

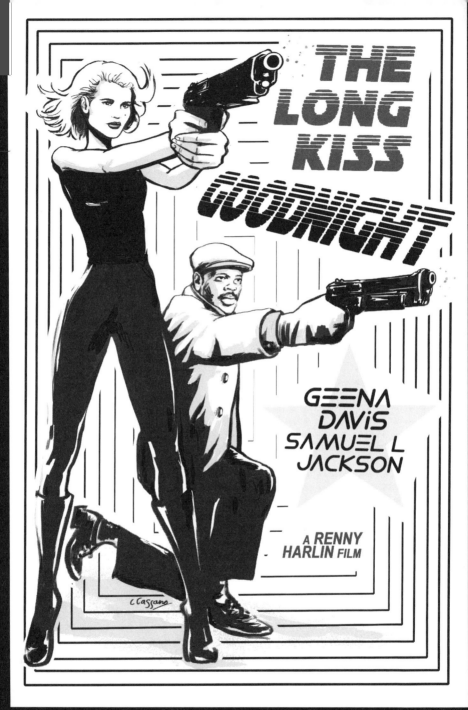

THE LONG KISS GOODNIGHT

GEENA DAVIS
SAMUEL L JACKSON

A RENNY HARLIN FILM

Christa Cassano.

hile **Samuel L. Jackson was filming** his career-defining role in *Pulp Fiction*, he was also, astonishingly, working a second job. At night, he went to the Coast Playhouse in West Hollywood to star in a production of *Distant Fires*, Kevin Heelan's play about race and class conflict on a construction site. It was Jackson's first appearance onstage in three years, and he worked insanely long hours to do both projects simultaneously—after a night at the theater, he sometimes arrived on location for *Pulp Fiction* at 5:30 a.m.—"but there was no way I was not coming in for this, because this is what gives me life," he said. He was attuned to the body language of live audiences: he could feel when they were leaning forward and getting carried along by the momentum of the drama.

On November 10, 1993, Jackson went out for dinner after the play, joined by three male friends, all actors, all Black. After the meal, the four of them stood outside the restaurant, still talking, enjoying the evening too much to get in their cars and go home. Then there was a bright light in their faces. Jackson looked around and realized they were surrounded: two police cars and sheriffs with their guns drawn, barking, "Hands up! Lay on the ground!"

"I guess we were standing there too long," he noted dryly. The police told them that they had a report of four Black men standing on the corner, holding guns and baseball bats. The cops searched the cars of Jackson and his friends but didn't find the phantom weapons. There was no apology, naturally, not even after the Black men wrote letters to the police department. Jackson's conclusion: "If you're Black and you're in America, you're going to get hassled by the cops eventually."

Before *Pulp Fiction* was released by Miramax in 1994, Quentin Tarantino kept trying to lower the company's expectations. It had a budget of about $8.5 million (kept down by paying all the principal actors the same salary, $20,000 per week), and he repeatedly pointed to the forgettable Damon Wayans romance/thriller *Mo' Money*, which grossed about $40 million, as a reasonable benchmark of commercial success. Instead, *Pulp Fiction* became one of the defining films of the decade, winning the Palme d'Or at Cannes, grossing over $100 million domestically (and as much again internationally), inspiring legions of copycat screenplays, and giving an adrenaline shot into the career of everybody involved with it.

The movie was nominated for seven Academy Awards, losing most of them to *Forrest Gump*. In the best supporting actor category, Jackson lost the Oscar to Martin Landau. When twelve-year-old Anna Paquin opened the envelope, Jackson could be seen on camera, natty in a tuxedo and very obviously saying "Shit!" ("I didn't care," Jackson said of the obscenity. "It was no reflection on Martin Landau.") But while Landau was able to spend the rest of his life without having total strangers regularly walk up to him and spout dialogue at him from a 1994 film (*Ed Wood*, in his case), that was not the case for Jackson.

People would demand that Jackson recite Ezekiel 25:17, or ask him "You know what they call a Quarter Pounder with Cheese in Paris?" (often rendering the line as "in France"). He would usually respond with "They don't call it a Quarter Pounder with Cheese?" Once in a while, the person speaking with him was astute enough to recognize that as the next line of dialogue in the scene and to respond with the following line ("No, they got the metric system. They wouldn't know what the fuck a Quarter Pounder is")—when that happened, Jackson would also continue, sometimes reenacting the entire scene with a total stranger.

The most common *Pulp Fiction* question was about the briefcase and its extremely desirable but unseen contents: they wanted to know exactly what the MacGuffin inside it was. (One popular theory: it was Marsellus Wallace's soul.) Most often, Jackson would just say, "I don't know, I never looked in it." (True: the only characters to peer inside the briefcase during the movie were those played by John Travolta and Tim Roth.) If he was feeling more expansive, he would explain, "John did ask Quentin Tarantino exactly what was supposed to be inside and Quentin said, 'Whatever you want it to be.' So I assumed it was something that, when people looked at it, seemed like the most beautiful thing they had ever seen or their greatest desire. When I looked inside, between scenes, I saw two lights and some batteries."

Six years after Jackson was dragged the length of a subway platform, his lawsuit against the MTA reached a courtroom. "By the time we got to court, I had started to do some larger films," Jackson noted. The jury felt bad enough for his pain and suffering to award him $540,000, but since he had become a movie star, he said "they didn't feel bad enough to award me millions." The 1994 verdict, appealed by the MTA, was finally upheld in 1996.

Jackson was now working steadily, even if most of the roles he was being offered had originally been intended for one of two other Black actors: Denzel Washington if it was a studio movie or Forest Whitaker if it was an indie movie. He didn't mind seeing other actors' fingerprints on the screenplays he was sent—it was a step up from scripts with characters so obviously disposable that he would read them wondering "which page I was killed on." He emphasized to his agents that he wanted to stay busy, and he was happiest if he had at least two projects lined up after the movie he was currently shooting.

In New York City filming *Kiss of Death*, Jackson was waiting to hear back about a recent audition, for the sure-to-be-a-blockbuster *Waterworld*. On the set, he was approached by the producers of the third *Die Hard* movie, who told him that Laurence Fishburne had gotten the *Waterworld* role he wanted, but that meant Fishburne had dropped out of *Die Hard with a Vengeance*, which was shooting very soon—did he want the role? Jackson didn't hesitate: "Fuck yeah! Yes! I'll take that job!"

His agents were unhappy, Jackson said—not about the job offer but that by lunging at it, he had eliminated their negotiating leverage. "My agents cursed me out and said, 'You never take a job without talking to us.' I was like, 'Fuck.'" (Dennis Hopper ended up playing opposite Kevin Costner in *Waterworld*, which became the most expensive film production ever but did middling business; Fishburne successfully sued the *Die Hard* producers, saying they had reneged on a verbal deal for him to appear in the film because they realized they could cast Jackson more cheaply.)

The raw material of *Die Hard with a Vengeance* was a screenplay called *Simon Says*, but it got adapted on the fly to become a John McClane vehicle. Jackson remembers, "Some days we'd get to work, but we wouldn't actually have dialogue. We would go to Bruce's trailer, and they'd say, 'Okay, you have to go from 168th Street to 97th Street today. We're going to do it in the cab, and Sam, you say this. Bruce, what do you want to say?'"

Jackson figured out the secret to playing the sidekick to an international action hero: he was the audience's representative onscreen, there to hang with the star and be amazed by his astonishing feats.

Done right, he was an essential foil; done wrong, he was a "Black Tonto." In *Die Hard with a Vengeance*, Jackson played a shop owner in Harlem who gradually sheds his prejudices when he leaves his Black neighborhood to team up with a white cop. "Zeus Carver was the most like me of any character I ever played," Jackson said.

While the movie was shooting on a construction site in Brooklyn, the writer Nelson George ran into Jackson and his body double on a street corner, both wearing the same shirt, waiting for the next setup. George had recently sent Jackson something he had written for *The Village Voice* weekly newspaper, a righteous, poetic meditation on race called "To Be a Black Man." He asked Jackson if he would star in a short film adapting it. Jackson agreed, and so on Saturday morning, he visited George's apartment on the bottom floor of a nearby brownstone, where the writer had set up a makeshift recording studio in a walk-in closet. "He really didn't let me direct him very much," George said. "He said, 'I got it,' he went in the closet, and he recorded several versions of the narration. Then we went out into the neighborhood and walked around with a 16mm Bolex. And then he went and played golf. He was a huge star already, but he took the time to do a short film that would play at a couple of festivals—something about the material spoke to him and that was enough for him to do it."

Die Hard with a Vengeance ended up being the number one movie at the box office in 1995, both in the United States and globally, but major motion pictures with plum roles for Black characters remained scarce—so Jackson went looking for characters that he could make his own, even if they were originally intended to be white. If he wanted to play a character, he would ask his representatives to set up a meeting with the movie's producers. "They call and the producers go, 'Sam Jackson! We never thought of going that way. Wow! That's interesting.' Sometimes they ask me to come in to discuss it, and I end up convincing them that the dynamics of the story won't change because I'm African American."

His one-man campaign for colorblind casting, centered on the career of one Samuel L. Jackson, didn't always succeed. He had a strong audition for *The Getaway*, the thriller starring Alec Baldwin and Kim Basinger, trying out for the role of Rudy (ultimately played by Michael Madsen), who has consensual sex with Jennifer Tilly's character while her husband is tied up—only to be told by the filmmakers that it would "change the politics of the movie" if they cast a Black man in the role.

Jackson objected strenuously: "But if I was raping her, it would be OK, right? Get the fuck out of there. It's a bullshit excuse, and they used it."

When Jackson read the script for the Geena Davis vehicle *The Long Kiss Goodnight*, about a suburban housewife unaware of her past as a government assassin, he dug the story—and the character of Mitch, a sketchy private investigator. The role of Mitch was originally written for a white man, but Jackson campaigned for the part, finally running into director Renny Harlin (Davis's husband) at a dinner party and closing the deal. In this case, Jackson was the one who lobbied against an interracial love scene. "At one point there was a tryst between the two characters," he said. "They fell into bed and had sex. But I wasn't in favor of it. It had nothing to do with race. My reasoning was that it was better to keep the tension. If they started fucking, there was nowhere to go with it—like in most relationships."

Jackson similarly convinced director Kevin Reynolds (recovering from the *Waterworld* debacle) over the course of a ninety-minute meeting that the inner-city-school drama *One Eight Seven* would be better served by having a Black man (e.g., him) play the lead. Jackson's logic: audiences had recently seen minority students tangle with a white teacher in *Dangerous Minds* with Michelle Pfeiffer. "If you put somebody like me in the school and students still rebel, it's more interesting," Jackson pointed out. "Reynolds got it, but not until I talked to him."

Both *One Eight Seven* and *The Long Kiss Goodnight* underperformed at the box office: Jackson blamed the Warner Bros. marketing department. He thought that Warners got squeamish about *One Eight Seven* and buried it after the son of the Time Warner chairman, Gerald Levin—a high school teacher in the Bronx—was tortured and killed by a former student. And although Harlin believed racism was at the root of *The Long Kiss Goodnight*'s anemic ticket sales, Jackson thought the studio made a mistake marketing the movie to men instead of women. "Women like seeing themselves empowered," he observed. "Instead of buying commercial time on football games, they should have bought time on daytime soaps."

Jackson wasn't blind to the movie business's racism. Often, the people behind it didn't bother to be subtle. The poster for the international release of *White Sands* featured an image of Jackson running through the desert with a briefcase—only his skin tone had been changed to Caucasian. The marketing executive behind that decision claimed he was trying to avoid spoiling the plot of the movie.

The most obvious disparity was in Jackson's paychecks. "I get paid like a B-list white actor," Jackson said flatly. He heard plenty of excuses and justifications for why he didn't merit the big bucks, despite his Oscar nomination, his obvious abilities, and his presence in massive global blockbusters: *Die Hard with a Vengeance* was actually a Bruce Willis movie. *Pulp Fiction* was actually a John Travolta movie. *Jurassic Park* was actually a velociraptor movie. "That's how they keep you in place," he said. "But, by the same token, I make a lot more money than I've ever made in my life."

For *A Time to Kill*, the adaptation of the hit John Grisham novel, Jackson was paid $2.6 million. Off camera, he told newcomer Matthew McConaughey, who was starring in his first major movie, that by the following year, McConaughey would be making more money than him.

McConaughey just laughed. "No, I won't," he said. "Come on, you're the man."

"Yeah," Jackson replied, "but you're the white man."

Jackson thought that his perfect work schedule would be two movies and three plays a year. His onstage opportunities were limited in Los Angeles, so he compensated by making as many movies as he could— he was featured in five movies in 1996—and constantly looking for the next job, as if he were still a starving actor in New York. In 1996, Jackson ran into Quentin Tarantino at a party. "When are you going to write something else for me?" Jackson demanded. In fact, Tarantino already had a project in mind: six months later, he sent Jackson the script for *Jackie Brown*.

For his third feature film, Tarantino again cast an array of big names (Michael Keaton, Bridget Fonda, Robert De Niro) and forgotten favorites (Pam Grier, Robert Forster)—the one significant carryover from the *Pulp Fiction* cast was Jackson. He played the movie's villain, Ordell Robbie, with a distinctive chin braid and gleeful amorality. "He's a great friend to have, but he's definitely the wrong guy to cross," Jackson said of Ordell. (Tarantino said that after writing the script, he identified so hugely with Ordell that he considered playing the role himself; Jackson treated this suggestion with the lack of seriousness that it deserved.)

De Niro played Ordell's best friend, Louis Gara, fresh out of jail. This was their second movie together, but in *Goodfellas*, their characters didn't speak to each other, so similarly, the actors never had a conversation. "Bobby didn't really deal with people he didn't have to deal with,"

Jackson said. This time, they interacted more—enough for Jackson to note how quiet De Niro was when the camera wasn't rolling. "He just wouldn't talk a lot," he said. "Every now and then, he'd say something, and you'd kind of go, 'Did he say something? Is he talking?'"

One night, Jackson was awakened from a dead sleep by a four a.m. phone call from Tarantino. "Hey, you have to work," Tarantino told him.

"I have to come to work?" Jackson sleepily replied.

"Nah, you know that conversation you have with Bob on the phone?"

"Yeah."

"Well, he won't do it with me. He'll only do it with you."

"So I have to come in and talk to him?"

"No, all you have to do is stay on the phone now and do the scene with him."

Jackson didn't need to fumble for a script: as usual, he had memorized all his lines before shooting started. He ran the lines with De Niro—but before he could roll over and go back to sleep, Tarantino told him that he'd have to do it again for De Niro's close-up. Jackson stayed on the phone until six a.m. as De Niro's long-distance scene partner: "Dude would not let me hang up."

Most actors making a phone call in a movie have to play out the conversation without the benefit of a human being on the other end of the line. In fact, many actors won't even show up to feed lines to a scene partner who's doing close-ups; if they're not visible on camera, they'll head for their trailers, letting that work fall to a stand-in or a production assistant. Even when he wasn't showing respect to De Niro, Jackson stuck around the set to play his half of the scene off-camera, both out of a sense of professionalism and because he enjoyed it. "There are only so many acting opportunities in a lifetime," he noted, "so you've got to take them."

LaTanya Richardson's opinion was that Jackson still had an addictive personality: he had just redirected its focus onto acting. "It's his drug. He had to replace it with *something*," she said. "As long as Sam has read a script or the camera is there, he feels as if he's been fed that day."

In the throes of that thespian addiction, Jackson once again delivered a brilliant performance in a Tarantino movie while moonlighting on a second job. This time, it was up in San Francisco, where Barry Levinson was filming the underwater sci-fi thriller *Sphere* with Dustin

Hoffman and Sharon Stone. The two sets had extremely different atmospheres, Jackson said, and not just because Levinson's featured huge tanks of water: "Barry's very quiet, whereas Quentin fills the room, you know he's there, he'll laugh out loud during a take. Quentin's set is like a party. Barry's is like an interesting workplace where everybody's doing their job and enjoying themselves but nobody's doing it out loud." Jackson said he didn't have any problem shifting from one character to another: "I would put the hair and the braid on and I would immediately be back as Ordell."

Jackson rated Tarantino's ear for how Black characters talk as excellent, not perfect: he rated it at ninety-five percent. "Quentin thinks he writes great Black dialogue," Jackson said. "He writes interesting Black dialogue, but it's not pure." Sometimes Jackson would tell Tarantino that he hadn't gotten a Black idiom correct and the director would respond, "Now don't be telling me what's ebonic." But Tarantino so trusted Jackson that he was the one actor he would let modify his dialogue (not improvisationally—Jackson would discuss tweaks with Tarantino first).

Jackson attempted to adjust Tarantino's pronunciation in the famous "dead nigger storage" scene in *Pulp Fiction*, where the director made a cameo as a friend of Jules, angry that he has to contend with a bloody corpse in his garage at 8:15 a.m. ("When you came pulling in here, did you notice a sign on the front of my house that said 'Dead Nigger Storage'?" he asks. "It ain't there because storing dead niggers ain't my fucking business!"). Jackson advised him, "Quentin, as long as you say 'nigger,' it's going to be like fingernails on a chalkboard. You've got to say 'N-I-G-G-A-H, nigga.' That means you're familiar with the use of the word and you've used it in mixed company, not just with some white guys." Tarantino deliberately kept the more abrasive pronunciation of the slur in that scene but cast a Black actress (Venessia Valentino) as his wife to soften the impact.

Jackie Brown contained an even higher density of the word "nigger" in the dialogue; Jackson took responsibility for some of that, saying, "With Ordell, I may have said it three times more than Quentin wrote, because that was who Ordell was." Some viewers objected to its frequency—characters in the movie say the word thirty-eight times—including filmmakers such as Allen and Albert Hughes and Spike Lee. "I'm not against the word, and I use it, but not excessively," Lee said. "And some people speak that way. But Quentin is infatuated with that word. What does he want to be made—an honorary black man?" This was the crux of Lee's objection: Tarantino was a white filmmaker using a racial slur not only for verisimilitude but to establish his own street cred. "Because Sam Jackson kisses his butt, that means Black people love him?" Lee demanded. "That's wrong. I am not the only African American in this world who has a problem with this excessive use of the N word."

Tarantino defended his pulp diction: "As a writer, I demand the right to write any character in the world that I want to write," he said. "And to say that I can't do that because I'm white, but the Hughes brothers can do that because they're Black, that is racist." Tarantino had once made a cameo appearance in a Spike Lee movie (*Girl 6*), but now the feud between the two loudmouth geniuses escalated—and Jackson emphatically took Tarantino's side.

"I hate to say it, but I think Spike's pissed off with Quentin because he made this interesting Black movie, and Spike hasn't done that in a few years," Jackson said, not actually sounding like he hated to say it. "In my opinion Spike's the last person who should try and censor somebody's artistic endeavor. People have tried to do that to him for years and for him to do the same is ridiculous." Jackson made it personal, revealing that he and Lee had fallen out when he turned down *Malcolm X* in favor of *White Sands*. "Most of the actors who've passed through Spike's films actually outgrow him in a couple of ways. One of the ways is that we won't work for nothing anymore. Especially if you realize, 'Okay, well, Spike's got this house in New York, he's got this office in New York, and he's building this house in Martha's Vineyard and he wants me to work for scale.' What's wrong with this picture?"

On the N word itself, Jackson wasn't bothered by its growing prevalence, and not just because he peppered his daily speech with it. When he heard young people of assorted skin colors using it, he regarded that as vindication of Lenny Bruce's philosophy: "You take the power from a word by overusing it." While he recognized that the word had a dictionary's worth of meanings, depending on context, he himself defiantly employed it to lay out the parameters of his own identity.

He explained, "I have let people know that I'm an actor, I'm a nice guy, and there are a lot of things that we can get along with, but the first thing you need to know about me is I'm a nigger. And they look at me like, 'What?' And I go, 'I'm not just, you know, a really nice colored fella. I'm a nigger.' And they go, 'What? Sam, I really don't understand.' I'm one of those guys you really really really don't want to mess with. So I've done things that, you know, people go to prison for, I guess. I'm really not just going to punch you in the face. I'm going to do some niggerly shit to you."

And he defended Tarantino's right to use the word in his films, both as a racial slur and as an in-the-club password for his characters, Black and white. He said that the Hughes brothers, with whom he made *Menace II Society*, asked him the same question that Lee raised publicly. They phrased it more pithily: "What the fuck is up with Quentin and this 'nigger' thing?"

Jackson replied, "And how many times did you use it in *Menace II Society*?"

"Oh, that's different."

"Bullshit. You wrote your script; he wrote his."

Jackson knew very well that Ordell's frequent use of the word made viewers uncomfortable. As he saw it, that was a large part of the point: you shouldn't feel comfortable around a character like Ordell Robbie. He could have objected, and if he had thought the language was offensive, he would have. "Quentin's not a racist. I'm not a racist. I'm going to be true to that character and say what that character says, no matter what anybody out there thinks."

Jackson particularly reveled in one piece of *Jackie Brown* dialogue, when Ordell's speaking with Beaumont Livingston, the character played by Chris Tucker: "I hate to be the kind of nigga that do a nigga a favor and then—*bam!*—hit the nigga up for a favor in return, but I gots to be that kind of nigga."

"It's like *boom!*" Jackson said, fully aware of the excess and the impact of a single sentence. "But wouldn't Ordell say that?"

SPHERE

Kevin Bannister.

Losing Isaiah (1995)

Kadar Lewis
MOVIE: 4/10 **SLJ FACTOR:** 5/10 **MINUTES UNTIL HE SHOWS UP:** 42

How to tell which of two rival mothers *Losing Isaiah* wants you to sympathize with at any given moment: who's getting the Hollywood glamour treatment. At the beginning of the movie, when Halle Berry is a crack addict who abandons her baby and Jessica Lange is a social worker with saintly motives, Berry looks like a strung-out mess while Lange glows. Later

> *"This goes way beyond you. Black babies belong with Black mothers."*

on, when Berry's character has gotten clean and is trying to reclaim the baby that Lange's character adopted, Berry is styled like a catalog model and Lange looks like an unkempt fishmonger.

The movie has some fine performances and affecting moments, and doesn't lapse into melodrama as often as it could have, but it ultimately can't figure out its point of view—which is how it ends up with an unsatisfying split-the-difference conclusion that feels lazily focus-grouped, not Solomonic.

The director, Stephen Gyllenhaal, and the writer, Naomi Foner, ended up more famous for another collaboration: they're the parents of the actors Maggie and Jake Gyllenhaal. The movie was practically a couples retreat: Samuel L. Jackson and his wife LaTanya Richardson play opposing counsel in the custody battle. Richardson portrays a Black attorney hesitantly representing the white family, while Jackson is the high-priced lawyer working pro bono to reunite a Black biological mother with her child. Although Jackson and Richardson both deliver fine performances in the courtroom scenes—she's warm while he's supercilious, which makes for a good contrast—they disappointingly never face each other down toe-to-toe.

"Because she has been acting on the stage since she was a kid, she is a lot more knowledgeable than I am," Jackson said of Richardson. "All of a sudden we were in a situation where I could be helpful to her. Telling her to keep it simple because she'd have to repeat the same thing over and over again. How to hit a mark, find her light, and help the cameraman. It was enlightening for her to see that I had learned so much and was so comfortable doing it and that I could help her find a comfort zone. The only insistence I had was that we have separate dressing rooms and bathrooms. That way, I'd always be on time. I wouldn't be if I had to share a bathroom with her."

Kiss of Death (1995)

Calvin

MOVIE: 7/10   **SLJ FACTOR:** 5/10   **MINUTES UNTIL HE SHOWS UP:** 12

EXPLETIVES NOT DELETED: assholes, fucking, shit (x2), fuck (x2), bitch

Jimmy (David Caruso), a crook trying to go straight, reluctantly helps his cousin in an auto heist; Calvin (Samuel L. Jackson) is a law enforcement officer who busts that heist. When the operation goes sour, they get hit by the same bullet: Jimmy in the hand, Calvin in the face. Initially antagonists, they become uneasy allies and eventually friends, but despite the violent origin story, their relationship feels bloodless. Forced to become a confidential informant, Jimmy is buffeted by the demands of the criminals and the cops; as played by Caruso, he's watchable but not really believable. As Calvin, meanwhile, Jackson seems to spend the entire movie dabbing at his weeping right eye, injured in the bust.

> *"You see this eye here? Runs all the time—I can't make it stop. I got a third of my hearing in this ear. And when I want to go to the beach, like take my kids to the beach and play with them and shit, strong direct sunlight gives me a migraine so bad I cry like a baby. They don't know why—it just does."*

This remake of a 1947 film noir classic, directed by Barbet Schroeder, has a classy cast that includes Helen Hunt, Ving Rhames, and—doing great work as a ball-breaking district attorney—Stanley Tucci. The best thing about the movie is Nicolas Cage's indelible performance as Little Junior, a small-time crime lord who bench-presses strippers, advocates for the inspirational value of having your own acronym (his is "B.A.D.: Balls. Attitude. Direction"), and abhors the taste of metal utensils in his mouth. Muscular and asthmatic, he's a murderous roid-rage nightmare who's lonely and vulnerable in the wake of his father's death.

A few years later, Jackson named Cage as the most unpredictable actor he had ever worked with: "He likes to constantly change. He doesn't like to do the same thing over and over. And once you realize that, it's kind of like, 'Oh my god, what is he going to do now?' I'm the opposite. I'm constant."

This was the moment in Cage's career when he was utterly riveting onscreen, just before his fondness for eccentric character choices and overacting would boil over into self-parody in action blockbusters like *Con Air* and *Gone in Sixty Seconds*. The other principal actors here don't try to match his quirky intensity—which might be for the best, honestly—but in comparison, everything they do seems rote and wan.

Die Hard with a Vengeance (1995)

Zeus
MOVIE: 7/10   SLJ FACTOR: 8/10   MINUTES UNTIL HE SHOWS UP: 8
EXPLETIVES NOT DELETED: shit (x25), fuck (x19), goddamn (x6), asshole (x2), fucking (x11), goddammit (x2), motherfucker (x3), motherfuckers

"We drive a lot, we run a lot, we duck a lot, we curse a lot, and we bleed a lot," Samuel L. Jackson said of the third *Die Hard* movie. "And occasionally we stop to act." Jackson plays Zeus Carver, an electrician who, against his better judgment, comes to the defense of John McClane, a white man standing on a Harlem sidewalk in his boxer shorts, wearing a sandwich board with the message "I Hate Niggers" on it. (McClane [Bruce Willis] is there because of a mad bomber [Jeremy Irons] with a master plan for tormenting him and stealing a huge quantity of gold from the Federal Reserve.) Zeus is prickly, intelligent, and brave—but refreshingly unskilled in the life of an action hero, not even knowing how to disengage the safety on his gun.

> *"My name is Zeus. Yeah, Zeus. As in father of Apollo, Mount Olympus, don't fuck with me or I'll shove a lightning bolt up your ass—Zeus!"*

The movie, directed by John McTiernan (who directed the original *Die Hard* but skipped the first sequel), runs out of steam halfway through and has plot holes big enough to drive fourteen dump trucks through, but there's popcorn-movie fun in abundance: the condescending villainy of Irons, a particularly inventive heist, lots of New York City color, and especially, the dynamic between Willis and Jackson. Their eventual friendship is inevitable, but Zeus's initial disdain for

McClane, racially charged, has more zing: "You mean to tell me I'm in this shit because some white cop threw some white asshole's brother off a roof?"

For his part, Jackson rejoiced in the scenes where they drive through Central Park at breakneck speed, with Willis actually behind the wheel, zipping along pedestrian paths and through Sheep Meadow: "I'd always wanted to do that when I was sitting in traffic," he said.

Gratuitous *Pulp Fiction* reference: as Willis and Jackson approach a pay phone on 72nd Street, McClane explains that during his suspension from the NYPD, he's been "smoking cigarettes and watching Captain Kangaroo," a quote from the Statler Brothers' "Flowers on the Wall," the song Willis's Butch was singing along to as it played on his car radio, just before he hit Marsellus with his Honda.

Fluke (1995)

The Voice of Rumbo
MOVIE: 3/10   SLJ FACTOR: 2/10   MINUTES UNTIL HE SHOWS UP: 15 (voice)

You say you're not interested in *Fluke*? What if I told you that it starred Matthew Modine as a workaholic businessman who dies in a car crash and is reincarnated as a dog? (Wait, come back! Now stay. Sit.) The handsome mutt named Fluke, with thoughts voiced by Modine, has canine adventures that range from escaping from a pound to escaping from a cosmetics testing lab. Fluke travels across the country, employing the combo technique of running through freshly plowed fields and hopping on a freight train, so he can reunite with his wife and son (Nancy Travis, Max Pomeranc) and take revenge on his business partner (Eric Stoltz), whom he unfairly blames for his untimely death. The movie is too goofy for adults, too somber for kids, and too weird for anybody who just wants to watch happy puppies having charming escapades. You decide which is more unsettling: the scene where a dog avenges himself by attacking an innocent man from the back seat of the car, making him crash into a brick mailbox, or the scene where a dog sneaks into bed so he can lie next to his human widow?

"You can't be sorry about what's been, squirt—you got to be."

Samuel L. Jackson provides the voice of Rumbo, the streetwise older dog who teaches Fluke how to avoid the dogcatcher, where to scrounge sausages, and how to lift up one leg to piss. Rumbo was once a "two-legger" himself but doesn't want to admit it. For his part, Jackson sounds like he can't believe he's saying four-legger dialogue like "That's one way of getting rid of your fleas." While it's hard to fault him, the movie isn't improved by his performance, which is saturated with incredulity and spiced with an undertone of "as soon as I get out of this recording session, I am totally firing my agent."

The Great White Hype (1996)

Reverend Fred Sultan
MOVIE: 6/10   SLJ FACTOR: 9/10   MINUTES UNTIL HE SHOWS UP: 6
EXPLETIVES NOT DELETED: fucking (x4), shit (x4), fuck (x3), motherfucker, shitless, motherfucking, bitch, bullshit

Everything about the Reverend Fred Sultan is phony: his name, his promises, his concern for the boxers he manages. He's a ruthless operator who hides his intelligence behind a façade of piety covered by a veneer of buffoonery, all overlaid with a patina of showmanship. But Samuel L. Jackson plays this charlatan with such enthusiasm, he makes an uneven comedy come alive whenever he swans into the room, wearing yet another outrageous outfit accessorized with a turban. "I love you," Sultan tells the heavyweight champion he handles (Damon Wayans). He says it with sincerity, and then he repeats it, emphasizing that he thinks of the boxer as his brother—but the third time he says it, the fighter knows he's getting financially screwed.

> *"Don't give away what you can sell!"*

Tony Hendra (the actor-writer best known as the manager in *Spinal Tap*) conceived the jaundiced premise: a promoter looking for a white opponent to goose interest in a title match against his Black prizefighter (a scenario played as drama in *Rocky*, as comedy here). Originally intended to be improvised, the idea was turned into a screenplay by Ron Shelton (the writer-director with a specialty in sports comedies such as *Bull Durham*). When Shelton left the project to direct *Tin Cup*, Reginald Hudlin took over as director: the resulting movie has lots of good ideas but not enough punch lines, and although the cast includes Jeff Goldblum, Jamie Foxx, and Corbin Bernsen, their various plotlines never cohere. Jackson said that studio meddling didn't help the movie's zigzag creation. "I always thought of it as this interesting kind of satire, but it turned out to be this not-so-great comedy," he said. "I think that maybe there was more than one film being shot there at the time."

Odd *Pulp Fiction* reference: the Reverend spots a guy with greasy black hair at the prizefight and jokes, "Vincent, how you doing, baby, you seen Jules?"

The Search for One-Eye Jimmy (1996)

Colonel Ron
MOVIE: 2/10   SLJ FACTOR: 2/10   MINUTES UNTIL HE SHOWS UP: 27
EXPLETIVES NOT DELETED: fucking, dick

The Search for One-Eye Jimmy features a startling number of rising stars, including Samuel L. Jackson, Steve Buscemi, John Turturro, Sam Rockwell, Tony Sirico (Paulie Walnuts on *The Sopranos*), and Michael Badalucco (Jimmy Berlutti on *The Practice*)—not to mention Jennifer Beals and Anne Meara. Unfortunately, writer-director Sam Henry Kass, later a member of the *Seinfeld* writing staff, had more connections than

> "I'm being disrespectful? What are we talking— the Pope or a gas station attendant? I believe this little rodent suffers from delusions of grandeur."

chops—which is probably why this amateurish indie comedy, made in 1993, went unreleased for three years. The shaggy-dog narrative rambles aimlessly and the jokes mostly fall flat.

The story, such as it is, centers on a film student who returns to his working-class Brooklyn neighborhood to make a documentary movie and thinks he's found a story in a missing-person case—which falls apart when it turns out that the titular One-Eye Jimmy locked himself in the basement while he was doing laundry. Along the way, we meet a sampler platter of unemployed eccentrics and lowlifes, which means we see a lot of talented actors working hard to sell subpar material.

Buscemi, playing a sad sack trying to convince people to pose with his cardboard cutout of a pro wrestler, has some moments, as do Sirico, doing malevolent schtick as a local mobster who recently lost two hundred pounds, and Turturro, showing off his moves as an obsessive disco dancer. Jackson doesn't fare so well playing a Vietnam vet with blacked-out teeth and a tree branch attached to his helmet, fishing in the Gowanus Canal. Portraying a character with mental issues, Jackson doesn't figure out how to make the role compelling, but at least he's smart enough not to overdo it. The best thing about Colonel Ron is his contempt for all the other characters in the movie—an attitude that seems totally earned.

"We were in Red Hook, Brooklyn, back when it was a shithole," said the movie's leading man, Holt McCallany. "We had terrible locations, terrible food, and no fucking money. But Sam didn't care." McCallany remembered that although Kass didn't encourage improvisation, Jackson had more leeway to do it because of his stature. "He kept telling me how badly my breath stinks," McCallany said. "In the back of my mind, I felt some insecurity: does my breath really stink?"

A Time to Kill (1996)

Carl Lee Hailey
MOVIE: 7/10   SLJ FACTOR: 9/10   MINUTES UNTIL HE SHOWS UP: 5
EXPLETIVES NOT DELETED: shit

"The first time I saw the film, I almost walked out," Samuel L. Jackson said of *A Time to Kill*. "I have a lot of mixed feelings about that film. I know it's a powerful film, and it's great. But we shot a lot of stuff that's actually not in that movie, which taught me the power of editing."

Jackson's character, Carl Lee Hailey, works in a sawmill in a small Mississippi town. When his ten-year-old daughter Tonya is brutally raped and assaulted by two white-supremacist locals, Carl Lee, fearing they will be acquitted by rural jurors, shoots and kills them before they can go to trial. In a starry cast that includes

> "America is a war, and you on the other side. How a Black man ever going to get a fair trial with the enemy on the bench and the jury box?"

Kevin Spacey, Donald Sutherland, Sandra Bullock, Ashley Judd, Chris Cooper, and Charles S. Dutton, Jackson laps everybody: his anguished performance feels raw, riveting, and extremely real. While *A Time to Kill* is an old-fashioned Hollywood entertainment (directed by Joel Schumacher, adapting a hit novel by John Grisham), the movie has an old-fashioned Hollywood problem: even in a story about race and the Klan, the Black experience gets pushed to the side so the camera can focus on a white actor. So the protagonist isn't Carl Lee, it's Jake Brigance, the young white lawyer defending him (Matthew McConaughey, in his first leading role); the supporting characters mostly orbit around Jake and he gets the film's most dramatic moments.

Jackson said, "There was this huge scene I did, when I go to Jake's office before killing the guys. I'm talking to him about what happened to my daughter. I tell him the story he tells the jury at the end of the movie. About what they did, how she looks. When I finished the scene, everybody in the room had broken down. They said it was awesome. It was one of those feelings when you've done something and you think, 'I nailed the thing. Damn.' That particular speech was my moment. I'm very good in the rest of the film, but that particular moment would have killed."

When Jackson first saw the edited movie, however, he said, "I'm like, 'Wait a minute! The whole fucking scene's gone!' I had no idea. *A Time to Kill* would have been different. When I was doing it, it was a story about a man who loved his daughter so much he was willing to make this kind of sacrifice so the world would be a safe place for her. If her attackers were sent to prison, she would never feel safe, because they could get out. He had to kill them so she would know those two guys would never hurt her again. Every reference to his thought process was gone by the time the movie came out. It became a film about a guy who took the law into his own hands, and now he's trying to find a way to get out of it. That's not what I was doing, and it's my only deep regret about the film."

Trees Lounge (1996)

Wendell
MOVIE: 7/10   SLJ FACTOR: 6/10   MINUTES UNTIL HE SHOWS UP: 41
EXPLETIVES NOT DELETED: fucking (x6), shit (x3), bullshit

For reasons both aesthetic and financial, a huge swath of indie movies in the 1990s had a baggy, lived-in quality: the camera followed a main character around while they encountered friends and strangers, sometimes with dramatic payoffs, but often not. *Trees Lounge*, the first film written and directed by prolific character actor Steve Buscemi, is that sort of movie, centered on the Long Island bar of its title. When Samuel L. Jackson wanders into the bar for a beer, nothing particularly eventful

> *"You got yourself a little lawn you can piss on, so what? Wonder Bread town, everybody looks alike, running around like they all happy and shit when they're really fucking miserable."*

happens in his three-minute scene, but we're happy to see him anyway.

Jackson and Larry Gilliard Jr. play two furniture movers in red

T-shirts who have rear-ended the car belonging to Tommy (Buscemi) and cracked his taillight. In the bar, they find their boss Mike (Mark Boone Junior), who is looking unhealthy and unshowered, having basically taken up residency at the Trees Lounge while his marriage falls apart. A friendly Jackson razzes him and reminds him that he and his wife were never going to be happy in the suburbs.

Mike, like Tommy and the other regulars at the Trees Lounge, is drowning in his beer glass. The movie begins when Tommy's life is at a low point (he's been fired from his auto mechanic job for stealing from the till, and his girlfriend of eight years is now married to his former boss, although she may be pregnant with Tommy's baby)—but somehow he keeps making it worse, snorting coke at his uncle's funeral, making out with his ex's seventeen-year-old niece (Chloë Sevigny), and drinking, drinking, always drinking. But although Buscemi has said that the movie is a portrait of how his life might have turned out if his acting career hadn't happened, the movie is more than a cautionary tale about addiction, or a collection of vignettes—it's a classical tragedy. Tommy knows his fate as an alcoholic but hurtles toward it anyway.

The Long Kiss Goodnight (1996)

Mitch Henessey
MOVIE: 7/10   SLJ FACTOR: 10/10   MINUTES UNTIL HE SHOWS UP: 6
EXPLETIVES NOT DELETED: ass-fucked, ass-fuck, ass-fucking, shit (x15), pussy (x2), shithole, motherfucker (x2), fuck (x10), fucking (x3), fucked, fucker, bitch (x2), motherfuckers

The Long Kiss Goodnight had essentially the same premise as *Buffy the Vampire Slayer*: a woman living an ordinary life discovers, to her surprise, that she's actually a killing machine. It's become a cult classic, but it underperformed at the box office when first released. Geena Davis stars as Charly Baltimore, a schoolteacher with a loving husband and a young daughter—and a bad case of amnesia. Trying to figure out her past, she hires a host of private detectives, including the low-budget Mitch Henessey (Samuel L. Jackson). When he stumbles on a suitcase with some of her personal documents, they go on a road trip, where she gradually awakens to her previous identity and skills as an elite CIA

> "I never did one thing right in my life. You know that? Not one. That takes skill."

assassin, and he has to outrun explosions, jump out of windows, and sometimes jump out of windows while outrunning explosions.

Mitch, an ex-convict and an ex-cop, is forthright about his failures in life, and he sings the wrong words to songs on the car radio, but he's loyal and good-humored in insane circumstances and he looks sharp in a yellow turtleneck and a green tam o'shanter. He was so appealing that the movie departed from the script—originally, his character was supposed to die. But at an early screening, test audiences rebelled: Harlin said that one viewer shouted out, "You can't kill Sam Jackson!" They quickly filmed a new ending, where Mitch survives the final action sequence, an attempted bombing at Niagara Falls, and goes on *Larry King Live* to brag about it.

Jackson has consistently cited Mitch as his favorite character in his long film career. "He's another dude that's in a job that he thinks is a con," he said. "I just love the sincerity of that dude, who becomes brave in the face of some shit that he knew he shouldn't even be talking about." A profane loudmouth pretending to be a tough private detective is rich territory that allows an actor to explore the gap between fantasy and reality. As it happens, Jackson spends a lot of his life in that gap: his job as an actor means that he routinely pretends to do more and be more than he's capable of in his personal life. That can be inspiring to other people—and it can be just as inspiring to him.

Hard Eight (1997)

Jimmy
MOVIE: 9/10   **SLJ FACTOR:** 9/10   **MINUTES UNTIL HE SHOWS UP:** 24
EXPLETIVES NOT DELETED: shit (x8), motherfucker, fucking (x4), pussy (x4), fucks, goddamn, fucked-up, fucked, bullshit (x2), asshole, fuck

Paul Thomas Anderson released *Hard Eight*, his first feature film as a director, when he was just twenty-six. It's impossible to watch it now without seeing all the ways in which it establishes his themes and habits: long tracking shots, problematic father figures, symmetrical two-person compositions, whip-pan camera movements, serious dialogue punctuated with flashes of absurdity, good-hearted but dim people who hatch criminal schemes that quickly spiral out of control, even a showcase role for Philip Seymour Hoffman (seen here in a short but

"You think, what, you can just walk through this life without being punished for it?"

memorable scene as an abrasive craps player). But it's more than the overture to a brilliant career—it's a riveting story of love and loyalty in the casino demimonde.

Philip Baker Hall plays an older gambler, Sydney; John C. Reilly is John, a wayward young man who goes to Vegas trying to win $6,000 to pay for his mother's funeral. Gwyneth Paltrow is Clementine, a cocktail waitress who John falls hard for; Samuel L. Jackson is Jimmy, a sleazy buddy of John's working security for a Reno casino. The movie is structured around Sydney's long conversations with the other three main characters: first John, who he treats like a surrogate son; then Clementine, who he also takes a paternal interest in; then Jimmy, who knows the secret of why Sydney has befriended John.

Jimmy is a counterpoint to the well-tailored, dignified Sydney: he's loud, self-important, crude. When he sits in his car, his leather jacket squeaks as it rubs against the vinyl upholstery. He can't be bothered to learn the correct pronunciation of Clementine's name. He knows that Sydney holds him in contempt, and that rankles him. Jackson carefully calibrates his performance of Jimmy: he's canny enough to squeeze $6,000 out of Sydney to keep his secrets (not coincidentally, the same amount that John needed at the beginning of the movie for his mother's funeral). And riding a hot streak, he parlays that cash into more money at the craps table. But he's not smart enough, or lucky enough, to avoid the consequences of that extortion.

Jackson has one particularly great line reading, after Jimmy asks Sydney what happened to a gun that he loaned to John for an ill-fated kidnapping attempt. Sydney informs him that he threw it away. "Oh, *damn*," Jimmy says, with the heartfelt emotion totally absent from his day-to-day operator persona. "I *love* that gun."

One Eight Seven (1997)

Trevor
MOVIE: 4/10   SLJ FACTOR: 6/10   MINUTES UNTIL HE SHOWS UP: 0
EXPLETIVES NOT DELETED: bullshit (x2)

Section 187 is the part of the penal code that refers to murder. Well, in California, anyway—when it first appears in this movie, scrawled threateningly on the pages of a high-school textbook, the action is happening in New York, where section 187 of the penal code addresses residential mortgage fraud.

Fun as it is to imagine Samuel L. Jackson playing a rogue mortgage-fraud investigator, he's actually cast as Trevor Garfield, a high school science teacher who bicycles across the Brooklyn Bridge, holds the attention of an unruly classroom in Bed-Stuy—and gets shanked by the student who defaced the textbook (Method Man), taking revenge for a failing grade.

"Like you, I used to think the world was this great place where everybody lived by the same standard I did. Then some kid with a nail showed me I was living in his world, a world where chaos rules, not order, a world where righteousness is not rewarded."

"A teacher wrote this movie" are the final words on the screen before the credits roll—but *One Eight Seven* (also known as *187*) is not an exposé of the war-zone conditions found in some urban high schools, or the tale of a teacher who inspires disadvantaged students to find a love for learning (although it nods at both of those tropes, and it was marketed as a serious film about educational issues). It's a high-gloss revenge fantasy.

Relocating to Los Angeles, Trevor gets a job as a substitute teacher in another blighted school, but now he deals summarily with the delinquents in his class. He secretly executes a student who's been threatening a fellow teacher (Kelly Rowan); when another one steals his watch and trashes his classroom, he retaliates by covertly shooting him with a hypodermic-tipped arrow, amputating his finger while he's comatose, and then tattooing the finger and delivering it to the hospital in an envelope. This is as lurid and nonsensical as it sounds—and we haven't even mentioned the climactic scene where Trevor plays Russian roulette with a student.

After his near-death experience, Trevor is fearful and jittery at some points, vengeful and sadistic at others. The movie squeezes as much drama as it can from the mystery of whether this upright teacher actually committed these brutal crimes, so Jackson's job is to play a character who could go either way, covering savagery with rectitude and justifying his actions as reasonable rather than gruesome insanity. Jackson mostly pulls it off, by focusing on the reality-based parts of the script.

A few years later, Jackson described Trevor as the most challenging role he had played up to that point. "I went to some inner-city schools and I rode around with a police crash unit. I came to realize that teachers today have the stress level of cops without the weapons," he said. "Here was a guy trying to rediscover himself and get back to doing the thing he loves most, which is teaching. It's the kind of role you internalize but also have to find a way to get it out to an audience so they can experience your anguish."

Eve's Bayou (1997)

Louis Batiste
MOVIE: 9/10   **SLJ FACTOR:** 7/10   **MINUTES UNTIL HE SHOWS UP:** 0 (silent and shadowy), 6 (speaking and dancing)

The opening lines of *Eve's Bayou*: "Memory is a selection of images: some elusive, others printed indelibly on the brain. The summer I killed my father, I was ten years old." Samuel L. Jackson is that father, a doctor with a weakness for extramarital affairs. But this movie belongs to his daughter Eve (a remarkable performance by the young Jurnee Smollett), trying to make sense of the adult world in a small Creole town in a swampy corner of Louisiana.

> "To a certain type of woman, I'm a hero. I need to be a hero sometimes."

The movie's air is thick with memories and prophecies, both of which prove to be unreliable and fraught. In one of the film's most striking sequences, Eve's aunt Mozelle (Debbi Morgan) gazes into a mirror and tells the story of how her lover shot her husband: we see her watching the action in reflection until she steps away from the mirror and enters her own memory, swallowed up by her past.

The film marked the directorial debut of Kasi Lemmons (now best known for the 2019 Harriet Tubman biopic, *Harriet*): set in the early 1960s, it's semi-autobiographical but unsentimental, full of tension and secrets. Jackson is credited as a producer, a title he said was largely nominal—it was a way for him to get paid that didn't bust the budget designated for the actors—but helped Lemmons get the green light for an unusual movie with a Black cast.

"I'm used to testosterone-driven sets," Jackson said. "All of a sudden, I was in an estrogen-fueled situation. There's someone in tears over here. And somebody is stomping around over there. And I had to walk around and be the big-hug man. Go, 'Look, she didn't mean that. Come on, give me a hug.'"

Jackson's philandering physician is full of charm and love for his children; he plays both that genuine warmth and the neediness that drives him to other women. "The movie hinges on Louis Batiste," Lemmons said. "It absolutely wouldn't work if he's not a sympathetic character." A kiss between him and his eldest daughter Cisely (Meagan Good) sends the family spinning off its axis, all its members trying to piece together not what happened, but what it meant. "My intention was, what if you explode the moment?" Lemmons said. "To me, it wasn't controversial: it was the story."

Jackie Brown (1997)

Ordell Robbie
MOVIE: 9/10   SLJ FACTOR: 10/10   MINUTES UNTIL HE SHOWS UP: 4
EXPLETIVES NOT DELETED: shit (x41), motherfucker (x21), fucking (x18), motherfucking (x11), motherfuckers (x4), bitch (x11), fuck (x15), goddamn (x19), every-motherfucking-thing, shitload (x2), dick, bullshit (x3), pussy, fucked, bitches, titty

When Quentin Tarantino was in his late twenties, he adapted a novel, *Rum Punch*, that Elmore Leonard wrote in his early sixties. The film (*Jackie Brown*) starred Pam Grier and Samuel L. Jackson (both in their late forties) and Robert Forster and Robert De Niro (both in their late fifties). It's not the movie you'd expect from a world-conquering young man who recently won his first Oscar: although the plot centers on a complicated heist of $500,000, the movie's really about growing older and realizing that life's opportunities have passed you by.

Tarantino tones down his flashy chronology shifting and ultraviolence in favor of spending time hanging out with his characters: letting them listen to soul music, letting them argue about where they parked the car, letting them think. That gives *Jackie Brown* a leisurely pace, but

"He put himself in a position where he was going to have to do ten years in prison, that's what he did. And if you know Beaumont, you know there ain't no goddamn way he can do ten years. And if you know that, then you know Beaumont's going to do anything Beaumont can to keep from doing them ten years, including telling the federal government any- and every-motherfucking-thing about my black ass. Now that, my friend, is a clearcut case of him or me. And you'd best believe it ain't gonna be me."

Tarantino wanted the movie to be an exemplar of the genre he called "hangout movies": films like *Rio Bravo* and *Dazed and Confused* that you can watch again and again, enjoying the company of the characters more than the plot.

"You don't watch it four times in a row," Tarantino said. "It's just that, for people who like it, I really wanted to give them a gift that they could watch for the rest of their lives. Every two or three years, put in *Jackie Brown* again, and you're drinking white wine with Jackie, and drinking screwdrivers with Ordell, and taking bong hits with Melanie and Louis."

Jackie Brown (Grier) is a flight attendant working for one of North America's worst airlines, with a sideline in smuggling cash out of Mexico for the small-time arms dealer Ordell Robbie (Jackson). It's Jackson's second murderous criminal in a row in a Tarantino film, but the differences between Jules and Ordell go much deeper than the hairstyles. While Jules Winnfield is a charming guy who puts on a fearsome aspect to do his job, Ordell Robbie is a ruthless, desperate operator who can adopt a mask of bonhomie if it helps him get what he needs.

As Jackson parsed the difference, "Jules is a moralistic kind of guy. Ordell Robbie has no morals. He has just one steadfast rule. Nothing and no one is going to get in his way."

The partnership between Tarantino and Jackson is fundamentally verbal: the actor feeds on big mouthfuls of theatrical dialogue, while the writer-director knows he can rely on the actor to unlock the rhythms and inner truths of monologues and one-liners alike. But although Ordell has plenty of memorable lines ("AK-47, the very best there is. When you absolutely, positively got to kill every motherfucker in the room, accept no substitutes"), Jackson's best moments here are the silences: Ordell in sunglasses, seated in the back of a courtroom, watching Jackie's bail hearing. Ordell methodically putting on his gloves before he executes his plan for the employee (Chris Tucker) he's convinced to get in the trunk of his car, letting the smallest of smiles play on his lips.

And, especially, the extraordinary pause when Ordell, knowing that someone's stolen his money, closes his eyes and thinks for over twenty seconds before correctly figuring out that it was Jackie Brown. On the day they filmed that moment, Jackson first played the scene at the pace you would see in most movies, taking a beat before reaching his conclusion. "Take your time," Tarantino told him, and so Jackson did the scene again, counting to five in his head. "No, no, no,"

Tarantino said, telling Jackson to actually go through Ordell's entire chain of deduction, sifting through the confusing mechanics of the double-cross. *"Take as much time as you want."*

"I just think that's amazing," Jackson said. "He trusts the fact that an audience is going to stay with you and start going through the process with you that long. Because a lot of times, people don't want dead air in a film like that, especially a thought process. They want to, you know, feed the audience the idea, feed the audience the answer really quick before they get—you know, before they lose their concentration. But Quentin trusts audiences like I do."

Sphere (1998)

Harry
MOVIE: 4/10   SLJ FACTOR: 4/10   MINUTES UNTIL HE SHOWS UP: 7

In theory, *Sphere* was a classy blockbuster: Barry Levinson directed an adaptation of a hit Michael Crichton novel about a team of experts (Dustin Hoffman, Sharon Stone, Samuel L. Jackson, Liev Schreiber) descending to the bottom of the Pacific Ocean to investigate a mysterious spaceship that crashed three centuries ago. They soon discover that's it's actually an American vessel from the future, propelled back in time by the power of an alien artifact: the enormous, shimmering golden orb that gives the movie its title.

"We're all going to die down here, you know."

The team's underwater base becomes Weird Shit Central: a bloom of giant jellyfish kills Queen Latifah's character, copies of *20,000 Leagues Under the Sea* are blank after page 87, an alien intelligence makes contact but throws a temper tantrum. The movie has some genuinely cool moments before it bogs down in the second half, and the A-list cast heroically sells one talky scene after another. Jackson plays a genius mathematician who doesn't get to do a lot of math. He does have great reaction shots when confronted with idiocy and he manages to make his sleeping face seem both placid and ominous. His best scene, however, is his comedic turn after he returns from visiting the spaceship and surprises everyone with his newfound enthusiasm for breakfast: "This toast? Good. Bacon? Better. But these eggs—these eggs are fantastic."

Science-fiction movies about making first contact with an alien species often have a stately, cerebral pace. Most viewers of *2001: A Space*

Odyssey, Close Encounters of the Third Kind, or *Arrival* are willing to accept a slow, simmering build because there's a mind-bending payoff that reorients everything that came before. In this case, unfortunately, the big twist is that the sphere is taking the unconscious fears and desires of the human beings and making them reality. This "makes sense" but is also deeply unsatisfying: it's the sci-fi version of "and then I woke up and it was all a dream."

Out of Sight (1998)

Hejira Henry (uncredited)
MOVIE: 10/10   **SLJ FACTOR:** 6/10   **MINUTES UNTIL HE SHOWS UP:** 114

Movie romances have bloomed in some unusual locations, maybe none more unlikely than the locked trunk of a Ford Thunderbird. That's where George Clooney, playing a career bank robber, and Jennifer Lopez, playing the federal marshal he takes prisoner, find themselves curled up together during a getaway from a prison break, talking about old movies and against their better professional judgment, falling in love. *Out of Sight* was a career-defining movie for both actors—and for director Steven Soderbergh, who on his seventh feature film figured out how to apply his arthouse aesthetic to movies that could anchor the multiplex. Soderbergh takes an antic Elmore Leonard story, adds French New Wave editing flourishes, and underpins it with old-school Hollywood glamour—and every single scene crackles with intelligence and wit.

"I prefer to think of it as an exodus from an undesirable place."

The insanely high-quality cast includes Don Cheadle, Viola Davis, Ving Rhames, Albert Brooks, Luis Guzmán, Catherine Keener, Steve Zahn, Dennis Farina, and Michael Keaton (reprising his character from *Jackie Brown*). So to play a character who doesn't appear until the final scene of the movie, Soderbergh said, "We all knew that you needed somebody powerful. The guy comes in, implies that he's the preeminent escape artist in the country, it's got to be somebody you believe." That was Samuel L. Jackson, who showed up the day after he wrapped *The Negotiator* and knocked out his two-minute scene in two hours. He plays a convict who's escaped from prison nine times ("ten if you count that prison hospital in Ohio I walked away from") who meets an imprisoned Clooney in the back of a transport van headed to a penitentiary in Florida. Effortlessly matching Clooney's charisma, Jackson knows how to control the scene by leaning back and withdrawing from it. Although Hejira is weary and wary of his fellow passenger, a friendship begins to blossom—one with the potential for freedom.

The Negotiator (1998)

Danny Roman
MOVIE: 6/10 **SLJ FACTOR:** 7/10 **MINUTES UNTIL HE SHOWS UP:** 0 (still photo), 2 (in the flesh)
EXPLETIVES NOT DELETED: fucked, fuck (x7), motherfucker (x2), fucking (x5), shit (x7), goddamn (x2), shitless, bitch (x2), bitches, bullshit, asshole

When the summer-movie spectacle of helicopters and gunfire and shattering glass dies down, you're left with Samuel L. Jackson and Kevin Spacey in a room together. Two master actors playing two master hostage negotiators—which is to say, two professional liars playing two professional liars—jockey for control of a high-stakes situation, while looking for a way to trust each other. Their scenes are so enjoyable, you don't mind the absurd plot machinations required to make them happen.

> *"You don't feel like talking? Well, we're going to stay here until you do. It's your choice. Because I'm not going to jail today."*

By his own account, director F. Gary Gray didn't have much to do with those scenes: "I found myself so intimidated," he said of his stars. "They started to use big words I didn't understand, and I was like, 'Fuck, if I open my mouth, I will make a fool of myself.' I had this vision of what I wanted to do, but I would get into rehearsals and not say anything for fear of looking stupid."

Jackson, in fact, was unimpressed by Gray—but because of a lack of preparation, not a lack of intelligence, he said. "People should come in every day to work, not confused about what they want to do or mistreating the crew by overshooting because they don't know what they want."

Spacey and Jackson essentially cast themselves when they met at an Oscars party, the night before Spacey won the trophy for his work in *The Usual Suspects*. They had gotten to act together in *A Time to Kill*, but only briefly. "We were just getting warmed up by the time *A Time to Kill* was over," Jackson said. "So when I saw him at the party I said, 'So, Kevin, are you reading *The Negotiator*?'" Spacey allowed that he was.

"And I said, '*And?*' And he says, 'I'll do it if you do it.' And I said, 'Well, *I'll* do it if *you* do it!' And that was that."

Jackson plays a Chicago police lieutenant, renowned for his skill with tense hostage negotiations. When he gets arrested for looting a police disability fund—a frame job—he storms into the internal affairs office and takes hostages of his own, looking to find the real culprits. Expert at defusing other people's rage, he gives in to his own. Knowing all the techniques of a hostage standoff, he demands to speak with a negotiator from across town (Spacey), since he can no longer trust anyone in his own precinct. The movie's way too long—it's a full hour before Spacey really joins the action—and yet the screenplay never takes the time to develop its characters, relying on talented actors (Paul Giamatti, David Morse, J. T. Walsh) to make them feel like more than cardboard cutouts. (It was originally developed as a Sylvester Stallone vehicle, which may have something to do with it.)

Jackson does what he can in the movie's margins to give the character the fingerprints of an individual: a man with red hair ("I was feeling Aboriginal," Jackson joked of the dye job) who's a good-natured stiff on the dance floor (we see him line-dancing at a birthday party). But what this movie mostly demands of Jackson is charisma and forward momentum—and he provides plenty of both.

de'Angelo Dia.

ow did **Samuel L. Jackson choose his roles?** Story and character, then look and location.

The story needed to be compelling: Jackson was keenly aware that he was in the entertainment business. If a script couldn't hold his attention, the resulting movie wouldn't hold the audience's attention. ("I just sit there and read it, and hope that I won't figure out what's going to happen thirty pages later," he said.) Then he considered the character he was being asked to play: "whether it lets me explore some aspect of me that I haven't explored." He preferred verbal characters, who expressed themselves through speech: "I look for monologues, big chunks of dialogue." And "if the character doesn't have some kind of edge, I'm really not attracted to him." If Jackson liked a screenplay but not the character he was offered, he would ask if a different role was available. Sometimes he would turn down a leading part, but volunteer for a supporting role—if the producers could keep his shooting schedule under ten days.

Jackson gave bonus points to characters he could outfit with exotic hair or accessories, and to movies that were shooting someplace he had never been before. One thing he didn't care about: balancing the types of movies in his career, whether that meant alternating studio movies with indie productions, dramas with comedies, or leading roles with supporting parts. "The one that's ready is the one that gets done next," he said.

"In a fair world, I'd probably have three or four Oscars," Jackson said. But he emphatically didn't pick roles that were awards bait: he wanted to make the types of movies that he loved when he was a kid. He was enthralled by John Wayne's war movies, so he made *Rules of Engagement*. He had always imagined what it would be like to get eaten by the monster in a horror movie, so he signed up for *Deep Blue Sea*. He had no real interest in making a romantic comedy, but as a Peter Sellers fan, he would have happily appeared in an Inspector Clouseau–style comedy. He dreamed of being in a gorefest like *The Texas Chainsaw Massacre*. The genre Jackson really longed to star in, however, was the western, so he could finally use all the fast-draw techniques he had practiced as a kid: "I want horses," he said. "I want to stand in the middle of the street and see if I'm faster than somebody. I want to pick people off rooftops. Doesn't that sound like a good time?"

Jackson also didn't have a wish list of directors that he hoped to work with, although people assumed he did and often asked him who was on it. The one time he answered that question was on a British talk show: he had heard George Lucas was gearing up to make three more *Star Wars* movies, so he said that he'd love to work with Lucas. (Jackson had seen the original *Star Wars* on opening day in 1977, in a New York City movie theater—he was blown away, and spent half the movie wondering, "Wow, how do you get in a movie like this? How? How? How?")

In the original *Star Wars* (aka *Episode IV—A New Hope*), when the movie cuts between rebel X-wing pilots attacking the Death Star, it's difficult to keep them all straight: it's basically a squadron of interchangeable pale-faced British actors. Lucas gradually increased the diversity of the population living in the galaxy far, far away, but usually by adding more aliens with brightly hued skin.

Somebody told Lucas about Jackson's interview; much to Jackson's surprise, the director then invited the actor to visit Skywalker Ranch, his lavish production facility in Northern California. When they met, Lucas said he admired Jackson's work but wasn't sure he had a part for him in the prequels. Jackson told him, "Look, man, I could be a stormtrooper. You could put me in one of those white suits, I'll run across screen, nobody even needs to know!"

Lucas told him that he would try to find him a better role than a stormtrooper, but warned, "It might just be the captain of the queen's guard who says 'Look out, run.'"

Two months later, Jackson got another call, summoning him to England: Lucas had found something for him to do. Without a script, or a clue about the story or his character, Jackson arrived at Leavesden Film Studios, just northwest of London. He was sent straight to the wardrobe department, where the costumers pulled out some clothes for a fitting: a big brown robe, a tunic, and black boots. "Wait a minute, that's a Jedi costume!" Jackson exclaimed. "Am I going to be a *Jedi*?"

He learned the name of his character when a production assistant handed him a slip of paper with "Mace Windu" written on it—and then he was led downstairs to a man who opened up an aluminum Halliburton briefcase. "Lightsaber handles," he told Jackson. "Pick one."

Amazed at his youthful dreams coming true, Jackson set a goal for himself: "Just don't piss anybody off. Don't get killed. Just stay alive."

Jackson succeeded well enough that his Jedi gig lasted for a long, long time—well, for the entire prequel trilogy, anyway. Lucas appreciated Jackson's talent and his uncomplaining professionalism; Jackson said that Lucas was more open and collaborative than his reputation suggested. Jackson, suddenly famous with a preteen demographic, was memorialized with his own action figure—and he got to keep his lightsaber handle, which the Lucasfilm artisans specially engraved for him with the initials B.M.F. Yes, it's the one that says Bad Mother Fucker.

When Jackson saw *Shaft* in 1971, it was a revelation: a protagonist who "kinda looked like me, sounded like me, dressed like I wanted to dress." As played by Richard Roundtree, he was not only an icon of blaxploitation but a hero for the civil rights era, a streetwise embodiment of the people struggling against authority. Jackson watched the movie over and over, and decades later he was still quoting deep cuts from the dialogue: "They just threw my man Leroy out the goddamn window. That's some cold shit, Shaft." Or he liked to tell a production assistant that he was actually a tool of the Man, and "When the Man say you be there, you be there, waiting."

So in 1999, when his agent sent him the script for an updated version, Jackson was interested, but curious: Who did they want him to play? Roundtree was only twenty-eight when the first *Shaft* movie was released, and Jackson was now over fifty (only five years younger than Roundtree himself). The answer, she said: "Well, maybe Shaft."

Jackson's cool factor outweighed his age, and his star power got him the role over Don Cheadle: he accepted the part for his biggest payday yet (reportedly $10 million). It was touted as his first solo starring role in a movie (meaning one where he was above the title and not in partnership with a white actor), which was true if you scrunched up your face and forgot about *One Eight Seven*.

The shoot was contentious; as Jackson told the story, it was because he, director John Singleton, producer Scott Rudin, and screenwriter Richard Price all had different visions of the iconic character. Shaft as Jackson saw him: "Handsome, very good street smarts, was very cool, had some mack ability with the ladies." An icon on a human scale, not a Black Superman, as apparently Singleton wanted him to be. Jackson thought the differing perspectives were a reflection of their ages: Singleton was three years old when he first saw the movie (on a double bill with Bruce Lee's *The Chinese Connection*), an age where it seemed like the hero could do anything. Jackson, however, saw it when he was twenty-two, an age where he felt like he could be Shaft himself, given the right wardrobe.

Jackson wanted to stay true to the core of the character, as summarized by Isaac Hayes in the theme song, the funkiest elevator pitch ever: "a black private dick who's a sex machine to all the chicks." So he objected to the movie basically making Shaft celibate: "I get to kiss a girl once and the rest of the time I just physically abuse people." Jackson lost the sex-machine battle, but he refused to play Shaft as a police officer. That was both because it betrayed the core of the character—Shaft should outwit the Man, not be the Man himself—and because, given how many acts of violence Shaft was committing in this movie, Jackson didn't want to look like he was endorsing police brutality. The plot was reworked: Shaft begins the movie as an NYPD detective, but quits the department in frustration.

Earlier in his career, Jackson probably would have gone along with what the producers wanted, partially because he worried that he might get fired. But after making more than sixty movies, he had not only discovered how much clout he had, he had noticed a surprising dynamic: on most movie sets, the person who has worked on the fewest movies is the director. "I know better than they do what works for Sam Jackson," he declared. "It wasn't about power with me—it was about common sense."

According to Jackson, his beef wasn't primarily with Singleton, but with Rudin, who had commissioned Price to rewrite the script Singleton authored with Shane Salerno—and then constantly leaned on the director to make sure that he didn't deviate from Price's rewrite. "I'd do it my way and then poor John would have Scott Rudin breathing in his ear demanding that he make me say the lines they'd paid so much money for." Finally, Jackson told Rudin "that I refused to say that white man's lines."

Jackson said he changed the dialogue so it would sound like a Black man, and that when Price objected that he had written the lines, he told him, "Yes, and you got paid for them. Now let me make you sound brilliant."

The racial dimensions of the conflict were obvious: while Rudin and Price were white, Jackson and Singleton were Black, and they were making sure that a Black icon didn't end up bleached of his personality. After so many years of spotting juicy characters conceived as white, reimagining them as Black, and making a space for himself in other people's movies, Jackson had to contend with the inverted cultural dynamic: white people with strong opinions about Black culture. After the conflict became public, Jackson did what he could to walk the racial aspects back: "There are untrue rumors flying around about issues of race, and how we didn't like Scott Rudin and Richard Price because they are white and we were doing a Black movie. It had nothing to do with race; it had to do with the artistic process."

Shaft was a solid hit, which benefited everyone who worked on the movie, although there wouldn't be another entry in the series for nineteen years (after Singleton had died from a stroke, only fifty-one). Jackson was right: he wouldn't get fired from a movie for flexing his muscles as the star, although it behooved him to do so discreetly. Another belief confirmed: despite starting his career late, he knew the mores of movie sets better than most of his directors.

"If a director doesn't hire me, I feel sorry for him," Jackson said. They often did hire him, of course: Jackson had worked with dozens of directors, enough to develop a personal taxonomy of the men behind the camera (and they were almost all men—the notable exception being Kasi Lemmons). He divided them into three different genera: technicians, writer-directors, and guys who were lucky to be there. Jackson loved the technicians, whom he also called the shooters: film school graduates much more concerned with the composition of their shots than the methods of their actors. They had hired him because they trusted him, and they generally left him alone to do his job. Writer-directors ran the gamut: some were brilliant, others less so—and some of them were persnickety about actors changing dialogue, even if the script needed improving. (A common problem: white writers not as fluent in Black vernacular as they thought they were. A related problem: Black characters whose speech patterns didn't match their level of education.) The guys who were lucky to be there? They were problematic, but they could work out: generally they were surrounded by professionals, and if they were smart enough to let the people on their team do their jobs, everyone could survive the movie without too much trauma.

It was rarely obvious at the table read that a shoot was going to be problematic. "It usually takes about a week," Jackson said. That was around when the realization sank in for him: "This dude talked a good game, but he's not very good, he's not prepared. This is not gonna be fun."

On location, he found that directors' egos could expand quickly: "I remember starting a film one time and I had talked to this director for a few weeks before we started. He had visited a few sets I was on, watched me work, so I figured he knew what the deal was. So I get to work, and the first thing that happens is that night, before we roll one inch of film, he comes to my trailer and says, 'Okay, when you're on set, you have to show me respect, you can't call me "motherfucker" or any of that shit.' I stopped and went like, 'What? How many films have you done?' And I counted in my head: 'Okay, you've done two movies, so I have to show you respect?' No, what you need to do is get out there and show *me* why I need to respect you."

Respect could come from unexpected quarters. On September 7, 2001, Jackson was in New York City, for a concert celebrating Michael Jackson's thirtieth anniversary as a solo performer (featuring stars such as Destiny's Child, Liza Minnelli, and the gloved one). Backstage at Madison Square Garden, Jackson was waiting to kick off the show by introducing the first performers—Usher, Mya, and Whitney Houston, covering "Wanna Be Startin' Somethin'"—uncertain of how he had ended up with this particular gig. Then he heard somebody behind him, reciting dialogue from *Jackie Brown*.

Jackson turned around. He was used to hearing quotes of his famous lines from overzealous fans—but not from one of the greatest actors of the twentieth century. Standing behind him, however, was Marlon Brando in a suit and tie. (Michael Jackson allegedly paid Brando a million dollars to appear onstage at the tribute: for his money, he got a rambling seven-minute monologue about the singer's humanitarian efforts that included the declaration "In the last minute, 100,000 children have been hacked to death with a machete." Things somehow got even weirder: according to some sources, after the 9/11 attacks a few days later, Michael Jackson fled New York City with Brando and Elizabeth Taylor, driving themselves west and making frequent stops for KFC and Burger King.)

While Brando and Samuel Jackson waited for the show to start, they discussed acting—a conversation that went well enough that Brando gave him a phone number and said, "Call me; we need to talk."

When Jackson got back home, he called that number—and reached a Chinese restaurant. Nonplussed, Jackson asked, "Is Marlon Brando there?"

"Hold on, hold on." Soon, Brando came to the phone; the two actors spent an hour talking.

The next time Jackson called, the person answering the phone said that he had called a Chinese laundry. Jackson, realizing that this was Brando's method of screening his calls, just said, "Is Mr. Brando there?"—and they were soon deep in conversation again.

Jackson didn't need such elaborate subterfuges. He had achieved what he considered the perfect level of fame: he enjoyed the ego boost of being recognized in public, but he still was able to walk around without an entourage, leading an ordinary life, riding the subway in New York City, driving his own car and pumping his own gas in Los Angeles. "Folks are always shocked when they see me in the grocery store," he said. When they asked "What are you doing in the store?" he would tell them the truth, obvious but still too strange for them to absorb: "Shopping!"

Keith Knight.

Star Wars: Episode I—The Phantom Menace (1999)

Mace Windu
MOVIE: 5/10   SLJ FACTOR: 4/10   MINUTES UNTIL HE SHOWS UP: 84

Some things were good about *The Phantom Menace*: the epic spectacle, from droid armies to Queen Amidala's costumes; the amazing three-way lightsaber battle between Darth Maul (Ray Park), Qui-Gon Jinn (Liam Neeson), and Obi-Wan Kenobi (Ewan McGregor); the joke where Qui-Gon's Jedi mind tricks fizzle.

> *"This is the clue we need to unravel the mystery of the Sith."*

Some things were bad: the joy-sucking premise of the central conflict being built around a trade dispute; the way setting so much of the movie on Tatooine made the *Star Wars* universe feel smaller; the racial stereotypes thinly disguised in extraterrestrial drag, most notably Jar Jar Binks as a floppy-eared version of Stepin Fetchit.

Some things were just weird: taking Darth Vader, one of the most formidable movie villains ever, and rendering him as a towheaded nine-year-old boy who likes to say "Yippee!"; revealing that he was conceived spontaneously without a father; discovering his affinity for the Force through a blood test for midi-chlorians, turning the mystical into the mundane.

It was a mixed bag of a movie, but many fans treated it like a personal betrayal—apparently, waiting sixteen years between *Star Wars* films made people a little nuts. Writer-director George Lucas said that many people working at Lucasfilm had tried to dissuade him from centering the movie on a prepubescent Anakin Skywalker: "Everybody said, 'That's insane, you're going to destroy the whole franchise.'" Lucas was rich and successful enough that he didn't care, saying that he didn't have the energy to make a hit movie just for the sake of making a hit movie. "I said, that's the story, that's what I wrote. And if I'm going to do it, I'm going to do it and not change it." He got his way, but explained, "That's one of the reasons why there was so much hype on the first film, because everybody was terrified."

Lucas's dialogue remained as wooden as the forest moon of Endor; some actors were defeated by it while others made it sing, and he didn't seem to care very much either way. Standout performers here included Neeson, and in small roles, Terence Stamp and Samuel L. Jackson. As a Jedi sitting on the Jedi Council, Jackson delivered exposition, didn't have much of a character beyond being bald, and played all his scenes alongside a puppet (Frank Oz as Yoda)—but he got to say "May the Force be with you" and he made being a mystical warrior bureaucrat seem like an intense calling.

The Red Violin (1999)

Charles Morritz
MOVIE: 6/10   SLJ FACTOR: 9/10   MINUTES UNTIL HE SHOWS UP: 3

Forty seconds. For forty long seconds, the camera gazes on a silent Samuel L. Jackson while he listens to somebody else play an antique violin. On his face, we can see a complex play of emotions: covetous desire for the instrument, fear that its value will be recognized and his scheme to filch it will be revealed, wet-eyed awe at the beauty of its sound. It would be an eternity with a less gifted or less intelligent performer, but Jackson—unblinking, barely moving—makes it a tour de force.

> "I guess I never thought I'd find it. The ultimate thing, as I see it. The perfect marriage of science and beauty. Impossible thing. Now what?"

"One of the most cerebral characters that I've played," Jackson said. His character, Charles Morritz, is an expert on antique musical instruments. Working for a Montreal auction house to appraise the contents of an upcoming auction, he becomes obsessed with the mysterious red violin. Morritz is rude, especially to hotel staff, and unethical, but he ultimately values the violin because of its beauty, not because of its financial worth.

The movie tracks the history of the violin in five vignettes, ranging from a seventeenth-century Italian workshop to the Cultural Revolution in China. Following an object through an anthology film, a narrative trick also employed in movies such as *Tales of Manhattan* (1942, a tailcoat), *The Yellow Rolls-Royce* (1965, a car), and *Twenty Bucks* (1993, a $20 bill), is a reliably entertaining gimmick. Unfortunately, while *The Red Violin* always looks sumptuous, long stretches of it are shallow and sometimes silly. Particularly risible: the sequence where the nineteenth-century British violinist Lord Frederick Pope (Jason Flemyng), a dissolute nobleman in the Byronic mode, achieves new heights of inspiration by playing the red violin while his naked lover (Greta Scacchi) slithers up and down his body.

The final chapter, set in the modern day and anchored by Jackson, is the movie's strongest: the various storylines weave together at the auction of the titular instrument. Jackson plays his pivotal role subtly enough that viewers can parse the difference between stealing the instrument and liberating it, and might even be moved to consider the meaning of beauty in human lives. Director François Girard said, "I was very impressed with Sam's skills, building this continuity and keeping track of the evolution. It's a hard character to play because it's a mental journey that he's going through and most of it's alone."

Jackson prepared for the role by immersing himself in the world of violin manufacturers. On the set, when screenwriter (and supporting actor) Don McKellar offered a few pointers from his own research into violin making, Jackson made it clear he had already done his homework, politely but firmly telling McKellar, "I know that."

Deep Blue Sea (1999)

Russell Franklin
MOVIE: 5/10   SLJ FACTOR: 8/10   MINUTES UNTIL HE SHOWS UP: 4
EXPLETIVES NOT DELETED: shit, goddamn, asshole

Jaws with more teeth but less bite: *Deep Blue Sea* is the story of genetically engineered sharks busting out of a high-tech aquatic research facility and attacking a cast that looks like it was randomly captured with a net on the red carpet of the People's Choice Awards (Saffron Burrows, Michael Rapaport, Aida Turturro, LL Cool J). This would be a classic B-movie setup, except that it almost completely lacks a sense of humor—director Renny Harlin thought he was making a nail-biting horror classic and didn't want to break the serious mood.

"When the avalanche came, it took us a week to climb out. And somewhere, we lost hope. Now I don't know exactly when we turned on each other. I just know that seven of us survived the slide and only five made it out."

The only *Deep Blue Sea* scene that anyone remembers is Samuel L. Jackson's final monologue—with good reason. He plays the president of the board of Chimera Pharmaceuticals, which has sunk $200 million into shark research (Alzheimer's breakthrough, yadda yadda), and he's come to check on his investment before he shuts the Aquatica facility down. He shows up in rich-guy casual clothes and is unfazed by the antipathy of the staff: when the cook (LL Cool J) serves him some product-placement vodka, it comes with an extra twist of class resentment. He even takes it in stride when Aquatica is flooding and the sharks start eating people.

When it's time for Jackson's big speech, he lays out the backstory that explains why: he's the survivor of an avalanche in the Alps. He delivers a stem-winder (a variation on Robert Shaw's monologue about the USS *Indianapolis* in *Jaws*) that stops the squabbling and inspires the survivors to pull together, telling them in high Jackson dudgeon, "Nature can be lethal, but it doesn't hold a candle to man." And then, just as he's getting ready to lead them to safety, a shark jumps out of the water and eats him like a handful of gummy worms.

According to Jeff Okun, the visual effects supervisor on the movie, Jackson's speech was originally supposed to be much longer: "seven pages of the worst dialogue you've ever heard in your life."

Harlin defended it: "I knew the audience would be groaning and saying, 'Oh come on, this is pompous,' but it *had* to be pompous for the surprise to work. It had to take you to a place where you get a little uncomfortable and start squirming in your seat."

On the set, Jackson and Okun and Harlin debated the pace of the scene; Jackson wanted to move into shark-bait position as quickly as possible. "Renny, have you read this dialogue?" he asked the director. "I don't want to say it."

Jackson's bottom line: "The sooner you kill me, the happier I'll be."

Nevertheless, Harlin's original cut kept most of the monologue—and bombed with audiences. ("Renny Harlin, you suck!" said one irate audience member at a test screening.) When the movie got recut with a lighter touch, the editor cut Jackson's monologue short, the way he had wanted—with a great white attack that sucker-punched audiences.

Okun said that after seeing the new version, Jackson called him up, delighted. "It is my favorite death," the actor said. "Best. Death. Ever."

Rules of Engagement (2000)

Childers

MOVIE: 4/10   **SLJ FACTOR:** 5/10   **MINUTES UNTIL HE SHOWS UP:** 1

EXPLETIVES NOT DELETED: motherfucker (x2), motherfuckers (x4), goddammit (x3), bitch, bullshitting, shit (x3), fuck (x2), bullshit, fucking, goddamn

Some of the problems with *Rules of Engagement,* an overwrought military courtroom drama: The long prologue in 1968 Vietnam, a sequence that forces the fiftysomething stars Tommy Lee Jones and Samuel L. Jackson to play twentysomething lieutenants, and lingers pornographically on the bloody massacre of a platoon of soldiers. The way the movie consistently treats Arabs as a violent mob and thereby justifies the pivotal plot point where Colonel Terry Childers (Jackson) orders his Marines to shoot into a crowd of them outside the American embassy in Yemen, slaughter-

> *"You think there's a script for fighting a war without pissing somebody off? Follow the rules and nobody gets hurt? Yes, innocent people probably died. Innocent people always die. But I did not exceed my orders!"*

ing eighty-three. The crucial plot threads that get resolved in a few lines of text, just before the credits roll. Guy Pearce's accent, which sounds like Taika Waititi with his jaw wired shut.

The reason it's watchable at all is that two great actors anchor it: Jackson as the Marine colonel undergoing a court-martial and Jones as his old buddy defending him. They don't have a lot of personal chemistry—you never feel like their characters have actually been pals for three decades—but you can tell the actors are old pros who respect each other. Jones said of Jackson, "His preparation enables him to create the illusion of absolute spontaneity." Jones, playing a mediocre military lawyer with a drinking problem, is more fun to watch. While Jackson spends most of the movie playing a paragon of military rectitude, he gets one great scene: when he's testifying at his own court martial, he shouts down the prosecutor (Pearce) goading him.

Apparently the movie's creation was defined by battles between director William Friedkin, producer Scott Rudin, screenwriter Stephen Gaghan, and writer James Webb (formerly secretary of the navy under Reagan, later a U.S. senator [D] from Virginia). Friedkin later said of Webb, "At times he can be argumentative and mean-spirited, but in fairness, he describes *me* as the only man in the country with a temper worse than his." Creative conflict can benefit a film production—but here, everyone was so busy staking out turf, they forgot to make a good movie.

Shaft (2000)

John Shaft
MOVIE: 6/10   SLJ FACTOR: 8/10   MINUTES UNTIL HE SHOWS UP: 0
EXPLETIVES NOT DELETED: motherfucker (x9), fucking (x4), goddammit (x2), fuck (x9), assholes, shit (x3), shitload, motherfucking (x4), dickhead, goddamn, asshole (x2)

Just talking 'bout *Shaft*: while this remake is a generic NYC crime drama, the movie constantly feels like it's wrestling with the legacy of the original and how much of it to include beyond a cameo for Richard Roundtree. Perhaps the biggest change is that Jackson's Shaft (identified as the nephew to Roundtree's character) is now more of an action hero and a brutal street enforcer, capable of dropping a dozen bodies in a firefight, happy to run in bad guys on trumped-up charges just to mess with them.

A bald Jackson glides through the movie, playing the role like he's been preparing for it since 1971. He's suave in a long leather jacket and cool enough to sell ludicrous dialogue such as "It's my duty to please that booty." He's surrounded by an excellent cast: Dan Hedaya, Vanessa Williams, Busta Rhymes, and especially an intense Jeffrey Wright (as a Latino drug lord) and a fleshy Christian Bale (as a wealthy killer).

> *"I remember when I took that job thinking I could fight the good fight from the inside, and you telling me about all the problems, that color thing—too black for the uniform, too blue for the brothers—about how justice gets tangled up in red tape or just bought off by the green. You were right. Fuck that job. Fuck the badge. I'll get that silver-spoon motherfucker and I'm going to get him my own way."*

Bale plays the son of a powerful NYC real estate developer who flaunts his money and privilege, resents his father's new wife, and resents being called out for his blatant racism: a character named Walter Wade Jr., but recognizable to anyone watching the movie today as a stand-in for Eric Trump. Bale does a great job of making his character more than a stereotypical villain while remaining completely unsympathetic—so much so that the most satisfying moment in this movie is John Shaft punching Eric Trump in the nose.

Unbreakable (2000)

Elijah Price

MOVIE: 7/10   SLJ FACTOR: 10/10   MINUTES UNTIL HE SHOWS UP: 25

Samuel L. Jackson signed up for *Unbreakable* in an unlikely way: he ran into Bruce Willis in a casino in Marrakech. The two actors knew each other well from *Pulp Fiction* and *Die Hard with a Vengeance*, but neither expected to see in the other in Morocco. Jackson wasn't even sure it was Willis at first—he had never seen him totally bald before—while Willis said, "Somebody over there is trying to impersonate Sam Jackson."

Once the confusion was resolved and the reunion was achieved, Willis told Jackson, "Sam, there's this guy who's writing a script for us." That was M. Night Shyamalan: Willis had just starred in the director's debut film, *The Sixth Sense*. So Willis called up Shyamalan in the United States and put him on the phone with Jackson. "This is amazing. I'm writing one of your scenes right now," Shyamalan told him.

"It was some crazy coincidence," Shyamalan remembered. "And you know me, as with everything: 'Oh, must be a sign!' I asked Sam if he liked the subject of comic books."

> *"Do you see any Teletubbies in here? Do you see a slender plastic tag clipped to my shirt with my name printed on it? Did you see a little Asian child with a blank expression sitting outside on a mechanical helicopter that shakes when you put quarters in it? No? Well, that's what you see at a toy store. And you must think you're in a toy store, because you're here shopping for an infant named Jeb. One of us has made a gross error and wasted the other person's valuable time. This is an art gallery, my friend, and this is a piece of art."*

Jackson was an avid comics fan and frequent shopper at the Los Angeles comic-book store Golden Apple. "So my answer was 'Yes' and 'I'll do it.'"

Shyamalan's reinvention of a comic-book origin story plays very differently two decades later, now that Hollywood has achieved Peak Superhero. At the time, making a movie about a superpowered do-gooder felt eccentric: in an effort to seem less marginal, Shyamalan even began the movie with a block of text about the importance of comic books.

Unbreakable is moody and built around long takes, often interrupted only by a scene fading to blackout. While its stately rhythms can drag, they suit a movie about the slow awakening of Bruce Willis's character David Dunn, working as a security guard, to the realization that he has unusual powers. Dunn is subdued and confused—a former football star now underemployed as a security guard, on the verge of separating from his wife (Robin Wright Penn)—and he is filmed with a drab color palette.

In this somber, overcast world, Elijah Price arrives like a rocket from another planet: he owns a gallery specializing in comic-book art, he often leans on a crystal cane because he has a rare genetic condition that makes his bones extremely fragile, he has a striking asymmetrical haircut, he dresses in purple and orange, he has soliloquies in which he explains his grand theory that superhero comic books are reflections of extraordinary individuals in the real world. It's a riveting performance by Jackson, capturing both Elijah's vulnerability and his arrogance and showing how his genius gradually curdles into monstrosity. By the end, Elijah has embraced the name Mr. Glass and his status as an archenemy, and we realize that we've been watching one of the best renderings of a supervillain ever in movies.

A pair of clever, subtle choices by Shyamalan: he often films Dunn through an aperture (a doorway, the space between two train seats), a visual reminder that he is in a box, unaware of his full abilities or how he might make an impression on the larger world. When he films Elijah Price, however, he frequently does it in reflections: the character is looking for a superhero, somebody he can befriend and be the mirror image of.

Jackson's best scene comes when Elijah declines to leave a comic-book store after it closes, and the clerk starts wheeling him out. Elijah remains silent—but deliberately, repeatedly swerves his wheelchair into the shelves, knocking over displays and scattering comic books everywhere. The ostensible stakes behind this act of defiance, not wanting to leave a comic-book store, are incredibly low, but what makes the scene riveting is the expression on Elijah's face, a rictus of attitude as fierce as a drag queen posturing on the runway. The scene feels like a metaphor for issues of gender, and disability, and race—any way in which the world judges people based on their biology. Elijah, who has been betrayed by the body and bones he was born with, is trying to create a different world, one full of exceptional people, through force of will. You can tell he'll do it, just by looking at Jackson's intense, unwavering stare.

The Caveman's Valentine (2001)

Romulus
MOVIE: 4/10   **SLJ FACTOR:** 8/10   **MINUTES UNTIL HE SHOWS UP:** 1
EXPLETIVES NOT DELETED: fuck, fucking (x2), bitch

Romulus Ledbetter: a brilliant Juilliard-trained pianist with schizophrenia, living in a cave in Central Park. Exterior view: Samuel L. Jackson with a billowing beard and dreadlocks halfway down his back. Interior view: "Inside his skull was dark and gloomy, the feeling of a ruined basilica," said director Kasi Lemmons.

> *"Don't you watch me! You think you're going to crawl into my brain and see a show?"*

The Caveman's Valentine reunited Jackson and Lemmons, collaborators four years earlier on *Eve's Bayou*, and the indelible portrait of Romulus they create together is built on mutual belief in each other's talents. Lemmons said of her star, "You can trust him and roll the camera."

As Romulus, Jackson has an unsteady but quick gait, looking as if he's always about to slip on the ice, and he gives his speech similar cadences, as lucid conversation skitters off into delusions about the green Z-rays being projected by his nemesis Stuyvesant from the top of the Chrysler Building. (He's so committed to this belief system that early in the movie, one wonders if this will be a science-fiction movie in which the character's delusions prove to be all too real.) In the hands of many actors, a role like Romulus would be offensive or just overwrought Oscar bait, but Jackson plays him with intensity and nuance. Lemmons buttresses his superb performance with visual evocations of his world, giving him triumphant fantasias at the piano and surrounding him with flying moth seraphs. The movie provides Romulus with a strong foil: his daughter (Aunjanue Ellis), a New York City police officer who loves him and is embarrassed by him.

Unfortunately, the movie also gives him a murder to solve. One winter morning, Romulus discovers a frozen corpse in a tree outside his cave, which leads him to shave and shower, track down a suspect, and bluff his way into a fancy art-world party upstate thrown by a world-famous photographer (Colm Feore). The mechanics of the mystery are dull and arbitrary—and Romulus as a private detective isn't as charming a conceit as the filmmakers seem to believe. What works about that plotline are his scenes with the glitterati, where his blunt opinions are treated as authentic and his core decency gets him seduced by the photographer's sister (Ann Magnuson). It was Jackson's first real on-camera love scene, but it's punctuated by his character's delusions. Afterward, he sees a hallucination of his ex-wife, who scoffs, "Some white girls'll fuck any kind of Black man."

"For a lot of reasons, this was a lot of fun for me to put onscreen," Lemmons said. The black-and-white sequence is sensual and shows Jackson at his most vulnerable. "Love scenes are always awkward for the actors and very voyeuristic for the director," Lemmons added. "It always seemed unbelievable to me that Samuel Jackson, a big, handsome movie star, had never done a love scene. I couldn't understand it, so I was delighted to give him his first love scene."

XXII

THE RED VIOLIN

Malachi Lily.

When **Samuel L. Jackson and LaTanya Richardson** first arrived in Los Angeles, they assumed that their stay would be temporary: they were a family of New Yorkers who just happened to be three time zones away from home for a while. "Then *Pulp Fiction* happened," she remembered. "Sam's agent said, 'Oh no, darling, you don't live in New York anymore.'"

Nevertheless, the family flew east soon after that—and discovered that there is nothing like a full-blast New York City winter to teach you how acclimated you've become to California weather. A dismayed Jackson discovered that he would need to chop away the ice on the front steps of their Harlem brownstone. Although they still loved New York, the family bought a house in L.A., staying in unfashionable Encino.

Richardson stopped in the middle of the street when she spotted her dream home: a 4,500-square-foot Tudor house with sharply raked gables and leaded windows. Jackson was skeptical, because the walls were covered in white paint. He had spent too many hours refinishing and repainting their brownstone to do it again, he told Richardson: "I'm not stripping another thing."

"No no no, you don't have to do that now," she assured him. "You can pay somebody."

After they bought the house for $1.1 million in the summer of 1995, they also paid craftsmen to install more leaded glass and work crews to knock down walls—and hired Wesley Snipes's interior designer to adjust their décor. They also bought the property next door and turned a small ranch house into a guest cottage. Jackson had recently started playing golf; a backyard swimming pool got converted into a putting green.

"We wanted our daughter to live in a homey environment," Jackson said. "My wife and I are essentially just very southern people raised in middle-class households." They could now, however, afford to fill their home with African American and African art, including the onyx statues of Italian Moors that he had bought in Paris.

The house had no fewer than seven TV sets—including a small black-and-white set in the kitchen that reminded Jackson of his childhood at 310½ Lookout Street. Jackson liked to watch the *Today* show,

Chicago Hope, and *ER*—and lots of sports, especially golf and basketball. The biggest screen, however, could be found in his greatest indulgence: his personal screening room, located in the guest house. The screening room had green velvet walls, a humidor, an old-style popcorn machine, and rows of leather rocking chairs. "This is Sam's room," Richardson said. "I don't care what he does in here. He earned it. He and his boys can come over and smoke cigars and watch whatever they want."

Jackson owned over six thousand movies on laser disc; what he favored was old *Twilight Zone* episodes, Hollywood classics from the 1940s and 1950s, and especially Asian movies. He had become obsessed with Hong Kong action movies (his four recommendations for newcomers: *Hard Boiled*, *Drunken Master*, *My Father Is a Hero*, and *The Bride with White Hair*), and then discovered that he actually preferred Hong Kong crime movies. ("I can't do any of that kicking stuff—I'm too old," he joked.) He gradually branched out even further, becoming an aficionado of Korean and Thai cinema.

On location, Jackson was accustomed to predawn call times that got him into the makeup trailer before most people even hit the snooze button. When he was home and not shooting a movie, he liked to keep the same schedule, waking up early and hitting the golf course at 6:30 a.m. He'd be home by 10:30 a.m., and could happily spend the rest of the day around the house, reading scripts, watching movies, or puttering around.

He did household chores and drove Zoe's car pool, picking up his daughter and her friends from school. He opined, "Being an actor is like everybody else who has a job, and it's a lot less important job than being a teacher or a sanitation worker. You go to work, you come home, and somebody's gotta cook. It's more normal than people would like to believe."

Richardson booked occasional acting jobs, including episodes of *Party of Five*, *NYPD Blue*, and *Ally McBeal*, and she started a production company with her friend Pauletta Washington (Denzel Washington's wife). But it was obvious that her professional star had been eclipsed by her husband's. "Sometimes it gets really sickening, the way it's *him him him* all the time," she complained. "But it's not Sam who's changed; it's just the way Hollywood is."

Jackson, at least publicly, shrugged off that imbalance. "For a long time she was a lot more successful than I was, and I dealt with that," he said. "So it's OK."

Staying clean and sober was relatively straightforward for Jackson: he knew how troubled his life had been when he was using drugs and how much success he had achieved after getting clean. But when he slept at night, he still sometimes had drug dreams, where he would be holding a lump of cocaine the size of a softball and getting high with all his friends. "You wake up the next day feeling horrible even though you only dreamed you were sneaking around," he said. He took the dreams as flashing red warning lights: he had to stay diligent if he didn't want to relapse.

Asked how his marriage had stayed together while he was using, Jackson honestly said that he had no idea. "It wasn't something I was doing to make it stay together."

Jackson was no longer a destructive presence in his family's life, but Richardson sometimes felt alone in the marriage. Jackson had learned to get in touch with his inner self onscreen, and acted with both precision and passion. But at home he was, she said, "emotionally disconnected," and she felt abandoned during his long absences—he could be on location more than half the year. If she called him while he was away and told him that she missed him, his answer would be something like "Oh, okay." (Their phone conversations didn't last very long.)

"That's not good enough?" he asked when challenged. "I don't think you should say things expecting a response."

When Richardson was asked for the secret to their marriage staying together, she replied, "Amnesia."

Jackson, maybe surprisingly, agreed: "You need to forget some of the shit you do to each other. If you've been together as long as we've been together...we know how to hurt each other like nobody else can hurt us."

Zoe mostly grew up away from the public eye, cosseted in the privileged environment of Los Angeles private schools. When she got her own phone line, Jackson wasn't sure if that was excessive: when he was growing up in Chattanooga, there was only one phone line in his entire neighborhood. "There's very little that she's denied if she achieves in school," Jackson said. When Zoe turned sixteen, she expected that she was going to get a car—but to get a flashy car, she had to earn good grades. When Jackson bought himself a Porsche convertible, he made sure to get it with stick shift, so that she wouldn't be able to borrow it. Similarly, Jackson zealously guarded his stash of berry Popsicles in the family's freezer, like a hapless sitcom dad. "I like Popsicles," he said, "and I think people should buy their own. I count them when I come home to be sure they're all there. It's not a very good night when the Popsicles are gone."

Father and daughter had family rituals—they watched *Buffy the Vampire Slayer* together when he was home—but Jackson conceded that Zoe, like her mother, might feel somewhat disconnected from him. "I'm sure that there have been many instances where Zoe has felt neglected by me," he admitted. "Occasionally we have to fish around for ways to have a conversation about certain things." She liked rap music, so her father started listening to hip-hop, just to keep track of what she was thinking about.

When Zoe was seventeen, she visited her father on a movie set. One of his costars, the rapper Busta Rhymes, leered at her and said, "Your daughter's looking real fine."

Jackson stared him down and instructed him, "You better stay as far away from her as possible."

Zoe went east for college, attending Vassar. Soon after she left the house, Richardson took a job as a regular cast member on a TV series, a time-consuming gig that she had steered clear of since *Frannie's Turn*. On the A&E legal drama *100 Centre Street*, produced by Sidney Lumet, she played a conservative lesbian judge who had an unlikely friendship with a liberal judge played by Alan Arkin.

Although Jackson knew he was not a perfect human being, he also cherished his daily existence as a husband and father. He bristled when people said that he wasn't a good role model because he often played foul-mouthed murderers in movies: as he saw it, that was just him doing his job (and doing it well). If people wanted to judge him as a role model, he pointed to what happened after the director said "cut": the quotidian details of his life, how he carried himself with dignity, and how he supported his family. That had less impact on the culture at large, but it had the advantage of not being make-believe.

"I help her with her homework," he said of Zoe. "I make up beds. I take out the garbage. I graduated from college. I can read and write. I can speak correctly. I treat everyone with respect. I pay my taxes. I've never been to jail. I think that's the stuff of a role model."

In the 1990s, Bill Cosby was still considered an exemplary role model. Jackson ran into his former employer when he attended a Sixers game in Philadelphia, "maybe five years or so after I got famous." Although they had never spoken on the set of *The Cosby Show*, beyond exchanging pleasantries, when Cosby saw Jackson at the game, he recognized him immediately: "Sam! Hey! You working? I need a stand-in!"

.

.

THE INCREDIBLES

R. Sikoryak.

Changing Lanes (2002)

Doyle Gipson
MOVIE: 7/10   **SLJ FACTOR: 9/10**   **MINUTES UNTIL HE SHOWS UP: 1**

"Sam normally plays the King of Cool roles. And he is supremely cool both on and off the screen," director Roger Michell said. "But in *Changing Lanes*, we were asking him to play somebody very different: an anonymous guy, a clumsy, awkward, baffled, ordinary Joe whose world is being ripped up in front of his eyes. Sam jumped on the material. We did a costume fitting before rehearsals and he found a scruffy old hat in a cardboard box in the back of the fitting room. That and a shabby old raincoat and pair of totally ungroovy black-rimmed specs, and the character was just suddenly there, staring back at him in the mirror."

> *"You think I want money? What I want is my morning back. I need you to give my time back to me. Can you give me back my time? Can you give my time back to me? Huh? Can you?"*

That character is Doyle Gipson, a middle-class insurance salesman on his way to a custody hearing when he gets in a fender bender with Gavin Banek, a hotshot corporate attorney played by Ben Affleck with healthy dollops of hair gel and self-regard. Gavin rushes off to a court date, neglecting to exchange insurance information or to offer Doyle a lift—and leaves behind an important legal document. Although the two lead characters share barely any time onscreen, they spend the movie obsessed with each other, engaged in escalating acts of revenge. Both want to do the right thing but keep failing, for different reasons. Gavin's grown too accustomed to taking the path of least resistance in his privileged life; Doyle thinks his problem is that he's an alcoholic, but by the end of the movie we learn that he's actually hooked on rage and chaos.

The screenplay methodically raises the stakes as the two antagonists continue their vendettas, but the movie's believability suffers along the way. What's good about this surprisingly engaging movie are the quieter moments, like Affleck discussing ethics with Sidney

Pollack (playing Gavin's slippery father-in-law, a senior partner at his law firm). Jackson's best scene comes after Doyle's terrible morning in family court. He goes into a bar, hesitantly orders bourbon, straight up with a twist, and then stares at the glass, fearfully contemplating it. Underneath Doyle's rumpled exterior, Jackson deftly shows us, there's a man contemplating his willingness to destroy his own life.

Star Wars: Episode II—Attack of the Clones (2002)

Mace Windu
MOVIE: 6/10   SLJ FACTOR: 6/10   MINUTES UNTIL HE SHOWS UP: 4

As Mace Windu, Samuel L. Jackson played the majority of his scenes in the *Star Wars* movies opposite Yoda; he felt fortunate that before the wrinkled and green Jedi master went full CGI, he got to do one movie with the puppet version of Yoda. "There was a person operating his right hand, a person doing his left hand, somebody else operated his eyes, and Frank [Oz] did the voice," he said. That gave him a sense of Yoda as a physical creature, "so when it got into CGI on the next film, I had a good gauge on where he was and how he moved, and I followed that."

> "You must realize there aren't enough Jedi to protect the Republic. We're keepers of the peace, not soldiers."

(Lucas, as is his wont, reedited *Episode I* a decade later, replacing puppet Yoda with a digital version.)

That was just a warmup exercise: *Episode II* builds to an epic melee where the Jedi stop pontificating and start kicking ass, in a battle royale with droids and clone troopers. Jackson said that George Lucas warned him that actors doing battle with green-screen effects determined their own fate by how much they gave the editors to work with: "You can make yourself look like a badass, or you can screw it up," Lucas told him. So, Jackson said, "having fought a lot of imaginary things as a child in my room, I went back to that space."

(Such is the mythic hold of *Star Wars* on our imagination that some actors have to unlearn old childhood habits. As Hayden Christensen said, "Anyone who picks up a lightsaber just automatically starts making the whooshing noise. In fact, Ewan [McGregor] and I were never really able to refrain from doing it. When we were filming, George would have to come up to us after some takes and say, 'Listen, guys, that was really great, but you're both moving your mouths when you're moving. Really, we can add that noise in post, so don't worry about it.' ")

Mace Windu makes impossibly high leaps, commands battalions of soldiers, and finally activates his lightsaber—which, much to viewers' surprise, was purple. (Previously, Star Wars lightsabers came in three colors: blue and green for the good guys, red for the bad guys.) Jackson said he asked Lucas for a purple lightsaber for a reason that was both practical and vain: he wanted to be able to be able to pick himself out of the crowd in a massive fight scene. "I'm the most powerful Jedi in the universe," he told Lucas, "and I think it would be an interesting thing for me to have a different color lightsaber than anybody else."

"No, that's ludicrous," Lucas said. But months later, when Jackson was called back to the set for some reshoots, Lucas told him, "I tried something, and it's already causing a shitstorm online, so I don't know if we're going to keep it." Then he showed him footage of Windu wielding a violet blade. That color made the final cut—Mace Windu even used that purple weapon to decapitate the bounty hunter Jango Fett.

When Mace Windu isn't onscreen, which is most of the time, *Attack of the Clones* is both very good and very bad. Ewan McGregor comes into his own as Obi-Wan Kenobi, delivering a sly leading-man performance, while Count Dooku (Christopher Lloyd) has a glorious lightsaber battle with an unexpectedly nimble Yoda. Unfortunately, the movie's central plotline is the romance between Anakin Skywalker (now a bratty teenager played by Hayden Christensen) and Amidala (a still bored Natalie Portman), which not only is tedious but seems to be written and acted by people who don't like each other and have only learned about the concept of love from educational filmstrips.

XXX (2002)

Agent Augustus Gibbons
MOVIE: 5/10   SLJ FACTOR: 4/10   MINUTES UNTIL HE SHOWS UP: 3
EXPLETIVES NOT DELETED: assholes

If you enjoyed *The Fast and the Furious* movies but thought the franchise was too realistic, then *XXX* is the movie for you. Abandoning the laws of physics and the United States alike, and not even pretending to be acquainted with common sense, it tells the story of Xander Cage (a glowering Vin Diesel), whose viral video stunts (e.g., stealing a state senator's car and driving it off a bridge for clicks and lolz) get him recruited by the National Security Agency. He's sent on a mission to Prague, where he snowboards his way through a gunfight, escapes from another gunfight by turning a restaurant tray into an improvised skateboard, and incidentally breaks up a terrorist plot. Director Rob Cohen, who also directed the first *Fast and Furious* movie, finds an aesthetic that's equally extreme sports and video game.

> *"I inspired you— I'm an authority figure, that's what I'm supposed to do."*

Diesel plays many scenes opposite Asia Argento, but his real costar is the shearling jacket with a sheepskin collar that he wears in the second half of the movie. Samuel L. Jackson sports a huge facial scar, which apparently substitutes for the screenwriter coming up with actual character development. He plays Gibbons, the NSA handler who recruits Xander, on the premise that "the best and brightest of the bottom of the barrel" won't smell like undercover agents. "Why is it always the assholes who pass the test?" Gibbons complains. Cohen said that casting Jackson opposite Diesel, he wanted to see "the King of Cool butting heads with the Prince of Cool." Ultimately, Jackson's job here is to be just tough enough for Diesel to seem a little edgier when he defies his authority.

Formula 51 (2002)

Elmo McElroy
MOVIE: 8/10   **SLJ FACTOR:** 9/10   **MINUTES UNTIL HE SHOWS UP:** 1
EXPLETIVES NOT DELETED: bitch (x2), motherfucker (x3), fucking (x4), motherfucking (x3), fuck-up, fuck (x8), shit (x10), Liverfuckingpool, goddamn (x4)

When Samuel L. Jackson signed on to this action comedy as star and executive producer and tailored the project to his own desires, his protagonist ended up with a bag of golf clubs on his back (used for hitting both balls and people), an amazing hairpiece (cornrows), and memorable clothes (a kilt). "Most days I wore [the kilt] traditionally—sans underwear," Jackson said. "But on days where I had to run and jump, they made me wear something so we didn't have to spend money to CGI, you know, nasty parts."

Jackson struts through *Formula 51* as a fast-talking, ass-kicking recreational-drug chemist who double-crosses his crime-boss patron (Meat Loaf) and travels to Liverpool to sell the formula for a potent blue pill that he's invented. He teams up with a local fixer, Robert Carlyle:

pairing the two actors effectively but unsubtly announces that the movie is aiming for a cross between *Pulp Fiction* and *Trainspotting*. (That means it probably should have been directed by Guy Ritchie, who specialized in that particular fusion cuisine, but it's actually Hong Kong veteran Ronny Yu behind the camera.) It's not as inventive or as smart as either of those two landmark movies, but it's relentlessly entertaining—in no small part because Jackson's so obviously enjoying himself.

The movie, a British-Canadian co-production, was tailored for UK audiences: released in Great Britain a year before it played in the United States, it debuted under the name *The 51st State* (a sardonic term familiar to Brits, capturing how England sometimes acts like a colony of the United States, its former tributary). Although the movie was partially inspired by Liverpool's historical role in the transatlantic slave trade, the result mostly plays the American-British relationship for culture-clash comedy. Jackson's Californian character wonders if "black pudding" is edible (the answer depends on how you feel about fried pig's blood) and asks—in the middle of a car chase, because it's that kind of movie—"So let me get this straight: 'Bollocks' is bad, whereas 'the dog's bollocks' is good?"

> *"MDMA utilizes serotonin. Opiates like heroin utilize dopamine, sort of like the same sensation you get after sex. Amphetamines increase adrenaline, and cocaine gets those synapses in the brain firing really fast. My product is fifty-one times stronger than cocaine, fifty-one times more hallucinogenic than acid, and fifty-one times more explosive than Ecstasy. It's like getting a personal visit from God."*

Basic (2003)

West

MOVIE: 3/10　SLJ FACTOR: 6/10　MINUTES UNTIL HE SHOWS UP: 2
EXPLETIVES NOT DELETED: dicks, fuck (x3), dick, fucking (x2), motherfucking, goddamn (x2), motherfuckers, shit (x2), bitches, shitty

When *Pulp Fiction* came out in 1994, Quentin Tarantino spoke in awed tones about the magic that happened when Samuel L. Jackson and John Travolta were onscreen together as Jules Winnfield and Vincent Vega. "It's rare to actually see this natural comedy team—and that's what they are," he said. "I mean, I'm almost tempted to do a series of

Jules & Vincent movies: *Jules & Vincent Meet Frankenstein*, *Jules & Vincent Meet the Mummy . . ."*

Unfortunately, it took Jackson and Travolta nine years before they appeared in the same movie again—and in *Basic*, a military thriller, they're barely ever in the same scene. Travolta plays a DEA agent investigating deaths and drug trafficking in an Army Ranger unit based in Panama; Jackson appears in flashback as the hard-ass sergeant who mercilessly rode his charges until he got fragged in the jungle. Jackson, unsurprisingly, is good at playing an intimidating drill sergeant, although he doesn't come up with a performance as iconic as R. Lee Ermey in *Full Metal Jacket* or Louis Gossett Jr. in *An Officer and a Gentleman*.

> *"Those of you I find lacking will quit. And those of you who refuse to quit will have a training accident. This base suffers three training accidents a year: unfortunate accidents that I will not hesitate to repeat if you cross me."*

John McTiernan directs *Basic* with one hand on the volume knob: the movie is full of yelling and helicopter roar and howling winds. The movie's superficially watchable because of the charismatic cast (also Taye Diggs, Connie Nielsen, and Giovanni Ribisi), but it's hard to care about any of it because the screenplay is organized around a roulette wheel of arbitrary POV shifts. Roughly every fifteen minutes, we find out that everything we've seen previously is bullshit: presumably, the filmmakers were aiming for a mind-bending *Rashomon* feeling, but the cumulative effect is to make us feel like suckers for trying to follow the action. By the end, it makes less sense than *Abbott and Costello Go to Mars*.

S.W.A.T. (2003)

Sgt. Dan "Hondo" Harrelson
MOVIE: 5/10   **SLJ FACTOR:** 6/10   **MINUTES UNTIL HE SHOWS UP:** 15
EXPLETIVES NOT DELETED: shitlist, shit, bitch (x2)

A quick history of the LAPD's S.W.A.T. unit, one of the first in the nation: it was founded because of unrest in the Black neighborhood of Watts. Its first real mission, in 1969, was to take on a small group of Black Panthers (the cops used grenade launchers; the Panthers were acquitted). In short, S.W.A.T. is Exhibit A for the militarization of the urban police and for those tactics being applied on Black and brown populations.

This movie doesn't want to engage with that history, beyond one scrap of dialogue after our heroes handcuff and manhandle a suspect in South Central. It's delivered by the great Octavia Spencer in a tiny role: "Don't y'all got nothing better to do than to be hauling another Black man off to jail? Just perpetuating the cycle, ain't you?" We also meet one cop who's never had a civilian complaint filed against him; in this world of big-budget propaganda for military-style policing, that makes him a figure of mockery.

> *"You've been in that cage six months, shining boots and fixing weapons, waiting for a second chance. I got one and I'm offering it to you."*

The movie isn't out to raise social awareness—it just wants to make blockbuster summer entertainment out of a vaguely familiar brand name. (The show *S.W.A.T.*, part of the Aaron Spelling TV factory, was best remembered for its theme song, which hit #1 in 1975; it's reprised here multiple times.) Samuel L. Jackson plays Hondo, an LAPD vet who recruits a team of young go-getters: LL Cool J, Michelle Rodriguez, Colin Farrell. (Jackson said he checked out the up-and-coming Farrell before filming started: "I knew he was a hot young Irish actor who was good looking and I talked to a couple of people about him.")

After an extended training sequence, the team embarks on its real mission: escorting a French drug lord to federal custody after he offers $100 million ("one hundred *meeleeon* dollars") on live television to anybody who will help him escape, which attracts a colorful array of local criminals with surprising levels of organization and firepower. Through the fusillades of gunfire and the crashing helicopters, Jackson stays steady and good-humored, like an encouraging sports coach; he may tangle with the LAPD brass, but he never gets in high dudgeon.

The song playing over the closing credits, by the Nashville rock band Hot Action Cop, is actually called "Samuel Jackson" (rhymed, repeatedly, with "hot action"). Inspirational lyrics: "How does he get so smooth?"

No Good Deed (2003)

Jack Friar
MOVIE: 5/10   **SLJ FACTOR:** 4/10   **MINUTES UNTIL HE SHOWS UP:** 0
EXPLETIVES NOT DELETED: shit, shit-for-brains

Bob Rafelson had a colorful Hollywood résumé: he co-created the Monkees, he produced *Easy Rider*, he directed his pal Jack Nicholson in the classic film *Five Easy Pieces*, and he once got Dennis Hopper out of a mental institution. Which makes it a bummer that the last movie he directed was this by-the-book film noir thriller that could have gone straight to cable: what was he doing hangin' 'round? *No Good Deed* is based on the 1924 Dashiell Hammett short story "The

> *"You know what happens to cops who have ten million dollars? They eat their service revolvers."*

House in Turk Street," starring his hard-boiled detective the Continental Op. The cultural references have been updated here—eight decades later, there are cell phones and compact discs—but the archetypes feel musty. There's a cruel, manipulative crime boss (Stellan Skarsgård), a femme fatale playing all the men in the gang against each other (Milla Jovovich), and a stoic, upright man of the law (Samuel L. Jackson).

Jackson's character is now a Delaware cop, working in grand theft auto, who looks into a missing-person case as a favor to a neighbor. While doing that, he helps an elderly woman with her groceries in a rainstorm, leading him to enter the house of a gang planning a bank heist; the robbers assume he has shown up looking for them and truss him up. It's a strangely passive role for a movie protagonist—our hero spends the bulk of the movie tied up or with a gun pointed at him—and Jackson gives a mostly disengaged performance to match. He does get one big laugh: as the criminal plot falls apart and the body count climbs, he shakes his head and comments, "This is a well-oiled machine."

Two details make Jackson's character not utterly generic: he's diabetic and he's a frustrated cellist. Those facts set up a scene where Jovovich's character saves his life by injecting him with insulin, and then (absurdly) frees him briefly so they can play music together. The moment where he wraps his arms around his captor to teach her the fundamentals of cello is ludicrous but has still has real erotic heat.

Twisted (2004)

John Mills

MOVIE: 3/10   SLJ FACTOR: 6/10   MINUTES UNTIL HE SHOWS UP: 7

EXPLETIVES NOT DELETED: fucked, fucking (x2), bullshit, shit, asshole

Twisted, after some second-unit footage of foggy San Francisco, opens on Ashley Judd with a knife to her neck. The man holding the knife gropes her and whispers creepy endearments for a minute or so before she slams him to the ground and cuffs him: she's a cop. There's no reason she couldn't have taken control of the situation earlier—except that the script wanted the thrill of upending expectations.

> *"What kind of moron tries to flush body parts down the toilet? Especially when he's got a perfectly good furnace out back."*

That sets the mood for this psychological thriller directed by Philip Kaufman, where logic and common sense are constantly battered by arbitrary twists and reversals. It's the sort of movie that rotates through its main cast as suspects until it runs out of misdirection and lurches to a conclusion. The pert Judd is miscast as a hard-bitten detective who loves her job and booze and picking up strangers in bars. She investigates a series of murders where she's the best suspect: the victims are all former sexual partners of hers and lately she's been drinking to the point of blacking out, making her wonder if she killed them without remembering it.

The high-caliber cast squandered on this inanity includes Andy Garcia as her partner, Camryn Manheim as a forensic scientist, David Strathairn as a police psychologist, and Samuel L. Jackson as the commissioner of the San Francisco Police Department. Jackson plays an old-school cop who doesn't take any guff—"Back up, you're breathing my air," he warns—and a father figure to Judd's character (he and her dead father were partners). Walking through the movie with a commanding air, unflustered by its stupidity, he's believable even when the screenplay isn't.

In My Country (2004)

Langston Whitfield

MOVIE: 4/10   **SLJ FACTOR:** 5/10   **MINUTES UNTIL HE SHOWS UP:** 10

EXPLETIVES NOT DELETED: fuck (x2), fucking (x3), shit (x3), bullshit

After decades of oppression (and revolution) in South Africa, the 1994 election of Nelson Mandela overturned the nation's apartheid regime. The new government had a quandary: What to do with the vast number of citizens who had once carried out policies of white supremacy? The solution was the Truth and Reconcilia-

> *"It's ironic, you teaching me about Africa."*

tion Commission, which offered amnesty to those who gave full and accurate confessions at its hearings. Those dramatic, harrowing stories of racist violence—and the grace with which many South Africans forgave their oppressors—were clearly why director John Boorman wanted to make this movie.

That material, however, was insufficiently boffo at the box office, so Boorman hired two movie stars (Juliette Binoche and Samuel L. Jackson) to play journalists reporting on the hearings. In a subplot that was likely intended to evoke interracial reconciliation but was nevertheless colossally misguided, a romance blooms between them. It's tone-deaf to have the hearings provide a Hollywood meet-cute, and it's offensive to watch the two of them nuzzling each other as they sit and listen to testimony about police brutality.

The movie is told mostly from the POV of Binoche's character, Anna Malan, a white poet from an Afrikaner farming family who has to confront her country's failings (it's an adaptation of Antjie Krog's memoir *Country of My Skull*). Jackson plays a wary *Washington Post* reporter, baffled as to why the guilty aren't being held accountable. That lets Binoche, with a shaky accent, educate him on the African value of ubuntu, a Nguni word meaning "unity," or more precisely, "I am, because you are." (A few years later, the term became familiar to American sports fans as the philosophical underpinning of a Boston Celtics title run.)

Charlize Theron, who grew up in South Africa, wanted to play the lead role, but Boorman said that he cast Binoche for her mixture of strength and vulnerability. "Ah, hire a French woman so they need to get a dialect coach," Jackson wisecracked. "That's cool." There's not much chemistry between Jackson and Binoche; their characters feel like mouthpieces for their respective political philosophies more than actual human beings. Jackson's best scenes come when he interviews a particularly brutal army colonel named de Jager (Brendan Gleeson); they spar with intelligence and mutual contempt. Reconciliation is an admirable value, but conflict makes for better movies.

Kill Bill: Vol. 2 (2004)

Rufus

MOVIE: 9/10   **SLJ FACTOR: 4/10**   **MINUTES UNTIL HE SHOWS UP: 3**

Kill Bill, Quentin Tarantino's blood-spattered four-hour tour de force (split into two halves) is most obviously about revenge: as it careens from one genre to another, the unifying plot thread is Uma Thurman's character, The Bride, seeking vengeance on her former lover Bill and his minions. (Her motivation: after she left Bill for another man, they attacked her so brutally that she was in a coma for four years.) But the movie has humanity and so another motif is resurrection: The Bride awakes from her coma, The Bride fights her way out of a coffin buried in a grave, The Bride plays dead when her daughter pretends to shoot her and then springs back to life.

> *"I was a Drell, I was a Drifter, I was a Coaster, I was part of the Gang, I was a Bar-Kay. If they come through Texas, I done played with them."*

The second half of *Kill Bill* has less Kill and more Bill than the first half. Samuel L. Jackson appears in a flashback as the organist at a small El Paso church where The Bride is having her wedding rehearsal—a scene that ends when Bill and his Deadly Viper Assassination Squad show up and gun down everyone at the rehearsal. (*Kill Bill* is full of snake names. Fun fact: Kobe Bryant borrowed his "Black Mamba" nickname from Thurman's character in this movie.)

The flashback was originally scheduled for two days of shooting— but as they were filming in the small town of Lancaster, California, on the edge of the Mojave Desert, a helicopter landed and disgorged executive producer Harvey Weinstein. The film company chairman had a brief conversation with Tarantino and producer Lawrence Bender, reminding them that they were behind schedule and over budget. After he left, Tarantino went for a long walk with his assistant director William Paul Clark; when they returned, they excised the sequence where the Deadly Viper Assassination Squad gunned down everyone in the chapel. "We were all supposed to get killed," said Bo Svenson, who played the reverend. "Makeup, and squibs, and all that kind of visual effects that we've seen in movies many times." Instead, the camera pulls back from the chapel and floats up as we hear gunfire: when we see a sheriff's car come into the frame, the camera returns to ground level to find all the dead bodies. "Absolutely brilliant problem solving," Svenson raved.

In the scene just before the massacre, Jackson casts a cool penumbra over the action as a musician sitting in the corner, smoking a cigarette and suggesting "Love Me Tender" as a wedding song. It's little more than a cameo, but he does get one memorable bit of dialogue, detailing his musical history with Rufus Thomas and a bevy of R&B groups. Jackson's close enough to Tarantino that they try to work together as often as possible, but that doesn't mean the director will write a role for the actor in every movie. "There was nothing for me to do in *Kill Bill*," Jackson complained. He nevertheless got a copy of the screenplay before Tarantino began shooting: "I read through it twice and I found, 'Oh, yeah, I can be this piano player guy.'"

The Incredibles (2004)

Lucius Best/Frozone
MOVIE: 9/10   SLJ FACTOR: 8/10   MINUTES UNTIL HE SHOWS UP: 1 (voice)

To play a suave superhero with ice-based powers, *Incredibles* director Brad Bird cast the coolest guy around, Samuel L. Jackson. But in the booth, Jackson didn't opt for the obvious earmarks of vocal "cool": growly, or bass-heavy, or otherwise evocative of a Curtis Mayfield rap. Lucius Best (aka Frozone) has a higher-pitched timbre than Jackson's usual speaking voice—but he's got Jackson's suave attitude and impeccable comic timing. "Lucius is this really cool dude. He shows up, he hangs out, he's got a solution," Jackson said.

The Incredibles, the sixth animated feature film from Pixar, is Bird's affectionate tale of superheroes trying to

"Super-ladies, they're always trying to tell you their secret identity. Think it'll strengthen the relationship or something like that. I say, 'Girl, I don't want to know about your mild-mannered alter ego or anything like that. I mean, you tell me you're Super Mega Ultra Lightning Babe, that's all right with me. I'm good."

settle down into civilian life. It has visual panache, wit, and a light dusting of Ayn Rand's objectivist philosophy. While our protagonist Mr. Incredible struggles with his identity as middle-aged Bob Parr, his pal Frozone, untormented by memories of his adventures as a Nietzschean superman, is content to chill.

Jackson's best scene comes near the end, when the giant robot Omnidroid is threatening the city of Metroville. Lucius tries to rush into action—but can't find his Frozone outfit. "Honey, where's my super-suit?" he asks, trying to sound cool and civic-minded, but not quite succeeding. Honey—that's actually the name of his wife—doesn't know, but doesn't want him battling the Omnidroid, because they have dinner plans. "You tell me where my suit is, woman!" Lucius finally explodes. "We are talking about the greater good!"

Kimberly Adair Clark, who gives a brief but brilliant performance as the unseen Honey, has no film credits as an actress outside the *Incredibles* movies: she worked in the human resources department of Pixar. But with the mounting panic in his voice, Jackson sets her up perfectly to deliver the best line of the movie: "Greater good? I am your *wife*! I am the greatest good you are ever going to get!"

Formula 51

Samuel L. Jackson

Robert Carlyle

Emily Mortimer

Pia Guerra.

S amuel L. Jackson grew up just two miles from the Chattanooga Golf and Country Club, one of the oldest golf courses in Tennessee—but its Tudor clubhouse was half a world away, on the other side of the Tennessee River, in the wealthy Riverview neighborhood. From the vantage point of 310½ Lookout Street, Jackson said, "Golf seemed an old man's game and a white man's game."

Jackson maintained his apathy toward the game until the summer of 1994, when he was forty-five years old; that's when some friends dragged him onto the golf course and forced him to play a round with them. Even though Jackson believed he was the best athlete in the foursome, they beat him soundly—the perfect way to stoke his competitive fires. "These guys aren't athletes," Jackson thought. "They can't beat me playing anything else. I've got to get this game down."

Jackson came back for another eighteen holes, and then eighteen more—and before he knew it, he was hooked. Even as a grown man, he defined himself as an only child, and so the sport perfectly fit his personality. "I like solitary kinds of things," he said, "and no matter how many people you're playing with, you're playing golf by yourself. It's you, the ball, and the golf course. It's not a team sport. You can't blame anybody else for your mistakes, and you take all the credit for the good things that happen."

He marveled at how different golf was from the team sports he grew up playing, like baseball and basketball. The ball lay motionless on the ground, but hitting it seemed like one of the hardest things in the world to do well. Early on, Jackson got frustrated when he shanked a shot and angrily hurled his club across the green. His caddy told him, "You're not good enough to get mad." Lesson learned: Jackson never threw a club again.

Learning the game, he played most of his golf on public courses, not country clubs: near his home in Encino, there were four different public courses for him to choose from. He would play with everyone from eighty-year-old women to teenagers to a dozen Black policemen who were happy to welcome him to their group, so long as he was willing to gamble with them. "You can find out a lot about people in four hours," Jackson said—even if sometimes he ended up detesting his partners, the experience was always fascinating. "And half the time they don't know who the fuck I am," he said.

Sometimes it would take a while for his playing partners to recognize him, and then, around the ninth tee, somebody would say, "You're that actor guy, aren't you?" Jackson would concede that he was. They'd respond, "Laurence Fishburne, right?"

Other times, Jackson got to golf with people who knew exactly who he was. Not long after he started playing the game, he went to a party at his agent's house. He was walking past a sofa when a voice quietly commanded him, "Sam, come here." Jackson looked down and saw Sidney Poitier. Stunned that his childhood hero even knew his name, Jackson joined him on the sofa. They chatted about the business of Hollywood for a while, and then Poitier told him, "Call me tomorrow—we're going to play golf." They did, even though Jackson was keenly aware of the voice shouting in the back of his head: "God, I'm actually friends with Sidney Poitier."

Jackson got obsessed. He called golf "my new drug of choice"—one that wouldn't burn a hole in his septum. He had a clause written into all his movie contracts: on location, the producers had to get him access to a local country club, pay his greens fees, and carve out time in his shooting schedule for him to get in at least two rounds every week. He kept frequenting funky public courses, but he also visited the finest links around the world. He said the best wrap gift anyone ever gave him was from director Joe Roth at the end of the *Freedomland* shoot: two rounds of golf at Augusta National, "which was awesome." Roger Michell, who directed Jackson in *Changing Lanes*, first met the actor on the set of *Formula 51* in Liverpool, where he saw the actor regularly hop on a helicopter so he could go play golf on the hallowed Scottish course of St. Andrews. "I think he sees his filmmaking as an adjunct to golf tourism," Michell dryly observed.

Jackson bought a cap or a shirt from every club he played at, which meant that he owned hundreds of golf shirts from different courses. He played at Turnberry and Loch Lomond in Scotland, at the New South Wales Golf Club in Australia, and, while filming *Rules of Engagement*, at a scraggly course in Morocco. "I've never met a course I don't like, even that one in Morocco," he said. "We lived on that course. The only green thing on it were the greens. There were animals everywhere, ants hitching a ride on our golf ball to see where it would take them."

One morning, Jackson was sleeping in a hotel room in London when he received an unscheduled six a.m. wake-up call.

"Hey, it's MJ," announced the voice on the telephone—meaning Michael Jordan.

"Where are you?" Jackson said blearily.

"Downstairs. We're going to play golf. Get up, let's go!"

That was how Jackson spent the morning at the Wentworth Club, next door to Windsor Castle, playing golf and talking trash with Michael Jordan and Ahmad Rashad. "I didn't even take my sticks with me [to London]—I didn't know they were there," Jackson said. "I had to go out and beat them down with some rental clubs."

Jackson followed the rules of the game scrupulously: "Golf's a very moral game," he observed. The code of golf meant not only that you didn't cheat, but that you policed yourself more carefully than an outside judge would. But he was utterly indifferent to the uptight standards of stodgy golf establishments or the clenched-jaw white supremacy of WASP culture: other players could witness him driving his golf cart at maximum speed and loudly peppering his early morning play with his favorite all-purpose word, "motherfucker."

"People know me for it all over the golf course," he bragged. "If I hit a bad shot, I'll go 'motherfucker!' and golfers who didn't even know I was there go, 'Alright, Sam's over there.' Or if it's a great shot—pow, right on the pin—I'll go, 'Yeah, motherfucker!' and they'll actually know the difference."

Jackson put serious thought into his golf outfits, assembling them the night before a round and superstitiously retiring certain combinations if he golfed poorly in them. And as he joked on the stage of Radio City Music Hall while hosting the ESPY Awards, "The golf course is the only place I can go dressed like a pimp and fit in perfectly. Anywhere else, lime-green pants and alligator shoes, I got a cop on my buns."

Jackson's golfing partners included Charles Barkley, Kenny G, Darius Rucker, Justin Timberlake, Joe Pesci, Don Cheadle—and Bill Clinton, famous on the golf course for his liberal use of mulligans. "Clinton is just having fun," Jackson said. "He'll hit the ball six times and be like, 'Ah, give me a five.'"

The first time Jackson played golf with Tiger Woods was at St. Andrews. Woods shot 72, while Jackson shot 78—but Jackson's handicap was a hefty 15, so he won. Jackson gave Tiger Woods some acting advice, and in return, Woods gave him some golf tips. "But you can't tell it by my game," Jackson said. He gradually whittled down his handicap to 6, and then 2.3, before a back injury took him off the golf course for a while and his game regressed a bit. Jackson's goal: "to be a scratch golfer for at least one month in my golf career."

Jackson cared at least as much about golf as he did about acting—and given a choice, he would have much rather won an event on the PGA Tour than an Oscar. "Golf and acting have certain mechanics you need to know to be able to play the game," he said. "In golf, you have to visualize the play before you make it. In acting, you have to visualize the character." He believed that the less you thought about either activity while you were doing it, the better off you'd be—but in order to work by instinct, you first had to learn your craft.

Jackson came to golf late, just as he came to movie stardom late. Acting made him a better golfer, by ensuring that he never worried about spectators or suffered from stage fright. And golfing made him a better actor, by calming him and centering him. Jackson observed, "Films get in the way of my golf, but they have afforded me the chance to play a lot of golf."

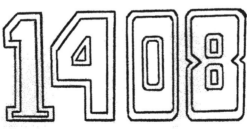

Coach Carter (2005)

Coach Ken Carter
MOVIE: 7/10   SLJ FACTOR: 9/10   MINUTES UNTIL HE SHOWS UP: 0
EXPLETIVES NOT DELETED: shit, goddammit

Ken Carter on being portrayed by Samuel L. Jackson: "I watched him transition into me within the first 15 minutes of us meeting. It was amazing. I'm looking at him do me, with my hand movements and my speech pattern."

Both the real and the fictional Coach Carter are stern basketball coaches with high expectations for their inner-city students. The turning point of this movie is when the coach sends his players to the library because some of them are failing their classes, locking them out of the gymnasium and forfeiting games until they raise their GPAs. Jackson inhales every particle of role-model inspiration contained in the screenplay, playing the coach with confidence and dignity. Carter isn't an especially complicated character, but Jackson makes him a compelling one—even though scenes about the coach's inner life are fleeting. When we're away from the basketball court, we follow the players instead, watching them grapple with after-school-special issues like teenage pregnancy, gang violence, and unauthorized house parties.

"I want you to go home and look at your lives tonight, and look at your parents' lives, and ask yourself, 'Do I want better?' If the answer is yes, I'll see you here tomorrow. And I promise you, I will do everything in my power to get you to college and to a better life."

It's engaging, if familiar to anyone who's ever watched a sports movie—or the high-school-basketball TV show *The White Shadow*. (Director Thomas Carter [no relation] was a *White Shadow* cast member.) The biggest surprise is that the Richmond Oilers lose a climactic game that the team won in real life: the movie passed up an easy triumph in favor of emphasizing that the team's most important victories came away from the court.

Jackson was also a role model to the young ensemble cast, which included a couple of notable performers making their film debuts: Channing Tatum (then better known as an Abercrombie & Fitch model) and the singer Ashanti. Jackson led by example, showing the younger actors how to act professionally (know your lines, show up on time, learn the names of crew members), and stood up for them. As he recounted, "Sometimes I'm a defender of them when too much is being asked of them, because they don't know how to say 'No, I can't do that now'—and especially in a basketball situation where people can get hurt."

Jackson criticized what he saw as slack behavior by director Carter—as usual, he wanted everyone else on the set to be as prepared as he was, even though he knew that was unrealistic. On the day Jackson had to film a crucial three-page monologue, one of the producers checked in with him, making sure that he was ready to go. "Man, no worries," he responded. "I'm working with my favorite actor tonight: *me*."

XXX: State of the Union (2005)

Agent Augustus Gibbons
MOVIE: 4/10   SLJ FACTOR: 4/10   MINUTES UNTIL HE SHOWS UP: 2
EXPLETIVES NOT DELETED: bitch (x2)

With Vin Diesel opting out of the sequel and the producers jettisoning the extreme-sports gimmick, what was left of the *XXX* action-movie franchise was the brand name and the presence of Samuel L. Jackson. Once again, Jackson, playing NSA boss Gibbons, recruits a nontraditional agent: in this case, Ice Cube, playing Darius Stone, a former Navy SEAL now serving twenty years in a military prison. Ice Cube can be a slyly funny actor, but here he's mostly called on to glower. Darius establishes his street bona fides by quoting Tupac, which plays oddly, given that Ice Cube himself is a major rapper of the same generation.

"Your turn to do the dying, General."

The plot, such as it is, centers around a secretary of defense (Willem Dafoe) who plans to overthrow the U.S. government and put himself in charge. Along the way, we get an explanation for the scars on Gibbons's face, but it's as half-baked as the rest of the movie. (The scars seem to come and go, depending on the scene.) The best moments between Ice Cube and Jackson are when Darius quotes Gibbons's lines from the first movie back at him, making it clear that he knows his schtick and he isn't buying it. That's amusing, but it makes the character of Gibbons less intimidating—more of a sidekick than a master manipulator. To compensate, Jackson gets some action scenes, and even gets in a fire-fight with one pistol in each hand.

In retrospect, Jackson's performance as Gibbons was the first draft of his performance as Nick Fury in the Marvel movies: the tough boss of a super-secret spy agency who has a facial disfigurement, recruits loose-cannon operatives with extraordinary abilities, and survives his own (apparent) death. Given better material as Fury, Jackson gave that character gravitas; here he just hit his marks. The best thing you can say about this movie is that it's over in a reasonably brisk 100 minutes.

Star Wars: Episode III—Revenge of the Sith (2005)

Mace Windu
MOVIE: 7/10   SLJ FACTOR: 6/10   MINUTES UNTIL HE SHOWS UP: 24

Revenge of the Sith was hamstrung by wince-inducing dialogue and the callow version of Anakin Skywalker at its center, but it's still the best of the *Star Wars* prequels because it's where three decades of plot outlines and narrative machinery finally clicked into place, giving the big action sequences a mythic grandeur. One pivotal set piece was a scene where Mace Windu (Samuel L. Jackson) confronts Chancellor Palpatine (Ian McDiarmid), secretly a Sith Lord who has been gathering power while pretending to preserve democracy. An attempt to take him into custody turns into a lightsaber fight—a remarkably balletic one considering it pits a fifty-six-year-old (Jackson) against a sixty-year-old (McDiarmid).

"In the name of the Galactic Senate of the Republic, you are under arrest, Chancellor."

Jackson remembered the fight as comprising ninety-seven separate moves, shot over three days. "You've got a month to learn that fight," he said. "You start off with your saber, and you show up with your sneakers on, and real slowly, you learn the moves so you can see that you can do it. And you've got it, you've got the fight down pat. And then they show up with your boots, and you're like, 'Right, this is very different from my sneakers.' So you have to re-learn the fight with your boots on. And after you learn *that*, they show up again with the long-ass robes with your long-ass sleeves on it *and* your boots. I went,

'Oh, shit. I've got to learn the fight *again*.' Then you learn how to figure out how to keep your sleeves out of the way of your lightsaber. It's a process."

Lucas told Jackson that he needed to kill a character and the only important prequel character that he didn't need for other plot reasons was Mace Windu. So, the director informed him, "Your wish for a spectacular death is going to come true."

Mace Windu meets his demise halfway through the movie's running time: after Anakin lops off his right hand, Palpatine blasts him out of a high window. But in recent years, Jackson has insisted that his character didn't die, arguing that Jedi can fall safely from extreme heights. Jackson ran his theory past George Lucas, and says that Lucas told him, "I'm okay with that. You can be alive." But, Jackson conceded, "George doesn't have anything to do with it anymore."

The Man (2005)

Derrick Vann
MOVIE: 4/10   SLJ FACTOR: 7/10   MINUTES UNTIL HE SHOWS UP: 3
EXPLETIVES NOT DELETED: shit (x8), bullshit (x7), bitch (x9), assholes, shitstain, fuck, goddamn (x2), asshole

An action comedy so formulaic that it feels like it was written with a copy of the *Save the Cat!* screenwriting manual open at all times, *The Man* stars Eugene Levy and Samuel L. Jackson as mismatched partners busting some gunrunners. Both are playing versions of their onscreen archetypes: Levy is a nebbishy sales rep for dental equipment, while Jackson is a scarred Detroit cop in a leather jacket.

> "It's these repetitive asswhippings that cause guys like me to burn out on the job."

The pleasure of the movie is watching the two actors team up: even when a scene is underwritten (which is most of the time), their rhythms mesh well. A totally deadpan Jackson plays the role of the streetwise Derrick Vann completely straight, as if he were starring in a low-budget *Shaft* knockoff. That lets Levy make the most of the comedy as Andy Fiddler, a square guy who stumbles into a violent situation way beyond his ken. "Why do you swear so much? Do you think it makes you sound tougher when you just swear all the time?" Fiddler asks indignantly. "I could go around all day saying eff you, eff this, and eff that, and effing this, you mother-effer. But I don't, because there has to be some civility in the world." (Vann just replies "Fuck you.")

In the movie's best scene, Fiddler asserts himself in front of the bad guys by slapping Vann and calling him a bitch. "Let me tell you, did I enjoy smacking him across the pooper!" Levy said. "I'm the only guy in the history of movies who's ever slapped Sam on screen and lived to tell about it."

Freedomland (2006)

Lorenzo Council
MOVIE: 4/10   SLJ FACTOR: 8/10   MINUTES UNTIL HE SHOWS UP: 2
EXPLETIVES NOT DELETED: shit (x7), fucking (x5), fuck (x5), bitch (x2), motherfucking, brotherfucker

Samuel L. Jackson made four movies between 1989 and 2006 where Richard Price was credited as a screenwriter, all of them containing some good moments but none of them a career high point for either man, including *Sea of Love*, *Kiss of Death*, and *Shaft*. *Freedomland* had the most potential but was the worst of the lot. Price adapted his own gripping novel, the best-selling story of what happens in two adjacent New Jersey towns—one largely white, one largely Black—when a white mother stumbles into an emergency room saying that a carjacker in the projects has not only stolen her car but abducted her four-year-old son in the back seat. Her story doesn't add up, but the situation spirals out of control anyway.

"Twenty-two years of policing in this city—things I see day in, day out, makes it very, very hard to have faith in humanity."

In a vanity move, the studio executive Joe Roth directed the film himself. His basic idea appears have to been "make it look like a feature-film version of *The Wire*," a series that Price also wrote for—unsubtly, Roth even cast a bunch of the show's ensemble. Although the movie covers a lot of the same territory as the HBO series (poverty, police work, and racial conflict in the urban eastern seaboard), it lacks the show's nuance and internal logic. Many individual scenes work, but they seem disconnected from each other.

This morass contains some strong individual performances. Edie Falco, in a supporting role, nails the movie's best scene: trying to convince the missing child's mother (Julianne Moore) to confess that she knows more than she's telling, she delivers a hypnotic monologue about her bereavement after her own child was kidnapped years ago. And Jackson stars as detective Lorenzo Council. His character's more richly rendered in the novel, where Price writes of his "cracked bellow" as Lorenzo addresses a community meeting: "He was a big man—six foot three, 240 pounds—with a royal gut, a pendulous and chronically split lower lip, and thick glasses. In situations like this, loud and angry usually did the trick." Jackson substitutes his own movie-star physique for Price's prose, but he honors the character with a vivid performance: even as the movie loses its way, we empathize with Lorenzo balancing his allegiances between the police department and the people he serves in the Armstrong housing project.

Julianne Moore, one of the all-time greats, is curiously misused in this film, giving an off-key performance as the puffy, agitated mother who may be complicit in her own child's disappearance. Nevertheless, Jackson loved working with her, admiring the way she could switch effortlessly from off-camera gossip about *American Idol* to on-camera histrionics. He remembered their running joke through the shoot, which began when they were filming a particularly intense scene that ended with her buckling at the knees and Jackson catching her. After one take, Roth called "cut"—and then a wide-eyed Moore looked up at Jackson and in a little-girl voice implored him, "Carry me, carry me." Jackson cracked up, he said, "and every day from that point on, she would look at me and go, 'Carry me, carry me,' and I would fall out laughing. As a wrap gift, I actually gave her a dog tag with diamonds on it, and I had *CARRY ME* put on the back of it."

Also in the cast was LaTanya Richardson, marking the first time Jackson had acted with his wife in over a decade, since *Losing Isaiah* in 1995. They hung out together off-camera, although Jackson declined her offer to run lines together. Richardson knew that Jackson was number one on the call sheet and she wasn't, but it was still a shock for her to see how different their trailers were, and how fully her husband received the star treatment. "Occasionally I let her ride in my car from the trailer to the set," Jackson joked. "You got to keep them in their place, though—you can't let them get used to that."

Snakes on a Plane (2006)

Neville Flynn

MOVIE: 6/10   **SLJ FACTOR:** 8/10   **MINUTES UNTIL HE SHOWS UP:** 6

EXPLETIVES NOT DELETED: bullshit, ass (x2), shit (x7), goddamn (x2), fucking (x2), motherfucking (x2), motherfucker, fuck

Samuel L. Jackson on how he took the lead role as an FBI agent in *Snakes on a Plane*: "When I opened up that script and I saw that title, I said, 'Oh, I'm doing this.' I didn't even need to read it. And then I read it, and it was all cool, and I get to production and they start talking about *Pacific Flight 121*. And I'm like, 'Excuse me, what is that?' And they said, 'Oh, you know, we don't want to give away too much to the audience.' What the fuck are you talking

> *"I have had it with these motherfucking snakes on this motherfucking plane!"*

about? How do you expect to get people into the theaters? You really think people want to see *Pacific Flight 121*? As opposed to *Snakes on a Plane*? 'Well, we're kind of noodling it, and we're going to do a whole poll.' I said, 'You don't need to do a fucking poll!' When I picked up the script, I took this job, because it said *Snakes on a Plane*. I didn't have to read the script. I just knew, okay, you got a plane, and you got a plane full of snakes. That's all I need to know. It's not about 'this is *Pacific Flight 121* and we're flying from here to there.' No! Nobody cares about that shit. You're either afraid of flying or you're afraid of snakes. And if you're afraid of both, hey, you're in the perfect place."

The heyday of disaster movies was the 1970s, when producer Irwin Allen concocted star-heavy spectacles such as *The Poseidon Adventure* and *The Towering Inferno*. Tragedy repeats itself as farce, and disaster movies now survive in their parodies (*Airplane!*) and in over-the-top takes on the genre such as the *Sharknado* series and this movie. There was so much pre-release buzz for *Snakes on a Plane*, basically on the strength of the title and Jackson's presence, that producers commissioned a week of reshoots that would push the movie further into the R-rated absurdity that fans wanted. To wit, Jackson's most famous line (see above) wasn't in the original script, but was added after a fan-edited trailer included a Jackson soundalike saying "I want these motherfucking snakes off this motherfucking plane!" According to Jackson, he had told the producers that he should say exactly that line, and that they should film him saying it if only to have more options in the editing room, but they originally "wanted a PG rating for the movie, so they would never let me say it."

The movie delivers pretty much exactly what you expected, if what you expected was an airplane full of character sketches that includes Julianna Margulies as the senior flight attendant working one last Hawaii–to–Los Angeles redeye before she goes to law school, Kenan Thompson as the bodyguard for a rap star, and a plane full of CGI snakes. (You probably don't care why the snakes are on the plane, but the reason is "a gangster put them there to kill a witness who's planning to testify against him.") A woman dies when a snake bites her nipple; a man dies when a snake bites his penis; a snake dies when a flight attendant shoves it in a microwave oven that, amazingly enough, has a preset "SNAKE" button. Jackson shows up bald and badass, unflustered by the cavalcade of ophidian death. His confident presence makes the passengers believe that they will make it through the flight alive, and audience members believe that they will make it through the movie entertained. There's some turbulence along the way, but he delivers.

Home of the Brave (2006)

Will Marsh
MOVIE: 4/10   **SLJ FACTOR:** 6/10   **MINUTES UNTIL HE SHOWS UP:** 2
EXPLETIVES NOT DELETED: fuck (x2), fucked

In the Iraq war, the gap between expectation and execution was the distance between "we will, in fact, be greeted as liberators" (Dick Cheney, 2003) and the bloody morass that the conflict became. The filmmaking equivalent might be booking a movie into a few theaters at the end of a calendar year to make it eligible for the Oscars and hurriedly withdrawing it when it becomes clear that it's more likely to contend for the Razzies. That's what happened with the well-intentioned but wooden *Home of the Brave*.

An unofficial remake of William

"Do you want to know what a blast wound looks like? What an OR in the desert smells like? What really happens to them, how they die? You really want to know? You want us to come back like nothing ever happened. You don't want to get your hands dirty with the details."

Wyler's 1946 masterpiece *The Best Years of Our Lives*, the movie begins with a twenty-minute sequence in Iraq where a military convoy gets ambushed; the action then shifts to Spokane, where four of the soldiers involved try to adjust to civilian life, without much success. Rapper 50 Cent is assigned back pain and a guilty conscience; soap actor Brian Presley receives unemployment and anomie; Jessica Biel gets a rubbery prosthetic right hand and an ex-boyfriend who tells her, "I guess it takes only one good hand to push people away." Samuel L. Jackson plays a lieutenant colonel (and surgeon) experiencing sleeplessness, alcohol abuse, and suicidal urges.

Jackson can't transcend the predictable, awkward script, but he makes strong choices, playing his doctor as a towering oak tree of a human being who's wobbling in gale-force winds. He nurses his pain and shuts out his wife—Jackson has the gift of making an impassive face look like more than a blank expression. A scene where he drunkenly brings three lawn workers home to share his family's Thanksgiving table seems inventive and promising but goes off the rails around the time he rips the lip piercing out of his son's face.

Irwin Winkler has a first-rate CV as a movie producer, with credits including *Rocky*, *The Right Stuff*, and *Goodfellas*. He didn't have the same gift as a director, although he helmed seven films; this movie ended his directorial career.

Farce of the Penguins (2007)

Narrator
MOVIE: 2/10   SLJ FACTOR: 3/10   MINUTES UNTIL HE SHOWS UP: 0 (voice-over)
EXPLETIVES NOT DELETED: bitches (x2), asshole, shit, fuck, motherfuck, motherfuckers, pussy-whipped, bitch

Everybody in Hollywood has a dream project: to make it happen they'll do whatever it takes and call in every favor they're owed. Who would have guessed that Bob Saget's holy grail was a foul-mouthed parody of a penguin nature film?

In 2005, the French documentary *March of the Penguins* became an unexpected blockbuster, earning over $125 million around the world. The American version featured Morgan Freeman as the narrator, explaining the lives and mating rituals of emperor penguins, and

"The sun is setting earlier now; the weather is getting colder. And I can't wait to finish recording this shit and go play golf."

won the Best Documentary Oscar. Saget (famous for his G-rated work on *Full House* and *America's Funniest Home Videos*) watched the movie in a friend's screening room and cracked up everyone there with his own raunchy voice-over. That inspired him to release his commentary as an actual movie: when he couldn't get the rights to *March*, he licensed other penguin footage instead. Saget recruited an all-star vocal cast (Jason Alexander, Whoopi Goldberg, etc.), most of whom deliver just a few lines, generally as penguins kvetching about the opposite gender. The demented ambition it took to make this weird feature film come together is genuinely impressive; unfortunately, the schtick gets tired after five minutes.

Saget and Lewis Black provide the voices of the lead penguins, with major roles also filled by Mo'Nique and Tracy Morgan (whose exuberantly offensive performance is the funniest in the movie). The marquee star is Samuel L. Jackson, taking Morgan Freeman's seat as the narrator: the movie is sometimes billed as *Farce of the Penguins as Told by Samuel L. Jackson*. To do the narration, Jackson showed up in a gray Adidas hoodie sweatshirt, with reading glasses and Kangol hat, and knocked out a performance that was dignified scene-setting, except with obscenities: for example, he gives a sonorous line reading to "Meanwhile, back at the mating grounds, the air is colder than a well digger's asshole."

"You're going to miss me so bad," Saget joked with Jackson as the recording session wound down.

Jackson laughed. "You're going to miss *me*, dude," he responded. "Because you gotta write some more. You're going to have motherfuckers in here who don't think as fast as I do!"

Black Snake Moan (2007)

Lazarus
MOVIE: 8/10   SLJ FACTOR: 9/10   MINUTES UNTIL HE SHOWS UP: 2
EXPLETIVES NOT DELETED: shit (x14), motherfucker (x5), goddamn (x5) fuck (x3), bitch, dick, shithole, motherfucking

Given the choice between a thoughtful film about personal redemption or a movie where Samuel L. Jackson chains a scantily clad Christina Ricci to a radiator, writer-director Craig Brewer decided to have it both ways.

Jackson plays Lazarus Red, a farmer scraping by in rural Tennessee and formerly a bluesman of local repute. After his wife leaves him for his own brother, he plows under her rose

"God seen fit to put you in my path. And I aim to cure you of your wickedness."

garden and wallows in his own grief and rage—until the morning when he finds Rae (Ricci), who has been assaulted and left on the country road by his home. She's battered, unconscious, and wearing only a flimsy pair of panties and a cut-off T-shirt. (Her shirt features both the American and Confederate flags, another having-it-both-ways move.) Lazarus takes Rae into his home and nurses her back to health, but padlocks a chain around her waist to keep her from wandering off in her delirium. When he discovers that she's a damaged human being, known as the town's nymphomaniac wild child, he keeps her chained, healing her spirit through both the Bible and the blues.

As you might expect, his efforts are also a balm for his own troubled soul. What's surprising is the complexity of the relationship between the pair (nonsexual despite Rae offering to fuck him): sometimes a father-daughter drama, sometimes a screwball bondage comedy, sometimes an electric blues song that slides between sin and salvation. S. Epatha Merkerson and Justin Timberlake do excellent work in supporting roles, but the core of the movie is the layered dynamic between Jackson and Ricci. "During the rehearsal period, Christina and I developed this really interesting bond, and interesting trust, that kind of allowed her to go anywhere she wanted to," Jackson said. While he recognized that her state of undress was titillating, he said he was unfazed by it on the set: "After an hour of looking at Christina in those little panties and that shirt, you kind of get over it."

Jackson had a six-month crash course on guitar (he learned to play while shooting *Freedomland* and *Snakes on a Plane*), making himself into a credibly rough-voiced Delta bluesman. But more impressive is how he fully inhabits Lazarus's broken-down body. "My grandfather's brothers were farmers and they didn't move very fast," he said. "They were doing backbreaking work in the fields and drove tractors. As it's very hot and muggy in the South, you conserve your energy. The weight of all that work makes you walk a certain kind of way. You also have aches and pains at a certain age and so you have to find a way to walk so your body doesn't creak."

Cedric Burnside played drums in a scene where Lazarus finally resurrects himself and returns to a local juke joint to play the electric blues. "At first his strengths weren't so strong," Burnside said of Jackson's musical abilities. He watched Jackson turn himself into a respectable musician, while shooting two other movies and flying back and forth from Mississippi to Los Angeles. "I thought I was a determined person, but I didn't know what 'determined' means until I met that guy."

1408 (2007)

Olin
MOVIE: 8/10 **SLJ FACTOR:** 7/10 **MINUTES UNTIL HE SHOWS UP:** 15
EXPLETIVES NOT DELETED: dammit, fucking

Although Samuel L. Jackson is nominally the costar of *1408*, the movie is basically a one-man show: John Cusack stars as Mike Enslin, a man determined to check into a hotel room where dozens of grisly deaths have happened over the years. (He writes books about haunted hotels, which is his way of processing his grief from the death of a young daughter.) Jackson has one big scene as Gerald Olin, the manager of the Dolphin Hotel, who does everything he can to dissuade Enslin: persuasion, bribery, a recitation of the room's brutal history. Jackson plays him suavely, and with just a hint of menace.

"My concern here is not for the hotel. My concern here is not for you. Frankly, selfishly, I don't want you to check into 1408 because I don't want to clean up the mess."

According to Cusack, audience responses to Jackson's character broke down along gender lines. "The guys think Olin's evil and the girls think he's not," he said. "All the girls I've talked to said, 'No, he's a good guy, he's trying to help you out.' And the guys are like, 'No, he isn't. He's the crypt keeper. He's the one who set you up.'"

A heedless Enslin settles into room 1408, apparently unaware that in Stephen King adaptations like this one, writers don't fare well in hotels. Mild jump scares escalate to phantoms and indoor snowstorms and agonizing memories. The movie, legitimately spooky, was an old-fashioned horror film—counterprogramming to the trend of torture porn movies like *Saw* and *Hostel*.

Because the filmmakers wanted a PG-13 rating, they could include only one major curse. To maximize its impact, they assigned it to Jackson, who summed up the movie in five memorable words: "It's an evil fucking room." Cusack, who had to endure various ordeals in the room during a fifteen-week shoot, lamented that during those extended solo scenes, "all you want to do is swear. You want to go 'Fuck! Shit!' But you can't, because Sam got the one 'fuck' that we could use."

Resurrecting the Champ (2007)

Champ

MOVIE: 6/10   **SLJ FACTOR:** 10/10   **MINUTES UNTIL HE SHOWS UP:** 2

EXPLETIVES NOT DELETED: shit (x2), bitch

Betrayed by his body, betrayed by his mind, a man wanders the streets of Denver, shadowboxing with his own memories. Samuel L. Jackson plays the former heavyweight known as Champ—as he explains to a young journalist (Josh Hartnett) who stumbles on him, it's because he's the boxing legend Bob Satterfield, a 1950s-era pugilist who was one victory away from a title fight. As Champ, Jackson speaks in a high-pitched wheeze; his body posture can flip from shambling to crisp, when muscle memory overcomes years of homelessness. It's a riveting portrait of a man living on the borderlands of society and his own consciousness: at times, you'll swear you can see the light flicker in Jackson's eyes, only to dim again.

> *"I went from up-and-coming to has-been, with nothing in between."*

"Everybody's got a story. They didn't just spring up out of the sidewalk as a homeless person," Jackson said. To render Champ as a specific human being, rather than a generic homeless person, Jackson considered the physicality of a boxer who was too old to exercise but stayed in shape just by jogging and carrying his stuff around. "That's his fighter's movement," he said. Staring in a mirror, thinking deeply about Champ, Jackson remembered a voice: it was his grandfather's. "He had this kind of high-pitched whisper that always made me lean over and say, 'What did you say, Pop?'" Jackson remembered. "He was always pulling me toward him with his voice." He realized that voice could do the same thing for the people in Champ's life—even when he smelled rancid, they would have to lean in to hear what he had to say—and for an audience watching the movie.

When his wife, LaTanya Richardson, watched the movie, she started shaking her head during his first scene, and he knew exactly why: she was worried that he wouldn't be able to maintain the voice. "We've watched so many films where people start something and they don't finish it," he said. "They start out limping on their right foot and before you know it, they're limping on their left foot."

Jackson sustains his remarkable performance through the entire film; unfortunately, the movie's focus is not on Champ, but on Erik

Kernan Jr., the journalist interviewing him. Kernan is an ambitious but plodding sportswriter for a Denver newspaper, willing to cut corners with the truth if it impresses his bosses or his six-year-old son. His bouts with journalistic integrity and the legacy of his own family are interesting only to the degree that they parallel Champ's—but the movie nevertheless plays out every predictable beat of his emotional growth. (The movie is based on an extraordinary *Los Angeles Times Magazine* article by J. R. Moehringer, about his friendship with the real-life Champ and his journey into the truth about Bob Satterfield; Moehringer did a superior job striking a balance between reporter and subject.) When we first meet Champ, he's a victim, being assaulted in an alley by some affluent young white assholes eager to prove their manhood. As the movie unfolds, we learn the ways in which Champ is actually the author of his own fate: all the while, Jackson makes us lean in closer to hear more of his secrets.

Samuel L. Jackson and LaTanya Richardson showed off their Encino house in the April 2000 issue of *Architectural Digest*—with lots of photos and puffery such as "The home speaks for LaTanya and Sam as a total spirit"—but once the home was memorialized in the magazine's high-gloss pages, Richardson was ready to move on. "My wife just bought a new house," Jackson said in a radio interview only two months later, not sounding enthusiastic. "She's moving."

That meant he was moving too: they spent $8.9 million to buy a house in a gated community adjacent to Beverly Hills. The house, originally owned by a British lord and most recently occupied by the sitcom star Roseanne, had nine bedrooms and ten bathrooms; the two-acre property also featured a pool, a tennis court, a rose garden, and a two-bedroom guest house. Their neighbors included plutocrat Sumner Redstone and their old pals Denzel and Paulette Washington; Magic and Cookie Johnson lived across the street.

The Jacksons and the Johnsons became good friends, attending the same church. Every summer, the Johnsons would invite the Jacksons to join them for a group vacation on their yacht, and they would cruise through the Amalfi Coast and the Côte d'Azur for three weeks. Jackson would bring a suitcase stuffed with classic movies and new Asian flicks, while, he said, "the ladies watch whatever series that they didn't binge-watch all year." One of the few luxuries Jackson lacked on the yacht was golf, so he'd get his fix by driving a bucket of biodegradable balls into the Mediterranean Sea.

One of the other pleasures not available at sea: public adulation. Johnson said, "If we want to hear the roar of the crowd, we get off the boat and walk around. It's crazy to have both of us in Portofino. They don't know who to start with."

At Vassar, Zoe Jackson majored in psychology and graduated in 2004. Her father gave the commencement speech in Poughkeepsie, New York, telling 616 graduates, "Find something that moves you or pisses you off, and do something about it. Put yourself out there. Be brave. Be bold. Take action. You have a voice. Speak up, especially when something tries to keep you silent. Take a stand for what's right. Raise a ruckus and make a change. You may not always be popular, but

209

you'll be part of something larger and bigger and greater than yourself. Besides, making history is extremely cool."

Zoe went on to attend the French Culinary Institute in New York City before becoming a film and TV producer, ultimately combining her kitchen expertise with her showbiz knowledge to work on reality cooking shows such as *Chopped*.

"She has a very strong social conscience," Jackson said, proud that Zoe had paid attention to her parents' backgrounds as revolutionaries and inherited their desire to make the world a better place. He couldn't help but laugh, however, when she told him that she had attended the Occupy Wall Street protests with a friend from Vassar: the actress Anne Hathaway. Jackson said, "You went to Occupy Wall Street—*with Annie Hathaway?*"

Richardson acted only intermittently but didn't lose any velocity on her fastball. She played the censorious church treasurer in the musical *The Fighting Temptations* (starring Beyoncé and Cuba Gooding Jr.), bringing complexity to the movie's villain, and earned a Tony nomination for her work in the Broadway revival of *A Raisin in the Sun*. (She played Denzel Washington's mother, although in real life, he was only five years younger than her.) She also managed the Jackson family's charitable donations, redirecting some of her husband's Hollywood-studio paychecks to causes that included the NAACP legal defense fund, a reading room at Spelman College, and Ingwavuma Orphan Care in South Africa. "She has this benevolent spirit that needs to be fed," Jackson said appreciatively. "People get to me by getting her, which is fine, because I can be a little self-centered and she keeps me, you know—she keeps me focused on the world."

Richardson also did more work to maintain the couple's relationships outside the marriage, since Jackson was often absent, geographically or emotionally. Even after Jackson and Spike Lee had their dramatic public rupture, Richardson remained close with Tonya Lewis Lee, Spike's wife. When Lewis Lee wrote and produced a movie for the Hallmark Channel, *The Watsons Go to Birmingham* (based on a historical children's novel by Christopher Paul Curtis), Richardson acted in it. As a result, both couples went out for dinner together on a regular basis, and Jackson said, "our relationship healed"—which paved the way toward Lee and Jackson working together again on *Oldboy* and *Chi-Raq* and the AT&T commercials that run incessantly during television coverage of March Madness.

Jackson couldn't be in every single movie that got released, but it wasn't for lack of trying. His appetite for work being what it was, and Hollywood being the fickle type of industry that it is, he was attached to plenty of projects that got announced but never happened.

A handful of the most intriguing: *Truck 44*, about firemen who rob a building by setting fire to it, was canceled after 9/11. In the comedy *Man That Rocks the Cradle*, Jackson would have played a live-in nanny. *Black Phantom* would have starred Jackson and Kevin Hart as double-crossing hit men. George C. Wolfe wanted to direct an update of the 1961 Danish film *Harry and the Butler*, where Jackson would have played a New Orleans jazz musician and roller-coaster mechanic who falls on hard times and lives in a converted train caboose—but when he inherits a big chunk of money, he hires an out-of-work British butler (Michael Caine).

He also turned down some movies that went on to be hits with other actors, such as *Kiss the Girls*, a thriller where Morgan Freeman ultimately costarred with Ashley Judd. "Too misogynistic," Jackson said. Paul Thomas Anderson invited Jackson to play Buck Swope in *Boogie Nights*, but Jackson had already committed to another film; the role went to Don Cheadle (who also starred in *Hotel Rwanda* when Jackson passed on that script). Jackson was attached to *The Matrix* for years but got tired of waiting for the Wachowskis to make the movie happen, so he took other work; when he was unavailable, they cast Laurence Fishburne as Morpheus.

Weirder than any of those never-happened projects was an animated film that was over a decade in the making (and depending on how you think about it, still might not be finished): *Quantum Quest: A Cassini Space Odyssey.* Co-director Harry Kloor was a double PhD (in physics and chemistry) who had a personality better suited to Hollywood than the academy; he touted his multiple black belts in modern martial arts and his Nissan 300ZX Twin Turbo sports car. Kloor wrote for the TV show *Star Trek: Voyager*—and in 1996, he was approached by NASA and JPL to see if he could make an educational film about the Cassini-Huygens mission (a probe, launched in 1997, that ended up in orbit around Saturn to collect massive amounts of data on the gas giant and its rings).

The NASA boffins wanted to do a movie about the journey of a photon, taking a million years to go from the core of the sun to the surface, then eighty-seven minutes to travel through space to bounce off Saturn and reach the Cassini probe. Kloor convinced them that while they might be fascinated by this journey, it wouldn't particularly appeal to kids: Why not turn the photon and other scientific concepts into colorful characters and make an animated movie? NASA bought the pitch, giving him $100,000 in seed money.

Kloor wrote a script for a sixty-five-minute educational movie, called *Quantum Quest*, about the adventures of Dave the Photon; working all his contacts and leaning hard on the educational angle, Kloor recruited an improbably high-caliber cast of Hollywood talent who worked for scale, recording voice performances for under a thousand dollars each, including John Travolta, Christian Slater, Sarah Michelle Gellar, James Earl Jones, and Samuel L. Jackson. Then NASA revised their plans: they wanted the movie to incorporate actual images from the Cassini-Huygens mission. The probe wasn't reaching the neighborhood of Saturn until 2004, however, and it would take years to get usable data after that. Essentially, Kloor said, they wanted him to wait a decade before he made the movie.

So *Quantum Quest* went into hibernation until 2007, when Kloor recruited a co-director experienced in animation, Daniel St. Pierre, and found a studio in Taiwan called Digimax that provided a substantial production budget. Kloor gave the seed money back to NASA with a return on investment. "It's the only project NASA's ever made a profit on," he bragged. "They put a hundred K in and they got two hundred K back, and for years, they kept calling me to say, 'Something's gone wrong, because we got more money.'"

Digimax had no animators, so St. Pierre spent many months in Taiwan, teaching its employees the necessary skills, "training a studio to make this film." The company wanted to do a full-length feature, so Kloor heavily revised his script, expanding it to around one hundred minutes. That meant returning to his actors a decade later and asking them to record new dialogue: most declined (or were never even told about it by their agents). Undeterred, Kloor recruited a second cast, including William Shatner, Mark Hamill, Jason Alexander, Amanda Peet, and Chris Pine. Jackson was one of the few actors to stay with the project.

"Unlike a lot of other people, Sam immediately said, 'Yeah, I'll do it,'" Kloor said. "I think Sam truly cares about kids and he loves science fiction." In both versions of the script, Jackson played a character called Fear, a sentient embodiment of antimatter and the general of the armies of evil, in the service of a villain called the Void. Jackson was agreeable and generous on the day he came to do his voice recording—although he did nickname St. Pierre "Four Eyes" and mock Kloor mercilessly when the writer made the mistake of suggesting a line reading.

Back in Taiwan, the filmmakers edited the material together and worked on character design. St. Pierre said, "The way Sam played Fear was quite serious; he has a sharp, thorny aspect to him. So we put these spikes that could grow out of his shoulders and back and the more excited and agitated he got, the more these spikes would grow."

They were about to start animating *Quantum Quest* when St. Pierre was called into an executive meeting: Digimax wanted to cut the movie down to forty-three minutes. (Digimax was funded by the Taiwanese government; as far as Kloor and St. Pierre could tell, the company fell victim to local politics and had its budget unexpectedly slashed.) They cut the movie to the bone, ending up with forty-nine minutes plus credits. Digimax had the distribution rights in Asia and released the movie there: St. Pierre and Kloor believe it did well in those territories but have no hard data.

In the United States, they had an odd property: a star-studded movie too short to play multiplexes but not educational enough to be booked at most science museums. And the animation, reminiscent of the video game *Skylanders*, was uneven at best. "The Taiwanese team rose to the occasion to the best of their ability," St. Pierre said. "I have nothing bad to say about the artists and technicians." In one more feat of recruiting, they signed up Jon Anderson (of the band Yes) to perform the movie's theme song, "Sing."

The movie played at a few IMAX theaters, including the screens at the Saint Louis Science Center and the Kentucky Science Center, and then vanished, although it remained available to be booked by educational institutions. Kloor says the movie's target audience is "kids in the third, fourth, fifth grade—or college students who are stoned." In the streaming era, *Quantum Quest* became newly valuable and Kloor has been approached about getting it onto Netflix or Amazon—maybe even restoring it to its intended length. "It would cost a fraction of what people normally spend to have a full-length feature," he pointed out.

The Cassini probe was destroyed in 2017, burning itself up in the upper atmosphere of Saturn so it wouldn't contaminate any of the planet's moons. If *Quantum Quest* ever gets completed as a feature film, it will have had a journey even longer than the plutonium-powered orbiter. Its saga is a useful reminder that every single movie Jackson has appeared in has required extraordinary effort by countless professionals across a period of years, which makes it even more extraordinary that he's been in over 140 of them.

Years later, St. Pierre still remembered the advice Jackson gave kids when the filmmakers interviewed him on camera. "Read as much as you can, whatever you can, all the time," Jackson said. "Fill your mind with thoughts and ideas and other people's words and philosophies."

The reason Samuel L. Jackson liked to read was the same reason he liked to act: it was escapism that took him away from his own too-familiar identity, at least for a little while. So he was an avid reader his entire life, favoring science fiction and thrillers and comic books. Phil LaMarr, who appeared with Jackson in *Pulp Fiction*, periodically ran into his fellow actor at the Golden Apple comic-book shop in Los Angeles.

LaMarr remembered a day when he was browsing in the adult section of Golden Apple, with his back to the curtain that separated it from the kid-friendly titles. He was interrupted by a familiar voice: "*A-ha!* Caught you!"

"Oh, goddamn you," LaMarr thought when he turned and saw Jackson. "When you're looking at the Milo Manara stuff, you're not really in a conversational mode."

The store's main room, on the other side of the curtain, contained a full array of superhero comics, including Marvel titles that featured Nick Fury. Jackson was fourteen years old in 1963, when Fury debuted in Marvel comic books in *Sgt. Fury and His Howling Commandos* #1. Nick Fury had an eye patch; he chomped on cigars; sometimes he led a squadron in World War II and sometimes he commanded the immensely powerful spy agency SHIELD. But whether he was drawn as a square-jawed war hero by Jack Kirby or with secret-agent op-art stylings by Jim Steranko, he was a white guy. When the character appeared in a TV movie that aired on Fox in 1998, *Nick Fury: Agent of S.H.I.E.L.D.*, he was played by David Hasselhoff.

That changed in 2001, when Nick Fury appeared in Marvel's Ultimates line, wherein Marvel rebooted their entire continuity, discarding decades of storylines and reimagining favorite characters. (The original versions still existed in their own comics, which was sometimes confusing.) Fury was still a super-savvy high-tech secret agent with an eye patch, but now he was African American. Soon after his Ultimates debut, writer Mark Millar and artist Bryan Hitch made the comic-book character look like the spitting image of Samuel Jackson.

Millar explained the inspiration: "I wanted an African American Nick Fury to be director of SHIELD because the closest thing in the real world to this job title was held by Colin Powell at the time. I also thought Nick Fury sounded like one of those great 1970s blaxploitation names and so the whole thing coalesced for me into a very specific character, an update of the cool American super-spy Jim Steranko had done in the 1970s and based on the Rat Pack, which seemed very 1960s and due for some kind of upgrade."

So why Jackson? Millar said, "Sam is famously the coolest man alive and both myself and artist Bryan Hitch just liberally used him without asking any kind of permission," Millar said. "What we didn't know was that Sam was an avid comic fan and knew all about it."

When Jackson first spotted his own face in an Ultimates book, he was confused: had he given permission for Marvel to use his image and forgotten about it? He called up his agent and manager, who were similarly perplexed. His reps threatened legal action for the unauthorized use of his likeness—but when Marvel offered to cast him as Fury should the character ever appear in a movie, they accepted the offer. It seemed like a cheap way out for the publisher. "You have to remember this was 2001," Millar pointed out. "The idea that this might become a movie seemed preposterous, as Marvel was just climbing out of bankruptcy at the time."

When Marvel Studios, under the leadership of Kevin Feige, started making its own movies instead of just licensing out characters like the X-Men, they kicked off the Marvel Cinematic Universe, or MCU, with *Iron Man* in 2008. In that movie, they kept their promise from years earlier: Jackson appeared as Nick Fury in a brief scene after the credits. "We put it at the end so it wouldn't be distracting," Feige said.

Trying to keep the scene secret, director Jon Favreau filmed it with a skeleton crew and kept it off preview prints; the first time anyone saw it was at the movie's premiere. "It's only fun if it's a surprise," Favreau said.

It turned out that Jackson playing Nick Fury was fun even when people expected him to show up: two years later, the actor signed a long-term deal to play the character in nine MCU movies. He barked orders, he manipulated superheroes into doing what he wanted, he looked formidable in a long leather coat. He gave a jolt to every movie he appeared in—and sometimes he even got to kick ass. Even if Fury, beset by aliens and idiots, wasn't always having a good time, Jackson clearly was. "Who wouldn't want to be a superhero?" he asked.

Once Jackson embodied the Bond-meets-Shaft vision of Nick Fury, it became hard to imagine the character any other way. Marvel, bowing to popular pressure and wanting to diversify their pages, even made the character dark-skinned in the non-Ultimate comics. The somewhat convoluted plot mechanic that made it happen: it was revealed that Nick Fury had fathered a biracial son, known as Nick Fury Jr., who grew up to lose an eye (hello eye patch!) and become director of SHIELD once his father retired. Presto!

When Millar finally met Jackson, the first thing Millar did was tell the actor that he hoped that he didn't mind how he exploited his appearance in the comic. Jackson replied, "Fuck, no, man. Thanks for the nine-picture deal."

Jackson exceeded the bounds of that nine-picture contract, appearing in eleven MCU movies through *Spider-Man: Far from Home* in 2019, but publicly lobbied Marvel to keep him in the role; the studio seemed receptive, even developing a Nick Fury TV series. Jackson declared that he'd be happy to wear the eye patch for another decade, into his eighties: "I could be the Alec Guinness of Marvel movies."

His only regret about the character? "I wish Nick Fury could curse."

African Cats

Joan LeMay.

Jumper (2008)

Roland

MOVIE: 3/10   **SLJ FACTOR:** 7/10   **MINUTES UNTIL HE SHOWS UP:** 12

For a YA novel about a teenager who discovers he has the power to teleport, *Jumper* was quiet and even a bit contemplative. Doug Liman's movie version, in contrast, is loud and fast and empty-headed: it takes the premise of Steven Gould's book and grafts on a global war between the teleporting Jumpers and the Paladins who ruthlessly hunt them down. Intended as the first installment of a franchise that never took off, the movie lacks recognizably human

> *"You are an abomination. Only God should have the power to be all places at all times."*

characters and basic logic, but it has one cool trick: the teleporting fight scenes, where the action can shift from Rome to Tokyo to a Chechnya war zone in split seconds. Those sequences are fun to watch for a while but eventually feel like the action-movie equivalent of channel-flipping late at night, when resting on any program for more than a few seconds will confirm that there's nothing good on.

The movie stars Hayden Christensen (not great, but better than when he's being directed by George Lucas); the performers also include Kristen Stewart (in a small part just before she became famous for *Twilight*), Tom Hulce (his last acting role before he retired in favor of theatrical producing), and Samuel L. Jackson's hair. A glorious crown of brilliant white, the hair evokes the R&B star Sisqó (famous for the 2000 hit "Thong Song"), if Sisqó were a secret government agent. The hair makes Jackson stand out in every scene, even more than the purple lightsaber did in *Star Wars*. His performance as the primary Paladin— sometimes quietly persuasive, sometimes brutally violent—is a menacing portrait of zealotry that almost lives up to the hair.

Iron Man (2008)

Nick Fury (uncredited)
MOVIE: 9/10   SLJ FACTOR: 5/10   MINUTES UNTIL HE SHOWS UP: 125

The cornerstone of the Marvel Cinematic Universe: Robert Downey Jr. as a dissolute playboy tech genius, riding through a war zone in the back of a Humvee with a tumbler of scotch in his hand, bantering with soldiers about his long string of hookups with *Maxim* cover models. *Iron Man* had a lot going for it (including

> *"You think you're the only superhero in the world?"*

excellent supporting work by Jeff Daniels and Gwyneth Paltrow), but it succeeded because of the lightly jaded comedic tone of Downey Jr.'s performance as Tony Stark, and the moviemakers' faith that this B-list comic-book superhero was compelling enough to carry a movie. The movie is so committed to Tony Stark's character that it spends more time showing him at work as an engineer—in two extended sequences, one of them in an Afghanistan cave, one of them in a posh Malibu workshop—than it does putting him in fight scenes in his Iron Man armor.

Samuel L. Jackson appears in a surprise post-credits scene that cemented the notion that when you see a modern blockbuster movie, you should stay until the very end. As Nick Fury, the director of the government agency SHIELD, he steps out of the shadows, sporting a black trench coat and an eye patch. He tells Stark that he's part of a "bigger universe" and says, "I'm here to talk to you about the Avenger Initiative."

When *Iron Man* was made, there was no guarantee that there would be follow-up movies starring Thor and Captain America; the notion of an *Avengers* movie that brought them all together was what producer Kevin Feige called a "pipe dream." (It seemed so improbable that Downey's contract stipulated a bonus in the neighborhood of $50 million if that movie ever got made.) The scene with Nick Fury was, more than anything, a promise to fans: *we want to do more of these movies and they're going to be cool.* In less than thirty seconds, Jackson didn't have much opportunity to establish Nick Fury's character beyond the eye patch. But with a firm yet understated delivery, he pitched the whole notion of the MCU—just as effectively as if he were pitching credit cards in TV commercials.

Cleaner (2008)

Tom Cutler
MOVIE: 7/10   **SLJ FACTOR:** 8/10   **MINUTES UNTIL HE SHOWS UP:** 0
EXPLETIVES NOT DELETED: shit (x7), fucking (x2), fucked

Tom Cutler can sterilize crime scenes and scrub away bloodstains, but he can't clean up the messes in his own life so easily. In a taut film noir, Samuel L. Jackson plays Cutler, a former police officer now running the Steri-Clean company, raising a teenage daughter alone after the murder of his wife. The movie's eighty-eight minutes are filled with plot twists and betrayals, some surprising, some less so. The plot kicks off when he takes care of the bloody viscera of a murder in a suburban mansion, letting himself in with a key left under the mat—but when he comes back to return the key the next day, he discovers that the woman living there (Eva Mendes) has no idea that anything untoward happened in her home.

> *"Death is tragic. But it's also big business. Some people deal with it spiritually, others deal with it legally, but what most people don't know is that when someone dies in your house, it's up to you to clean up the mess."*

Luis Guzmán plays the cop investigating the murder; Ed Harris plays Cutler's former partner. Portraying a man whose orderly habits aren't enough to disperse his personal miasma of regret, Jackson anchors it all with a subtle, restrained performance.

The producers sent Jackson the script because he was considering directing a movie: he decided that he didn't want to direct it, but he did want to play the lead. He suggested Renny Harlin as the director (their third time working together, after *The Long Kiss Goodnight* and *Deep Blue Sea*). That made for a high-efficiency set staffed by seasoned professionals, screenwriter Matthew Aldrich said: "From where I was sitting, the production was clockwork: there was no turmoil, no drama, no emergency lunchtime meetings about where the rest of the money was going to come from."

Aldrich, who was making his first movie, savored the scenes between Jackson and Harris, watching the economy and focus both brought to their work. "They were both really on when it was time to be on, and then they were both off when it was time to be off. They showed up, they executed, they did good work, and then they both went back to their corners."

According to Aldrich, Jackson had very few notes on the screenplay, but he did speak up when necessary. At one production meeting, Aldrich was lobbying for filming in New Jersey, in the cold, clear months between winter and spring. "I was advocating for it to look and feel cold, with ice still on the ground, and I was really hammering on the importance of it."

Jackson stared down the tyro screenwriter and said, "We'll wear coats."

Star Wars: The Clone Wars (2008)

Mace Windu
MOVIE: 5/10   SLJ FACTOR: 3/10   MINUTES UNTIL HE SHOWS UP: 1 (voice)

As drawn by the *Clone Wars* animators, Samuel L. Jackson is a semicircle and a trapezoid: the curve of his bald head and the angular jawbone jutting out from it. His Jedi avatar, Mace Windu, delivers a few inconsequential lines and then disappears: Jackson is here, along with Christopher Lee and Anthony Daniels, to establish some continuity from the *Star Wars* movies to this animated feature. The action

> *"I don't like it, dealing with that criminal scum. This is a dark day for the Republic."*

happens between *Episode II* and *Episode III* of the prequels but most of the recognizable characters (Obi-Wan Kenobi, Anakin Skywalker, etc.) are voiced by new actors.

As a movie, it felt like an extended pilot for a TV series—which, in fact, it was. The show it launched ultimately ran for seven seasons, on the Cartoon Network and other platforms, artfully filling in the gaps between movies and fleshing out a multitude of characters. This initial outing leaned heavily on big action scenes: since so many prequel characters already existed only as CGI, this was less a reinvention and more an adjustment of animation style. The dialogue was clunky, but that was a *Star Wars* tradition. The plot revolved around the Jedi currying favor with Jabba the Hutt by retrieving his kidnapped son, a Huttlet named Rotta. Baby Hutt was cute enough; a decade later, however, Lucasfilm used his prototype to achieve thermonuclear levels of adorable with Baby Yoda.

Lakeview Terrace (2008)

Abel Turner

MOVIE: 8/10   **SLJ FACTOR:** 8/10   **MINUTES UNTIL HE SHOWS UP:** 2
EXPLETIVES NOT DELETED: shit (x5), bullshitting (x2), goddamn (x2), asshole (x2), bitch, pussy

Neighbors yelling at each other through a fence, arguing over whether trees in one backyard violate the property line: that's real-life drama more intense than most Hollywood thrillers. When it happens here, it's particularly potent, because one of the yelling neighbors is Samuel L. Jackson—and he's wielding a chain saw.

> *"You and your little chocolate drop picked the wrong time to move, the wrong place."*

For a while, *Lakeview Terrace* keeps its conflict at a human scale: bright lights shining into a neighbor's window, cigarette butts getting flipped over a fence. Because it's directed by Neil LaBute and it stars Jackson, Patrick Wilson, and Kerry Washington, it's a riveting little drama; the danger builds slowly, like the Los Angeles wildfires that begin the movie miles away and end up next to the cul-de-sac where our main characters live. Jackson is an LAPD cop who takes an immediate dislike to his new neighbors because they're an interracial couple: his being Black upends the expectations of that scenario somewhat. He's the villain of the movie, but Jackson makes him a complicated character, filled with offhanded authority, wounded pride, and a single parent's concern for his children.

LaBute said, "Sam knew a lot more about guns and police work than many other people associated with the movie, because he has a lot of experience and does a lot of research. But it's not just that. It's that he knows that real people aren't two-dimensional."

Early in the shoot, they filmed a scene where his character got out of bed. Jackson promptly got on his knees to pray and LaBute questioned the choice: "Whoa, you think this guy would do that?"

"He prays every day," Jackson flatly told him, an actor who knew the mind of his character.

Eventually *Lakeview Terrace* bows to the demands of its genre and the action escalates to home invasions, fistfights, and shootouts. But before it hits those predictable beats, you see three people trapped in a few square feet of adjoining sun-drenched real estate, revealing their worst selves to each other.

Soul Men (2008)

Louis Hinds
MOVIE: 7/10   SLJ FACTOR: 8/10   MINUTES UNTIL HE SHOWS UP: 0
EXPLETIVES NOT DELETED: shit (x27), goatfucker, motherfucking (x3), fuck (x11), motherfucker (x19), motherfuckers (x2), fucked (x4), goddamn (x2), pussy, fucking (x3), goddammit (x3), bitch (x3), asshole, fucker, dumbshit

Soul Men is the rarest of movies: one where another actor says "motherfucker" more often than Samuel L. Jackson. Bernie Mac utters those four syllables twenty-nine times in one hundred minutes, plus eight uses of "motherfucking," for a total of thirty-seven. Jackson, for once, is outpaced, with just twenty-four uses of "motherfucker" and its variations. They both are maestros of the "motherfucker," but in this movie, Jackson uses the word more like a percussive instrument, executing R-rated paradiddles, while coming out of Mac's mouth, it sounds like a profane aria.

> *"You barely got offstage before you ran your ass back out there. Look, an encore is at the audience's discretion. You're supposed to wait for it!"*

"Nobody said 'motherfucker' or 'fuck' better than Sam and Bernie. Nobody on earth. They should patent the word," testified director Malcolm D. Lee. He admitted that many more uses of the word got snipped out in editing: "It got to the point where we really had to extract as many curses as we could—they were saying 'fuck' with everything. Fucking coffee, fucking this, fucking that, fucking, motherfucking this—after a while, people get tired of it or they get immune to it."

The two actors shared more than a fondness for profanity: what makes this movie work is the joy they take in sharing the screen, playing characters who provoke each other in the way that only old friends can do. Their different acting styles meshed extraordinary well: Jackson's grounded by-the-script approach freed Mac to cut loose. "Keeping Bernie to a script is somewhat difficult," Jackson confessed. They developed a system where Mac would improvise but always return to a designated line, cueing Jackson to continue with the scene as written.

Before this movie, the actors had known each other for years: Jackson used to host an annual charity golf tournament in Bermuda that included a comedy night, hosted by Mac. After Mac became famous, first from the *Original Kings of Comedy* movie in 2000, and then from his eponymous TV show, the old friends wanted to work on a movie together. Their original idea, that they would costar as rival barbecue joint owners, shifted when they were pitched this movie's concept: two backing singers in an R&B group (Marcus Hooks and the Real Deal) are reunited decades after their heyday when the lead singer (played by John Legend) dies. Mac's character Henderson, the prosperous owner of a car wash, longs for his bygone fame, while Jackson's character Hinds, a convicted felon who has found serenity in the philosophy of Lao Tzu, just wants to be left alone. As they drive across the country to perform at the funeral, do they gradually put aside their old grudges and grievances? Of course they do.

Many of the movie's jokes and emotional beats are predictable, but it doesn't matter when you're spending time with Mac and Jackson, watching them in a procession of outlandish stage costumes and era-appropriate wigs. The sweetest scene comes when they're stuck by the side of a highway in the southwest, changing a tire—and then their old hit "I'm Your Puppet" comes on the radio. Henderson starts singing along and doing their old choreography; a grumpy Hinds joins in, reluctantly losing himself in the music, finding himself in the friendship.

Bernie Mac died of complications from pneumonia on August 9, 2008, between the completion of *Soul Men* and its release. He was fifty years old.

The Spirit (2008)

Octopus
MOVIE: 2/10   SLJ FACTOR: 4/10   MINUTES UNTIL HE SHOWS UP: 8

Three comic-book geniuses whose output gradually turned into tracts for their crankish philosophies: Steve Ditko (the co-creator of Spider-Man, later interested mostly in advocating for Ayn Rand's philosophy of objectivism). Dave Sim (whose magnum opus *Cerebus* got swamped by his theology and misogyny). And Frank Miller (author of *Elektra: Assassin*, *Sin City*, and *300*—and increasingly, a toxic right-wing xenophobe).

> *"I'll have to explain why a criminal mastermind like myself doesn't provide his employees with medical insurance."*

One comic-book genius who was a pioneer of the form and by most accounts a mensch: Will Eisner, creator of *The Spirit* and one of Frank Miller's heroes. So after Miller got a co-director credit on Robert

Rodriguez's *Sin City* movie, he adapted *The Spirit* as his first solo directorial project. Miller was aiming for Eisner's mix of humor and hard-boiled detective stories; lacking the necessary cinematic skill to bring it off, he ended up with a hodgepodge of clichés from various genres. While *The Spirit* features some top-notch actresses (Eva Mendes, Scarlett Johansson, Paz Vega) playing femme fatales of various stripes, the best thing about this painfully dull movie is the overall look (human actors overlaid with heavy CGI; lots of black-and-white silhouettes with splashes of color). However, since that's a variation on the *Sin City* approach, it doesn't feel particularly inventive here.

Samuel L. Jackson had long wanted to work with Miller, and even had tried to acquire the rights to one of his properties. He said, "I spent a lot of time in comic book stores, always have, since I was a kid, and I was never able to contact him, but he knew of my interest. When they did *Sin City*, I was talking to Quentin [Tarantino, who directed one segment of it] and I told him, 'How can you do this thing and I'm not in it?' And he told Frank, and Frank was impressed that I even, you know, knew what it was and wanted to be a part of it. So when *The Spirit* came up, he said I was the person that he thought of to play the Octopus."

Jackson bites into the Octopus, the movie's criminal mastermind, like a hungry man with a plate of calamari. And he has one memorable sequence where he marvels at his own freakish laboratory creation: a hopping foot that's sprouted a tiny head. But the whole movie feels awkward and tentative, like an amateur theatrical where you're relieved if everyone remembers their lines. Jackson does fully commit to the outré look of his character (facial tattoos; Morse-code eyebrows; even, in one scene, a Nazi uniform and monocle). If this movie's only strength is its surface appearance, he's determined that nobody will have a better surface than him.

Afro Samurai: Resurrection (2009)

Afro/ Ninja-Ninja
MOVIE: 8/10   SLJ FACTOR: 7/10   MINUTES UNTIL HE SHOWS UP: 0 (voice)
EXPLETIVES NOT DELETED: shit (x10), bitch (x5)

When a Black samurai called Afro slices up everyone standing in his way, the blood flows as freely as the RZA's beats on the soundtrack: it's a hip-hop remix of anime. In the *Afro Samurai* mythology, the warrior with the Number One headband has great power and can be challenged only by the warrior wearing the Number Two headband. In the single season of the TV series, Afro travels from town to town, wearing the Number Two headband and facing off against various foes (brigands; kidnappers; his best friend from childhood, now a cyborg with a teddy-bear head) until he's ready to confront Number One, who killed Afro's father. The stoic Afro is accompanied by his sidekick Ninja-Ninja (possibly a figment of his imagination) who provides loud-mouthed color commentary. Samuel L. Jackson did the voices for both Afro and Ninja-Ninja: with rumbling superego and high-pitched id, Jackson created his own version of the Chuck D./Flavor Flav dynamic. Ninja-Ninja is the more entertaining character, but Jackson said that as an only child, he identified more with the taciturn Afro.

"The legendary Number One headband: it promises power, omnipotence, immortality. But at what cost? One that is greater than any man can imagine and heavier than any man can bear."

This movie comes after the series: the Number One headband is stolen by the bootylicious Lady Sio (voiced by Lucy Liu), who wants revenge on Afro for all the dead bodies he's left in his wake—so once again, he needs to reclaim the headband. The performances by Jackson and Liu give the movie a surprising amount of emotional weight, but the real appeal is visual: Afro's asymmetrical tuft of hair, headbands that ripple in the wind, and monochromatic characters who battle in vividly colored landscapes.

Jackson, also credited as executive producer, couldn't quite believe that his obsessions with anime and Asian cinema had migrated from the fringes of American culture to the mainstream. "It's an amazing time for animation and action movies and comics, all of it," he said. "I'm loving it."

Gospel Hill (2009)

Peter Malcolm
MOVIE: 4/10   SLJ FACTOR: 4/10   MINUTES UNTIL HE SHOWS UP: 1 (visible); 11 (first dialogue)

Veteran character actor Giancarlo Esposito explained his approach to directing *Gospel Hill*: "I've been an actor for 43 years and actors are narcissistic," he said. "However, as a director, I can understand that."

Apparently that perspective helped him recruit an impressive array of talent for his directorial debut, including Angela Bassett, Danny Glover, Taylor Kitsch, Nia Long, Adam Baldwin, Julia Stiles, and the RZA. The movie, a kaleidoscopic view of race and class and family in a South Carolina town of indeterminate size, is ambitious and well-intentioned. It's also superficial and overflowing with clichés. The cast is gifted enough to make many scenes work as vignettes, but the movie is a buffet of empty emotional calories.

> *"Don't hate the sheriff, y'all. Y'all need to pity him, 'cause he can't see what's coming. And it's going to roll right over him, along with everybody else who don't realize we all the same. It's right around the corner, and it's called freedom."*

The *Gospel Hill* plot is built around two events. One is a rezoning decision, prompted by a rapacious corporation that's buying up homes of local families so it can demolish a lower-class neighborhood in favor of a golf course, assisted by an unscrupulous local doctor (Esposito himself). The other is the fortieth anniversary of the assassination of a local civil rights hero, forcing his son (Glover) to confront his father's legacy and how he's spent his life afraid to carry it forward.

Samuel L. Jackson plays that civil rights leader, whose murder went deliberately unsolved by a racist sheriff. He appears fleetingly in black-and-white flashbacks and "archival" footage, being earnest and inspirational, even when he's arrested for a lunch counter sit-in. We see only his public persona, but Jackson brings enough charisma to this cardboard character that we can believe the town would still be mourning him four decades later.

Jackson's character is called Paul Malcolm throughout the movie—until the final credits roll, when his name is rendered as Peter Malcolm. Tempting as it is to expound on this as a sophisticated gambit that plays off the phrase "robbing Paul to pay Peter," it's more likely a sloppy blunder, and not one that would appeal to any actor's narcissism.

Inglourious Basterds (2009)

Narrator (uncredited)
MOVIE: 10/10   SLJ FACTOR: 3/10   MINUTES UNTIL HE SHOWS UP: 28 (voice-over)

By dispensing with the war-movie convention that all characters, even Nazis, speak English to each other, Quentin Tarantino not only found fresh takes on stock scenarios, he exploited linguistic gaps to ratchet up the tension. So the thrilling, bloody *Inglourious Basterds* features a British secret agent (Michael Fassbender) tipping off the enemy because of his shaky German accent, Brad Pitt speaking comedically bad Italian with a Tennessee drawl, and the brilliant SS colonel Hans Landa (an Oscar-winning performance by Christoph Waltz) conducting dazzling multilingual interrogations.

> *"The reason for Hugo Stiglitz's celebrity among German soldiers is simple: as a German enlisted man, he killed thirteen Gestapo officers. Instead of putting him up against the wall, the high command decided to send him back to Berlin to be made an example of. Needless to say, once the Basterds heard about him, he never got there."*

One might say that *Basterds* is about World War II movies more than it's about the war itself, but more precisely, its characters use movies as their weapons of war: Goebbels (the Nazi minister of propaganda) with his German sniper movie *Nation's Pride*; Shosanna (a young Jewish Frenchwoman) with her own short film declaring her revenge on the Nazis, to be projected while she immolates them with reels of nitrate film stock. Tarantino seems like a combatant himself, crafting a narrative that indulges our desire to watch Hitler get assassinated—so thoroughly so, three separate plans to kill him at a movie house all succeed. For Tarantino, cinema wins over history.

Samuel L. Jackson hoped to play the role of Marcel, a Black Parisian working at the movie house Le Gamaar (and the lover of our heroine, Shosanna), but Tarantino wanted somebody younger who actually spoke French. When Tarantino asked Jackson if he knew any Black actors in France, his answer was, "Well, yeah: me! If you take me over there, I'll be there!" Jackson reasoned that he could learn to speak French phonetically; when he failed to convince Tarantino, he successfully lobbied for a small voice-over role instead. Jackson delivers two brief but engaging exegeses, one on the backstory of the fictional character Hugo Stiglitz, the other on the inflammable nature of nitrate film.

Astro Boy (2009)

Zog

MOVIE: 6/10   SLJ FACTOR: 3/10   MINUTES UNTIL HE SHOWS UP: 65 (voice)

Samuel L. Jackson's performance in this animated movie consists of just ten words, divided into four lines of dialogue: "I'm old-school," "Not just people," "The blue stuff," and "No big-gie." That doesn't give an actor much room to

"I'm old-school."

work, but Jackson's rumbling delivery complements the visuals of his character: an enormous robot abandoned on the surface of Earth, given a spark of life by Astro Boy, visiting from the floating utopia of Metro City.

Astro Boy balances the exuberance of a child superhero with the character's melancholy origin: he's a robot, built by a brilliant scientist (Nicolas Cage) as a replacement for his dead son. (In the 1951 manga where the character debuted, he was originally called "The Atom," a particularly evocative name in post-Hiroshima Japan, and one that underlines the character's tragic undertones.) The character here has been aged, from six to thirteen, and Americanized, in both attitude and appearance. While the movie has some low-key charm, it feels muddled and uncertain; it flopped hard enough to put the Hong Kong production studio that made it, Imagi Animation, out of business.

In a movie where many of the jokes feel like they were cobbled together from spare parts left over from other movies, the funniest characters are a blast of zany invention: the three ringleaders of the Robot Revolution Front, haplessly fighting for the rights of automata while hamstrung by their harm-no-humans programming. The RRF crew even get off one great *Pulp Fiction* gag, when they open a briefcase and gaze with awe upon its glowing contents. Then they reveal what was inside the briefcase: a flashlight.

Mother and Child (2010)

Paul

MOVIE: 7/10   SLJ FACTOR: 6/10   MINUTES UNTIL HE SHOWS UP: 3

In a movie full of complicated women trying to figure out their relationships with each other, the two central characters are both very good at their jobs and very bad at connecting with people. They are mother and daughter, although they don't know each other: thirty-seven years ago, Karen (Annette Bening), then only fourteen years old, gave birth to Elizabeth (Naomi Watts) and gave her up for adoption. Bening and Watts are excellent playing demanding women, both of them casually cruel, whose absence from each other's lives has defined the cartography of their interior landscapes. The movie, which also features Kerry Washington and LaTanya Richardson, has emotional complexity but unsteady pacing: many scenes cut off just as they seem to be getting started.

> *"Sometimes when you fall, it's hard to get up."*

Writer-director Rodrigo García lavishes his attention on his female characters; the men in their lives are mostly overwhelmed by their passions and needs. Samuel L. Jackson plays Paul, one of those men, the senior partner at a high-powered Los Angeles law firm who hires Elizabeth. They embark on an affair, but one where she is careful not to lose control. The first time they go to bed together, she mounts him and gives instructions like an offensive coordinator.

"I was really scared, because I wanted the sex scenes to go well. And they were shot right away, there were no massive rehearsals or time to bond," Watts confided—the two actors basically "shook each other's hands and went straight to work." She said that she loved working with Jackson: "He's just the most gentle, careful man. You know, just because he wears a different sweatsuit every day of the week, it doesn't mean he's just that kinda tough guy or street urchin."

In a movie that careens between subtle and didactic, often in the same scene, Jackson maintains an even keel. He plays Paul as a cautious, intelligent man who is plausibly both attracted to Elizabeth and afraid of losing himself in her. His look: a salt-and-pepper beard with a bowtie. "I think he's a very good romantic lead," Garcia said. "A lot of women audience members have found him very attractive as a realistic, almost 'nerdy sexy' version of Sam."

Iron Man 2 (2010)

Nick Fury
MOVIE: 7/10   SLJ FACTOR: 7/10   MINUTES UNTIL HE SHOWS UP: 61

"We still haven't moved Nick Fury into the badass zone," Samuel L. Jackson said when *Iron Man 2* came out. "He's still just kind of a talker." But what a talker: in a movie where Robert Downey Jr.'s Tony Stark spends most of his screen time as the walking embodiment of a midlife crisis crossed with the military-industrial complex, Jackson plays the one authority figure who can get him to sit up straight.

When a hungover Stark blearily wonders whether Fury is just a hallucination, the reply pins his ears back: "I am very real. I'm the realest person you're ever going to meet." Jackson makes Fury imposing and impervious to mockery, even when Stark asks whether he should be looking at the eye or the patch.

"Sir! I'm going to have to ask you to exit the doughnut!"

Iron Man 2, like most Hollywood sequels, was bigger, louder, and more bombastic than the original. Compare the bad guys: in the original *Iron Man*, Jeff Bridges's Obadiah Stane put on a suit of armor to fight Stark, but otherwise seemed like a reasonably normal corporate executive. Here, Mickey Rourke's Ivan Vanko is a Russian tech genius covered with tattoos, accessorized with electric whips, gold teeth, and a white cockatoo, and suffering from a vitamin deficiency that can be counteracted only with extensive chewing of scenery. But it's easy to forgive the movie's excesses as overexuberance: it was trying to stuff two hundred pounds of blockbuster into a hundred-pound suit.

Unthinkable (2010)

H

MOVIE: 5/10   SLJ FACTOR: 8/10   MINUTES UNTIL HE SHOWS UP: 3 (in a surveillance photograph), 4 (in the flesh)
EXPLETIVES NOT DELETED: fuck (x4), fucking (x2), fucks

The thrilling but morally vacuous question at the core of *Unthinkable*: If a terrorist planted a nuclear bomb in an American city, would you torture him to find out where it was? That fictional scenario has long been a favorite device for torture apologists and writers of the TV series *24* (but I repeat myself). It's so well-worn, *Unthinkable* needs to raise the stakes by having the terrorist hide *three* nuclear

"Are you ready for this? No, no one ever is."

devices and by making its government-sanctioned torture particularly graphic. While characters in this movie argue both sides of the issue like they're on a high-school forensics team, the filmmakers stack the deck: to save millions of fictional lives in ninety-seven quick-paced minutes, they make torture abhorrent but necessary.

This straight-to-video production was done on such a low budget that the government's secret interrogation center is very obviously a high-school gymnasium. But the producers wisely spent their money on a talented cast: Carrie-Anne Moss (the protagonist, an FBI counterterrorism expert with a conscience), Stephen Root, Michael Sheen, Martin Donovan, and in the crucial role of the interrogator, Samuel L. Jackson. His role, the man known as H, is written as an enigma in a sweater vest. He's a torturer who loves his children—that's a pop-culture cliché—but H is also a de facto prisoner of the CIA who has the impunity to assault other federal officers, a man who inventively inflicts pain but doesn't appear to be a sadist, and a cynic who believes deeply in the value of his job. Jackson skillfully binds these contradictions together in a performance that is more than the sum of its parts: he makes American black-site horrors all too human.

The Other Guys (2010)

P. K. Highsmith
MOVIE: 4/10   SLJ FACTOR: 8/10   MINUTES UNTIL HE SHOWS UP: 1
EXPLETIVES NOT DELETED: shit

Here's how it starts: Dwayne "The Rock" Johnson and Samuel L. Jackson play Danson and Highsmith, action-movie versions of New York City cops. "Tell me again why I decided to get on this roof?" the Rock asks, clinging to the top of a getaway vehicle.

"I think you can chalk that up to bad life choices," Jackson replies via walkie-talkie, driving the car in hot pursuit. In his first minute of screen time, Jackson shoots his gun, crashes his car into a double-decker tourist bus, and shouts, "Did someone call 9-1-holy shit?"

> *"You have the right to remain silent, but I want to hear you scream!"*

Less than fifteen minutes later, both cops overconfidently jump off a twenty-story building without a good landing spot, smack into a city sidewalk. With them dead, that leaves the rest of the movie to be carried by a more hapless pair of cops: Will Ferrell as an NYPD forensic accountant and Mark Wahlberg as an officer who got the nickname "Yankee Clipper" after he mistakenly shot Derek Jeter. Ferrell and Wahlberg are consistently entertaining actors, but they have very little onscreen chemistry here. They especially suffer in comparison with Johnson and Jackson: while Danson and Highsmith are clichés walking on two legs, they're a lot more fun to watch than the rest of this movie.

The Other Guys gets off a few good jokes—a discussion of lion-versus-tuna warfare, a schoolgirl who comes for a ride-along in a high-speed police chase and gets flung around the back seat of the car—but most of the time, director Adam McKay is going through the motions. The one part with real passion is the animated infographic that runs through the closing credits, laying out statistics on just how bad American income equality is, an eye-popping sequence that has almost nothing to do with the movie we just saw. Five years later, McKay directed *The Big Short* (and won an Oscar for co-writing the screenplay), about the financial crisis of 2008—clearly, that's the movie he wanted to be making.

The Sunset Limited (2011)

Black
MOVIE: 5/10   SLJ FACTOR: 7/10   MINUTES UNTIL HE SHOWS UP: 0
EXPLETIVES NOT DELETED: shit (x7), bullshit (x2), shitting (x2), bitch (x2)

The Sunset Limited locks three men in a room, but only two of them appear on camera. Tommy Lee Jones directs and plays a white man named White; Samuel L. Jackson, cast as the Black man named Black, discusses theology and epistemology and life with him. The third man is Cormac McCarthy, author of the play that this TV movie adapts—he provides the relentless stream of words, reaching for bleak poetry but more often hitting the level of late-night dorm bullshit.

> *"The light is all around you but you don't see nothing but shadow."*

White is a college professor who, convinced of the futility of life, throws himself onto the tracks of an oncoming train. Black is a religious ex-convict who saves him, takes him back to his cheap apartment, and tries to convince him that life has greater meaning, or at least delay his suicide. After an hour and a half of circular arguments, White hits Black with a firehose blast of nihilism and exits, presumably to kill himself, leaving Black alone with his Bible and his doubts.

The movie hints that Black might be a guardian angel who has pulled off an according-to-Hoyle miracle in the rescue of White, but then skitters away from that notion. Similarly, the suicide attempt apparently happened at the 155th Street subway station in New York City, but the train that almost killed White is the Sunset Limited, an Amtrak line that runs between New Orleans and Los Angeles. This mood of theatrical unreality might have worked onstage but doesn't translate well to the screen.

In a scenario where he's physically constrained, Jackson carefully employs his hands—clasping them, pointing, opening his palms for benediction—making even small gestures feel significant. Jones is even stiller, letting his weatherbeaten face tell the story of a man who's been battered into despair. Together, the actors gracefully dance through the talky script like old minuet partners. *The Sunset Limited* reunited SLJ and TLJ a decade after *Rules of Engagement*, and they eagerly seized the opportunity to film a philosophical play with a deluxe budget.

"We rehearsed it for eight or nine days while they built the set," Jackson said. Once they started shooting, they ripped through eleven to fourteen pages of screenplay every day.

Jones said, "The HBO people stopped by for a few days to make sure we weren't wasting their money, but they mostly sat quietly in the corner with their hands folded in their laps. We worked out the language, I diagrammed the camera angles, and then directed the movie. What is there not to be happy about?"

Thor (2011)

Nick Fury
MOVIE: 5/10   SLJ FACTOR: 4/10   MINUTES UNTIL HE SHOWS UP: 113

Thor has a strong cast, and its sci-fi Wagner schtick is fitfully entertaining, but the franchise wouldn't hit its stride until its third installment, when Taika Waititi, the director of *Thor: Ragnarok*, surgically grafted a sense of humor onto the Thunder God. This movie is, however, a showcase for actors in eye patches, since it also features Sir Anthony Hopkins as the All-Father Odin, patriarch of the Norse gods who plucked out his right eye in exchange for divine wisdom. Sadly, Odin never faces off against Nick

"Legend tells us one thing, history another. But every now and then we find something that belongs to both."

Fury for a one-eyed staring contest: Fury, once again, doesn't appear until after the credits roll. SHIELD plays a substantial role in *Thor*, but its man on the scene in New Mexico is Clark Gregg's Agent Coulson (or as Thor calls him in the movie's best line, "son of Coul").

Jackson's appearance here as Fury feels particularly pro forma. He scowls and looks imposing in a dark suit, but while he can stop men dead in their tracks with a single unblinking eye, he can't do much to salvage this movie in its final ninety seconds. The best thing about his scene is that Nick Fury unveils the Tesseract (which proves to be an important MacGuffin in a whole skein of Marvel movies) by popping open a metal suitcase to reveal the magical artifact in all its iridescent blue glory. Ever since *Pulp Fiction*, any time Samuel Jackson opens up a suitcase and there's something glowing inside, we want to know what it is; this time we get to find out.

Captain America: The First Avenger (2011)

Nick Fury
MOVIE: 8/10   SLJ FACTOR: 6/10   MINUTES UNTIL HE SHOWS UP: 112

Stan Lee, Jack Kirby, Steve Ditko, and the other inventors of Marvel superhero comics were geniuses. They were also products of their era, and some aspects of the comic books they created in the 1960s have aged better than oth-
ers. For example, their heroes are overwhelmingly male and white; it took decades for the Invisible Girl to change her name to the Invisible Woman, stop getting routinely kidnapped by bad guys, and assert herself as the most powerful member of the Fantastic Four. Their comics seemed to have more white characters with "Black" in their superhero handles (e.g., Black Bolt, the Black Widow) than actual Black characters.

"At ease, soldier."

Captain America (created by Kirby and Joe Simon) has aged surprisingly well: despite periodic misgivings over the decades, most people have settled on the notion that he stands for belief in the best ideals of the USA, not unthinking acceptance of everything the country does.

His comic books first appeared in 1941 (just before the United States entered World War II); their popularity waned after the war ended and they were canceled. So when he was revived in 1964, the backstory was that Steve Rogers (the Captain) had been frozen in a block of ice and missed two decades of American history. That was poignant—but by the time of this movie (a fleet-footed origin story set in a comic-book version of World War II), the gap between V-E Day and the present era had become heartbreaking. As Nick Fury tells a bewildered Steve Rogers, standing bewildered in the middle of twenty-first-century Times Square, "You've been asleep, Cap, for almost seventy years."

(In the comics, Nick Fury also has a backstory as a World War II soldier, leading the Howling Commandos—the explanation for his being fit and youthful decades later is something called the Infinity Formula, which is apparently *much* better than Grecian Formula.)

Samuel L. Jackson is onscreen for less than a minute and has only a few lines of dialogue, but he has the gravitas to deliver the news to Steve Rogers that everyone he ever knew and cared about is gone. Blunt but sympathetic, Jackson has a sufficiently commanding presence that he doesn't have to introduce himself: Captain America immediately knows he's speaking with a superior officer. And from the color of Jackson's skin, it's obvious that the world has changed since 1945 in ways that extend past the Lindy Hop going out of style.

Arena (2011)

Logan
MOVIE: 4/10 **SLJ FACTOR:** 4/10 **MINUTES UNTIL HE SHOWS UP:** 1
EXPLETIVES NOT DELETED: fuck (x3), assholes, shit, motherfuckers, pussy-whipping, fucking, bitch, bullshit

Not so much a movie as it is a delivery system for blood, violence, and tits, *Arena* is centered on the Death Games, a modern gladiator league that kidnaps its participants and then pits them in lethal combat against each other, live-streaming the matches around the world. Director Jonah Loop has a good eye and the screenplay has a surprising number of grace notes (in this context, "surprising number" = "any number greater than zero"), but the only person in this lurid exploitation flick who looks like he's having fun is Samuel L. Jackson.

"In my mind, just watching those poor fools lose wasn't enough, so I've upped the ante."

His character runs the Death Games start-up (with the help of two sexy young women whose duties range from managing the network servers to staging S&M shows). He wears velvet and leather, nibbles on decadent meals, and blithely oversees a snuff-film assembly line. But he's never happier than when he gets an opportunity to say the *Cool Hand Luke* line "What we've got here is failure to communicate": Jackson does his best impression (misquoting the line slightly) and then shouts with glee, "I have always wanted to say that! I love Strother Martin!" Jackson, who had played roles like this villain before, brought nothing new to this one: apparently, he made the reasonable decision that *Arena* was not a project that demanded invention or nuance.

Lee Herrera.

uentin Tarantino and Samuel L. Jackson didn't realize right away how much they had in common. Although Tarantino is fourteen years and four months younger than Jackson, he also is an only child who spent the earliest years of his life in Tennessee, living with his grandparents. (Tarantino's movies are, not coincidentally, riddled with Tennessee references, from the origin of Butch's gold watch in *Pulp Fiction* [a general store in Knoxville] to the steak dinner shared by Major Marquis and the Hangman in *The Hateful Eight* [in Chattanooga].) Although Jackson got excellent grades in high school while Tarantino dropped out of the ninth grade, they both spent the better parts of their childhoods inside their own heads, obsessed with comic books and movies.

Tarantino is capable of carrying on normal human conversations about subjects other than movies, but really, he's just marking time until the moment when he can have an in-depth discussion of obscure Canadian horror films or the westerns of William Witney. So the moment when Tarantino and Jackson bonded, beyond a professional appreciation of each other's talent, centered on movies. It came one day on the set of *Pulp Fiction*. Tarantino passed by Jackson's trailer and heard the distinctive sound effects of a Hong Kong action movie; the genre was still unfamiliar to most Americans, but Jackson had brought a stash of videos to work.

"He couldn't believe I was watching this movie," Jackson said. After that, Tarantino visited every day to see what was playing at the Samuel Leroy Jackson Repertory Film Theater. And the director blew Jackson's mind by arranging for Sonny Chiba, star of dozens of kung fu movies, including *The Street Fighter*, to visit the set.

Tarantino could afford to be relaxed: the *Pulp Fiction* shoot was going extremely well. Fittingly for a movie that plays with time, they began on the first day by filming the ending: the diner scene, marked by Jackson's virtuoso performance. "He's doing this almost *Richard III* storm sequence kind of thing—except he's in a coffee shop, bent over, sitting in a booth," Tarantino said of Jackson. "He's dominating the entire room while never getting up from that booth. Sam's just really remarkable."

Jackson also thought of *Pulp Fiction* in theatrical terms, believing that Tarantino had bridged the stage and the cinema. He favorably compared Tarantino to another writer he was familiar with: playwright August Wilson. "They're both very literary and expository in getting ideas out there and moving an audience in a certain way oratorically rather than visually," Jackson said. "Doing monologues is so rare in movies. Watching *Jaws*, and seeing that shark story that Robert Shaw does, I always wanted to do that. It's really scary in a way. You don't have to depend on another actor being able to carry his emotional weight with yours. It's a great flying-by-the-seat-of-your-pants feeling."

When the *Pulp Fiction* shoot concluded, Jackson's wrap gift for his director was a token of their shared love of blaxploitation: a framed poster for the 1974 movie *Truck Turner*, starring Isaac Hayes and Yaphet Kotto, about an NFL player who becomes a bounty hunter.

After the release of *Jackie Brown* in 1997, Jackson went fifteen years without a significant part in a Tarantino film. They remained friendly; Tarantino would regularly invite Jackson over for movie nights at his house. And the director would send Jackson his screenplays, even when there wasn't a designated role for the actor. Jackson devoured them—"I read so much shit between books, comic books, scripts, and I'm usually 20 pages ahead of most writers because I know where they're going, but I'm never that way when I'm reading his stuff"—and when there were no obvious parts for him in *Kill Bill: Vol. 2* and *Inglourious Basterds*, he made a point of finding small roles to play so he could remain part of the Tarantino repertory company.

Jackson loved being on most movie sets, but Tarantino's were by far his favorite. Tarantino wouldn't let anybody bring electronic devices onto the set: no phones, no iPads, nothing with an on-off switch. "So when he says 'cut,' you talk to each other," Jackson enthused. Or between takes, Tarantino would hold forth about how he would have cast his movie if it had been made in a different decade, or the actors would have an impromptu dance party to the music playing over the PA. In the evenings, Tarantino would host movie nights or beer busts. "It's all about the collaboration," Jackson said. "I'd walk through fire for Quentin."

When Tarantino started writing the screenplay for *Django Unchained*, his 2012 western film, he thought he was writing a starring vehicle for Jackson: he planned to shoot a few scenes establishing Django's origin story as an enslaved person, and then the main action would happen after the Civil War, with Jackson playing an older Django. But the more Tarantino worked on it, the more he felt like he was skipping the most important part of the story: he needed to focus on a younger Django directly taking on slavery. Forty-four-year-old Jamie Foxx took the role of Django (after Will Smith turned it down).

After he sent the script to Jackson, Tarantino called him up. "As you can see, I kind of went a different way with the character," he explained. "You're about fifteen years too old for him."

"Yeah, I noticed that."

"So what do you think about Stephen?"

"What do you mean, what do I think about him?"

"Do you have any problem playing him?"

"Do I have any problem playing the most despicable Negro in cinematic history?" Jackson replied. He did not. He believed "there are some people who, when they call you, you don't care what they're doing—you just drop your shit and do it."

Jackson threw himself into the villainous role of Stephen, who runs the Candieland plantation for Calvin Candie (played by Leonardo DiCaprio). At first blush, Stephen appears to be a decrepit seventy-six-year-old house slave, bowing and scraping before Calvin, but he proves to be the conniving, torturing power behind the throne. Jackson explained, "Calvin's major concern is just to go out and stage Mandingo fights. Stephen, when you see him, he's sitting there writing checks. So he's the guy who makes that plantation run. Within those 75 miles that are Candieland, he understands he's king. He can do anything he wants to there. Even the white people obey him. But if he sets foot outside that 75 miles, he's just another slave in the South. He's smart enough to know he needs to keep up his own kingdom. The institution of slavery works for him."

Richard Gladstein, who worked as a producer or executive producer on three Tarantino-Jackson collaborations, observed that while Tarantino and Jackson spent considerable time discussing and rehearsing a movie, once they were on the set, they spoke very little. They were so in sync, they could communicate most of what they needed to say with eye contact and gestures and explosions of laughter. Gladstein said that of all Tarantino's actors, "Quentin provides Sam the most leeway in terms of slight alterations to the dialogue."

On *Django*, Tarantino was particularly impressed with an idea Jackson had for a scene where Stephen would repeat key words as Calvin

Candie gave a speech, like an antebellum hype man. "He knew exactly what line to do it," Tarantino raved, "so he wouldn't fuck up Leo or his monologue or his rhythms."

Tarantino left one particularly harrowing scene on the cutting-room floor, where Stephen tortured Django, trying to burn off his nipples with a hot poker. "People hate you enough," Tarantino told him. "I don't know if I want people trying to kill you on the street."

Jackson was disappointed: "I took time to do it and I felt great when I was doing it and I know what kind of impact it would have on an audience!" he complained. "When we were shooting it, I was thinking, 'This is going to be *awesome* when people see this.'"

In early 2014, a year after the release of *Django Unchained*, Tarantino sent Jackson a new script—but warned him that because it had already leaked online, he wasn't going to make the movie. He promised, "I'll write you something else."

Jackson dove into the screenplay for *The Hateful Eight* anyway. He knew that when he read a Tarantino script, "inside of this great thing is something that's going to challenge me, characters that have different personalities, intelligence, and intellect. They're all smart guys, but some are smarter in street ways, some are smarter in life ways, some are smarter intellectually. Some are just smart in the fact that they know how to exist in a world that's chaotic. For me, that's always exciting, and it's always a compliment that he thinks I can make them live."

Actor Tim Roth, also a member of the Tarantino repertory company, said, "It feels, to me, that Quentin's leading man is Sam. And I think that's an extraordinary circumstance, for a white man, however talented, to be able to write for a leading man, a Black actor, and give him such a range of roles."

The character designated for Jackson, Major Marquis Warren, was particularly smart and memorable—but what stung for Jackson was that Marquis was, in many ways, the old-fashioned western hero that he had been fantasizing about playing since he was a child watching cowboy movies in Chattanooga: a bounty hunter in Wyoming armed with a six-shooter and his wits. He called up Tarantino and demanded, "Dude, how are you not going to make this movie?"

Fortunately, Tarantino changed his mind. Most of the action in *The Hateful Eight* takes place in a log cabin full of characters with suspect motives, all seeking shelter from a snowstorm together. Tarantino's inspiration was old episodes of western TV shows where a viewer didn't know whether the guest star wore a white hat or a black hat (and apparently, John Carpenter's 1982 sci-fi movie *The Thing*)—but the central theme was race in America, and the through line from the Civil War to the twenty-first century. The skin color of Jackson's character, a Civil War veteran, wasn't an incidental detail: it forced everyone trapped in the room to confront how much divided them, even after the war nominally ended at Appomattox.

Tarantino said, "This could almost be a post-apocalyptic movie, to some degree or another. It's like this frozen wasteland, and the apocalypse has destroyed every semblance of their society and their way of life, and these survivors are huddled together in this pitiless wasteland shelter. And suddenly they're all blaming each other for the apocalypse, but the apocalypse *is* the Civil War. But that wasn't what I was necessarily thinking about on page 72 in my bedroom when I was writing it."

The shoot, largely on location in freezing cold Colorado, was arduous, but the cast (which also included Jennifer Jason Leigh, Bruce Dern, and Walton Goggins) bonded so thoroughly that they kept a group text as the "Haters" going long after the movie wrapped. Jackson got to sink his teeth into his most epic monologue yet in a Tarantino film, where his character attempts to relate an anecdote so vividly that it'll provoke Dern's character into shooting him. In a movie where everybody's telling stories about themselves and the audience has to judge which ones are true, the winners are the people who are the best at telling stories. Jackson told Tarantino, "This is my *Iceman Cometh* and that's my Hickey monologue."

Jackson wasn't in the habit of showering his directors with praise: "I heard him say action and I heard him say cut" was how he dismissed one. Maybe that was because most of them suffered in comparison to Tarantino. Their two decades of collaboration made Jackson unusually effusive. "There's so much to say about Quentin: the passion, the knowledge, the joy and enthusiasm while he's working, the sheer cinematic encyclopedia that he is, is just joyful. The poetry of his words is infectious. I love speaking his dialogue," Jackson said. "There's just something very natural in our connection in terms of his art and my talent that mesh in a beautiful and wonderful and creative, joyous, ecstatic, orgasmic kinda way."

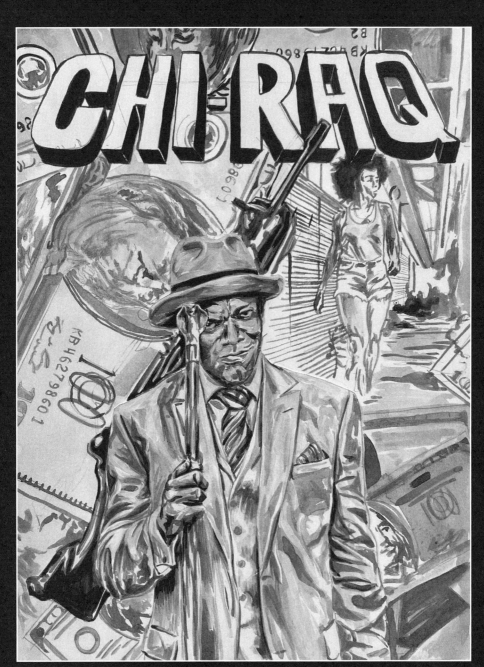

Dionis Ortiz.

The Avengers (2012)

Nick Fury

MOVIE: 9/10   **SLJ FACTOR: 8/10**   **MINUTES UNTIL HE SHOWS UP: 1**

Samuel L. Jackson defended *The Avengers* against critics, but he understood what genre of movie he had made: "Noise and toys, that's all it is," he conceded. Nevertheless, in a movie where Nick Fury fires a rocket launcher at a fighter jet and jumps out of a helicopter that's on fire, Jackson's best scene is a quiet one. Agent Phil Coulson has just been killed, so Fury confronts Iron Man and Captain America with a bloody handful of vintage trading cards owned by Coulson—not thundering at the two of them, but softly speaking of the old-fashioned values

> *"I recognize that the Council has made a decision, but given that it's a stupid-ass decision, I've elected to ignore it."*

of heroism and shaming them into working together. He neglects to tell them that the cards weren't on Coulson's person when he died.

As *Avengers* writer-director Joss Whedon said, "The idea that Nick Fury lost someone we all know he was close to, that we love, and then his first thought was to go to that guy's locker, take his prized possession, and cover it in blood so he could trick the heroes of the movie into being the heroes of the movie—I'm sorry, that's a guy I love."

Whedon did masterful work in *The Avengers*, bringing together six disparate superheroes from four film franchises and making the result feel like an organic delight rather than a corporate imperative. He yanked Nick Fury from the post-credits shadows and put him at the dead center of the movie: partially for the sensible plot reason that he had recruited all those heroes into the Avengers Initiative, and partially because Jackson could handle both character subtleties and the noise-and-toys moments. "He does look so good with a rocket launcher," Whedon said wistfully.

Whedon added, "We always wanted him to be pushing the boundaries of what is right, so that we could believe he might do something truly terrible. And in fact, he is lying and manipulating everybody."

Even though he's in a comic-book movie, Jackson delivers something in *The Avengers* that we hadn't seen in his previous four appearances as Nick Fury: moral chiaroscuro, dressed up in a black trench coat.

Meeting Evil (2012)

Richie

MOVIE: 3/10   SLJ FACTOR: 5/10   MINUTES UNTIL HE SHOWS UP: 7
EXPLETIVES NOT DELETED: shit, fuckbeast, cunt, cocktease, pussy, fucking (x7), bitch (x2)

John (Luke Wilson) is having a bad day: he got fired from his job, his marriage is on the rocks because of his infidelity, and he has a stack of unpaid bills (helpfully stamped *FINAL NOTICE* on the envelope). But it's about to get worse: when the dapper stranger Richie (Samuel L. Jackson) knocks on his door, asking for help getting his car started, John complies—and somehow finds himself in the passenger seat for an over-the-top killing spree. Richie murders just about anyone who crosses his path, for reasons as trivial as their wanting to see an ID with a credit card. *Meeting Evil* looks like a sun-baked neo-noir, but it plays like a horror movie that stars a shark or a Babadook who just keeps coming. It's constantly ominous, but hardly ever entertaining.

> *"People like that just want to be fooled—it's their nature. Once you know that, you can take anything you want from them."*

Jackson looks sharp in a suit and fedora and his performance is a Tootsie Pop with a chewy center of menace—even when he's being superficially charming, you can taste the underlying threat. He makes every individual moment believable, but he can't find the underlying logic of a role that has none. Writer-director Chris Fisher planned this movie as a straight-to-video production costing roughly a million dollars; the presence of Jackson and Wilson elevated it, but not as much as one might have hoped. "I would have been interested in seeing Sam play the sad sack and Luke play the maniac," Fisher said, which actually might have shaken up the film's rote feeling—he should have fought for that.

Wilson got cast after Jackson; he believed he made the cut because they had played golf together a few times, but he was still intimidated. Wilson compared the experience to acting with Gene Hackman in *The Royal Tenenbaums*: "You have to concentrate and not be in awe of this person." In an early scene, however, an angry Wilson was supposed to shout at Jackson and knock his fedora from his head. But when the cameras were rolling, Wilson didn't want to lay his hands on Jackson's person, or even his wardrobe: "I just yelled at him, and the director was like, 'Did you forget to knock Sam's hat off?' I was like, 'No, I just couldn't bring myself to do it.'"

The Samaritan (2012)

Foley
MOVIE: 7/10   **SLJ FACTOR:** 7/10   **MINUTES UNTIL HE SHOWS UP:** 1
EXPLETIVES NOT DELETED: shit (x4), goddamn (x3), fucking (x2), fucked-up

A neo-noir thriller should have a quality twist, and *The Samaritan* features a big one. Admittedly, it's been used in other movies, but it's particularly effective here because of its placement: we discover a shocking secret halfway through the movie, not in the closing minutes. So instead of throwing a plot grenade and then rolling the credits, director David Weaver (who wrote the screenplay with Elan Mastai) forces his characters to confront the past and fumble their way through the consequences.

Samuel L. Jackson stars as the former con man Foley, just done serving a twenty-five-year prison term (an angry mark forced him to murder his partner in crime). Most

> "If you keep on doing what you've always done then you'll keep on being what you've always been. I used to share a cell with a guy who had those words tattooed across his chest in Japanese characters. After ten years, the guy gets out: a week later, he gets himself killed for being what he'd always been. Those words are still on his skin, buried in a box somewhere."

of his friends have died or moved away; the few who remain want nothing to do with him. While Foley tries to go straight, even getting a construction job, the son of his dead partner (Luke Kirby) keeps trying to recruit him for an $8 million grift.

The movie's a genre exercise, but a skillful one. Weaver takes equal care with the mechanics of the con and the mundane details of Foley's lonely life in Toronto. (For once, the city plays itself, rather than standing in for New York.) Jackson gives a solid, unflashy performance as Foley; a few moments, where he indulges himself in Jacksonian righteous indignation, feel schticky, but mostly he plays a man who has come out of prison with all his glib charm stripped away and is trying to figure out what remains. Jackson's surrounded by an excellent cast, especially Tom Wilkinson as a crime boss and Ruth Negga as a young woman who needs saving but has some secrets of her own.

A tough-minded plot builds to a satisfyingly bloody climax, but according to Jackson, the original script went even further. "It had a much darker ending, which was the thing that totally sold me on it when I read it," he said. "They pulled back on it in a lot of ways, which upset me. It's flawed for those reasons: the film needs to be full bore."

The title refers to a particular con that is central to the movie—but it's no accident that it strips the "Good" out of "Good Samaritan." In this movie, the impulse toward charity is constantly mixed up with base motives and dark consequences.

Django Unchained (2012)

Stephen
MOVIE: 9/10   **SLJ FACTOR: 9/10**   **MINUTES UNTIL HE SHOWS UP:** 85 (silent), 88 (in full effect)
EXPLETIVES NOT DELETED: titty, motherfucker (x3), goddamn (x4), shit (x3), bitch (x5), fucked (x2), motherfuckers (x2), fuck, fucking, shitfire

A small but telling detail from *Django Unchained*: writer-director Quentin Tarantino made the price of slaves unusually low but the bounties for dead men comparatively high, underscoring the bleak moral of many spaghetti westerns, that life is cheap but death is profitable.

Tarantino had wanted to make a spaghetti western for years, but what inspired this movie was his search for a setting that would best exemplify the nihilistic violence he was seeking. "Do you want to have that pitiless a landscape? Do you want that surreal quality?

"Your black ass been all them motherfuckers at the big house could talk about for the last few hours. Seem like white folk ain't never had a bright idea in they life was coming up with all kinds of ways to kill your ass."

Do you want a West that will put the characters to their extremes? In thinking what could fit the bill for that, I thought: *a slave in the antebellum South."*

While some critics argued that placing a genre film in that setting trivialized its horrors, Tarantino was looking for the same revisionist catharsis that he had found in *Inglourious Basterds*: these films are for anyone who agrees that the most satisfying thing a movie can do with history's greatest villains is to kill them in explosions of blood and fire.

Freed slave Django (Jamie Foxx) and silver-tongued Schultz (Christoph Waltz) team up as bounty hunters in 1858 and then go to free Django's wife Broomhilda (Kerry Washington), enslaved on the Mississippi cotton plantation Candieland—owned by Calvin Candie (Leonardo DiCaprio) and run by his aged, loyal slave Stephen (Samuel L. Jackson). The sequence where they ride into Candieland has the same foreboding air as *Apocalypse Now*, with our heroes traveling toward the headwaters of evil.

To play Stephen, Jackson made the provocative decision to darken his own skin tone, both for maximum contrast with his snow-white hair and to emphasize the character's unadulterated African bloodlines. On camera, Jackson employs an astonishing collection of penetrating glares, expressing disbelief, contempt, and calculated sadism, as necessary. To play a seventy-six-year-old, Jackson uses all his physical technique to minimize his robust six-foot-three frame and spends most of the movie leaning on a cane and quivering with palsy—which makes it genuinely shocking when he casts aside the cane and stands up straight, fully revealing himself as a master manipulator. As ever, Tarantino favors characters who are playing roles themselves.

"I love fucking Stephen," Jackson said. "It's awesome to be unapologetically evil."

Adventures in Zambezia (2013)

Tendai

MOVIE: 3/10   SLJ FACTOR: 4/10   MINUTES UNTIL HE SHOWS UP: 2 (voice)

Adventures in Zambezia targets the demographic of young children who like birds, animated movies, and bright colors. Parents who put it on to distract their kids won't be hauled off by Child Protective Services, but it's not well executed. The story drags; the jokes don't land; the computer-generated animation looks cheap. The plot is fine: Kai, a young peregrine falcon, moves to Zambezia, a utopian city in a hollow tree where almost every species of African bird lives in harmony. There he joins the city's elite force of avian defenders, the Hurricanes, and has to protect Zambezia from an evil lizard antagonist and broker a peace with the previously spurned marabou storks. Samuel L. Jackson plays Kai's overprotective father with restraint and sincerity. (He turns out to be co-founder of the Hurricanes, along with Kai's mother, who died in the line of duty.)

The movie, known just as *Zambezia* elsewhere in the world, was the first feature-length film from a small South African animation studio; you can respect their ambition while conceding that the results of their labor don't compare well to Hollywood movies such as *Rio* and *Zootopia*. The movie features the voices of some big-name actors, including Jackson, Leonard Nimoy, and Jeff Goldblum (who gives the film's most amusing performance, as the distracted commander of the Hurricanes)—which wasn't sufficient to get it into movie theaters in Canada, the UK, or the United States. Newbie director Wayne Thornley was nevertheless thrilled to work with the stars, citing one in particular: "I'm not sure how he does it, but when Samuel L. Jackson swears at you, you feel sort of honored."

Turbo (2013)

Whiplash
MOVIE: 6/10   SLJ FACTOR: 3/10   MINUTES UNTIL HE SHOWS UP: 26 (voice)

It's a movie law: if you're making a feature film about a snail that gains super-speed and wants to compete in the Indianapolis 500, then at some point a character needs to utter the line "There's nothing in the rule book that says a snail can't enter the race!" *Turbo*, as assembly-line children's entertainment, delivers on that

"Your trash talk is needlessly complicated!"

front. It doesn't, however, succeed in its efforts to launch a new catch-phrase: for some reason, "Snail up!" never caught on.

Turbo hews to the DreamWorks Animation formula: a goofy premise executed just well enough that parents don't gouge their own eyes out with their car keys, voiced by lots of well-known names. Ryan Reynolds plays the lead snail, Theo (aka Turbo), with Paul Giamatti as his anxious brother; the cast also includes Michelle Rodriguez, Michael Peña, Luis Guzmán, Maya Rudolph, and Snoop Dogg. The movie begins in a back-yard garden, owned by people who apparently don't care that snails are eating all their tomatoes. When the action shifts to a decrepit but ethnically diverse mini-mall in the Van Nuys neighborhood of Los Angeles, Samuel L. Jackson shows up as Whiplash, the intimidating leader of a gang of snail racers. A intra-mollusk rivalry is briefly explored and quickly forgotten; Whiplash and the other snails become Turbo's loyal pals and, at the Indianapolis 500, his pit crew. In less than a minute, Whiplash takes charge of a pit stop, marshaling the other snails to buff up Turbo and lubricate him with a tube of lip balm. The scene works because of Jackson's commanding presence—even though, in this movie, it's deployed through an eyedropper.

Oldboy (2013)

Chaney
MOVIE: 5/10   **SLJ FACTOR:** 8/10   **MINUTES UNTIL HE SHOWS UP:** 22
EXPLETIVES NOT DELETED: goddamn, motherfuckers, shit (x4), motherfucker (x5), fuck (x5), cocksucker, bitch (x2), fucking (x6), fucker, motherfucking

After *Jungle Fever*, Spike Lee made thirteen feature films over twenty-two years without casting Samuel L. Jackson. *Oldboy* marked their reunion, but the movie seemed driven by commercial motives more than sentimental or artistic ones. Even in the studio's own promotional materials, Lee gave the remarkably unenthusiastic quote "There's a million different stories you could tell. *Oldboy*'s going to be another one." (And after the producers chopped about thirty-five minutes out of his cut, he changed his credit to "A Spike Lee Film" instead of his trademark "A Spike Lee Joint.")

> *"No-dick, ass-licking son of a bitch! Fuck you! Booger-eating, piss-drinking motherfucker!"*

The movie is a violent thriller with a baroque revenge plot (Josh Brolin plays Joe Doucett, a drunken asshole who is kidnapped and imprisoned for twenty years and then has to find out why). The whole enterprise is stylish but superfluous: it's a faithful remake of the 2003 Korean film of the same name. (In a post-*Parasite* era, it's hard to fathom why the original didn't just get wider distribution.) So although there's a high level of craft on display, there's no reason to see this movie instead of the original unless you hate subtitles or really want to see some of the stars of *Avengers: Endgame* (Brolin, Jackson, Elizabeth Olsen) in a movie with more obscenity, blood, and skin than the MCU allows.

Jackson was a huge fan of the Korean movie, watching it eight or nine times a year. Whenever he met somebody who hadn't seen it, he made a point of sending them a copy of the DVD. When he found out about the remake, Lee said: "Sam called me up and said, 'I want to be in this!' So I sent him the script and said, 'Pick any role that you want except Josh's.' "

Jackson plays the warden of the secret nongovernmental prison that holds Brolin, and infuses the role with the amorality that a job like that would require. (It doesn't seem accidental that his character's name is pronounced like George W. Bush's vice president.) He's a dandy with a Mohawk, lip jewelry, and tailored red-and-black clothes. In a trick of movie editing, although Chaney torments Doucett for decades, he actually spends the majority of his time onscreen as Doucett's helpless prisoner. Impressively, Jackson remains a threatening force the whole time—even when he's screaming in pain because he's being tortured, literally getting salt poured in his wounds.

Reasonable Doubt (2014)

Clinton Davis
MOVIE: 3/10   **SLJ FACTOR:** 7/10   **MINUTES UNTIL HE SHOWS UP:** 18
EXPLETIVES NOT DELETED: fucked

Here's a hot tip for aspiring screenwriters: Keep the characters in your thriller sketchy and underdeveloped. That way, when you want them to engage in behavior that makes no sense, at least nobody can tell you they're acting inconsistently.

Screenwriter Peter A. Dowling leans hard on that shortcut in *Reasonable Doubt*, and also seems to have lost a bet that required him to stuff in as many howlers on legal procedure

> *"You could've ruined my life or ruined yours, but yet you found a third option."*

as possible. There is a high-concept plot, however: an assistant district attorney, driving home drunk, hits a pedestrian and leaves the scene of the crime. His victim dies that night—and the ADA (Dominic Cooper) has to prosecute the citizen (Samuel L. Jackson) who had the body in the back of his van, headed to the hospital, because the ADA can't reveal his own guilt. (Did you guess that Jackson's character is not as blameless as he first seems? Congratulations!)

"I'm not really sure what it's about," said Jackson. The movie was enough of a mess that director Peter Howitt pulled his name in favor of the pseudonym Peter P. Croudins, but Jackson nevertheless gave the film some teeth. His menacing performance, calm and understated and methodical, feels all too real.

The movie, set in Chicago, has multiple references to the tough neighborhood of Riverdale, unintentionally hilarious if you're thinking of Archie and Jughead and the gang at Pop's Chock'Lit Shoppe. Winnipeg doubled (unconvincingly) for Chicago—which meant that the movie sometimes filmed outside at night during the Manitoba winter. "Your lungs hurt," Cooper said of the subzero temperatures. "I'm trying to do an accent and my face froze."

For his part, Jackson ranked it as only the third-coldest movie he had ever shot, after *The Long Kiss Goodnight* and *The Red Violin*. But, he noted, "they were all in Canada!"

RoboCop (2014)

Pat Novak
MOVIE: 5/10   **SLJ FACTOR:** 7/10   **MINUTES UNTIL HE SHOWS UP:** 0
EXPLETIVES NOT DELETED: none (he gets bleeped as he says "motherfucker" and "horseshit")

The original *RoboCop*, released in 1987, was the first Hollywood movie by the Dutch director Paul Verhoeven, beginning a remarkable run of films (including *Total Recall*, *Basic Instinct*, *Showgirls*, and *Starship Troopers*) that were smart, satirical, crass, excessive—usually all those things simultaneously. In his hands, the sci-fi story of a policeman turned into a crime-fighting cyborg was a canny harbinger of our current era of fast-twitch media and governments in thrall to corporations.

"Has the U.S. Senate become pro-crime?"

This big-budget reboot feels like the filmmakers read the Wikipedia entry on *RoboCop* but never figured out how to update it when so much of its dystopian perspective had become reality. Director José Padilha (the man behind the excellent Brazilian documentary *Bus 174*) gives the movie a slick, expensive sheen. The script gestures in the direction of satire but doesn't have any particular point of view. There's plenty of action scenes, but they all feel like they're lifted from video games.

What's good: the cast, including Michael Keaton, Jennifer Ehle, and Michael K. Williams. Gary Oldman shines as the scientist behind the RoboCop program, gradually succumbing to corporate pressure and cutting ethical corners until he realizes the human cost of his compromises.

Samuel L. Jackson plays a blowhard conservative TV personality, the host of a show called *The Novak Element*. (The movie's two primary predictions for its near-future world, aside from mechanized police, are that the United States will occupy Iran and that Fox News hosts will get some seriously high-tech graphics.) Novak wears expensive suits, seems perpetually indignant, and cuts off interviews when a guest says something he disagrees with. Although Jackson plays the role with gusto, the archetype is familiar to the point of cliché. Jackson's best moment comes in the movie's opening moments, before Novak goes on the air. We hear him blowing raspberries and saying "ma-ma-ma-ma," doing vocal exercises to prepare for another performance—and revealing the entertainer behind the pious pose.

Captain America: The Winter Soldier (2014)

Nick Fury
MOVIE: 8/10   SLJ FACTOR: 9/10   MINUTES UNTIL HE SHOWS UP: 13

In *The Winter Soldier*, Nick Fury has devoted disciples, is betrayed by one of his closest colleagues, and comes back from the dead—and has never seemed less Christ-like.

For his sixth movie as Fury, Samuel L. Jackson shows the depths of his deceptions. As the actor noted, "Almost everything that comes out of Nick Fury's mouth is a lie in some sense." He also finally gets to cut loose—when Hydra agents impersonating police officers try to assassinate him, he stars in a car chase that weaves through D.C.'s streets and sidewalks. Bloody and enraged, Fury unleashes some serious firepower.

"Last time I trusted someone, I lost an eye."

Perhaps most importantly, when film legend Robert Redford shows up, Jackson looks like he belongs in the same frame. Redford (cast as a villainous senior official of SHIELD) is only thirteen years older than Jackson, but he had been a movie star for two decades before Jackson could get his parking validated at a Hollywood studio. The two actors had never performed together before, although Jackson had been introduced to Redford on numerous occasions, especially when he was a younger actor in movies playing at the Sundance Film Festival. So on the morning of their first scene, Jackson made a point of sitting down with Redford: "We talked about golf. We talked about life. We talked about movies. So by the time we got on set, it did look like we spent time together, or had some past."

Fury's scenes nod at racial inequities. He tells Captain America a story about his grandfather's job as an elevator operator, in an era when that was a plum job for an African American man, and a detail drawn from Jackson's real life: his own beloved grandfather Edgar Montgomery was an elevator operator in a hotel in Chattanooga. And just before the Hydra agents open fire on his vehicle, Fury thinks he's being profiled by racist cops assuming that a Black man wouldn't be driving a fancy car. These moments are small, but they stand in contrast to the rest of his MCU work, even if nobody paints *BLACK LIVES MATTER* on the side of a SHIELD helicarrier.

This movie is a comic-book version of the political thrillers Redford headlined in the 1970s, like *Three Days of the Condor* and *All the President's Men*. It doesn't go all the way with those movies' paranoid mindset, and doesn't even go as far as the *Captain America* comic books: in a 1974 sequence of issues, Cap discovered that the "Number One" leader of the "Secret Empire" syndicate was actually Richard Nixon: unmasked in the Oval Office, the president of the United States committed suicide.

Here, we have to settle for SHIELD collapsing and Fury reluctantly coming to terms with the knowledge that he surrounded himself with traitors. Jackson plays that failure as a question of Fury's self-awareness: "He has to ask, is he even lying to himself too? He has a very good idea of what's going on but his paranoia keeps him from believing some of it."

Pulp Fiction reference: when Fury pretends to be dead, an apposite biblical passage is carved into the marble of his gravestone: "The path of the righteous man," from Ezekiel 25:17.

Kite (2014)

Lieutenant Karl Aker
MOVIE: 3/10   SLJ FACTOR: 4/10   MINUTES UNTIL HE SHOWS UP: 4
EXPLETIVES NOT DELETED: shit

Samuel L. Jackson joined the cast of the live-action remake of *Kite* because he was a fan of the bloody 1998 anime about a schoolgirl assassin. Given that that the original version was hentai, the subgenre of Japanese animation distinguished by its sexual content—and was banned in some countries as child pornography—maybe Jackson shouldn't have

"Looks like somebody used a land mine to clear their sinuses."

been surprised that the material got toned down, but he was nevertheless disappointed. "We didn't tell it quite as hard as I wanted to tell it, but now it has been told, so here we are," he complained. "I like dark."

When Jackson signed on, the movie was going to be directed by David R. Ellis, the former stuntman who had helmed *Snakes on a Plane*—but Ellis died a month before the cameras were about to roll and was replaced by Ralph Ziman. Despite that tragedy, Jackson didn't drop out: "Once I commit to a project, I always see it through," he said.

In a dystopic future, a young woman, Sawa (India Eisley), fights against the "flesh-cartels" that are pressing children into prostitution. Jackson plays the cop secretly providing her with weapons and the drug that is blotting out her memories. Jackson's subdued performance feels like an echo of his work in better movies, as does his look (shaved head and trench coats, evoking *Shaft*). The movie has some visual brio but riffles through clichés before ending with an unsurprising twist, where an ally turns out to be a betrayer. Ziman seems to have genuine enthusiasm for the gory deaths—and not much else.

The most surprising thing about *Kite*: it was filmed in Johannesburg, still underused as a film production location. That gave it some unusual texture, from the urban architecture to the accents of supporting actors. It also resulted in an amusing line in the closing credits; after plugs for "Car Services for Samuel L. Jackson" and "Hotel Services for Samuel L. Jackson," we learned who provided "Escort Services for Samuel L. Jackson." Either that term means something very different in South Africa or the producers were being unusually frank about where the star directed his libidinal hentai impulses.

Kingsman: The Secret Service (2015)

Valentine
MOVIE: 8/10   **SLJ FACTOR:** 8/10   **MINUTES UNTIL HE SHOWS UP:** 7
EXPLETIVES NOT DELETED: fucked (x2), fucking (x4), fuck (x9), goddamn, shit (x9), bitch, goddammit, son of a bitch, bullshit, motherfucker (x2)

"I always felt the old Bond films were only as good as the villain," Colin Firth's old-school secret agent says in one of *Kingsman*'s rare quiet moments. That proves to be exactly correct with *Kingsman*, a twenty-first-century version of classic spy movies, cheeky and fun and over the top but not quite a parody—just like its antagonist, Richmond Valentine. He's a tech billionaire with eyeglasses and a permanently askew baseball cap; the screenplay describes him as "nerdily preppy—Bill Gates meets Tiger Woods." He's extremely squeamish about violence, which hasn't stopped him from concocting a plan to have most of humanity kill itself in an electronically induced orgy of brutality.

The most conspicuous choice Samuel L. Jackson made in playing Valentine is that he gave him a lisp. Director Matthew Vaughn initially resisted that idea, until Jackson reminded him that one of the toughest people on the planet had a lisp (boxer Mike Tyson) and explained how his own youthful stutter motivated him: "If you're Steve Jobs and you've got everything—you've got money, you've got power, you've got everything you want—but you've still got this goddamn stutter and lisp, and people aren't 100% taking you seriously, it can take you to that next level of going mad."

"So freaky how there's no recognizable name for the Chinese secret service. Well, that's what you call a secret, right?"

So the speech impediment is more than a flourish; it deliberately contrasts with the utter confidence that Jackson otherwise gives to Valentine. Jackson plays a mogul who's used to bending reality to his own ends. When he's counting down a clock to the apocalypse, he does so with such exuberance that he gets a roomful of his followers to ignore the impending genocide and start partying instead. When he calmly explains the rationale behind his master plan—"Global warming is the fever. Mankind is the virus."—he makes it sound like a public-minded TED Talk.

Kingsman is inventive, witty, and visually dazzling—but its treatment of race is, frankly, embarrassing. The only two notable roles filled by performers of color are the two bad guys, Valentine (Jackson) and his murderous minion Gazelle (the Algerian-French Sofia Boutella). Granted, part of the premise of the Kingsmen is that it's an old-fashioned institution that's traditionally recruited from the British upper crust. But the new recruits who supposedly bring the modern world crashing in? A white guy and a white girl. That's not much of a contrast with the old days. If the UK can drag itself into a multicultural twenty-first century, its spy movies should be able to do the same.

Avengers: Age of Ultron (2015)

Nick Fury
MOVIE: 7/10   **SLJ FACTOR:** 5/10   **MINUTES UNTIL HE SHOWS UP:** 22 (still photo), 70 (full motion)

Age of Ultron is a sleek spandex catsuit that looks good but keeps riding up in all the wrong places. The obligatory action set pieces—the Avengers versus hundreds of evil robot minions, the evacuation of a floating city, Hulk battling the oversized Hulkbuster armor—all feel like you're getting pummeled by ill-conceived CGI. The best moments in this superhero movie are when writer-director Joss Whedon works on a human scale: a budding romance between the Hulk and the Black Widow is surprisingly moving, and it's worth the price of admission to see the off-duty Avengers having a party, swapping stories and arguing over who is worthy enough to lift Thor's magic hammer.

> *"Here we all are back on earth, with nothing but our wit and our will to save the world."*

When Hawkeye brings the other heroes to his farmhouse in Missouri and introduces them to his family, it's in the finest tradition of middle management organizing an off-site retreat, hoping that chopping wood and throwing darts will bring the team together. And there's a surprise motivational speaker: Nick Fury shows up to give them a pep talk, which feels superfluous but stirring. After *Captain America: The Winter Soldier*, Fury lacks the resources of SHIELD (although he somehow commandeers a mothballed helicarrier), but Samuel L. Jackson looks great in a knit cap and shawl collar pullover sweater and remains utterly commanding when he tells Tony Stark to "look me in the eye."

Barely Lethal (2015)

Hardman
MOVIE: 4/10   **SLJ FACTOR:** 7/10   **MINUTES UNTIL HE SHOWS UP:** 4

The premise: nobody's more ruthless than teenage girls. So a spy agency called the Prescott Academy has trained orphan girls from a young age to be secret agent killing machines. When Agent 83 (Hailee Steinfeld) tires of the assassin life, she goes AWOL, gives herself a regular name (Megan), and enrolls at a typical

> *"It's all about putting holes in the subject."*

suburban high school. She prepares for the experience by watching movies better than this one (*Clueless*, *Mean Girls*) but discovers that proficiency in hand-to-hand combat hasn't prepared her for cliques and bullies and emotionally distant boys. It's mild but palatable entertainment aimed at preteens for whom high school is a source of both longing and dread. (Which makes the porn-inspired title doubly icky.)

Samuel L. Jackson plays the bluntly named Hardman, head of the Prescott Academy—sending up his own work in the MCU and *XXX* movies. Jackson knows that the comedy is maximized if he plays it perfectly straight, so we see him barking at grade-school girls ("007-year-olds," as villain Jessica Alba quips) while they're learning to defuse bombs and stab people in the carotid artery. That military bearing makes it even funnier when he puts on a ludicrously fake mustache and sideburns and shows up as Megan's bus driver. ("Martin Van Buren called and wants those sideburns back," she tells him. He responds, "Marty Van B died in 1822, fourteen years *before* the invention of the telephone.") It also means that after the final firefight, when he gives Megan permission to go to homecoming, we get the emotional payoff a teen action-comedy needs: before our heroine dances with her true love, she gets a hug from her emotionally distant father figure.

Big Game (2015)

President
MOVIE: 5/10   **SLJ FACTOR: 6/10**   **MINUTES UNTIL HE SHOWS UP: 3**
EXPLETIVES NOT DELETED: shit (x2), motherfucker (but not in the American version of the movie—while he said it in the Finnish release, the word was truncated to get a PG-13 rating in the USA)

Samuel L. Jackson never aspired to be the president, or even to play him on film. "The kind of films that I watched, as a kid, didn't make me go, 'Wow, I can't wait to play the president,'" he explained. And this Finnish movie, where Air Force One is downed over the Nordic wilderness, has a very European perspective on the American president: he's well-meaning but not particularly effective or popular, and being pursued by assassins doesn't transform him into an action hero. In fact, William Alan Moore, the leader of the free world, spends most of the movie tramping around the woods with only one shoe, his only protector a young Finnish boy. Jackson recognized that he was signing up to play a feckless president, not an idealized national patriarch, and requested only one moment of competence: that at a key moment, he got to kick an adversary in the balls.

The protagonist of *Big Game* is that Finnish boy: Oskari (a fine performance by Onni Tommila), sent into the woods with a bow and arrow for his thirteenth birthday and expected to come back with a hunting trophy to show that he is now a man. This movie has more holes than plot, but it has one heartbreaking scene. Oskari finds that his father has killed a deer and left the head for him to claim as his own trophy: shamefully, not even his own father believes in him. (He ultimately triumphs by bringing home the POTUS, the biggest game of all.)

> *"A few hours ago, I could order the greatest armed force on the planet to invade any country in the world. And now, I can't even order a pizza."*

In the most expensive Finnish movie of all time, Jackson headlined a strong cast that also included Jim Broadbent, Felicity Huffman, and Victor Garber. They presumably signed up on the strength of the previous film directed by Jalmari Helander (uncle of Tommila): *Rare Exports*, a delightfully twisted Christmas horror movie about feral prehistoric Santa Clauses. Helander, who had previously worked only with actors he knew personally, had to adjust to life with a Hollywood star, which terrified him a bit. "We had really fun times and sometimes he could be a little bit difficult," Helander said. "And when he comes into a room, you definitely feel that he's in the room."

Jackson kept his performance here on a human scale because he understood what movie he was making: "It's an interesting little film for kids who are tweeners, in that particular place where they want to be something, but they don't believe, or people around them don't believe, that they can."

Chi-Raq (2015)

Dolmedes
MOVIE: 7/10   SLJ FACTOR: 8/10   MINUTES UNTIL HE SHOWS UP: 5
EXPLETIVES NOT DELETED: shit (x6), titty, shitty, goddamn (x2), motherfucking (x2), motherfucker, bullshit, fucking, pussies

Every movie should have Samuel L. Jackson as the onscreen narrator, wearing a natty yellow suit, cracking dirty jokes, and commenting on the action—but so far, *Chi-Raq* is the only one that does. Jackson's primary job here is to explain the high concept of this Spike Lee joint: it's a retelling of the Aristophanes play *Lysistrata*, updated from 411 BCE Greece to modern-day Chicago, but still told in verse (sometimes rhyming). The Spartans and the Trojans are two rival gangs, clad in purple and orange respectively, brought into the twenty-first century with text messages and hip-hop music. The fierce and foxy Lysistrata (Teyonah Parris) organizes a sex strike by the women of Chicago (and later, the world), using the slogan "No Peace, No Pussy."

> *"Cops and gangs, black and brown folks stuck in the middle / Shit's on fire, y'all. I can hear Nero's fiddle."*

A satire of modern gun violence, the movie is inspired and overheated, righteous and ridiculous. Jennifer Hudson, the emotional center of the movie, gives an extraordinary performance as the mother of a young girl murdered by a stray bullet: shattered, she not only has to bury her, she has to scrub her daughter's blood off the pavement. Later, after a group of women occupy a military armory, there's a standoff between the genders featuring a dance routine to the Chi-Lites' "Oh Girl."

It falls to Jackson to guide the audience through this ambitious, messy movie, and he does so with glee. His character, Mr. Dolmedes, has a name halfway between "dolmades" (the Greek dish of stuffed grape leaves) and "Dolemite" (the blaxploitation character created by Rudy Ray Moore). The X-rated rhyming of Dolemite seems to be the inspiration for some of Jackson's dialogue: "No more punani, nookie pie, beehive, or honeybun / No coochie, no nappy dugout—that's right, you gets none." Jackson has the outsized presence to boast that he "was weaned on Thunderbird from my mama's titties" and to sum up the movie's themes while standing in front of a giant American flag (à la George C. Scott in *Patton*). And he has the weight of his own film history: once again, Lee has Jackson reprise his most enduring dialogue from *Do the Right Thing*, imploring the audience to "wake up."

The Hateful Eight (2015)

Major Marquis Warren
MOVIE: 8/10   SLJ FACTOR: 10/10   MINUTES UNTIL HE SHOWS UP: 5
EXPLETIVES NOT DELETED: goddamn (x5), horseshit, bitch (x10), fucking, motherfuckers (x2), fuck (x2), shit (x4)

Outside Minnie's Haberdashery, it's 1870s Wyoming and a blizzard is raging. Inside, where most of *The Hateful Eight* unfolds, it's intense and claustrophobic and cold. Director Quentin Tarantino "actually refriger-ated the whole stage," Samuel L. Jackson said. "The cast was there in coats. It was like 30 degrees in there. We drank tea so you could see our breath when we talked, and we're in our costumes, freezing. We'd run outdoors and stand in the sun."

"Them peckerwoods left their homes and families and come up this snowy mountain looking for me and fortune. Ain't none of them found fortune. The ones you ain't never heard of no more? They found me."

The Haberdashery, a large log cabin, is filled with various disreputable guests waiting out the storm, many of them veterans of the Civil War and/or earlier Tarantino films (including Kurt Russell, Tim Roth, and Michael Madsen). The scenario plays like a cross between the nihilistic westerns of Sergio Corbucci ("His characters roam a brutal, sadistic West," Tarantino said) and the locked-room mysteries of Agatha Christie (featuring detectives such as Hercule Poirot). Jackson plays Marquis Warren, a bounty hunter who's the smartest man in the room, carefully deducing who's lying about what and getting other characters to do his bidding: the actor and the director nicknamed the character "Hercule Negro."

The movie is thrilling and excessive in almost equal proportions. Some of its overabundance comes in forms that will be familiar to Tarantino fans—buckets of blood, characters drunk on their own words—but with greater volumes than he employed previously, and with less dramatic justification. Tarantino also found some new ways to go over the top: he filmed the movie in Ultra Panavision 70 format, a widescreen format perfect for gorgeous landscapes, and then set most of his western in a dark room. (The 70mm print played in theaters as part of a deluxe "road show" presentation, complete with intermission and program. That 187-minute cut is no longer available for public viewing; you currently have a choice between the 168-minute general-release edit and an expanded 210-minute version divided into four episodes, like a TV miniseries. While the extended version adds some interesting moments and retains the necessary tension, the movie doesn't feel rushed or incomplete in its theatrical cut. If you're watching the movie for the first time, you probably want the shorter version.)

Everybody in *The Hateful Eight* is lying about something, but the most important lie is the one Warren keeps in his pocket: the Lincoln Letter. It's his most cherished possession, a piece of personal correspondence from the sixteenth president of the United States—and it's a fake. When called out, he explains, "This letter had the desired effect of disarming white folks." Warren had a price of thirty thousand Confederate dollars on his head and regularly had to contend with Southerners hoping to collect the bounty—but as a Black man living in the United States, he knew that not all of his foes were going to be obvious. The forgery is so artful, it gains him the trust of suspicious strangers and even the admiration of people who know its mendacity.

The ending of the movie suggests that despite politics and skin color, even the most bitter foes can become allies—but it'll take a really good lie to bring them together, and the effort will probably kill them.

Jen Ray.

July 11, 1989: Sir Laurence Olivier died.

Also on July 11, 1989: Samuel L. Jackson, forty years old and recovering from a serious leg injury after getting dragged along a subway platform, stayed home and watched TV. On the news, he saw a tribute to Olivier that included images of the nonpareil actor in movies ranging from *Hamlet* to *Marathon Man*, and he marveled at how different each character looked, and how each image evoked an entire performance. Undeterred by the fact that Olivier had amassed more Oscar nominations for acting (ten) than Jackson had speaking roles in feature films (five), Jackson set a goal for himself.

"I made a decision that as an actor, I would find a way to be different, to be another guy each time, so that when my time came, an audience could sit there and think about how great Sam Jackson was as all those different characters," he said. Just seeing the panoply of Olivier's roles, Jackson realized that "the first thing you remember about most characters is what they look like."

In the theater, Jackson had to do his own makeup, but in the movies, he realized, "Well, shit, they've got better makeup artists." It took him a few years to take advantage of their expertise; aside from one memorable Jheri-curl wig, most of his early movie hairstyles were mundane. Jackson first implemented the Olivier Initiative on the 1996 boxing comedy *The Great White Hype*. He was playing a crooked boxing promoter, clearly based on Don King, so director Reginald Hudlin wanted him to look like King, with a huge shock of gray hair. Jackson resisted: he wanted his character to be an original creation, not a parody. So he made an unusual choice—he would rock a variety of turbans and a silver Julius Caesar wig. "And from that point on, I just decided, I had this great wigmaker, so I just found hairstyles that I felt would be distinctive for every character," Jackson said.

That wigmaker was Robert Louis Stevenson, who first met Jackson on the Atlanta set of the 1976 movie *Just an Old Sweet Song*, where Jackson was working as a stand-in, and collaborated with the actor on over thirty movies. Some of the distinctive looks they came up with included the asymmetrical haircut in *Unbreakable* ("I was thinking Frederick Douglass," Jackson said. "It informed my character very well because he's a thinker"), the dreadlocks in *The Caveman's Valentine* ("He grows this hair as a source of heat and as a mask that he can hide under"), and the cornrows in *Formula 51* ("He was going into this situation to look like what a British audience would typically think of as a black hip-hop kind of gangster"). The shaved head of Mace Windu in the *Star Wars* prequels "was just one of those things that happened," Jackson said. "It isn't that Mace is this ethereal dude who takes his lightsaber and goes 'rrrr-owww,' runs it over the top of his head."

Jackson's favorite movie hair, though, belonged to Ordell Robbie in *Jackie Brown*: a relaxed hairdo reminiscent of Ron O'Neal's style in the blaxploitation film *Super Fly*. The logic was that *Super Fly* was Ordell's favorite movie and he aspired to be that type of player. Jackson said, "I could wear it straight down or I could tie a French braid in the back or I could rock a ponytail." Even more arresting was Ordell's facial hair: a skinny braid protruding from his chin. The distinctive look was inspired by Jackson's love for the outlandish villains in Hong Kong movies.

Before shooting a movie, Jackson, his long-term makeup artist Allan Apone, and Stevenson would sit down at Apone's computer. "Al has this great program," Jackson said. "He can put my blank face on his computer screen and we can, like, pull hair from places and put it on and do stuff to my face." If they came up with something particularly elaborate during their cut-and-paste brainstorming, like the battered, weathered visage of Jackson's former boxer in *Resurrecting the Champ*, it could require up to three hours to make up Jackson every day. He didn't care: he slept in the makeup chair, never stirring, even when people were attaching prosthetics and pulling on his face.

Even as Jackson became a bona fide movie star, he maintained the character actor's love for disguises. "I'll put on a wig, I'll put a scar on, I'll do things to myself, because it takes me away from being me," he said. His agents and managers sometimes would yell at him to stop covering his handsome, valuable face with scars.

While he was working with his team on a character's exterior, Jackson would also be diving into the interior. If there was source material beyond the script, he would read it; if not, he would make up the essential details of his character's life: "The kind of foods that he eats, educational background, parents, the kind of friends he had, the kind of friends he developed, how he started making money..." The list went on. By the time Jackson was done writing up the biography of his character—a technique taught to him by the theater directors Lloyd Richards and Douglas Turner Ward, and one that could take a week or two—he would often have so many pages that they would need to be bound, like a companion volume to his screenplay.

"All my characters have lives outside the things you see them doing onscreen," Jackson said. He put particular thought into his relationship with the other characters in the movie, how he should carry himself physically, where he was coming from before a scene started—and where he was headed when it was over. If Jackson was doing his job right, the audience would want to come along with him when he left a scene.

By the time Jackson showed up on set or in a rehearsal room, he would have his lines memorized—and usually, everybody else's lines as well. "I unreasonably expect everyone to be as prepared as I am," he said. But one thing he wouldn't have done: said that dialogue out loud. Jackson would read a script silently: generally, by the third time through, he would have the lines down perfectly. Then he would start playing with variations, mentally trying out emphases and inflections. They would always sound somewhat different when he said them out loud for the first time—but he knew that his tone and volume would change anyway, when people and scenery and props entered the picture. He was happy to fine-tune his efforts to get in sync with his collaborators, but he wouldn't kowtow to directors and he would ignore notes that he thought were dumb.

"Sam can be quite intimidating," confessed John Boorman, director of movies such as *Point Blank*, *Excalibur*, and the Jackson-starring *In My Country*. "People are very wary of him because he's very professional and expects everyone else to be that way. He is on top of everything and won't suffer fools at all—he caught me out a couple of times! One day on set, I told him to do something. And he said, 'When we were rehearsing, you said quite the opposite.'"

Jackson didn't seek a director's approval between takes: he was confident in his own abilities, and assumed that if there was a problem, he'd hear about it. Similarly, he wouldn't go to the monitor to watch a scene in playback. He could judge how a scene was working when he was standing inside it—and although he loved watching himself act, he was happy to wait until the movie was completed to see it. He prided himself on hitting his marks: he executed every take with precision, walking across a room at the same time, picking up a prop on the same word. He knew that his consistency would later make it easier for the person editing the movie.

Thomas Jane's first big studio film was the shark movie *Deep Blue Sea*, and so he carefully watched Jackson on the set. "He gave me little pointers now and then, which I thought was cool," Jane said. "We'd do a scene and he'd say, 'Lay back on it a little.'" But more important was how Jackson expected everyone to be ready. When the actors were summoned to the set, they would have to gear up in wetsuits, Jane said, "and we'd end up sitting around for at least half an hour, sometimes an hour. Sam took that for about a day and a half. And then he was like, 'You know what, motherfuckers? If I'm on the set, it's going to be time to roll. If I'm not fucking rolling, then I'm going back to my trailer.' And he would leave."

This wasn't just a diva move, Jane said: "He set the tone for everybody, the other actors and the crew too. He let everybody know he was there to do business. In a way, he ran that part of the operation. He didn't like any fucking around—or waiting around. 'Let's shoot!' That came out of Sam's mouth I don't know how many times. 'Let's shoot! Let's shoot it!' And everybody would hop to it."

As Jackson got further into his career, he became less interested in giving directors a menu of options to choose from. He would usually cap his number of takes at three, and if asked to take a different approach to a scene, he would politely but firmly decline. His logic: "I don't get to go to the editing room, but you do. And you're going to put that thing that you asked me to do in there, because that's the thing you like. So if I don't do it, I don't have to worry about you fucking with my performance."

One situation where Jackson had to fuck with his own performance: recording the TV edit for his R-rated movies, replacing profanity with family-friendly words that would sync up with his mouth movements when he cursed. So instead of "motherfucker," he would substitute "melon farmer" or "Maryland farmer." He said, "You end up making up a lot of stupid shit like 'monkey fighters' and 'motor scooter.'"

Jackson believed in an actorly code of professionalism and modeled it for younger actors: be on time, know your lines, learn the names of crew members, treat everyone with courtesy. If the cast included children or novice actors who didn't know their rights, he made a point of looking out for them, making sure that they weren't exploited or put in hazardous situations.

Something that boggled Jackson's mind: some movie actors, even famous ones, had never acted in a play. He considered his theatrical experience to be the backbone of his success, and his career advice for most young actors was to do as many plays as possible (moving to New York City if necessary). And so it rankled him when studios cast rappers who had no acting experience whatsoever. He turned down movies such as the 50 Cent biopic *Get Rich or Die Tryin'* that starred a rapper and were looking to add some actorly credibility. "I can't see validating some rappers' acting careers when I have friends who can act who can't get jobs because they're not household names," he said. "Acting deserves a lot more respect than it gets. There are no naturals in this business. You can fake it for a while, but the audience catches on."

He often dismissed rappers with acting careers as "Ice Box, Ice Tray, and Ice Pick"—but he actually costarred with Ice Cube in the second *XXX* movie and worked alongside other hip-hoppers, including LL Cool J, Busta Rhymes, and Queen Latifah. Basically, if a fellow cast member demonstrated intelligence and a good work ethic, Jackson was willing to overlook past success on the *Billboard* charts.

Jackson took acting seriously because he loved it—which was also why he appeared in so many movies. He didn't understand why people were surprised by his making as many movies as possible: "The average person goes to work every day except for maybe two weeks of vacation a year. I do it and everybody says I'm a workaholic, but what's the difference?" Making movies wasn't the most strenuous job in the world— he could literally go to sleep between takes in his trailer if he felt like it—but that wasn't the point. Jackson did it because it was what he was supposed to do, the same way writers needed to write and painters needed to paint. As far as he was concerned, acting was no different. "It's a job," he said, and then he corrected himself. "It's a calling."

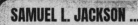

Rafa Orrico Diez.

Cell (2016)

Tom McCourt
MOVIE: 6/10   **SLJ FACTOR:** 7/10   **MINUTES UNTIL HE SHOWS UP:** 11
EXPLETIVES NOT DELETED: shit (x5), goddamn (x2), fuck, fucker (x2)

In the decade between the publication of Stephen King's novel *Cell*, about people turned into shambling mindless husks by a malign signal from their mobile phones, and the release of its film adaptation, pop culture was overrun by hordes of zombies, from *The Walking Dead* to *World War Z* to *Pride and Prejudice and Zombies*. So this movie felt late to the brain-eating party, with one good high-concept joke—our cell phones are literally turning us into shuffling zombies—and not much else. It got slammed, both by fans of the novel disappointed that King's mythological excesses had been trimmed and by zombie aficionados looking for more innovative thrills. It deserved better, but one of the morals of zombie movies is that we don't always get what we deserve.

> *"Us three are like bugs who had the dumb luck to avoid the stomp of the giant's boot."*

Cell kicks off with a great set piece: at the Boston airport, people go feral and attack each other, with a K-9 police officer even eating his dog. After that, it finds a predictable rhythm, with a small group of uninfected humans fleeing and hiding and meeting other survivors, hoping to find a safe haven in a world gone mad. What makes its ninety-eight minutes fly by is that our plucky band includes John Cusack and Samuel L. Jackson (reuniting on another King adaptation a decade after *1408*) and the great character actor Stacy Keach. Cusack stars as a graphic novelist named Clay Riddell (because "Malleable Mystery" would have been too obvious) whose imagination may have unleashed this technological apocalypse. Jackson plays the buddy that Clay meets along the way, a subway train driver who gets drunk in moments of safety and beautifully recites Psalm 40 in moments of despair. The zombie apocalypse isn't conducive to sharing life stories, but Jackson makes us believe in his levelheaded Vietnam vet with just a few lines of dialogue: "Lost most of my money in the Great Collapse of '08. And I lost my emotional stability in the Great Divorce of '09. You know, at the time, I thought *that* was the end of the world."

The Legend of Tarzan (2016)

George Washington Williams
MOVIE: 4/10   **SLJ FACTOR:** 4/10   **MINUTES UNTIL HE SHOWS UP:** 8
EXPLETIVES NOT DELETED: shit

The premise of Tarzan is inherently racist. From the character's beginnings (Edgar Rice Burroughs's ripping yarns, printed in pulp magazines and books beginning in 1912), the mythos has long designated a white man to be Africa's lord of the jungle, reducing the Black people who actually lived on the continent to native color or savage tribal adversaries. So although the character has a long history onscreen—"I've seen maybe six different Tarzans throughout my lifetime, from Lex Barker to Johnny Weissmuller to Gordon Scott," Samuel L. Jackson said—it's not clear why anyone would want to spend hundreds of millions of dollars in the twenty-first century propping up this particular pillar of intellectual property.

"Well, I'm not going to drink some foaming cup of you-know-what-it-is-and-won't-tell-me."

The filmmakers are aware of the character's problematic nature: their solution is to tell the story of Lord Greystoke aka Tarzan (Alexander Skarsgård) and his wife Jane (Margot Robbie) returning to the Belgian Congo circa 1890 as allies in the fight against the colonial regime of King Leopold II of Belgium. Joining Woke Tarzan is Jackson as George Washington Williams, a real-life Black American journalist and crusader whose "Open Letter to His Serene Majesty Leopold II" exposed the horrors of the Belgian exploitation of the Congo, and the enslavement and torture of its natives. Williams would be a fascinating figure to center a historical movie on, but here he's just Tarzan's sidekick: his job in this rote entertainment is to let the hero explain what's going on (a role that screenwriters sometimes call "the ear") and to marvel at how, like a buff Dr. Doolittle, Tarzan can speak to the animals.

"Sometimes I just do movies that I would've gone to see when I was a kid," Jackson said. "I would always think of myself as one of the Africans, 'cause they didn't have Black heroes then. The Africans were either the guys who Tarzan was fighting because they were doing some bad shit in the jungle, or the guys who were dressing up like tigers."

Jackson rocks a great Billy Dee Williams mustache here, but he spends most of his screen time running after Tarzan in the jungle, panting and trying to keep up. None of those jungle scenes are authentic, by the way—this is a movie about Africa that was filmed in England and Canada. (It's also a movie about the plight of people getting crushed by rapacious capitalism whose executive producer was Steven Mnuchin, Donald Trump's future treasury secretary.) Ostriches, hippopotami, and even butterflies are all computer-generated: in this movie, Tarzan is King of the CGI Apes.

Miss Peregrine's Home for Peculiar Children (2016)

Barron
MOVIE: 8/10   SLJ FACTOR: 8/10   MINUTES UNTIL HE SHOWS UP: 5

It must be the teeth: a full mouthful of shining white pointed incisors, flashing malevolently whenever Samuel L. Jackson grins. In this movie, Jackson also sports a shock of white hair and ivory eyes with tiny black pupils, but it's the carnivorous choppers that announce his evil intentions. Jackson accepted the role of Mr. Barron while filming *The Hateful Eight*,

> *"These children must be as insane as their headmistress!"*

and promptly asked for Barron's teeth so he could practice his elocution, learning to say "the teeth, the lips, the tip of the tongue" with something unfamiliar in his mouth. That also let Jackson test-drive the teeth with the *Hateful* cast and crew. "When I put them in and I was all bloody," he said, "I'd talk to them and they'd go, 'Oh my God!' It was kind of fun."

Miss Peregrine's Home for Peculiar Children is a late entry in the enduring genre of "outcast children with unusual powers grow up in a fabulous old house together," a category that also includes the X-Men, *The Umbrella Academy*, and the wizards of Hogwarts. Because this example is the eighteenth feature film directed by Tim Burton, it's also a valentine to society's misfits, full of visual snap and Gothic whimsy.

This was Jackson's first movie with Burton—it was, astonishingly, the first leading role ever for an actor of color in Burton's long career—and as always, he enjoyed working with a sure-footed director who knew which shots he needed.

At their first rehearsal, Burton responded to Jackson's performance by saying, 'Oh my God, I love that direction. Can you go further that way?'" Jackson was surprised but happy to comply—he played the principal villain with the gusto appropriate for a character who's evil enough to hunt down children and feast on their eyeballs. His Mr. Barron is a shapeshifter full of bluster and menace but isn't especially smart, regularly getting outwitted and tongue-tied by his prey. His best moment comes when he recounts the indignity of remaining in disguise in Florida for three weeks: "Have you ever *been* to Florida?"

Although Burton has a dour reputation, Jackson said the director didn't lack for enthusiasm, regularly clapping his hands and saying, "That was amazing! Do you want to do another one?"

"Only if you want to," the actor would tell him.

Jackson said, "His cinematic sense is almost the same as Quentin [Tarantino]. He knows what shots he wants to do and he knows how he wants to do them, and he gives you a scenario and asks you to fill that space in whatever way you want to fill it."

XXX: Return of Xander Cage (2017)

Augustus Gibbons

MOVIE: 6/10   SLJ FACTOR: 7/10   MINUTES UNTIL HE SHOWS UP: 3

EXPLETIVES NOT DELETED: shit (x3), bullshit

When Vin Diesel declined to make a second XXX movie, the filmmakers went ahead without him and spitefully killed off his character Xander Cage—in dialogue, and more definitively in a short film included as a DVD extra. But *XXX: State of the Union* flopped, so twelve years later, the mutual desire for another hit movie brought Cage back from the grave. Surprisingly, this resurrection is the most enjoyable XXXcapade, probably because it leans even harder into the ludicrous "James Bond, but with extreme sports" nature of the franchise. Where else are you going to see movie stars surfing big waves—on motorcycles?

> "This is some pretty surreal shit, being at your own funeral."

XXX: Return of Xander Cage followed the successful template of *The Fast and the Furious* franchise: ignore the dud installment except for one character (Ice Cube gets a great cameo here, just as Sung Kang became a regular after *The Fast and the Furious: Tokyo Drift*), bring Diesel back, and surround him with a photogenic crew of international rebels. The best member of the ensemble? The impossibly suave Hong Kong star Donnie Yen.

Even the dialogue is sharper: Samuel L. Jackson gets his best scene ever as Gibbons, kicking off the movie with a loose, funny monologue where he tries to recruit the real-life Brazilian soccer star Neymar for the XXX program, recapping the movie *Dogtown and Z-Boys*, advocating for the value of dumplings at breakfast, and discussing the capitalist conflict between liberty and safety. He's interrupted by a satellite falling from orbit and crashing into their noodle shop, killing them both in a fiery explosion. In a series like this, it shouldn't be surprising that Gibbons doesn't stay dead: at the end of the movie he shows up at his own funeral to give Cage a pep talk.

A huge missed opportunity: How could they not call this movie *XXX III*?

Kong: Skull Island (2017)

Preston Packard
MOVIE: 7/10   SLJ FACTOR: 7/10   MINUTES UNTIL HE SHOWS UP: 10
EXPLETIVES NOT DELETED: shit (x2), bitch (x2) (also, Kong interrupts him halfway through "motherfucker")

You wouldn't guess it from the haircuts, but *Kong: Skull Island* is set in 1973. Although the 1976 *King Kong* starring Jessica Lange was a turgid mess, the 1970s turns out to be an excellent era to set a Kong movie in. That's not just because it's almost possible to imagine Skull Island going undiscovered until the advent of satellite photography but because Kong movies map well onto the template for Vietnam movies: overconfident Americans with heavy ordnance crossing the Pacific Ocean and getting obliterated by the natives.

> *"It's time to show Kong that man is king."*

The *Skull Island* filmmakers underline those parallels in ways that are subtle (the boat going upriver into hostile territory, like a monster-movie version of *Apocalypse Now*) and not (the soldiers serving in Vietnam who get deployed as escorts on a Skull Island survey mission).

The cast is full of veteran actors giving their all for their paychecks, knowing full well that they're going to be upstaged by the giant lizards and the 104-foot-tall gorilla. Particularly engaging are John Goodman as a reckless scientist and John C. Reilly as a pilot who has been living on Skull Island for three decades, parachuting onto it after a dogfight in

World War II. And Samuel L. Jackson plays Preston Packard, the commander of the U.S. Army's 3rd Assault Helicopter Company, a military man on the verge of being rotated home who's grateful to have one more mission. When his squad of helicopters fly into the hurricane-force storm surrounding Skull Island, he exhorts them with the tale of Icarus: "The United States Army is not an irresponsible father, so they gave us wings of white-hot, cold-rolled Pennsylvania steel, guaranteed not to melt."

"This is my homage to Gregory Peck," Jackson said. "I'm Ahab and King Kong is the white whale." After Kong wipes out most of his men, Packard finds the purpose his life has been missing: he's hell-bent on taking down Kong. Jackson plays the obsession with such force, you can see why other characters go along with him, even knowing that they're on a suicide mission. Two characters in the movie can look Kong in the eye without fear: Brie Larson's photojournalist, because she makes a genuine connection with the primate, and Samuel L. Jackson's lieutenant colonel, because he's that much of a badass.

The Hitman's Bodyguard (2017)

Darius Kincaid

MOVIE: 6/10   SLJ FACTOR: 7/10   MINUTES UNTIL HE SHOWS UP: 11

EXPLETIVES NOT DELETED: fucking (x17), motherfucker (x19), fuck (x9), bitch (x6), shit (x32), dickhead (x3), shitwagon, motherfuckers (x2), bullshit, dick (x3), goddamn (x2), titty (x2), pussy, fucked (x2), fucked-up

Two months before the cameras rolled, *The Hitman's Bodyguard* was going to be a dramatic thriller, heavy on the action. Then the producers realized that they had cast Samuel L. Jackson as the hit man and Ryan Reynolds as the bodyguard, both of whom bring the funny, and commissioned a frantic two-week rewrite to retool the movie as an action comedy.

"While all you guys are wasting your time planning and aiming and deducing, I just do my thing. And my thing has always been better than your fucking thing."

The result, unsurprisingly, feels like a rush job: the tone is light, but the script is full of chuffa instead of jokes. (The Hollywood-writer term "chuffa," as defined by Mindy Kaling when she was writing and acting in *The Office*: "Chuffa is filler that seems like it's funny but isn't really a joke. It's just kind of an attitude.")

The action scenes deliver: the body count is large, the car chases are high-speed, and Jackson even takes the helm of a speedboat for an extended sequence in the canals of Amsterdam. (Jackson: "The great thing about the speedboat is the faster it goes, the safer it is.") And Gary Oldman, whose role as the murderous dictator of Belarus appears to have been untouched by the rewrite, makes for a compelling villain.

Jackson is Darius Kincaid, a foul-mouthed assassin who enjoys life and believes in love, while Reynolds is Michael Bryce, an uptight security expert who's very good at his job and very bad at the rest of his life. (Does Bryce learn life lessons from his time with Kincaid? Have you ever seen a movie before?) While Jackson and Reynolds are playing underwritten versions of their star personas, they have good chemistry, and sometimes that's enough. When Jackson improvised a gospel blues song on camera, "Nobody Gets Out Alive" (opening lines: "Life is a highway and it's mighty fucking long"), Reynolds expressed just the right amount of frustration before singing counterpoint with Ace of Base's 1994 hit "The Sign."

Similarly, Salma Hayek plays Kincaid's fierce and foul-mouthed wife—except that her character is in a Dutch prison for most of the movie. That's a shame, since she and Jackson have a good rapport when they're together.

Blurring the actors with their characters can pay dividends, as when Bryce, bitching about Kincaid to a confused Dutchman, complains, "This guy single-handedly ruined the word 'motherfucker' "—it seems much more like Reynolds taking a poke at Jackson.

"I thought it was hilarious," Jackson said. "Most people say I glorify the word. That's the first time I've heard someone say I ruined it."

Avengers: Infinity War (2018)

Nick Fury (uncredited)
MOVIE: 8/10   SLJ FACTOR: 4/10   MINUTES UNTIL HE SHOWS UP: 147
EXPLETIVES NOT DELETED: none (he dematerializes halfway through saying "motherfucker")

Culminating ten years of Marvel Cinematic Universe movies, the storyline of *Infinity War* is cosmic: despite the best efforts of dozens of superheroes and gods, the large purple bad guy Thanos collects the Infinity Stones, becomes omnipotent, and following the philosophy of

Thomas Malthus (1766–1834), decides to solve the universe's ills by eliminating half of all living beings with the snap of a finger.

Although the movie juggles an absurd number of stars and plotlines, it's surprisingly witty and nimble, and it makes sure just about everyone in the cast gets a moment of glory. Nick Fury once again appears in a post-credits scene, this one dramatizing the damage that happens *"Still no word from Stark?"* when half the world's population suddenly disappears: not only do superheroes turn into clouds of dust, but helicopters, suddenly lacking pilots, crash into buildings in balls of flame. In a short scene, Samuel L. Jackson plays a man who somehow is both overwhelmed and decisive. Nick Fury has a few seconds of life before he gets dusted himself—just long enough to send a distress call to Captain Marvel. Fury, the great manipulator and master architect of the MCU, is visibly pushed out of the action here: his disappearance is a vivid demonstration that Thanos has an even greater plan.

Incredibles 2 (2018)

Lucius Best/Frozone
MOVIE: 9/10   SLJ FACTOR: 8/10   MINUTES UNTIL HE SHOWS UP: 5 (in action on a plume of ice); 8 (speaking)

Incredibles 2 director Brad Bird claimed that he had to make this movie because Samuel L. Jackson "went out and started telling people that we were doing it before I knew that we were. We were like, 'What? Sam said what? Oh, I guess we better get to work on it!'"

"You need major life realignment on a number of levels, starting with Baby Superfreak here!"

While it's fun to imagine a world where Jackson's enthusiasm is enough to green-light a $200 million movie, Bird didn't make the sequel until he was ready: it came out fourteen years after the original *Incredibles*. (The action, however, begins moments after the first movie ends, a trick pulled off by only a few other sequels, including *Halloween II* and *Crank: High Voltage*.) As in the first movie, the master plan of the villain (here: Screenslaver) barely makes sense. And again, it doesn't matter, because there's so much to enjoy—a backyard battle between the superpowered baby Jack-Jack and a raccoon, astonishingly creative fight scenes that use the physics of teleportation in unexpected ways, even an overwhelmed Mr. Incredible at home, trying to be a good father. In Bird's hands, the well-worn tropes of sitcoms and superheroes, when combined, somehow both feel miraculously fresh.

Jackson once again plays the best friend whose finest moments come when he's struggling to maintain his cool—and does nothing to diminish the idea that a Frozone spinoff movie would be a frosty delight. Asked for his favorite character in the movie, Jackson didn't shine the spotlight on himself, for once—he nominated the pint-size fashion-designer tornado Edna Mode (voiced by Bird). "Edna is just the dopest. She's just, you know: wise, cool, dry, unaffected by the world," Jackson said. "The world revolves around her."

Life Itself (2018)

Himself
MOVIE: 5/10   **SLJ FACTOR:** 7/10   **MINUTES UNTIL HE SHOWS UP:** 0 (voice-over), 4 (in person)
EXPLETIVES NOT DELETED: motherfucker (x2), shit (x5), asshole, fuck (x2)

Let's talk about the first five minutes of *Life Itself*: Samuel L. Jackson, our narrator, doesn't just comment on the action—he tries to take control of the movie, demanding camera movements and music cues. When the story takes an abruptly gruesome turn on a New York City street, Jackson rises up in a gaggle of horrified bystanders, shouting "Holy shit!" He then declares, "I'm out," and departs the movie. (This turns out not to be strictly true—he shows up again later when a clip from *Pulp Fiction* plays—but it's far from the most deceptive maneuver this movie has in store, so we'll let it slide.) If all you want to see is five entertaining minutes of a "Sam Jackson unreliable-narrator screenplay," as this movie-within-a-movie is revealed to be, this would also be a fine moment for you to exit.

> *"Now, like any great hero, our hero wasn't perfect. She smoked, first of all—which they normally don't let you show in movies anymore, even though we all still smoke sometimes."*

Now let's talk about the next 112 minutes: writer-director Dan Fogelman (best known for the TV show *This Is Us*) tells a love story that encompasses multiple generations, Bob Dylan's 1997 album *Time Out of Mind*, and an unrelenting assault of parental death (disease! guns! traffic accidents!). A superb cast (Oscar Isaac, Mandy Patinkin, Annette

Bening, Antonio Banderas, Olivia Wilde, Alex Monner) does top-notch work. The movie is expertly crafted, it has lots of solid jokes, and it carefully uses its metafictional flourishes to land its emotional punches. It's also glib, manipulative claptrap. A cheap melodrama dressed up in fancy postmodern clothes, it turns out, is still a cheap melodrama.

KINGSMAN

THE SECRET SERVICE

Crixtover Edwin.

Jalmari Helander, who directed Samuel L. Jackson in *Big Game*, vividly remembered the day he flew from Austria to Germany with his lead actor. They were escorted through the airport like they were walking the red carpet at a movie premiere: all doors were opened for them, all lines were cut, all seats in first class were reserved for Jackson and his traveling party. "It's easy to go through the airport if you're Samuel Jackson," Helander concluded.

Jackson cruised through life the way he went through airports. He kept striding forward—enjoying the luxuries and comforts of his celebrity, and accepting them as the result of the hard work he had put into being Samuel L. Jackson. He turned sixty-five in 2013, which didn't slow down his work schedule but did earn him a senior-citizen rate when he went to movie theaters. When *Kingsman: The Secret Service* was released in 2015, featuring his lisping turn as a billionaire supervillain, Jackson saw it eight or nine times with live audiences, flashing his ID at the box office each time. "I'm not too proud," he said of the discount. "I've earned it."

Most years, Jackson made four or five movies, ranging from the latest MCU installment to children's cartoons to arthouse turns (and with an increasing amount of straight-to-video thriller dreck to keep him busy). He still gravitated toward high-quality studio popcorn movies, preferably ones he would have enjoyed as a child, and he was paid handsomely for them: his work in *Kong: Skull Island* earned him around $5 million.

Even more lucrative were his endorsements and commercials, most notably for Capital One credit cards. His Capital One TV ads, which began in 2013, ranged from hard sells to goofy buddy-comedy spots about going on a road trip with Charles Barkley and Spike Lee. For that ongoing campaign, which he referred to as "my real job," he was paid over $10 million per year, putting a precise value on how much his aura of cool was worth. Jackson explained, "Sometimes they make you an offer you can't refuse." Not that he was especially conflicted about the gig: at home watching sports on TV, he used to see Jimmy Fallon and Alec Baldwin shilling for Capital One, and wondered how he would deliver the trademark line "What's in your wallet?"

himself, experimenting with emphasizing each of the four words in the catchphrase.

Jackson also continued a sideline in narrating documentary films, on subjects ranging from writer James Baldwin (*I Am Not Your Negro*) to heavyweight boxer Jack Johnson (*Unforgivable Blackness*) to lions and cheetahs (*African Cats*). Director Morgan Neville very much wanted Jackson to narrate his documentary on Stax Records (*Respect Yourself*) but got nowhere until the well-connected Norman Lear called in a favor with Jackson's agent. When Jackson arrived at the recording studio, he wasn't friendly, Neville reported. "He wasn't mean—he was just all business. Highly intimidating, but a pro." Neville handed Jackson the script: the actor then stepped up to the microphone and nailed one perfect line reading after another.

Within half an hour, Jackson completed the job and was out the door. The sound engineer exhaled and told Neville, "I've been doing this for twenty years and I've never seen anybody do what he just did."

A couple of years later, Sam Moore—of the Stax Records duo Sam & Dave and the hit single "Soul Man"—sued the Weinstein Company and the producers of the movie *Soul Men*, saying that it had appropriated elements of his own life. Since Jackson had starred in the movie alongside Bernie Mac, his familiarity with Moore's history and dance moves became a legal issue. Jackson testified in a deposition that he never actually watched *Respect Yourself*—and that, in fact, he hadn't seen many of the documentaries that he had narrated. (Moore lost the lawsuit.)

Jackson also narrated two audiobooks. One was *A Rage in Harlem*, a 1957 hard-boiled detective novel by the pioneering Black author Chester Himes. The other was *Go the Fuck to Sleep*, the foul-mouthed parody of picture books that so struck a chord with exhausted parents that it hit number one on the *New York Times* best-seller list. Jackson was the best possible person to recite poetry such as "The cats nestle close to their kittens, / The lambs have laid down with the sheep. / You're cozy and warm in your bed, my dear. / Please go the fuck to sleep."

Although his belief in live theater was the foundation of his worldview, Jackson's appearances onstage became increasingly rare. In 2011, he played Martin Luther King Jr. in *The Mountaintop* on Broadway, costarring with Angela Bassett in Katori Hall's play, set on the night before King was assassinated. (He got better reviews than the play.) A decade passed before he announced that he planned to return to the New York stage in 2022, directed by his wife, LaTanya Richardson (who now professionally used the name LaTanya Richardson Jackson). The timetable was uncertain, both because of the pandemic and because of the scandal-induced withdrawal of the rage-filled producer Scott Rudin, but the play was a classic of twentieth-century Black theater that Jackson knew extremely well: August Wilson's *The Piano Lesson*. Jackson would be playing Doaker Charles, not the role of Boy Willie that he had originated thirty-five years earlier, but he would finally be starring in *The Piano Lesson* on Broadway.

Jackson was born in the era when mass media meant radio and newsprint, but he embraced the twenty-first-century opportunities available to a multiplatform celebrity. On his Twitter feed, he was loud about sporting events, he corrected random people's grammar ("Somebody needs to," he said), and he spelled "motherfucker" as many different ways as his keyboard would allow. He played himself in *Funny or Die* videos (in one, produced by his daughter, he had a "sad-off" with Anne Hathaway, arguing over whether *Django Unchained* or *Les Misérables* was more depressing; in another, random people accosted him for all the ways in which their children had mimicked his bad onscreen behavior). He sang "Raspberry Beret" with Brie Larson on *Carpool Karaoke*.

In June 2021, the Academy of Motion Picture Arts and Sciences announced that Jackson would finally be getting his long-deserved Oscar in 2022. "Sam Jackson is a cultural icon whose dynamic work has resonated across genres and generations and audiences worldwide," said Academy president David Rubin. The golden trophy was overdue: Jackson had already been receiving lifetime-achievement honors for many years.

In 2000, Jackson received a star on the Hollywood Walk of Fame, at 7018 Hollywood Boulevard, near the stars of Meryl Streep and Wesley Snipes; six years later, Jackson's victory tour continued across the street, when he put his hands and feet in the wet cement outside the Chinese Theater movie house. "We got a little gray film around the heel and sole of the shoes," he reported. Richardson Jackson took his shoes after the ceremony so she could put them in a shadowbox, which meant that Jackson sacrificed a pair of Armani dress shoes. "It was her thought: they need to be really good shoes," he said. "Why? You get cement on 'em!"

Jackson took his shoes seriously. He had what he described as a "sneaker fetish," which meant that he owned hundreds of pairs, every box labeled with color and style. "It looks like a Foot Locker in my closet," he conceded. He knew the size of his collection made his wife nuts: "She's got a ton of shit, but she still thinks I have too much."

Once Jackson received a free pair of Tod's driving shoes in an awards-show gift basket (driving shoes are thin-soled moccasins with rubber nubs on the soles that increase your control over the car pedals). They didn't fit, so he visited the Tod's store in Beverly Hills, where a salesclerk said he could exchange them for any pair he wanted. He got excited when he spotted a pair of alligator Tod's—and pissed off when the clerk said, apologetically, that those were the one style that were off-limits, because they were $5,000 a pair. "Fuck it," he said. "Give me the black ones and the brown ones." He walked out of the store and thought, "How fucking stupid was that? I spent ten thousand dollars for two pairs of fucking alligator loafers. How did I let that happen?" He knew that he had let his arrogance get the best of him—but he figured that it had worked out in the long run, since he did wear the shoes.

Jackson's most famous style choice was his love of Kangol caps— wearing them was a habit he picked up from his grandfather—but he was a sharp dresser who always picked the right clothes for the occasion. "Every event has its own cachet," he said. "Going to the golf course in the morning, if it's hot, I put on some bright shorts and a very cool shirt and I blind the guys—they're always going, 'Oh my God.' Yeah, but I feel *good*. At the Bob Hope Desert Classic, I had these lime-green shirts and yellow sweaters and these throwback plaid pants. It was cool. Sometimes you want to be subtle—at the SAG Awards, I went with the whole penguin look, black black black, but I had this diamond stick-pin that was really awesome, so I said, 'Okay, I'll stick this in, because I don't want to be a penguin.' Every year when I go to the Academy Awards, I have a discussion with the people at Armani about a specific kind of material: we see if they can find a specific color, just so I don't look like everybody else." He integrated his past fashion choices into his adult style, encompassing both the Ivy League clothes that his mother bought for him when he was growing up and the tie-dye fashions he gravitated to when he went to college. "I end up wearing very traditional clothes with wild colors inside them," he explained. "I wear orange with a traditional herringbone suit."

Jackson's movie contracts not only carved out time off for him to play golf, they mandated that his trailer would be equipped with satellite television. Between scenes, he could indulge his daytime viewing of choice: judge shows. Not only did he watch one reality courtroom drama after another, he was good friends with Judith Sheindlin—better known as the acid-tongued Judge Judy.

They met at the house of Jackson's longtime agent, Toni Howard; Sheindlin and Jackson would sit in the backyard smoking cigarettes. When Sheindlin finally quit—her habit was so serious, she used to wake up in the middle of the night for a smoke break—she sent Jackson to the doctor who had helped her stop, who used a treatment involving sodium pentothal (aka "truth serum").

"Judy's awesome," Jackson said. "I've had tea with Judy at the Dorchester in London." They regularly went out for meals and sometimes flew across the country together on Sheindlin's private plane. At Jackson's star-studded seventieth birthday party, featuring Questlove as DJ and Stevie Wonder as the musical entertainment, she was the guest who pulled him away from his dinner and onto the dance floor.

Aside from enjoying her company, Jackson respected her earning power as one of the highest-paid people in television. (In 2018, she earned $47 million for fifty-two days of filming.) "She's straight-up clocking dollars," he said admiringly.

Jackson was often asked when he was going to direct a movie. He was overqualified for the job in many ways—smart, driven, attentive to detail, at home on a movie set—and his exceptional record at the box office meant that he wouldn't have trouble getting financing. After flirting with the idea for many years, he decided that he preferred his current job: instead of working for a year and a half on a single project, he would rather spend that time acting in a half-dozen different movies.

He did, however, flex his Hollywood muscle as a producer (via his company Uppity Films). Some of his ideas for TV series never got traction—for example, the sci-fi show about four immortal women guarding the world from the forces of evil—but he and Richardson Jackson were the executive producers of *Enslaved*, a British-Canadian documentary miniseries about the history of slavery in the United States. The show was built around footage of deep-sea divers exploring the wrecks of slave ships on the bottom of the Atlantic Ocean, where hundreds of thousands of captured human beings died as human cargo. That approach to the tragic history of the Middle Passage not only appealed to Jackson's sense of history, it tapped into his youthful fascination with oceanography. Jackson hosted; the series also showed him tracing his family roots to the Benga tribe in Gabon.

"To find out that I was part of a tribe that was still in existence was a revelation," Jackson said. When he visited Gabon, he was profoundly moved by how the Benga treated him like a returning son: "That made me feel like I was coming home." he said. He could look around, and every person he saw had a "familial look, like my uncles, my cousins."

Three decades after *School Daze*, Jackson and his parking-lot sparring partner Laurence Fishburne were still being mistaken for each other— "even though we don't look anything alike," Fishburne accurately noted. Jackson probably would have kept track of the credits of his old friend, but he didn't have any choice, because total strangers would ask him if he had played Cowboy Curtis on *Pee-wee's Playhouse* (nope, that was Fishburne) or shout "Matrix!" at him on the street (wrong again—that was Fishburne's most famous role, Morpheus in the *Matrix* trilogy).

Jackson usually brushed those mistakes off, but in February 2014, he was doing a live satellite interview about the *RoboCop* remake with the KTLA TV station in Los Angeles when entertainment reporter Sam Rubin asked him if he had gotten a lot of attention for his Super Bowl ad. The problem: Jackson didn't have any commercials in the Super Bowl that year—Rubin was confusing him with Fishburne, who had appeared in a *Matrix*-themed ad for Kia cars. "I'm not Laurence Fishburne. We don't all look alike!" Jackson yelled. "You're the entertainment reporter for this station and you don't know the difference between me and Laurence Fishburne? There must be a very short line for your job." Rubin, visibly squirming, tried to turn the subject of conversation to *RoboCop*, but Jackson wasn't ready to let it go.

"Hell no!" he said. "There's more than one Black guy doing a commercial. I'm the 'What's in your wallet?' Black guy. He's the car Black guy. Morgan Freeman is the *other* credit card Black guy. You only hear his voice, though, so you probably won't confuse him with Laurence Fishburne."

After decades of being polite to confused strangers and racist fools who couldn't tell him and Fishburne apart, Jackson treated Rubin, and millions of viewers, to the righteous blast of his fury. Everyone knew Jackson was good at playing fictional characters, but it turned out he was at his most powerful when he was telling the truth.

Similarly, Jackson warned American voters about Donald Trump before he was elected, delivering a factual report on the man's character from the setting where he had witnessed it in action: the golf course. Jackson told a reporter that he had received a bill for dues from the Trump National Golf Club, a place where he had never enrolled as a member, although he had played a round with Donald Trump. Asked which of the two of them was a better golfer, Jackson replied, "Oh, I am, for sure. I don't cheat."

Trump, predictably, threw a tantrum, asserting that Jackson had to cheat at golf himself because his swing was so bad, complaining that the actor did too many commercials, and claiming that he had never met the actor. Jackson, however, literally had receipts.

While Jackson was bothered by Trump's dishonesty, he wasn't especially concerned by his narcissism—that was a character flaw he shared. Jackson was offended by actors who couldn't cop to their own self-regard and complained "I hate watching myself": if you couldn't stand watching yourself in a movie, why would you expect other people to pay good money to watch you?

Fundamentally, he didn't believe his fellow performers when they feigned modesty: acting was a "look-at-me business," Jackson knew all too well. "It's all about the narcissism of being in something and watching yourself in it!" he said. When he was flipping through channels at home, if he came across a movie he was in, he would stop and savor it. "The whole time I was doing theater, I always wanted to watch the plays I was in, but I wanted to watch 'em with me in 'em. And now I'm in the perfect venue: I can watch myself work." We couldn't all be Samuel L. Jackson, but we could enjoy watching him almost as much as he did.

Glass (2019)

Elijah Price
MOVIE: 5/10   **SLJ FACTOR:** 7/10   **MINUTES UNTIL HE SHOWS UP:** 23 (left forearm only), 29 (full body)
EXPLETIVES NOT DELETED: bitch-ass

After a while, Samuel L. Jackson got tired of asking M. Night Shyamalan what was up with the sequels to *Unbreakable*. When they made the 2002 movie, Shyamalan had told him that it would be the first movie of a trilogy, but the director shelved those plans after it grossed "only" $248 million: a massive hit, but dwarfed by the $677 million of his debut, *The Sixth Sense*.

> *"Everything extraordinary can be explained away, and yet it is true."*

"I always assumed that the studio looked at it as a failure because it didn't make as much money as the 'I see dead people' movie," Jackson said.

Then in 2016, Shyamalan called up Jackson and asked him to go to a private screening for his latest movie, *Split*, but wouldn't explain why. *Split* starred James McAvoy as a kidnapper with twenty-four different personalities, one of them a superpowered cannibal called the Beast. The twist, revealed in its final moments by a cameo of Bruce Willis playing David Dunn: it takes place in the same world as *Unbreakable*.

Once *Split* was a hit, Shyamalan reunited many of the actors from both movies for *Glass*, the final film in the trilogy: not just Jackson, Willis, and McAvoy in the leading roles, but supporting actors reprising roles from seventeen years earlier, including Spencer Treat Clark as Dunn's son, Charlayne Woodard as Elijah's mother, and even Bostin Christopher as the clerk in a comic-book store. "Night still uses the same crew," Christopher said, "so the first AD was like, 'Hey, welcome back!'" The three leads spend most of the movie confined to a psychiatric ward run by Dr. Staple (played by Sarah Paulson), a psychiatrist working to convince them that superheroes aren't real.

One of *Glass*'s problems is that the previous two movies were in very different modes—slow-burn superheroics in *Unbreakable*, psychological horror in *Split*—and they don't mesh well here. Another is that although Jackson has the title role, for the first half of the movie, he plays a character in a catatonic stupor, not doing anything more physical than twitching some facial muscles. Jackson described his job on this movie as "trying to figure out an active way to be passive," saying that a common precept for acting is "listen; react." In this case, he said, "my basic job was to sit there and listen and not really react, because we don't want people to think he's that cogent."

Eventually Mr. Glass reveals that not only is he cogent, he has an elaborate plan. It's a relief when he starts speaking in complete sentences, even though he remains subdued. Jackson doesn't get to scale the operatic heights that he did in *Unbreakable*, but he has some nicely underplayed moments, none better than when he responds to McAvoy howling at him by calmly observing, "Well, that sounds like the bad guys teaming up."

Captain Marvel (2019)

Nick Fury

MOVIE: 7/10   SLJ FACTOR: 8/10   MINUTES UNTIL HE SHOWS UP: 28

EXPLETIVES NOT DELETED: none (but he does say the excellent coinage "mother-Flerkin")

The twenty-first feature film in the Marvel Cinematic Universe was the first one to put a woman front and center: Oscar winner Brie Larson plays Carol Danvers, aka Captain Marvel, the most powerful superhero in the MCU.

The bulk of the movie is set in 1995, allowing for Elastica on the soundtrack and AltaVista

"If toast is cut diagonally, I can't eat it."

on the computer screens. Danvers comes to Earth on a mission for an alien race called the Kree and teams up with a young SHIELD bureaucrat named Nick Fury—Samuel L. Jackson, made to look twenty-five years younger through the power of digital special effects. The good news is that CGI has improved to the point where its presence doesn't make viewers cry blood. The bad news is that it's still distracting, because we know what Jackson looked like in 1995 and this isn't quite right. (It looks better than Robert De Niro digitally shaving off five decades in *The Irishman* the same year, though.)

The most important friendships in the movie are between women: Carol Danvers and her pilot pal Maria Rambeau (and Maria's young daughter, Monica). But the section where Danvers and Fury bond is a low-key delight. It's a reprise of Jackson's great work on *The Long Kiss Goodnight*, going on a road trip with a young woman who is slowly remembering her past and discovering her extraordinary abilities. In both cases, Jackson seems completely comfortable playing second banana, building a relationship on a foundation of friendship and humor rather than lust.

The movie is also an origin story for Fury: the turning point in his life when he decided that Earth needed superheroes. Jackson does an excellent job calibrating his performance, showing a protean version of Fury, a former soldier born in Alabama who isn't running things yet but doesn't waste much time freaking out when he discovers that aliens are real. He bonds quickly with a tabby cat named Goose—who knew Fury was a cat guy?—and barely misses a step when Goose turns out to be an incredibly powerful extraterrestrial known as a Flerkin. Jackson said, "The cat we worked with the most, Reggie, was pretty professional. Reggie was pretty good about hitting his mark, and you'd…talk softly to him and give him a snack after he does his thing." Jackson noted that Reggie wasn't that different from human performers: "Kind of like us, with a check!"

Unicorn Store (2019)

The Salesman
MOVIE: 8/10   **SLJ FACTOR:** 8/10   **MINUTES UNTIL HE SHOWS UP:** 21
EXPLETIVES NOT DELETED: shit (x2)

Rainbows and glitter and unicorns: the aesthetic that made Kit happy as a little girl doesn't serve her so well when she grows up and goes to art school. Flunking out, Kit moves back home to wallow in young-adult depression: sleeping in her parents' basement, working at a stultifying temp job, confiding in her Care Bears. But then she gets an invitation to The Store, a magical venue that exists for her

> *"Graph paper can't love you back!"*

alone and promises to sell her exactly what she needs. The proprietor is Samuel L. Jackson, who favors brightly colored suits and a sparkly wig that looks like something Flip Wilson rejected for his Geraldine character. He is bubbly and weird and commanding, and he offers to sell Kit a real unicorn.

Unicorn Store is incredibly twee, but it's also charming and laugh-out-loud funny. Brie Larson, who stars as Kit, directed the movie, her first feature; she proves to be confident and gifted behind the camera. Like Michel Gondry, she takes the visual language of whimsy and uses it to tell a human story: in this case, a woman figuring out how much of herself she'll have to give up to be an adult. The cast also includes Mamoudou Athie, screenwriter Samantha McIntyre, and doing exceptional work as Kit's parents, the peppy leaders of a wilderness skills/encounter group called Emotion Quest, Bradley Whitford and Joan Cusack.

Larson auditioned for the role of Kit circa 2012 but didn't get the part. That version of the movie (directed by Miguel Arteta and starring Rebel Wilson) never got made, but five years later, the producers came back to Larson. She began preproduction while she was in Hawaii and Vietnam, filming *Kong: Skull Island* with Jackson. "He found out I was directing and on the *Kong* set started begging for the job, which is a very surreal experience," she said. "There's a reason he's one of the greatest and most successful actors of our time; he's incredibly hardworking and creative and collaborative. He designed this character, everything down to the tinsel in his hair. I think he went to a Beyoncé concert and she had tinsel in her hair and he came back and said, 'I need that.'"

Avengers: Endgame (2019)

Nick Fury
MOVIE: 9/10   SLJ FACTOR: 2/10   MINUTES UNTIL HE SHOWS UP: 158

As the conclusion of a story stretching across twenty-one previous Marvel Cinematic Universe movies, *Avengers: Endgame* is a crowning pop-culture achievement unlike any other, even if it's not recommended for people who aren't fans of the MCU. A three-hour epic, it's split fairly evenly between time-travel hijinks, an enormous CGI battle, and, surprisingly, sorrow: our heroes spend most of the movie's opening hour soaking in grief, lamenting the half of the world's population that doesn't exist anymore because of their failure to stop Thanos. Somehow this added up to the highest-grossing movie of all time (unless you adjust for inflation, in which case it was still *Gone with the Wind*).

After the Avengers assemble, there are worldwide celebrations for the return of the vanished, which contrasts with a silent lakeside memorial service for Tony Stark, who nobly sacrificed himself. A total MCU flex: for that four-minute sequence, they got two Oscar winners (William Hurt, Marisa Tomei) to show up for cameo appearances, reprising their previous characters without any dialogue—not to mention three additional silent Oscar nominees (Samuel L. Jackson, Angela Bassett, and Michelle Pfeiffer). Jackson is the final figure in a long tracking shot, gazing off into the distance for a few seconds. Jackson's presence in an eye patch is required more than his acting skills here; he could be pondering Tony Stark's legacy, or wondering when Nick Fury will get a solo movie, or thinking about his tee time.

Shaft (2019)

John Shaft
MOVIE: 5/10   **SLJ FACTOR:** 7/10   **MINUTES UNTIL HE SHOWS UP:** 1
EXPLETIVES NOT DELETED: fucking (x5), motherfucker (x20), fuck (x15), shit (x30), pussy (x8), shitbag, bitch, goddamn, motherfuckers (x5), fucked (x3), motherfucking, shitload, god-motherfucking-damn, dickhead (x2)

Blaxploitation movies kicked off in 1971 with *Sweet Sweetback's Baadasssss Song*, followed two months later by *Shaft*. The genre featured Black actors taking center stage as pimps, pushers, and private eyes, sticking it to a racist system. (Plus gratuitous sex scenes and some really good funk music.) Decades later, most of the genre's innovations and transgressions have been thoroughly mined by mainstream movies and gangsta rap—so how to continue its legacy? One way is to make a movie *about* blaxploitation (e.g., *Dolemite Is My Name*). Another, less satisfying one, is to repackage its characters in another genre: *Shaft* as an action movie in 2002, *Shaft* as a buddy-cop movie here. (Demonstrating how out of ideas this franchise is: three out of the five *Shaft* movies have the identical title of *Shaft*.)

"What do I want? Wow, it's been so long since somebody asked me that. Well, now that you ask, I want cheap over-the-counter erectile cream. I want Jodeci and Al Green to drop a Christmas album. I want twenty-four hours uninterrupted with Halle Berry—hence the erectile cream. But what I really want to know is why you didn't afford my son the respect associated with the Shaft family name."

The mismatched partners in this movie: Samuel L. Jackson as John Shaft, still on the job but gone to seed, and his previously estranged thirty-year-old son JJ Shaft (Jessie Usher), a nerdy FBI data analyst. The script, by two TV veterans (Kenya Barris and Alex Barnow), emphasizes the comedy of the situation: some jokes land, but long stretches are hokey and dull. And this movie turns John Shaft into an irascible sit-com dad; while previously, he was old-school but suave, now he's too often crude and clueless and homophobic. (The 1971 movie was more progressive when it came to gay characters!)

A gray-haired Richard Roundtree shows up to give the affair a little dignity, and seventeen years after he last donned the trench coat, Jackson provides some heart: underneath all the wisecracks and the firefights, we see glimmers of a man longing for a human connection. Some of the connections between the three generations of Shafts feel forced, like the matching suede jackets they all wear at the end. But one touch is elegant: all three Shafts routinely jaywalk into traffic, and every time they do, it recalls the opening sequence of the 1971 *Shaft*, when Roundtree strode across the busy streets of Times Square, walking with the confidence that comes naturally to a king of New York City.

Spider-Man: Far from Home (2019)

Nick Fury
MOVIE: 7/10   SLJ FACTOR: 7/10   MINUTES UNTIL HE SHOWS UP: 1
EXPLETIVES NOT DELETED: bitch, bullshit

A charming teenage superhero caper set in Europe, *Far from Home* is also an extremely self-conscious movie. That's partially because it's the first MCU installment after Tony Stark's death in *Avengers: Endgame*; Peter Parker wondering whether it's worth continuing with the super-hero gig certainly echoes the thoughts of the movie's creators (and viewers!) after the conclusion of an epic twenty-two-movie story.

The meta quality becomes even more explicit with the movie's villain, Mysterio (Jake Gyllenhaal): a showman who uses CGI to make people believe they're watching a costumed hero fight in historic cities, battling against a deadly threat to life and landmarks. If Spider-Man falling for Mysterio's gimmicks makes him a sucker, then what does that make the people who paid to watch this movie?

Samuel L. Jackson's performance as Nick Fury has a different

> *"I used to know everything. Then I come back five years later, and now I know nothing. No intel, no team, and a high-school kid is dodging my calls."*

emotional tenor than usual: he's still pulling strings and barking orders, but where he previously seemed indifferent to the feelings of the humans and superhumans he recruited, now he's a father figure: emotionally invested in the choices of Peter Parker and disappointed when Peter makes bad decisions during a school trip. The kicker, we find out at the end of the movie, is that we haven't been watching the actual Fury, but a shape-shifting Skrull impersonating him while the real one-eyed McCoy chills out on a spaceship. (Except for the sequence where it's actually Mysterio pretending to be Fury.)

Jackson does a good job with the unusual assignment of impersonating himself, simultaneously presenting both his public face and the vulnerability of somebody who's trying that persona on for the first time to see how it fits. It's almost like Jackson has spent years of his life with strangers walking up to him and repeating his most famous movie lines to him.

Star Wars: Episode IX—The Rise of Skywalker (2019)

Mace Windu
MOVIE: 7/10   **SLJ FACTOR:** 1/10   **MINUTES UNTIL HE SHOWS UP:** 117 (voice)

Jedi, like Weebles and Chumbawumba, get knocked down, but they get up again. When Rey (Daisy Ridley), last of the Jedi, is lying flat on her back, about to lose the climactic battle for the fate of the galaxy, she hears a chorus of eleven voices from the previous eight episodes of the *Star Wars* saga and the *Clone Wars* TV

> *"Feel the Force flowing through you, Rey."*

show: the "Voices of Jedi Past," including Liam Neeson, Mark Hamill, Ewan McGregor, and even Alec Guinness. Depending on how much you've bought into the franchise's mythology, it's a powerful reminder of her mystical lineage or a pep talk at an old-timers' game. Frank Oz as Yoda and Liam Neeson as Qui-Gon Jinn have the most distinctive voices, but Samuel L. Jackson, delivering two lines as Mace Windu, runs close behind.

The movie brings the third *Star Wars* trilogy to a lurching conclusion, full of remixed plot elements and guest stars from the original trilogy, and with noticeable course corrections between J. J. Abrams (director of *Episode VII* and this finale) and Rian Johnson (director of *Episode VIII*). The cast is engaging, the sweep is epic, the chemistry between Ridley and Adam Driver is real—but since the bad guy is

Emperor Palpatine (Ian McDiarmid), parachuting in from the afterlife and revealed to have been pulling the strings all along, it feels unsatisfying, as if Abrams is pleading the Sith.

The Last Full Measure (2020)

Billy Takoda
MOVIE: 6/10   SLJ FACTOR: 7/10   MINUTES UNTIL HE SHOWS UP: 18
EXPLETIVES NOT DELETED: shithole, shit (x2), assholes, goddamn

The center of *The Last Full Measure* is William H. Pitsenbarger, a real-life U.S. Air Force medic and pararescue jumper who came to the rescue of an Army division on a particularly bloody day in the Vietnam War. Nobly sacrificing his own life rather than helicoptering out of a heated battle, he may have saved as many as sixty soldiers. But the protagonist of this movie, for some reason, is a callow civilian lawyer in the Pentagon (Sebastian Stan), tasked with looking into why Pitsenbarger didn't receive the Medal of Honor. Does this investigation lead to a posthumous medal for Pitsenbarger and growing and learning and hugging for the lawyer? Yes, it does.

> *"I sit around year in and year out thinking about twenty seconds thirty-two years ago I wish to God I could have back."*

The movie was clearly a labor of love for writer-director Todd Robinson, who spent two decades bringing it to the screen (long enough that the credits collected twenty-nine producers of various stripes). It's well-intentioned, earnest, and mawkish; what elevates it is a world-class cast of older actors giving it their all. Christopher Plummer and Diane Ladd play Pitsenbarger's parents, while William Hurt, Ed Harris, and Peter Fonda (in his final film role) play aging veterans.

All of them are damaged by what happened in Vietnam, some more overtly than others. Jackson is one of those vets, now a bespectacled grandfather taking his grandchildren fishing; when he meets the lawyer, he throws his tape recorder into the water and deflects his inquiries with philosophical parsing. To play Billy Takoda, Jackson creates a complex character who deploys his natural charisma and comic timing as defense mechanisms. In the space of a couple of scenes, Jackson renders a man who's wry, understated, and doing anything he can to distract himself from the guilt he's been carrying on his back for decades.

The Banker (2020)

Joe Morris
MOVIE: 7/10   SLJ FACTOR: 8/10   MINUTES UNTIL HE SHOWS UP: 9
EXPLETIVES NOT DELETED: fucking, asshole, shit (x5), goddamn (x4), bitch

When you spend half your life on movie sets, you run into some of the same people over and over. Samuel L. Jackson has made seven films with Anthony Mackie, for example: four Marvel movies, plus *Freedomland*, *The Man*, and *The Banker*. Here, Mackie takes the lead role of the real-life financial wizard Bernard Garrett,

> *"Even a rigged game's fun to play."*

overcoming racism and redlining in 1950s Los Angeles to make a fortune investing in real estate. Garrett is dogged and ambitious, but the movie really hums when Jackson shows up: he portrays Joe Morris, a fleshy, louche nightclub owner who becomes Garrett's partner. He's full of cynicism about American society and full of glee when he can hold that society upside down and shake loose change out of its pockets.

Large chunks of the movie are occupied by the mechanics of real estate investments. These procedural sections are surprisingly entertaining, both because of the rapport between Mackie and Jackson and because seeing two Black investors snooker the ruling class of Los Angeles is like watching a heist movie, only with more math.

The action gets bumpier when they buy a bank in small-town Texas, liberalizing its loan policies to give the Black community access to capital—the movie spends too much time on the young white man (Nicholas Hoult) they hire to be the public face of their partnership. In segregated Texas, two rich Black men have to disguise themselves with menial jobs to keep an eye on their own bank: Garrett resentfully pretends to be the janitor, but Morris poses as a chauffeur with the glee of a child playing dress-up. You can feel the movie straining to extract a political moral from the duo's capitalist exploits, but Jackson's exuberant performance carries a more fundamental message: sticking it to the man can be fun.

Death to 2020 (2020)

Dash Bracket
MOVIE: 5/10   SLJ FACTOR: 6/10   MINUTES UNTIL HE SHOWS UP: 0
EXPLETIVES NOT DELETED: shit (x2), fuck, fucking (x3)

People like fake newscasts. People also like comedic recaps of the year that just happened. But there's more appetite for all of that when the headlines are a mix of triumph and tragedy, rather than an unceasing tornado of ordure. As Samuel L. Jackson says here when he's told that this show will relive the events of 2020: "Why in the fuck would you want to do that?"

He's playing Dash Bracket, a reporter for the *New Yorkerly News*, in this Netflix mockumentary directed by *Black Mirror* creator Charlie Brooker. Jackson's not the only star who showed up for a socially distanced one-day shoot: also offering talking-head commentary on the previous year's events in the United States and the UK are actors including Hugh Grant (as an eccentric historian), Leslie Jones (as a misanthropic psychologist), and Lisa Kudrow (as Kellyanne Conway, although she's given a different name).

> *"In some ways, I prefer the coronavirus to the police. Don't get me wrong, I fucking hate the virus but at least it doesn't pretend it's here to help. It doesn't drive around the neighborhood with 'Protect and Serve' painted on its side before it kills you."*

This seventy-minute special has high production values, a steady supply of moderately clever snark, and not a lot of laughs. Although Jackson offers some unusual jokes ("You watch *Jaws* backwards, it's the story of a shark that spits panicking white people into the sea"—which actually makes sense in context), he plays one of the least schticky roles in the ensemble. You could describe him as the de facto narrator, if it weren't for the sonorous Laurence Fishburne, who provides the actual deadpan narration. That gives Jackson fewer comedic bits than some of the other stars, but it allows him to describe the murder of George Floyd by the Minneapolis police straightforwardly—with the steely, righteous anger that it deserves.

Spiral: From the Book of Saw (2021)

Marcus Banks
MOVIE: 6/10   SLJ FACTOR: 5/10   MINUTES UNTIL HE SHOWS UP: 10 (framed photo on the wall), 25 (in the all-too-fallible flesh)
EXPLETIVES NOT DELETED: fucking (x4), shit (x5), motherfucker (x5), fuck (x5), goddammit, motherfuckers, goddamn, bitch

Back in 2007, when Samuel L. Jackson first heard of the horror genre "torture porn" in an interview, he got very excited. "What is it? Asian extreme, gonzo?" he asked. "I want to see it now!" Fourteen years later, he got to experience the genre up close, appearing in the ninth installment of the *Saw* franchise, a not-for-the-squeamish spinoff called *Spiral*.

> *"Where the fuck were all of you, huh? My son called for backup three times in eight minutes and none of you motherfuckers could get here?"*

The movie was full of the customary Grand Guignol death traps and bloody torments for sinners worthy of Dante's *Inferno*: people pelted with broken glass, fingers pulled off, skin flensed from bodies. It was even directed by Darren Lynn Bousman, who had helmed three previous *Saw* entries. Two elements set it apart from the average *Saw*: one is that it taps into the ACAB mindset, with an "all cops are bad" mastermind who punishes police officers for their abuses of the citizenry. (In fairness, he is the movie's villain.) The other distinguishing element: Chris Rock in the lead role of Zeke Banks, the police detective investigating the murders, giving a compelling performance light on the wisecracks and heavy on the embitterment.

Samuel L. Jackson plays Zeke's father, the retired chief of the police department who is largely estranged from his son. Jackson's performance in the modern day feels bloodless; he exhibits more passion in flashbacks, dealing with the fallout when Zeke turns in his corrupt partner and thereby alienates all his fellow cops. To help viewers keep the timelines straight, Jackson also sports a luxuriant mustache in those flashbacks that makes him look like he was moonlighting in a 1970s porn movie. Given the massive plot holes in *Spiral*, we can't totally rule that theory out.

Unexpected *Pulp Fiction* reference: the vault in the police department's evidence room was manufactured by the Vincent & Jules Safe Company.

The Hitman's Wife's Bodyguard (2021)

Darius Kincaid
MOVIE: 5/10   SLJ FACTOR: 5/10   MINUTES UNTIL HE SHOWS UP: 1
EXPLETIVES NOT DELETED: motherfucker (x17), motherfuckers (x5), fuck (x21),
shit (x18), bitch, fucking (x8), motherfucking (x3), bullshit, Mc-fucking-who, fuck-up,
pussy (x2)

In 1980, Samuel L. Jackson served as understudy to Morgan Freeman in a production of *Mother Courage* at New York's Public Theater, befriending the veteran actor and learning from him. In the following four decades, the two performers made well over 200 movies but somehow never acted together onscreen until

> *"Believe me, I have not begun to express myself."*

The Hitman's Wife's Bodyguard—where Freeman was cast not as somebody close to Jackson's character, hitman Darius Kincaid, but as the father of Ryan Reynolds's character, bodyguard Michael Bryce. (Okay, stepfather.)

The Hitman's Bodyguard was built on the conflict between Reynolds and Jackson, but in this sequel, they've settled into a familiar frenemy groove; the movie revolves around Reynolds, trying to take a sabbatical from violence. Even Salma Hayek, reprising her role as the titular wife, spends more time onscreen with Reynolds than with Jackson (her husband). This movie squanders Jackson's talents, putting him in the unusual position of being along for the ride, both metaphorically and literally.

The movie is loud, fast, and forgettable: the characters careen around Europe, trying to stop a high-tech terrorist plot (masterminded by Antonio Banderas as a Greek plutocrat) to overload the continent's power grid. For some reason, here that results in explosions and high body counts rather than rolling blackouts. Since this movie was conceived as an action comedy from the jump, it really ought to have more laughs. Jackson has one top-shelf comedic sequence, however: Darius walks into a bar in a foul mood, starts a fight, and then happily drinks while mayhem rages around him, confident that no harm can come to him because he's the coolest man in the room.

JURASSIC PARK

OPENING
1993

KUPER

D**ying is a happening thing,"** Samuel L. Jackson said. He ought to know. Jackson died dozens of times onscreen—frequently enough that he became a connoisseur of ways to shuffle off the mortal coil. He was impaled with a prosthetic limb, executed in a gas chamber, and devoured by a shark. "So far I haven't been hung or garroted," he said, "but I'm willing to learn."

Jackson brainstormed novel ways to meet a bloody end, even though most of the time he got shot: bullets in the gut, in the mouth, in the back of the head. "I don't think I've ever been guillotined," he said. (He was correct.) "One death I haven't done is a bullet-riddled body falling off a high building through a greenhouse roof into a shallow pool so that when I hit, the blood just spreads rapidly through the water." For years, he wanted to die with his eyes open, to see if he could make his eyes glaze over as he expired, making sure not to blink: he finally got his chance in *Jungle Fever*.

Although Jackson savored a memorable exit, his pragmatism gradually outweighed the pleasure he took in it: as his career progressed, he always wanted his character to be available to return for a sequel. So he refused to make the first *XXX* movie unless his character survived it, he lobbied for the notion that Mace Windu didn't actually die after being blasted and defenestrated, and he even pitched the idea that he had survived getting munched on by a velociraptor in *Jurassic Park*.

"I'm not necessarily sure I'm dead," he insisted. "See, in my mind, the dinosaur tore my arm off, and I bandaged myself and was in shock for a while. When I woke up, everyone was gone, and I made my way back to the lab. I took Mr. DNA and made a whole little tribe of myself, and we learned how to control the dinosaurs. And when they come back, they'll find a very angry one-armed Black man with about 60 more of us, fighting those velociraptors."

As Jackson entered his seventies, he had to consider his own mortality, even though his own end was unlikely to be as bloody or abrupt as his movie deaths. The relatives who raised him passed away, but most of them succumbed to Alzheimer's first: first his grandfather, then his uncle, then his mother, then his aunt. "I don't think anybody should suffer the heartbreak of having someone who has nurtured you, taken care of you, and loves you reach a point where they can't even call your name," he said. To his surprise, there were some lighthearted moments as his loved ones faded away. When his mother and aunt visited him, they would play charades—which they unfailingly enjoyed, even when they no longer understood what they were supposed to be communicating.

Jackson raised money for the Alzheimer's Association, even doing a grassroots campaign on Reddit where he pledged to record monologues chosen by users of the site when various levels of giving were reached. One of those videos, his menacing version of the "I am the one who knocks" speech from *Breaking Bad*, racked up millions of views on YouTube. Jackson acknowledged the uncomfortable truth: given his genetics, he might find himself in need of Alzheimer's research himself at some future point.

Knowing that, Jackson did everything he could to stay sharp mentally. "I read, I do crossword puzzles, I memorize lines for a living," he said. "Maybe that's why I continue to work—because I want to exercise my mind."

Jackson worked to keep his wits sharp, to get out of the house, to fulfill his childhood dreams, to entertain people. His lifetime record for the cumulative box office of his movies wasn't a quirk of Hollywood accounting, but a testament to his relentless efforts to make all kinds of movies better, through ability and hard work and a peerless talent for saying the word "motherfucker." Of all the improbable roles Samuel L. Jackson imagined, the greatest one may have been himself: he turned a stuttering bookish child from segregated Chattanooga into America's favorite movie star. And the world was a better, cooler place for it.

Given that legacy, I asked him, what did Samuel L. Jackson want on his gravestone?

"My name," he said. "Spelled right."

Acknowledgments

How was your pandemic year? Sometimes weird, sometimes tragic? Yeah, me too.

I started writing this book the same week Samuel L. Jackson went on *Jimmy Kimmel Live* to read the poem "Stay the Fuck at Home" and finished it the same week I got my first Moderna shot. In between, my pandemic year will always be "the year I saw 140 Samuel L. Jackson movies, many of them more than once."

In a time when the world was a particularly confusing and uncertain place, Samuel L. Jackson was the steadiest part of my existence. Watching good movies and bad, I knew I could count on him to show up and do his job: to entertain me, to illuminate the human condition, to kick ass. He wasn't just my biographical subject, he was my role model and my inspiration.

All my love to my amazing wife Jen and my kids Dashiell and Strummer. Dashiell lobbied for me to write this book for years, mostly so he could watch MCU movies with me—I'm very glad that I listened to him. Having a house filled with loud, opinionated people related to me was often distracting, between Zoom classes and conference calls and backyard croquet games, but it was also a constant source of joy.

Because of that full house, I needed to leave sometimes. I can barely express my gratitude to the friends who loaned me guest cottages and vacation homes so I could get away for uninterrupted writing time, without which you would not be reading this book right now. Thank you, a thousand times over, to Andy Dews and Tom Warshauer; to Charlotte and John Wickham; to Betsy Rosen and Liam Stokes; to Chuck Barger and the extended Barger family. Your generosity and hospitality will long be remembered.

Thanks to one bad motherfucker of an editor, Brant Rumble, who has been a champion of this book since day one and who has made it better in countless large and small ways. My name is on the cover of this book, but many other people worked hard on it, including Michael Barrs, Michelle Aielli, Amanda Kain, Sara Wood, Mollie Weisenfeld, Monica Oluwek, Fred Francis, Amy J. Schneider, Lauren Rosenthal, Zach Polendo, Ashley Kiedrowski, moukies, and especially Mary Ann Naples. I thank and salute them all—and everybody else at Hachette Books.

Thank you to Daniel Greenberg, my agent—a total pro and a first-rate human being—and all his colleagues at Levine Greenberg Rostan who look out for me, especially Tim Wojcik, Miek Coccia, and Melissa Rowland.

When you're quarantining and socially distancing, you value your friends even more, especially when you know you won't be able to see them in person anytime soon. I lack the space to name them all, but my special thanks to James Hannaham, Bill Tipper, Scraps deSelby-Bowen, and Steve Crystal. The awesome Rob Sheffield and Phil LaMarr both went the extra mile by reading early versions of the manuscript for this book: it is enriched by their wisdom just as I am enriched by their friendship.

This book is dedicated to Jeff Jackson, the person not related to me who I saw the most in the past year. Our socially distanced lunches in my backyard kept me sane, and his offhand suggestions on how to structure the book were invaluable. (He's also a brilliant novelist: you should pick up his *Destroy All Monsters*.) Jeff's a great guy who's turned me onto a million cool things and I'm proud to call him my friend.

Big love to the groups of excellent people who helped keep me sane this past year: the Slightly Difficult Reading Society (Chuck Barger, Shannon Barringer, Maggie Bean, Jeremy Fisher, Hannah Hundley, Jeff Jackson, and Alan Michael Parker); the Book Club of Two (that's just me and Marc Weidenbaum); the dozens of cool people in the Big Al Memorial Survivor Pool; Rob and Erin Janezic, the best neighbors I could have asked for; my Tuesday-night online board game group (which doesn't have a proper name but comprises Robert Rossney, Maloy Wilkes, and Kelly Jordan); and Team Palindrome (way too many people to name), which gloriously won the 2021 MIT Mystery Hunt.

All my love to my mom and dad; to Julian and Sharon; to Nick, Will, and Miranda; to Cynthia and Alex; to Megan, Trina, Zane, and Sage.

For essential research help, my heartfelt thanks to Andy Greene, Viveca Gardiner, David Gallo, Aimee Graham, Jan Egleson, Menzi Ngubane, Douglas Wolk, Bryson Woody, Pat Blashill, Anette Baldauf, Molly Ker Hawn, the Howard Stern organization, and the good people of the Margaret Herrick Library in Los Angeles (especially senior reference librarian Genevieve Maxwell).

Thank you from the bottom of my writerly soul to the dozens of people who shared their Samuel L. Jackson stories with me: not all the interviews made it into the final version of the book, but hearing about the time they spent in the man's presence, on movie sets and elsewhere, informed how I wrote about him. Most of all, my thanks to Mr. L. Jackson himself: when I interviewed him some years back, I had no idea I would write this book one day, but the time we spent in conversation helped me understand how he navigates his way through the world. Realizing that the world was a better place as a result? That was what made me want to write *Bad Motherfucker*.

o celebrate the career of **Samuel L. Jackson,** we commissioned twenty-six artists from all over the world to do new posters for his movies. (It was supposed to be twenty-five, but apparently I can't count.) I had worked with some of them before on an interactive book I edited, *The Beautiful Book of Exquisite Corpses*, while others were new collaborators, but we were all united in our appreciation of the Jackson oeuvre. In almost all cases, the artist chose the movie that they wanted to do the poster for—and it was amazing to learn that we had almost as many different favorite Jackson movies as artists.

These artists are all awesomely talented and I was honored that they took time out of their busy schedules for *Bad Motherfucker*. I want to tell you a little bit about each of them and I hope you will then check out their non-Jackson-related art: Google them, follow them on social media, buy things from them!

After I contacted **Ryan Milner** (p. ix), I discovered that we already had more artists than we had budgeted for (part of that whole not-so-good-at-counting thing I mentioned) and regretfully informed him that we wouldn't be able to work together this time. Undeterred and fueled by passion for Samuel L. Jackson, he sent me an amazing rendering of *Bad Motherfucker*'s title, with a dozen different images of Jackson—blowing us away so thoroughly that we found room for it in the front of the book, making him our twenty-seventh artist.

My family owns three bricks and two canvases painted by **Dammit Wesley** (p. 10): my favorite is his vision of "Post Racial Park." He's a pillar of the art scene in Charlotte, North Carolina, who founded a very cool gallery and collective studio space called BLKMRKTCLT. I can't stop looking this image of Samuel L. Jackson in *Black Snake Moan*—I think he captured a piece of the man's soul.

Nicole Goux (p. 20) is the gifted artist on *Shadow of the Batgirl* (among other titles) and the co-creator of *Fuck Off Squad*. I love this fractured poster for *Unbreakable*: in case you were wondering, some of those comic book covers are featured in the movie, while others are her own fictionalized versions of 1960s comics.

My wife is a museum curator (visit the Mint Museum the next time you're in Charlotte), which means that sometimes she invites cool artists over to our place for brunch, like **Ali Fitzgerald** (p. 32), who wanted to do one of Samuel L. Jackson's "creature-y movies" and so was happy to tackle *Snakes on a Plane*. You might know her comics in *The New Yorker*, but I first encountered her work through *Drawn to Berlin*, a graphic-novel memoir about teaching art classes to asylum seekers in German refugee shelters.

I learned about the work of graphic designer **Todd Radom** (p. 40) when he did the logos and uniforms for every team in Ice Cube's Big3 basketball league—but his design clients also include big-league names such as the Los Angeles Angels and Super Bowl XXXVIII. I love how his *Shaft* poster pays tribute to the New York skyline of 2000.

Nicole Goux was kind enough to introduce me to the illustrator **Nancy Chiu** (p. 53), who did the one piece of art in the book where I commissioned a specific idea (thank you for making my dream come true, Nancy!). I was looking for somebody who loved drawing birds to do a poster for *The Hitman's Bodyguard* that fully rendered the tattoo on the neck of Darius (Jackson's character)—that tattoo, we eventually discovered, also represents the origin story of Darius as a hit man.

I discovered the work of **Alixa Garcia** (p. 64) through an animated short she did for the *Messages for the City* video campaign (as seen in Times Square in New York City and in other locations, including uptown Charlotte, North Carolina), and then learned she's exhibited everywhere from the Museum of Contemporary Art in L.A. to the Kunsthal KAdE in the Netherlands. When I asked her to contribute to this book, she sent me an impassioned email lobbying for *Do the Right Thing* for multiple reasons: because she lived in Brooklyn for seventeen years, because it dovetailed with her activism with Climbing PoeTree, and because of a crucial moment in an airport: "I'm also a professional poet, and one day, heading out on tour, my creative partner and I were stopped by a TSA agent who made us take out our books to look through them. We heard a voice from behind say 'You hustling books?'—turns out it was Spike Lee! We offered him a copy of our book. He reached into his wallet and pulled out a hundred-dollar bill, saying 'I support the arts.'"

Liniers (p. 72) is an Argentinian cartoonist who now lives in Vermont. Only after he completed his poster for *Goodfellas* (he turned it around in twenty-four hours because he was having so much fun) did I ask him if he knew anything about my favorite Argentinian movie, *Relatos salvajes* (aka *Wild Tales*)—and it turned out he had done a poster for that too!

I first noticed **Justin Teodoro** (p. 87) when he contributed great illustrations to my pal Erin Carlson's book *Queen Meryl*: he does a lot of different stuff when he's not gracing the pages of Hachette Books, but I especially dig his high-energy murals. His first and only choice for a Samuel L. Jackson movie was *Pulp Fiction*, which I respected.

Lauren Purje (p. 98) is an artist living in Brooklyn who was excited to tackle *Fresh*—both because of its Brooklyn setting and because it's a great movie. I'm eagerly anticipating her upcoming comics zine, *People Are My Favorite Animal*.

My friend Dean Haspiel, a formidable artist in his own right, introduced me to his former studio mate **Christa Cassano** (p. 118), whose projects this year include a comic for MoMA's *Illustrated Lives* series, producing a documentary film, and doing large-scale paintings and drawings based on action figures. You can see some of that action aesthetic in her poster for *The Long Kiss Goodnight*.

Continuing a chain of fruitful introductions and referrals, Nancy Chiu turned me on to her pal **Kevin Bannister** (p. 129), a delightfully twisted artist and graphic designer living in Southern California. His poster for *Sphere* captured what was best about that movie—the atmosphere of silent foreboding—and stripped out all of the bullshit, so I'm going to argue that it's a more successful work of art than the movie was.

de'Angelo Dia (p. 149) is the biggest *Star Wars* fan I know; he's also a multimedia wizard who does amazing work with chalk, ink, and spoken-word poetry. It was a privilege to see him experiment with a variety of approaches to his poster of *Star Wars: Episode II—Attack of* *the Clones*, ultimately finding the perfect way to stencil his original photography.

Keith Knight (p. 157): the man, the myth, the legendary creator of *The K Chronicles*. (And because one comic strip apparently isn't enough, he also writes and draws *The Knight Life* and *(th)ink*, and works in other mediums: check out his TV show, *Woke*.) Somehow he also found time to create this poster for *The Caveman's Valentine*, deftly capturing the unsettling intensity of Jackson's performance.

Malachi Lily (p. 168) describes themself as "a shapeshifting, black, trans/agender poet, artist, animator, curator, and moth." I dug how they found ways to represent the spirit of *The Red Violin* without actually including a picture of a violin—and how you can see Samuel L. Jackson's eyes through the F-holes. We now have a standing date for a cup of tea.

I've had the honor of collaborating with **R. Sikoryak** (p. 174) on three other books I've written: *The Tao of Bill Murray*, *The World According to Tom Hanks*, and *Kindness and Wonder: Why Mister Rogers Matters Now More Than Ever*. He's got the uncanny ability to mimic the style of just about anybody else, from M. C. Escher to Beatrix Potter, and bend it to his own ends. (Check out the results in his own books, including *Terms and Conditions*, which turns the iTunes user agreement into a graphic novel.) He was eager to take *The Incredibles* back to their comic-book roots, imagining how they would have looked if drawn by Jack Kirby. And as if that weren't enough, he also did this book's amazing endpapers.

There were days during the Trump administration when nothing made sense except the satirical columns of Alexandra Petri and the scabrous political cartoons of **Pia Guerra** (p. 188). (She was also the co-creator of the comic book *Y: The Last Man*—I'm the proud owner of a stack of trade paperback editions.) I was extremely pleased that when she chose an action movie, she opted for one of my favorite sleepers, *Formula 51*.

You may know **Ray Billingsley** (p. 193) from his warm and wise work on the syndicated comic strip *Curtis*, still going strong after more than three decades. I was lucky enough to interview him recently (for a *New York Times* article about comic artists making work that grappled with the pandemic instead of pretending it wasn't happening), so I knew he had design talents that he didn't always get a chance to show off on newsprint: witness his evocative take on the horror film *1408*.

That *Times* article also gave me my first chance to speak with **Lalo Alcaraz** (p. 208), but I'd been reading his amazing comic strip *La Cucaracha* for many years. I was honored that he took time out from his overstuffed schedule (comics! TV! screenplays! murals!) to put Nick Fury front and center with *The Avengers*, where he belongs. (That's not a Life Model Decoy.)

I am crazy excited for the next book by **Joan LeMay** (p. 217), a collaboration with Alex Pappademas called *Quantum Criminals: Ramblers, Wild Gamblers, Babylon Sisters, and Other Soul Survivors from the Songs of Steely Dan*, to be published by the University of Texas Press in the fall of 2022. She gave me permission to share the story of her first draft of her poster for *African Cats* ("it is TOTALLY FINE to mention that because it is hilarious"): she centered it on a beautiful rendering of a Bengal tiger, and I had to gently remind her that tigers are actually Asian cats.

I first met **Lee Herrera** (p. 237) because he was drumming in the cool band Julian Calendar (among other musical gigs). If you like what he did here with *The Hateful Eight*, you owe it to yourself to look at one of his pieces up close: he does beautiful portraits and still lifes that he creates by painstakingly stippling the image with dots from a ballpoint pen.

The artist Christine Wong Yap turned me on to **Dionis Ortiz** (p. 243), whose oeuvre includes paintings, prints, vinyl floors, and modified album covers; most of his recent work is more abstract than what he did here for *Chi-Raq*, but he's obviously a huge figurative talent as well. He recently emailed me, "I am excited about making a new body of work that explores the space in between the body and the community around us through the making of woodgrain paintings, printmaking, and collage."

Another brunch guest courtesy of my well-connected wife: **Jen Ray** (p. 263), who is a visual artist and a performance artist. (The next time you've got twenty minutes to spare, go online and watch her majestic-yet-bonkers "Eyes as Bright as Diamonds," steeped in the history and culture of Texas.) I knew that she could include the whole vista of *Jackie Brown* without giving short shrift to the divine Pam Grier.

Rafa Orrico Diez (p. 269) posted on Twitter on "Portfolio Day": "I am a graphic designer who loves design and posters." Fair enough—but that didn't sufficiently prepare me for his remixed movie posters, filled with collage and riotous invention. He had already done a host of posters for Jackson movies in various styles, but this hypercreative Spaniard added one more with his treatment of *Kong: Skull Island*.

Crixtover Edwin (p. 280), who picked *Kingsman: The Secret Service*, is an artist from Lagos, Nigeria, and the founder of Koulture Kanvas, which specializes in paintings celebrating Black excellence. If you like his work in black and white, you'll love it in color.

Suzy Exposito (p. 288), astonishingly, did the poster for *Eve's Bayou* while she was moving across the country to take a new job—as a music reporter at the *Los Angeles Times*. "I loved getting to pay homage to one of my favorite movies, and especially a Southern gothic," she emailed me.

I've been working with **Peter Kuper** (p. 301) since the early 1990s, when we crossed paths at the late lamented *Details* magazine. He's ridiculously prolific, and his work covers everything from politics to *Spy vs. Spy*, but my favorite of his many books is the Eisner-winning *Ruins*. Look closely at his *Jurassic Park* poster to note exactly what the *T. rex* is smoking.

n case you're the type of person who likes fine print, here are some more details about the filmography: the release date of the movies (and their chronology within each year) is determined by their theatrical release in the United States (which sometimes can be many months after a debut at a film festival or in another country). If a movie was never released theatrically, I peg the date to the broadcast premiere, the streaming debut, or when it went on sale.

At the beginning of each filmography entry, each character name is printed exactly as it appears in the credits (even when the credits get it wrong, like in *Gospel Hill*). If Jackson's character goes unnamed in the credits, which happens now and then, I call him whatever the other characters call him.

Expletives not deleted: what exactly constitutes a curse word is a judgment call, of course, and standards are shifting all the time. I included "asshole," "bitch," "cock," "cunt," "dick," "fuck," "goddamn," "pussy," "shit," and "tits"—and compound or hyphenated words that included those terms, such as "pussy-whipping," "Liverfuckingpool," and, of course, "motherfucker." I counted plurals separately, so you may need to add up your "motherfucker" and "motherfuckers" to get the full picture. Longer unhyphenated phrases didn't get counted separately, so "fuck you" got tabulated as a "fuck" and "son of a bitch" as a "bitch." I didn't include "ass," "bastard," "blowjob," "damn," "piss," or other words that are taboo in various contexts, including "nigger" and other racial slurs.

The dialogue featured as a pull quote in each film entry is always said by Samuel L. Jackson himself.

While this isn't an academic work, I believe in letting people know my sources. If you're looking to do even more reading on Jackson, I encourage you to chase down the bibliographical entries that follow. And if you're a college professor teaching a class on Jacksonology, please email me at gavin42@gmail.com and let me know.

Introduction: Worth of the Cool

"I say 'cool' all the time": Author interview with Samuel L. Jackson.

"I never feel like": Author interview with Matthew Aldrich.

"didn't end up in my pocket": Pat Jordan, "How Samuel L. Jackson Became His Own Genre," *The New York Times Magazine*, 26 April 2012.

"I never even auditioned": Dave Gelly, *Being Prez: The Life and Music of Lester Young*, Oxford University Press, 2007.

"He was a living, walking poet": Ted Gioia, *The Birth (and Death) of the Cool*, Fulcrum, 2019. (See also Gioia, "How Lester Young Invented Cool," *The Daily Beast*, 12 April 2015.) Note that although Young is sometimes credited with coining even more slang terms, such as "crib" and "bread," the etymology on some of those seems more spurious. "Crib" as a term for one's home, for example, has a centuries-long lineage dating back to Shakespeare's *Henry IV, Part 1*.

"I'd like to cool you": Ernest Hemingway, "Night Before Battle," *Esquire*, February 1939.

"probably too young": Rob Sheffield, "The Eternal Sunshine of Harry Styles," *Rolling Stone*, No. 1331, September 2019.

"This is the mask": Robert Farris Thompson, "An Aesthetic of the Cool," *African Arts*, Vol. 7, No. 1 (Autumn 1973).

"He always looked aware": Author interview with Hugh Laurie, who was personally uncertain as to whether that detachment made Grant the greatest of all film actors, or if the crown should belong to the more traditionally committed James Stewart.

"Manifest within": Thompson.

"We were trying to sound": Miles Davis, *Miles: The Autobiography*, Simon and Schuster, 1989.

"What bothered them": John Leland, *Hip: The History*, Ecco, 2004.

"They're the same fucking guys": Carvell Wallace, "Samuel L. Jackson Operates Like He Owns the Place. (He Does.)," *Esquire*, April 2019.

"the greatest feeling": Davis.

"I was always afraid of needles": Gary Giddins, *Visions of Jazz: The First Century*, Oxford University Press, 1998.

"Most people would be": Stephen Rebello, "20 Questions: Samuel L. Jackson," *Playboy*, December 2006.

"At the time he turned sixty": Giddins.

"I use 'motherfucker'": Author interview with Samuel L. Jackson.

"leopard skin jacket": Leland.

"I'm comfortable": Rebello.

"I don't know where": Amy Kaufman, "Q&A: Ryan Reynolds and Samuel L. Jackson buddy up for 'The Hitman's Bodyguard,'" *Los Angeles Times*, 10 August 2017.

"It was no burden": Jordan.

1. Half a Piece of Candy

"My grandfather was my best friend": Dotson Rader, "He Found His Voice," *Parade*, 9 January 2005.

"I was never hungry": *The Howard Stern Show*, syndicated radio program, 22 June 2000.

"There'd be bullets": *Inside the Actors Studio*, season 8, episode 115, Bravo, 2 June 2002.

"I grew up with": Michael Angeli, "Samuel L. Jackson Climbs Among the Glittering Stars," *The New York Times*, 7 February 1993.

"But my world was full": *Inside the Actors Studio.*

"unscrew the lightbulbs": Alex Simon, "Samuel L. Jackson Tells It Like It Is," *Venice*, March 2005.

"a term of respect": Pat Jordan, "How Samuel L. Jackson Became His Own Genre," *The New York Times Magazine*, 26 April 2012.

"My grandfather was this old guy": John H. Richardson, "What I've Learned: Samuel L. Jackson," *Esquire*, January 2011.

"It was very dangerous": Rader.

"Everybody was out": Sanjiv Bhattacharya, "Play it again Samuel…," *The Observer Review* (UK), 27 October 2002.

"You had to learn": *Live! with Kelly and Michael*, syndicated TV program, 9 February 2015.

"My family would point": Stephen Rebello, "Playboy Interview: Samuel L. Jackson," *Playboy*, October 2013.

"we figured they weren't": Steve Weintraub, "John Cusack, Samuel L. Jackson, Lorenzo di Bonaventura, Mary McCormack and Mikael Hafstrom Interviewed—1408," *Collider*, 11 June 2007.

"I was acting": Rebello.

"We were always told": Jill Nelson, "The working man," *USA Weekend*, 18–20 July 1997.

"to see how": *The Howard Stern Show*, SiriusXM, 5 January 2016.

"I was always crying": David S. Cohen, "Jackson career a tour de Force," *Variety*, 28 August–3 September 2000.

"But there was": Megan Conner, "Samuel L Jackson: 'I create characters—it keeps me from being me all day,'" *The Observer* (UK), 25 January 2015.

"And I was a selfish child": Jordan.

"There are still days": Ibid.

"She always worked at sample shows": Author interview with Samuel L. Jackson.

"The ladies would give you": *Fresh Air*, NPR, 24 March 1995.

"We took the heat": Tom O'Neill, "The US Interview," *US*, March 1998.

"He told me": Mickey Rapkin, "Sam's Town," *Elle*, November 2012.

"She sent me": O'Neill.

"Segregation was just": Jordan.

"What's happening here?": "Samuel L. Jackson & LaTanya Richardson Jackson," *Beyond the Spotlight*, episode 3, HBO, 2020.

"All her kids": Rebello.

"There was a family": Ibid.

"There were only": Hilary De Vries, "Addicted to Acting," *Los Angeles Times Magazine*, 11 June 2000.

"Almost instantaneously": Christopher Wilson, "The Moment When Four Students Sat Down to Take a Stand," smithsonianmag.com, 31 January 2020.

"I would participate": Simon.

"They used to take": De Vries.

"my job was": Rader.

"We drank beer": Wallace Terry, "What Saved Me," *Parade*, 18 August 1996.

"I definitely didn't": Rebello.

"I had anger": Rader.

"I had read too many": Rebello.

2. Desk Lamp (with Bulb)

"Self-mastery": *Morehouse College Bulletin*, Vol. 34, No. 108, May 1966.

"We were told": *Fresh Air*, NPR, 24 March 1995.

"I went wild": Wallace Terry, "What Saved Me," *Parade*, 18 August 1996.

"I balled": Carvell Wallace, "Samuel L. Jackson Operates Like He Owns the Place. (He Does.)," *Esquire*, April 2019.

"For the first time": Dotson Rader, "He Found His Voice," *Parade*, 9 January 2005.

"I was there": *Fresh Air*.

"The reprobates": "Samuel L. Jackson & LaTanya Richardson Jackson," *Beyond the Spotlight*, episode 3, HBO, 2020.

"They ignored those people": *Fresh Air*.

"You guys need to study": Alex Simon, "Samuel L. Jackson Tells It Like It Is," *Venice*, March 2005.

"Like every sport": Stephen Rebello, "Playboy Interview: Samuel L. Jackson," *Playboy*, October 2013.

"I became a hippie": Author interview with Samuel L. Jackson.

"You guys have some": John H. Richardson, "What I've Learned: Samuel L. Jackson," *Esquire*, January 2011.

"We actually thought": Tom O'Neill, "The US Interview," *US*, March 1998.

"You don't think": *Beyond the Spotlight*.

"one of the worst": David Keeps, "Tell It on the Mountain," *New York*, 29 August 2011.

"We all thought": Samuel L. Jackson (as told to Andy Lewis), "How I Became an Usher at Martin Luther King Jr.'s Funeral," *The Hollywood Reporter*, 3 April 2018.

"I was angry": Rader.

"From the time": Rebello.

"ELEMENTARY PUBLIC SPEAKING": *Morehouse College Bulletin*.

"could act like": Jean Oppenheimer, "Action Jackson," *Los Angeles Village View*, 12–18 February 1993.

"on opening night": Stephen Schaefer, "Play It Again and Again, Sam," *Variety*, 1 December 2008.

"I was horrible": Hilary De Vries, "Addicted to Acting," *Los Angeles Times Magazine*, 11 June 2000.

"And I didn't have": Elyssa Lee, "Samuel L. Jackson," *inStyle*, May 2002.

"Morehouse was breeding": John Patterson, "Samuel L Jackson: 'I was a drug addict but I showed up on time and hit my marks,'" *The Guardian* (UK), 30 June 2016.

"SOMEBODY'S WATCHING": "Morehouse College Student Protest; 1969," as found in the digital exhibits of the Atlanta University Center Robert W. Woodruff Library.

"We had read about": Jackson (as told to Lewis). Also check out volume 3 of the *Ebony Pictorial History of Black America* (Johnson Publishing, 1971); page 136 has a full-page photo of the Morehouse protesters on the steps of Harkness Hall, including Jackson.

"Wherever somebody was": *Beyond the Spotlight*.

"It has been reported": Bob Goodman, "Changes: Morehouse," *The Great Speckled Bird*, 9 June 1969.

"Finally I was": *Beyond the Spotlight*.

"We fed kids": Jackson (as told to Lewis).

"I wasn't one": Richardson.

"I was never": Tom Ward, "Icon: Samuel L. Jackson," *Men's Health*, September 2016.

"Get on this plane": Jackson (as told to Lewis).

3. Little Cooked Onions

"I learned how": David Rensin, "20 Questions: Samuel L. Jackson," *Playboy*, April 1995.

"That bedroom look": Ibid.

"At a certain point": Ibid.

"It was pathetic": Mickey Rapkin, "Sam's Town," *Elle*, November 2012.

"I learned that": Rensin.

"He saw her reflection": *The Howard Stern Show*, SiriusXM, 5 January 2016.

"Hate Whitey Theater": *Inside the Actors Studio*, season 8, episode 115, Bravo, 2 June 2002.

"People were paying": *Fresh Air*, NPR, 24 March 1995.

"If you're going to do it," "The great ones": Hilary De Vries, "Addicted to Acting," *Los Angeles Times Magazine*, 11 June 2000.

"We started talking": Dotson Rader, "He Found His Voice," *Parade*, 9 January 2005.

"When you think about": Caitlin Moynihan, "LaTanya Richardson Jackson on Her Early Theater Love and What Convinced Her to Join *To Kill a Mockingbird*," Broadway.com, 24 April 2019.

"It's horrible to say": Tim Gray, "LaTanya Richardson Looks Back on Her Long Career," *Variety*, 31 March 2017.

"It was like living": Author interview with Albert Cooper.

"We would also": Express News Service, "When hell freezes over; an interview with Samuel L Jackson," *The New Indian Express*, 22 June 2019.

"I know what it's like": Author interview with Albert Cooper.

"It's important to me": Mark Dagostino, "Samuel L. Jackson Sounds Off," *People*, 5 March 2007.

"In the seventies": Elyssa Lee, "Samuel L. Jackson," *inStyle*, May 2002.

"It's scheduled": Author interview with Albert Cooper.

"Don't go looking": "Samuel L. Jackson Answers the Web's Most Searched Questions," *Wired*, 7 March 2017.

"It was the best": Samuel L. Jackson, "Fame, What's Your Name?," *Details*, February 1996.

"I've been told": Diane Goldner, "Harlem on His Mind," *People*, 1 July 1991.

"You definitely need": Gray.

"We pulled into": Michael Angeli, "Samuel L. Jackson Climbs Among the Glittering Stars," *The New York Times*, 7 February 1993.

"I saw a nun": Michael Fleming, "Playboy Interview: Samuel L. Jackson," *Playboy*, June 1999.

4. Bill Cosby's Sweaters

"In my country mind": Tim Gray, "LaTanya Richardson Looks Back on Her Long Career," *Variety*, 31 March 2017.

"I didn't have a gun": *Fresh Air*, NPR, 24 March 1995.

"If my résumé": Sanjiv Bhattacharya, "Play it again Samuel...," *The Observer Review* (UK), 27 October 2002.

"I thought this was like": Matthew Belloni and Stephanie Galloway, "The Actor Roundtable," *The Hollywood Reporter*, 4 December 2015.

"There's always a time": *Inside the Actors Studio*, season 8, episode 115, Bravo, 2 June 2002.

"Why don't you": Arion Berger, "Samuel Jackson," *Mirabella*, March 1993.

"Sam's rhythms were different": Author interview with Dyane Harvey-Salaam.

"The American ideal": Nancy Mills, "Mr. Confident," *Rave!* (in *Daily Breeze*), 31 July 1998.

"no-man's-land": David Keeps, "Tell It on the Mountain," *New York*, 29 August 2011.

"We worked off-Broadway": Lisa Rosen, "Colleagues rib, praise Jackson," *Los Angeles Times*, 3 December 2008.

"Everybody from age twenty": Michael Angeli, "Samuel L. Jackson Climbs Among the Glittering Stars," *The New York Times*, 7 February 1993.

"You have to ask him": *The Graham Norton Show*, episode 437, BBC, 16 October 2020.

"I married the smart boy": Pat Jordan, "How Samuel L. Jackson Became His Own Genre," *The New York Times Magazine*, 26 April 2012.

"That was a big": Carvell Wallace, "Samuel L. Jackson Operates Like He Owns the Place. (He Does.)," *Esquire*, April 2019.

"Stars don't come bigger": Stephen Rebello, "20 Questions: Samuel L. Jackson," *Playboy*, December 2006.

"I don't know why": Jordan.

"vibrant": Frank Rich, "Stage: 'District Line,' from Negro Ensemble," *The New York Times*, 5 December 1984.

"My agent said": Author interview with Steve Zeller.

"Cobb, the kinda women": Charles Fuller, *A Soldier's Play*, Samuel French, 1981.

"I had my dream": Angeli.

"The first few years": Carol Allen, "Samuel L. Jackson talks to Carol Allen about his role in Tarantino's new movie," *The Times* (UK), 12 March 1998.

"I cried like a banshee": Joy Bennett Kinnon, "Samuel L. Jackson & LaTanya Richardson," *Ebony*, March 2006.

"I want to show you": *The Howard Stern Show*, SiriusXM, 5 January 2016.

"You can't talk to me": *Fresh Air*, 1995.

"Are you calling to ask": Stephen Rebello, "Playboy Interview: Samuel L. Jackson," *Playboy*, October 2013.

"I'm not going to make": Michael Fleming, "Playboy Interview: Samuel L. Jackson," *Playboy*, June 1999.

"You're smart": Wallace.

"I was always watching": Jordan.

"Every year": "What I Watch: Samuel L. Jackson," *TV Guide*, 2 September 1995.

"We were the junior Huxtables": *Fresh Air*, 1995.

"I wore Bill's clothes": Ibid.

"You learn how to work": *The Howard Stern Show*, 2016.

"I didn't impose myself": Ibid.

"When Sam got that part": Author interview with Albert Cooper.

"He had a name": *Fresh Air*, 1995.

"They both taught me": Belloni and Galloway.

"You never know": *Inside the Actors Studio*, 2002.

"August writes three-hour plays": Paul B. Cohen, "The Fires Within," *Los Angeles Village View*, 3–9 December 1993.

"Y'all doing our lines?": Author interview with Ylonda Powell.

"I was okay with it": Jordan.

"I rocked that play": Ibid.

"It's frustrating knowing": *Fresh Air*, NPR, 27 June 2000.

"sat backstage": Margy Rochlin, "Tough Guy Finds His Warm and Fuzzy Side," *The New York Times*, 2 November 1997.

"The mounting frustrations": *Fresh Air*, 2000.

"I could go score": *The Howard Stern Show*, 2016.

"That's how people saw me": *Fresh Air*, 2000.

5. The Films of Samuel L. Jackson, 1977–1988

Uncle Tom's Cabin

"I liked the challenge": John J. O'Connor, "Uncle Tom's Cabin," *The New York Times*, 12 June 1987.

Eddie Murphy Raw

"I was a young guy": Jason Zinoman, "Eddie Murphy Is Bringing Eddie Murphy Back," *The New York Times*, 26 September 2019.

School Daze

"It's like the round": Commentary track, *School Daze*, Sony DVD, 2001.

6. Emergency Cord

"Spike Lee's Summer Film Camp": Alex Simon, "Samuel L. Jackson Tells It Like It Is," *Venice*, March 2005.

"The actors from New York": Spike Lee with Lisa Jones, *Do the Right Thing*, Fireside Books, 1989.

"Fish has decided": Ibid.

"You acting motherfuckers": Keith Staskiewicz, "Reunion: Do the Right Thing," ew.com, 18 October 2013.

"There were some guys": Simon.

"I'd be in there": Staskiewicz.

"I go to the audition": Michael Angeli, "Samuel L. Jackson Climbs Among the Glittering Stars," *The New York Times*, 7 February 1993.

"Hollywood call today?": John Patterson, "Samuel L Jackson: 'I was a drug addict but I showed up on time and hit my marks,'" *The Guardian* (UK), 30 June 2016.

"That was the character name": *Fresh Air*, NPR, 24 March 1995.

"Very un–New York–like": *Late Show with David Letterman*, CBS, 14 December 2012.

"going to be a sad Christmas": Ibid.

"I had no idea": *The Howard Stern Show*, SiriusXM, 5 January 2016.

"You feel like": "Samuel L. Jackson & LaTanya Richardson Jackson," *Beyond the Spotlight*, episode 3, HBO, 2020.

"He was looking sketchy": Author interview with Nelson George.

"I was a fucking drug addict": Patterson.

"In the multi-roomed": Author interview with Elyse Singer.

"always isolated": Michael Fleming, "Playboy Interview: Samuel L. Jackson," *Playboy*, June 1999.

"I paid my bills": Stephen Rebello, "Playboy Interview: Samuel L. Jackson," *Playboy*, October 2013.

"People who smoke crack": Fleming.

"I need some coke": Carvell Wallace, "Samuel L. Jackson Operates Like He Owns the Place. (He Does.)," *Esquire*, April 2019.

"I threatened to leave": Pat Jordan, "How Samuel L. Jackson Became His Own Genre," *The New York Times Magazine*, 26 April 2012.

"which was not working": Hilary De Vries, "Addicted to Acting," *Los Angeles Times Magazine*, 11 June 2000.

"I never thought": Fleming.

"I figured that": *Fresh Air*, NPR, 27 June 2000.

"I found the humility": Wallace Terry, "What Saved Me," *Parade*, 18 August 1996.

"I've done all the research": Andrew Anthony, "You can call him 'nigga' . . . just don't call him 'nigger,'" *The Observer Review* (UK), 8 March 1998.

"I will never come back": Fleming.

"The few friends": *Fresh Air*, 2000.

"I wanted him to look": "Cracking a Character," *The Hollywood Reporter*, 17 March 1993.

"When my character": Simon.

"like the petals": Rebello.

7. The Films of Samuel L. Jackson, 1989–1991

Do the Right Thing
"I knew I wanted": Author interview with Spike Lee.

Sea of Love
"Who could": Commentary track, *Sea of Love*, Universal DVD, 2003.

The Exorcist III
"He was always": *The Howard Stern Show*, SiriusXM, 5 January 2016.

Goodfellas
"there would be guys": Alex Simon, "Samuel L. Jackson Tells It Like It Is," *Venice*, March 2005.

Jungle Fever
"Generally, when you saw Gator": Katie Rife, "Random Roles: Samuel L. Jackson on Nick Fury, Mace Windu, and the power of a great wig," *AV Club*, 18 January 2018.

8. Brown Envelope

"I never made amends": Mickey Rapkin, "Sam's Town," *Elle*, November 2012.

"I had never put the name": Author interview with Jeff Stanzler.

"Probably gonna get": Alex Simon, "Samuel L. Jackson Tells It Like It Is," *Venice*, March 2005.

"I know people": *Fresh Air*, NPR, 24 March 1995 (a rebroadcast of a 1991 interview).

"Commercial agents": Lena Williams, "Samuel L. Jackson: Out of Lee's 'Jungle,' Into the Limelight," *The New York Times*, 9 June 1991.

"Look, other Black actors": Bob Ickes, "Jackson Heights," *New York*, June 10, 1991.

"Who is America's": Liz Smith, "Liz Smith," *Los Angeles Times*, 22 August 1991.

"Hollywood call today?": John Patterson, "Samuel L Jackson: 'I was a drug addict but I showed up on time and hit my marks,'" *The Guardian* (UK), 30 June 2016.

"The reality is": Author interview with Samuel L. Jackson.

"I don't have to worry": Veronica Victoria Chambers, "Cameos: Samuel L. Jackson," *Premiere*, May 1992.

"I spent a lot": "Just a Stereotypical Day," *People*, 8 March 1993.

"Even when we've": Samuel L. Jackson, "Fame, What's Your Name?" *Details*, February 1996.

"Gee, I'm not sure": Simon.

"Steven had": Ibid.

"I didn't realize": Jada Yuan, "Tarantino's Leading Man," *New York*, 24 August–6 September 2015.

"Any brothers in it?": Michael Angeli, "Samuel L. Jackson Climbs Among the Glittering Stars," *The New York Times*, 7 February 1993.

"I find that really bizarre": Paul B. Cohen, "The Fires Within," *Los Angeles Village View*, 3–9 December 1993.

"I started counting": Gordon Cox, "7 Things You Don't Know About 'Reservoir Dogs,' as Told by Quentin Tarantino and the Cast," variety.com, 28 April 2017.

"Yeah yeah yeah": Yuan.

"If you show this": Mark Seal, "Cinema Tarantino: The Making of Pulp Fiction," *Vanity Fair*, March 2013. (Telling this story, Jackson sometimes compresses the time between Sundance and his receiving the script to two weeks.)

"Is this as good": Kelley L. Carter, "After 30-plus years and 100-plus roles, Samuel L. Jackson ranks his own roles," *The Undefeated*, June 14, 2018.

"Wait, wait, wait, wait": *Fresh Air*, 2007.

"Me and Quentin": Seal.

"Dude, read the script": Ibid.

"We never really": *Fresh Air*, 2007.

"I had it in my mind": Chris Willman, "A Little Peace, A Little Menace," *Los Angeles Times*, 9 October 1994.

"All the gangbangers": Seal.

"We rehearsed": Michael Sheridan, "Q&A with Samuel L. Jackson," *Tail Slate*, 9 March 2005.

"My scenes were mostly": Author interview with Phil LaMarr.

9. The Films of Samuel L. Jackson, 1992–1994

Amos & Andrew

"I read the name": Donna Britt, "New 'Amos': Busting Guts, Stereotypes," *The Washington Post*, 19 February 1993.

Menace II Society

"a Monday after-school special": Mark Blackwell, "Niggaz4Dinner," *Spin*, September 1991.

Jurassic Park

"He wanted to make": Katie Rife, "Random Roles: Samuel L. Jackson on Nick Fury, Mace Windu, and the power of a great wig," *AV Club*, 18 January 2018.

Against the Wall

"We were very": Alex Simon, "Samuel L. Jackson Tells It Like It Is," *Venice*, March 2005.

Fresh

"I really wanted": Greg King, "FRESH—interview with director Boaz Yakin," filmreviews.net.au (originally published in *Beat* magazine, ca. 1994).

Pulp Fiction

"*Pulp Fiction* works": Gavin Smith, "When You Know You're in Good Hands," *Film Comment*, July/August 1994 (as reprinted in *Quentin Tarantino Interviews*, edited by Gerald Peary, University Press of Mississippi, 2013.)

"that was the hardest": Chris Willman, "A Little Peace, a Little Menace," *Los Angeles Times*, 9 October 1994.

"because he carried himself": Pat Jordan, "How Samuel L. Jackson Became His Own Genre," *The New York Times Magazine*, 26 April 2012.

"Deus ex machina": Carvell Wallace, "Samuel L. Jackson Operates Like He Owns the Place. (He Does.)," *Esquire*, April 2019.

10. Two Lights and Some Batteries

"but there was no way": Paul B. Cohen, "The Fires Within," *Los Angeles Village View*, 3–9 December 1993.

"I guess": Juan Morales, "Wham, Bam, Thank You, Sam," *Detour*, March 1995.

"I didn't care": Michael Fleming, "Playboy Interview: Samuel L. Jackson," *Playboy*, June 1999.

"I don't know": Author interview with Samuel L. Jackson.

"John did ask": David Rensin, "20 Questions: Samuel L. Jackson," *Playboy*, April 1995.

"which page": Pat Jordan, "How Samuel L. Jackson Became His Own Genre," *The New York Times Magazine*, 26 April 2012.

"My agents cursed": Katie Rife, "Random Roles: Samuel L. Jackson on Nick Fury, Mace Windu, and the power of a great wig," *AV Club*, 18 January 2018.

"Some days": Ibid.

"Black Tonto": Chris Willman, "A Little Peace, A Little Menace," *Los Angeles Times*, 9 October 1994.

"Zeus Carver was": Jordan.

"He really didn't": Author interview with Nelson George.

"They call and": Fleming.

"change the politics": Morales.

"At one point": Fleming.

"If you put somebody": Ibid.

"Women like seeing": Ibid.

"I get paid": Andrew Anthony, "You can call him 'nigga'...just don't call him 'nigger,'" *The Observer Review* (UK), 8 March 1998.

"No, I won't": Ibid.

"When are you": Jamie Malanowski, "A Man of Action Who Finds Power in Stillness," *The New York Times*, 14 April 2002.

"He's a great friend": Kelley L. Carter, "After 30-plus years and 100-plus roles, Samuel L. Jackson ranks his own roles," *The Undefeated*, June 14, 2018.

"Bobby didn't really deal": Alex Simon, "Samuel L. Jackson Tells It Like It Is," *Venice*, March 2005.

"He just wouldn't": Eric Layton, "Play It Again, Sam," *Entertainment Today*, 7 November 1997.

"Hey, you have to work": Rob Leane, "Samuel L Jackson & Salma Hayek interview: The Hitman's Bodyguard, and breaking into Hollywood," *Den of Geek*, 13 August 2017.

"There are only so many": Steve Weintraub, "Samuel L. Jackson Interview—Resurrecting the Champ," *Collider*, 21 August 2007.

"It's his drug": Malanowski.

"Barry's very quiet": Carol Allen, "Samuel L. Jackson talks to Carol Allen about his role in Tarantino's new movie," *The Times* (UK), 12 March 1998.

"Quentin thinks he writes": Fleming.

"Now don't be telling me": Margy Rochlin, "Tough Guy Finds His Warm and Fuzzy Side," *The New York Times*, 2 November 1997.

"With Ordell": Fleming.

"I'm not against": Army Archerd, "Lee has choice words for Tarantino," *Variety*, 16 December 1997.

"Because Sam Jackson": George Khoury, "Big Words: An Interview with Spike Lee," *Creative Screenwriting*, May/June 1999 (as reprinted in *Spike Lee Interviews*, edited by Cynthia Fuchs, University Press of Mississippi, 2002.)

"As a writer": *The Charlie Rose Show*, PBS, 26 December 1997.

"I hate to say it": Anthony.

"In my opinion": Allen.

"Most of the actors": Anthony.

"You take the power": Ibid.

"I have let people know": *The N Word*, Post Consumer Media, 2004.

"What the fuck": Fleming.

"Quentin's not": Tom O'Neill, "The US Interview," *US*, March 1998.

11. The Films of Samuel L. Jackson, 1995–1998

Losing Isaiah

"Because she has been": Michael Fleming, "Playboy Interview: Samuel L. Jackson," *Playboy*, June 1999.

Kiss of Death

"He likes to constantly change": Ibid.

Die Hard with a Vengeance

"We drive a lot": Juan Morales, "Wham, Bam, Thank You, Sam," *Detour*, March 1995.

"I'd always wanted": Katie Rife, "Random Roles: Samuel L. Jackson on Nick Fury, Mace Windu, and the power of a great wig," *AV Club*, 18 January 2018.

The Great White Hype

"I always thought": "Samuel L. Jackson still the man: Any questions?," *The Hollywood Reporter*, 16 June 2000.

The Search for One-Eye Jimmy

"We were in Red Hook": Author interview with Holt McCallany.

A Time to Kill

"The first time": Michael Fleming, "Playboy Interview: Samuel L. Jackson," *Playboy*, June 1999.

"I have a lot of": Kelley L. Carter, "After 30-plus years and 100-plus roles, Samuel L. Jackson ranks his own roles," *The Undefeated*, June 14, 2018.

"There was this huge scene": Fleming.

"I'm like": Ibid.

The Long Kiss Goodnight
"You can't kill": Pat Jordan, "How Samuel L. Jackson Became His Own Genre," *The New York Times Magazine*, 26 April 2012.

"He's another dude": Carvell Wallace, "Samuel L. Jackson Operates Like He Owns the Place. (He Does.)," *Esquire*, April 2019.

One Eight Seven
"I went to some": "Combat Zone," *People*, 18 August 1997.

"Here was a guy": "Samuel L. Jackson still the man: Any questions?," *The Hollywood Reporter*, 16 June 2000.

Eve's Bayou
"I'm used to testosterone-driven sets": Jamie Malanowski, "A Man of Action Who Finds Power in Stillness," *The New York Times*, 14 April 2002.

"The movie hinges": Commentary track, *Eve's Bayou*, Lionsgate DVD, 2004.

"My intention was": Ashley Terrell, "20th Anniversary Special: Cast of 'Eve's Bayou' Talks About Film's Lasting Legacy," essence.com, November 7, 2017.

Jackie Brown
"You don't watch it": Larissa MacFarquhar, "The Movie Lover," *The New Yorker*, 20 October 2003.

"Jules is a moralistic kind of guy": Carol Allen, "Samuel L. Jackson talks to Carol Allen about his role in Tarantino's new movie," *The Times* (UK), 12 March 1998.

"Take your time": *Fresh Air*, NPR, 27 June 2000.

"I just think": Ibid.

Out of Sight
"We all knew": Commentary track, *Out of Sight*, Universal DVD, 1999.

The Negotiator
"I found myself": Mike Fleming, "F. Gary Gray Q&A: The Hard Life Lessons That Led To 'Straight Outta Compton,'" *Deadline*, 13 August 2015.

"People should": Patrick Goldstein, "This top grossing actor has strict code," *Los Angeles Times*, 14 February 2006.

"We were just": Chris Nashawaty, "Kevin Spacey and Samuel L. Jackson," *Entertainment Weekly*, 7 August 1998.

"I was feeling": Pat Jordan, "How Samuel L. Jackson Became His Own Genre," *The New York Times Magazine*, 26 April 2012.

12. Engraved Handle
"I just sit there": Author interview with Samuel L. Jackson.

"whether it lets me": Jamie Malanowski, "A Man of Action Who Finds Power in Stillness," *The New York Times*, 14 April 2002.

"The one that's ready": *The Howard Stern Show*, SiriusXM, 5 January 2016.

"In a fair world": "Samuel L. Jackson," *Ebony*, November 2000.

"I want horses": Josh Tyrangiel, "His Own Best Fan," *Time*, 14 August 2006.

"Wow, how do you get": Kelley L. Carter, "After 30-plus years and 100-plus roles, Samuel L. Jackson ranks his own roles," *The Undefeated*, June 14, 2018.

"It might just be": Hilary De Vries, "Addicted to Acting," *Los Angeles Times Magazine*, 11 June 2000.

"Wait a minute": Alex Simon, "Samuel L. Jackson Tells It Like It Is," *Venice*, March 2005.

"Lightsaber handles": Carter.

"kinda looked like": Brent Simon, "Shaft's Big Score," *Entertainment Today*, 23 June 2000.

"Well, maybe Shaft": Ibid.

"Handsome, very good": *The Howard Stern Show*, syndicated radio program, 22 June 2000.

"I get to kiss": De Vries.

"I know better": "Samuel L Jackson confirms strife over Shaft," *The Guardian* (UK), 12 June 2000.

"I'd do it my way": Glenn Whipp, "Can Ya Dig It?," *Los Angeles Daily News*, 11 June 2000.

"Yes, and you got paid": Pat Jordan, "How Samuel L. Jackson Became His Own Genre," *The New York Times Magazine*, 26 April 2012.

"There are untrue rumors": "Samuel L. Jackson still the man: Any questions?," *The Hollywood Reporter*, 16 June 2000.

"If a director": Michael Fleming, "Playboy Interview: Samuel L. Jackson," *Playboy*, June 1999.

"It usually takes": Author interview with Samuel L. Jackson.

"I remember starting": Ibid.

"In the last minute": Roger Friedman, "Michael Jackson Flashback," *Showbiz 411*, 29 August 2019.

"Call me": Matthew Belloni and Stephanie Galloway, "The Actor Roundtable," *The Hollywood Reporter*, 4 December 2015.

"Folks are always shocked": Aldore Collier, "Samuel L. Jackson Talks About His Marriage, The Oscar Snubs, And Why He Works So Hard," *Ebony*, August 2003.

13. The Films of Samuel L. Jackson, 1999–2001

Star Wars: Episode I—The Phantom Menace

"Everybody said": Author interview with George Lucas.

The Red Violin

"One of the most cerebral": Kelley L. Carter, "After 30-plus years and 100-plus roles, Samuel L. Jackson ranks his own roles," *The Undefeated*, 14 June 2018.

"I was very impressed": Commentary track, *The Red Violin*, Lionsgate DVD, 2003.

"I know that": Ibid.

Deep Blue Sea

"seven pages": Ian Failes, " 'The Sooner You Kill Me, the Happier I'll Be': a VFX Oral History of Samuel L. Jackson's Shocking 'Deep Blue Sea' Departure," beforesandafters.com, 24 July 2019.

"I knew the audience": Erin McCarthy, "17 Facts About *Deep Blue Sea* for Its 20th Anniversary," *Mental Floss*, 27 July 2019.

"Renny, have you": Failes.

"It is my favorite death": Ibid.

Rules of Engagement

"His preparation": Kyle Smith, "Action Jackson," *People*, 3 July 2000.

"At times he can be": William Friedkin, *The Friedkin Connection*, Harper-Perennial, 2013.

Unbreakable

"Somebody over there": Joe McGovern, "An Oral History of M. Night Shyamalan's 'Unbreakable,' " ew.com, 17 January 2017.

The Caveman's Valentine

"Inside his skull," "you can trust him": Rob Blackwelder, "Lemmons in the Limelight," SplicedWire.com, 23 February 2001.]

"For a lot of reasons": Commentary track, *The Caveman's Valentine*, Universal DVD, 2001.

14. Berry Popsicles

"Then *Pulp Fiction* happened": Peter Haldeman, "Samuel L. Jackson," *Architectural Digest*, April 2000.

"I'm not stripping": Ibid.

"This is Sam's room": Ibid.

"I can't do any": David Cohen, "Chopsocky hits the spot for Jackson," *South China Morning Post*, 6 June 1998.

"Being an actor": Jill Nelson, "The working man," *USA Weekend*, 18-20 July 1997.

"Sometimes it gets": Ibid.

"For a long time": Tom O'Neill, "The US Interview," *US*, March 1998.

"You wake up": Stephen Rebello, "20 Questions: Samuel L. Jackson," *Playboy*, December 2006.

"it wasn't something": O'Neill.

"emotionally disconnected": Pat Jordan, "How Samuel L. Jackson Became His Own Genre," *The New York Times Magazine*, 26 April 2012.

"Oh, okay": Megan Conner, "Samuel L Jackson: 'I create characters—it keeps me from being me all day,'" *The Observer* (UK), 25 January 2015.

"Amnesia": Jordan.

"You need to forget": Mickey Rapkin, "Sam's Town," *Elle*, November 2012.

"There's very little": O'Neill.

"I like Popsicles": Allison Samuels, "Q&A: Samuel L. Jackson," *Newsweek*, 12 July 2002.

"I'm sure that": Margy Rochlin, "Tough Guy Finds His Warm and Fuzzy Side," *The New York Times*, 2 November 1997.

"Your daughter's looking": Kyle Smith, "Action Jackson," *People*, 3 July 2000.

"I help her": Michael Fleming, "Playboy Interview: Samuel L. Jackson," *Playboy*, June 1999.

"maybe five years": *The Howard Stern Show*, SiriusXM, 5 January 2016.

15. The Films of Samuel L. Jackson, 2002–2004

Changing Lanes

"Sam normally plays": David Mermelstein, "The Action's with Jackson," *Variety*, 1 December 2000.

Star Wars: Episode II—Attack of the Clones

"You can make yourself": Katie Rife, "Random Roles: Samuel L. Jackson on Nick Fury, Mace Windu, and the power of a great wig," *AV Club*, 18 January 2018.

"having fought a lot": Ibid.

"Anyone who picks up": Author interview with Hayden Christensen.

"I'm the most powerful": Rife.

Formula 51

"Most days": "Formula 51," ew.com, 17 March 2020 (originally published 2001).

Basic

"It's rare": Chris Willman, "A Little Peace, A Little Menace," *Los Angeles Times*, 9 October 1994.

S.W.A.T.

"I knew he was": Justin Mason, "That Samuel L. Jackson quote again," taint.org, 16 December 2003.

In My Country

"Ah, hire a French woman": Michael Sheridan, "Q&A with Samuel L. Jackson," *Tail Slate*, 9 March 2005.

Kill Bill: Vol. 2

"We were all": Author interview with Bo Svenson.

"There was nothing for me": *The Howard Stern Show*, SiriusXM, 5 January 2016.

The Incredibles

"Lucius is": Kelley L. Carter, "After 30-plus years and 100-plus roles, Samuel L. Jackson ranks his own roles," *The Undefeated*, June 14, 2018.

16. Rental Clubs

"Golf seemed": John Hopkins, "Showbusiness gets Jackson in mood to shoot from hip," *The Times* (UK), 27 September 2003.

"These guys": Michael Fleming, "Playboy Interview: Samuel L. Jackson," *Playboy*, June 1999.

"I like solitary": David S. Cohen, "Jackson career a tour de Force," *Variety*, 28 August–3 September 2000.

"You're not good enough": Hopkins.

"You can find out": Fleming.

"You're that actor guy": Ibid.

"Sam, come here": Jana Mobley, "Who Made You the Man You Are Today?," *Esquire*, October 2014.

"my new drug": Jill Nelson, "The working man," *USA Weekend*, 18–20 July 1997.

"which was awesome": Author interview with Samuel L. Jackson.

"I think he sees": Jamie Malanowski, "A Man of Action Who Finds Power in Stillness," *The New York Times*, 14 April 2002.

"I've never met": Hopkins.

"Hey, it's MJ": Author interview with Samuel L. Jackson.

"Golf's a very moral game": "Samuel L. Jackson Played Golf With Donald Trump and Learned Everything He Needed to Know," Associated Press, 10 August 2017.

"People know me for it": Stephen Rebello, "20 Questions: Samuel L. Jackson," *Playboy*, December 2006.

"The golf course is": *The ESPYs*, ESPN, 15 February 1999.

"Clinton is just": Jon Caramanica, "The Samuel L. Jackson Method," *The New York Times*, 3 August 2017.

"But you can't tell it": Allison Samuels, "Q&A: Samuel L. Jackson," *Newsweek*, 12 July 2002.

"to be a scratch golfer": John H. Richardson, "What I've Learned: Samuel L. Jackson," *Esquire*, January 2011.

"Golf and acting": Stephen Schaefer, "Play It Again and Again, Sam," *Variety*, 1 December 2008.

"Films get in the way": Hopkins.

17. The Films of Samuel L. Jackson, 2005–2007

Coach Carter

"I watched him": Noah Davis, "The Real Coach Carter: What It's Like to Have Your Life Made into a Movie," esquire.com, 19 November 2015.

"Sometimes I'm a defender": Brian B., "Samuel L. Jackson talks Coach Carter," *Movieweb*, 11 January 2005.

"Man, no worries": Patrick Goldstein, "The Big Picture: This top grossing actor has strict code," *Los Angeles Times*, 14 February 2006.

Star Wars: Episode III—Revenge of the Sith

"You've got a month": Katie Rife, "Random Roles: Samuel L. Jackson on Nick Fury, Mace Windu, and the power of a great wig," *AV Club*, 18 January 2018.

"Your wish": Chris Lee, "He's the $6-billion man," *Los Angeles Times*, 13 February 2005.

"I'm okay with that": Dalton Ross, "Star Wars: Samuel L. Jackson thinks Mace Windu is still alive," ew.com, June 29, 2016.

The Man

"Let me tell you": " 'The Man' Interviews: Samuel L. Jackson and Eugene Levy," hollywood.com, 7 September 2005.

Freedomland

"cracked bellow": Richard Price, *Freedomland*, Broadway Books, 1998.

"Carry me": Author interview with Samuel L. Jackson.

"Occasionally I let her": Wilson Morales, "Freedomland: An Interview with Samuel L. Jackson," blackfilm.com, February 2006.

Farce of the Penguins

"You're going to miss me": "Behind-the-Scenes Montage," *Farce of the Penguins*, Velocity/Thinkfilm DVD, 2007.

Black Snake Moan

"During the rehearsal period": Rebecca Murray, "Samuel L Jackson Talks 'Black Snake Moan,' Guitar, and Christina Ricci," liveabout.com, updated 15 May 2018.

"My grandfather's brothers": Jack Foley, "Black Snake Moan—Samuel L Jackson interview," *IndieLondon* (undated).

"At first his strengths": Author interview with Cedric Burnside.

1408

"The guys think": Steve Weintraub, "John Cusack, Samuel L. Jackson, Lorenzo di Bonaventura, Mary McCormack and Mikael Hafstrom Interviewed—1408," *Collider*, 11 June 2007.

"all you want": Ibid.

Resurrecting the Champ

"Everybody's got a story": Steve Weintraub, "Samuel L. Jackson Interview—Resurrecting the Champ," *Collider*, 21 August 2007.

18. Eye Patch

"The home speaks": Peter Haldeman, "Samuel L. Jackson," *Architectural Digest*, April 2000.

"My wife just bought": *The Howard Stern Show*, syndicated radio program, 22 June 2000.

"the ladies watch": Jada Yuan, "Tarantino's Leading Man," *New York*, 24 August–6 September 2015.

"If we want": Jon Caramanica, "The Samuel L. Jackson Method," *The New York Times*, 3 August 2017.

"Find something": Boris, "5 Most Famous Vassar Commencement Speeches," wpdh.com, 15 May 2015.

"She has a very strong": Alex Simon, "Samuel L. Jackson Tells It Like It Is," *Venice*, March 2005.

"You went": Stephen Rebello, "Playboy Interview: Samuel L. Jackson," *Playboy*, October 2013.

"She has this benevolent spirit": "Samuel L. Jackson & LaTanya Richardson Jackson," *Beyond the Spotlight*, episode 3, HBO, 2020.

"Too misogynistic": Margy Rochlin, "Tough Guy Finds His Warm and Fuzzy Side," *The New York Times*, 2 November 1997.

"It's the only project": Author interview with Harry Kloor.

"training a studio": Author interview with Daniel St. Pierre.

"Unlike a lot": Author interview with Harry Kloor.

"The way Sam played": Author interview with Daniel St. Pierre.

"kids in the third": Author interview with Harry Kloor.

"Read as much": Author interview with Daniel St. Pierre.

"Oh, goddamn you": Author interview with Phil LaMarr.

"I wanted an African American Nick Fury": Gus Lubin, "Samuel L. Jackson had the perfect response to the writer who made his 'Avengers' role possible," *Business Insider*, 27 April 2015.

"We put it at the end": Joanna Robinson, "Secrets of the Marvel Universe," *Vanity Fair*, Holiday 2017.

"It's only fun": Adam B. Vary, "Jon Favreau talks 'Iron Man,'" ew.com, 5 May 2008.

"Who wouldn't want": Pat Jordan, "How Samuel L. Jackson Became His Own Genre," *The New York Times Magazine*, 26 April 2012.

"Fuck, no, man": Lubin.

"I could be the Alec Guinness": Seth Abramovitch, "120 Movies, $13 Billion in Box Office: How Samuel L. Jackson Became Hollywood's Most Bankable Star," *The Hollywood Reporter*, 9 January 2019.

"I wish Nick Fury": Caramanica.

19. The Films of Samuel L. Jackson, 2008–2011

Iron Man
"pipe dream": Joanna Robinson, "Marvel Looks Back at *Iron Man*—the Movie That Started It All," *Vanity Fair*, Holiday 2017.

Cleaner
"From where I was sitting": Author interview with Matthew Aldrich.

Lakeview Terrace
"Sam knew a lot": David Mermelstein, "The Action's with Jackson," *Variety*, 1 December 2000.

Soul Men
"It got to the point": Commentary track, *Soul Men*, The Weinstein Company DVD, 2009.

The Spirit
"I spent a lot of time": Jerry Edling, "Action Jackson," *The Hollywood Reporter*, 1 December 2008.

Afro Samurai: Resurrection
"It's an amazing time": Geoff Boucher, "He's Mr. Cool," *Los Angeles Times*, 24 January 2009.

Gospel Hill
"I've been an actor": Eileen Casey, "The HIFF Premieres 'Gospel Hill' Directed By Giancarlo Esposito," hamptons.com, 16 October 2008.

Inglourious Basterds
"Well, yeah": Jerry Edling, "Action Jackson," *The Hollywood Reporter*, 1 December 2008.

Mother and Child
"I was really scared": Earl Dittman, "Actress Naomi Watts goes behind the scenes of 'Mother and Child,' " *Digital Journal*, 15 December 2010.

"I think he's a very good romantic lead": Nick Allen, "Interview with writer/director Rodrigo Garcia," *The Scorecard Review*, 7 May 2010.

Iron Man 2
"We still haven't moved": Rick Marshall, "Exclusive: Sam Jackson says Nick Fury Won't See Action in 'Iron Man 2,' " mtv.com, 30 June 2009.

The Sunset Limited
"We rehearsed it": Amy Chozick, "Samuel L. Jackson on His Role in 'The Sunset Limited,' " *The Wall Street Journal*, 4 February 2011.

"The HBO people": David Carr, " 'Tis Nobler to Dive in Front of a Train? Discuss," *The New York Times*, 10 February 2011.

20. Hot Poker

"He couldn't believe": David Cohen, "Chopsocky hits the spot for Jackson," *South China Morning Post*, 6 June 1998.

"He's doing this almost": Chris Willman, "A Little Peace, A Little Menace," *Los Angeles Times*, 9 October 1994.

"They're both very literary": Ibid.

"I read so much shit": Kristopher Tapley, "Hateful Mates," *Variety*, 8 December 2015.

"So when he says": Samuel L. Jackson and Michael Keaton, "On Rehearsing," *Variety*, 1 December 2015.

"It's all about": Alex Simon, "Samuel L. Jackson Tells It Like It Is," *Venice*, March 2005.

"As you can see": Henry Louis Gates Jr., "Tarantino 'Unchained,' Part 2: On the N-Word," *The Root*, 24 December 2012.

"there are some people": Tapley.

"Calvin's major concern": Anthony Breznican, " 'Django Unchained': Samuel L. Jackson on playing a 'hateful negro,' " ew.com, December 2012.

"Quentin provides": Richard N. Gladstein, " 'Hateful Eight' Producer: How Quentin Tarantino and Samuel L. Jackson Interact on Set," *The Hollywood Reporter*, 29 December 2015.

"He knew exactly": Tapley.

"People hate you": Jada Yuan, "Tarantino's Leading Man," *New York*, 24 August–6 September 2015.

"I took time": *The Howard Stern Show*, SiriusXM, 5 January 2016.

"inside of this great thing": Tapley.

"It feels": Yuan.

"Dude": Tapley.

"This could almost be": Jeff Labrecque, "Quentin Tarantino: The Hateful Eight interview," ew.com, 31 December 2015.

"This is my *Iceman Cometh*": Ibid.

"I heard him say": Steve Weintraub, "Samuel L. Jackson Interview—Resurrecting the Champ," *Collider*, 21 August 2007.

"There's so much": Simon.

"There's just something very natural": "What Samuel L. Jackson Learned From Working With Quentin Tarantino," masterclass.com, 16 November 2020.

21. The Films of Samuel L. Jackson, 2012–2015

The Avengers

"Noise and toys": Linda Barnard, "Samuel L. Jackson talks about The Samaritan and working with Quentin Tarantino again," *Toronto Star*, 17 May 2012.

"The idea that": Commentary track, *The Avengers*, Walt Disney DVD, 2012.

Meeting Evil

"I would have been interested": Christina Radish, "Director Chris Fisher Talks Meeting Evil, Warehouse 13, Person of Interest and More," *Collider*, 19 April 2012.

"I just yelled at him": Christina Radish, "Luke Wilson Talks Meeting Evil, Enlightened, and Possibly Returning for Anchorman 2," *Collider*, 8 April 2012.

The Samaritan

"It had a much darker": Linda Barnard, "Samuel L. Jackson talks about The Samaritan and working with Quentin Tarantino again," *Toronto Star*, 17 May 2012.

Django Unchained

"Do you want to have": Author interview with Quentin Tarantino.

"I love fucking Stephen": Carvell Wallace, "Samuel L. Jackson Operates Like He Owns the Place. (He Does.)," *Esquire*, April 2019.

"It's awesome": Kelley L. Carter, "After 30-plus years and 100-plus roles, Samuel L. Jackson ranks his own roles," *The Undefeated*, 14 June 2018.

Adventures in Zambezia

"I'm not sure": "Wayne Thornley Adventures in Zambezia Interview," girl.com.au, March 2013.

Oldboy

"There's a million": "The Making of Oldboy," *Oldboy*, Sony DVD, 2014.

"Sam called me up": Bruce Fretts, "Elizabeth Olsen is creeped out by her own movie, Spike Lee's remake of the Korean thriller 'Oldboy,'" *New York Daily News*, 24 November 2013.

Reasonable Doubt

"I'm not really sure": "Special Features: Interviews: Samuel L. Jackson," *Reasonable Doubt*, Artisan/Lionsgate DVD, 2014.

"Your lungs hurt": Steve Weintraub, "Dominic Cooper Talks Reasonable Doubt," *Collider*, 16 January 2014.

"they were all in Canada": "Special Features: Interviews: Samuel L. Jackson."

Captain America: The Winter Soldier

"Almost everything": Russ Fischer, " 'Captain America: The Winter Soldier' Panel Recap: Falcon Flies, Cap Fights the Modern World [Comic Con 2013]," slashfilm.com, 20 July 2013.

"We talked about golf": Christina Radish, "Chris Evans, Scarlett Johansson, Samuel L. Jackson and Kevin Feige Talk Captain America: The Winter Soldier, Evolution of Black Widow, and Much More," *Collider*, 27 March 2014.

"He has to ask": Fischer.

Kite

"We didn't tell it": Matt Sernaker, "Exclusive—Kite—Interview with Samuel L. Jackson," *ComicsOnline*, 2 December 2014.

Kingsman: The Secret Service

"If you're Steve Jobs": Sean O'Connell, "What Kingsman's Director Initially Hated About Samuel L. Jackson's Performance," *CinemaBlend*, February 9, 2015.

Big Game

"We had really fun times": Author interview with Jalmari Helander.

"It's an interesting little film": Christina Radish, "Samuel L. Jackson talks Big Game, Playing the President, The Blob Remake, More," *Collider*, June 25, 2015.

The Hateful Eight

"actually refrigerated": Samuel L. Jackson and Michael Keaton, "On Rehearsing," *Variety*, 1 December 2015.

"His characters roam": Quentin Tarantino as told to Gavin Edwards, "Quentin Tarantino Tackles Old Dixie by Way of the Old West (by Way of Italy)," *The New York Times Magazine*, 27 September 2012.

22. French Braid

"I made a decision": "Samuel L. Jackson still the man: Any questions?," *The Hollywood Reporter*, 16 June 2000.

"the first thing": Katie Rife, "Random Roles: Samuel L. Jackson on Nick Fury, Mace Windu, and the power of a great wig," *AV Club*, 18 January 2018.

"I was thinking Frederick Douglass": Chris Lee, "The hair club for Sam," *Los Angeles Times*, 14 February 2008.

"AI has this great program": Steve Weintraub, "Samuel L. Jackson Interview—Resurrecting the Champ," *Collider*, 21 August 2007.

"The kind of foods": Megan Conner, "Samuel L Jackson: 'I create characters—it keeps me from being me all day,'" *The Observer* (UK), 25 January 2015.

"All my characters": Jill Nelson, "The working man," *USA Weekend*, 18–20 July 1997.

"I unreasonably expect": Stephen Schaefer, "Play It Again and Again, Sam," *Variety*, 1 December 2008.

"Sam can be quite intimidating": Chris Lee, "He's the $6-billion man," *Los Angeles Times*, 13 February 2005.

"He gave me little pointers": Author interview with Thomas Jane.

"I don't get to go": Carvell Wallace, "Samuel L. Jackson Operates Like He Owns the Place. (He Does.)," *Esquire*, April 2019.

"You end up making up": Rife.

"I can't see": David Rensin, "20 Questions: Samuel L. Jackson," *Playboy*, April 1995.

"The average person": Hilary De Vries, "Addicted to Acting," *Los Angeles Times Magazine*, 11 June 2000.

"It's a job": Schaefer.

23. The Films of Samuel L. Jackson, 2016–2018

The Legend of Tarzan

"I've seen maybe": Mikey Fresh, "Samuel L. Jackson Plays a Historical Black Figure in 'The Legend of Tarzan,'" vibe.com, 26 July 2016.

Miss Peregrine's Home for Peculiar Children

"When I put them in": Nick Romano, "Samuel L. Jackson on 'Miss Peregrine,' Tim Burton's Style, and What's Next for Nick Fury," moviefone.com, 29 September 2016.

"That was amazing!": Ibid.

Kong: Skull Island

"This is my homage": Christina Radish, "Samuel L. Jackson on 'Kong: Skull Island' and the Future of Nick Fury," *Collider*, 13 March 2017.

The Hitman's Bodyguard

"Chuffa is filler": Author interview with Mindy Kaling.

"The great thing about": Rob Leane, "Samuel L Jackson & Salma Hayek interview: The Hitman's Bodyguard, and breaking into Hollywood," *Den of Geek*, 13 August 2017.

"I thought it was hilarious": Ibid.

Incredibles 2

"went out and started": "Original Cin Q&A w/ The Incredibles 2's Brad Bird: 'You Throw a Rock Now and You'll Hit a Superhero,'" *Original Cin*, 12 June 2018.

"Edna is just the dopest": Patty Holliday, "13 Surprises With Samuel L. Jackson," *My No-Guilt Life*, 13 June 2018.

24. Alligator Loafers

"It's easy": Author interview with Jalmari Helander.

"I'm not too proud": Jada Yuan, "Tarantino's Leading Man," *New York*, 24 August–6 September 2015.

"my real job": *The Howard Stern Show*, SiriusXM, 5 January 2016.

"He wasn't mean": Author interview with Morgan Neville.

"The cats nestle close": Adam Mansbach (illustrations by Ricardo Cortés), *Go the Fuck to Sleep*, Akashic Books, 2011.

"Somebody needs to": Stephen Rebello, "Playboy Interview: Samuel L. Jackson," *Playboy*, October 2013.

"Sam Jackson is": Antonio Ferme, "Governors Awards: Samuel L. Jackson, Danny Glover, Elaine May and Liv Ullmann Set for Honorary Oscars," variety.com, 24 June 2021.

"We got a little gray film": Author interview with Samuel L. Jackson.

"sneaker fetish": Rebello.

"Fuck it": Author interview with Samuel L. Jackson.

"Every event has": Ibid.

"To find out": John Eligon, "Samuel Jackson Traces the History of the Trans-Atlantic Slave Trade," *The New York Times*, 19 September 2020.

"even though we don't": Sarah Hughes, "Laurence Fishburne: 'People have been confusing Samuel L Jackson and me for 25 years,'" *The Guardian* (UK), 26 April 2014.

"Oh, I am, for sure": Bridget Read, "Apparently Samuel L. Jackson Has Seen Donald Trump Cheat at Golf," vogue.com, 1 April 2019.

"I hate watching": Josh Tyrangiel, "His Own Best Fan," *Time*, 14 August 2006.

"look-at-me business": Author interview with Samuel L. Jackson.

25. The Films of Samuel L. Jackson, 2019–2021

Glass

"I always assumed": Aaron Couch and Seth Abramovitch, "Samuel L. Jackson on How M. Night Shyamalan Mellowed From Being a 'Dictator' Director," *The Hollywood Reporter*, 11 January 2019.

"Night still uses the same crew": Author interview with Bostin Christopher.

"trying to figure out": Steve "Frosty" Weintraub, "'Glass': Samuel L. Jackson on Trying to Find an Active Way to Be Passive," *Collider*, 18 January 2019.

Captain Marvel

"The cat we worked with": Huw Fullerton, "Samuel L Jackson on Captain Marvel, his Spider-Man future—and why he'll never say goodbye to the MCU," *RadioTimes* (UK), 10 March 2019.

Unicorn Store

"He found out": Jenelle Riley, "Brie Larson on Her Directorial Debut 'Unicorn Store.' Premiering at Toronto Film Festival," *Variety*, 15 August 2017.

Spiral: From the Book of Saw

"What is it?": Steve Weintraub, "John Cusack, Samuel L. Jackson, Lorenzo di Bonaventura, Mary McCormack and Mikael Hafstrom Interviewed—408," *Collider*, 11 June 2007.

26. Greenhouse Roof

"Dying is a happening thing": Michael Angeli, "Samuel L. Jackson Climbs Among the Glittering Stars," *The New York Times*, 7 February 1993.

"I don't think I've ever": Katie Rife, "Random Roles: Samuel L. Jackson on Nick Fury, Mace Windu, and the power of a great wig," *AV Club*, 18 January 2018.

"One death": David Rensin, "20 Questions: Samuel L. Jackson," *Playboy*, April 1995.

"I'm not necessarily sure": Karen Schoemer, "The 'L' is for Lucky," *Newsweek*, 5 June 1995.

"I don't think anybody": Georg Szalai, "The Lives Changed by Hollywood," *The Hollywood Reporter*, 22 August 2014.

"I read": Ibid.

"My name": Author interview with Samuel L. Jackson.

Index

Note: Page numbers in *italics* indicate an illustration.

Abbott and Costello Go to Mars
  (movie), 180
Abrams, J. J., 295–296
Academy Theatre, 36
Adventures in Zambezia (2013), 248–249
Affleck, Ben, 101, 175
African Cats (documentary), *217*, 282
Afro Samurai: Resurrection (2009),
  225–226
Against the Wall (1994), 111–112
Aiello, Danny, 74
Ain't Supposed to Die a Natural Death
  (Van Peebles), 36
Airplane! (movie), 104, 200
Alba, Jessica, 258
Alda, Alan, 77–78
Aldrich, Matthew, 1, 220–221
Alexander, Jason, 203, 212
Ali, Tatyana, 61
All the President's Men (movie), 254
Allen, Debbie, 57
Allen, Irwin, 200
Ally McBeal (television series), 170
Alzheimer's disease, 161, 302–303
The American Short Story (television
  series), 55
America's Funniest Home Videos
  (television series), 202
Amos 'n' Andy (radio/television
  series), 13, 106
Amos & Andrew (1993), 92, 105–106
Anderson, Jon, 213
Anderson, Paul Thomas, 139, 211
Apocalypse Now (movie), 248, 274
Apone, Allan, 265
Arena (2011), 236
Argento, Asia, 178

Arkin, Alan, 172
Arquette, Alexis, 102
Arquette, Patricia, 109
Arquette, Rosanna, 103
Arrival (movie), 146
Arteta, Miguel, 292
Ashanti, 195
*Assault at West Point: The Court-Martial of
  Johnson Whittaker* (1994), 94, 110
Astro Boy (2009), 229
Athie, Mamoudou, 292
Attenborough, Richard, 108
Autry, Gene, 14
The Avengers (2012), *208*, 244–245
Avengers (movies), 219
Avengers: Age of Ultron (2015), 257
Avengers: Endgame (2019), 250,
  292–293
Avengers: Infinity War (2018), 276–277
Avery, Margaret, 82

"Back to the Land" (Young), 3
Badalucco, Michael, 135
Baldwin, Adam, 227
Baldwin, Alec, 101, 122, 281
Baldwin, James, 282
Bale, Christian, 163
Banderas, Antonio, 278–279
The Banker (2020), 297
Baraka, Amiri, 34, 42
Barely Lethal (2015), 257–258
Barker, Lex, 271
Barkin, Ellen, 75
Barkley, Charles, 191, 281
Barnow, Alex, 293
Barr, Roseanne, 209
Barris, Kenya, 293

Barton Fink (movie), 89

Basic (2003), 179–180

Basic Instinct (movie), 252

Basie, Count, 2

Basinger, Kim, 122

Bass, Fontella, 79

Bassett, Angela, 227, 282, 293

Beals, Jennifer, 135

Bean, Sean, 102

Beastie Boys, 3

Becker, Harold, 75

Bender, Lawrence, 92, 94–95, 185

Bening, Annette, 230, 278–279

Bernsen, Corbin, 133

Berry, Halle, 84, 85, 130

The Best Man (Vidal), 38

The Best Years of Our Lives (movie), 201

Betsy's Wedding (1990), 77–78

Beyoncé, 210, 292

Biel, Jessica, 202

The Big Bang Theory (television series), 92

Big Game (2015), 258–259, 281

The Big Short (movie), 233

Binoche, Juliette, 184

Bird, Brad, 186, 277–278

Birdman of Alcatraz (television movie), 111

Birth of the Cool (Davis), 5

Black, Lewis, 203

Black Arts Movement, 42

Black Arts Repertory Theater, 42

Black Cream (movie). *See Together for Days*

Black Image Theater Company, 34–35

Black Mirror (movie), 298

Black Panther (movie), 62

Black Panthers, 30

Black Phantom (proposed movie), 211

Black Snake Moan (2007), *10*, 203–205

Blacula (1972), 76

Blades, Rubén, 73, 78

Blatty, William Peter, 80

Blazing Samurai (movie), 54

Bogart, Humphrey, 49

Bond, Cynthia, 77

Bond, James, III, 77

Boogie Nights (movie), 211

Boone, Mark, Junior, 138

Boorman, John, 184, 266

Bousman, Darren Lynn, 299

Boutella, Sofia, 256

Bowie, David, 8

Boyz N the Hood (movie), 107

Brando, Marlon, 155–156

Breaking Bad (television series), 303

Brecht, Bertolt, 45

Brewer, Craig, 203

The Bride with White Hair (movie), 169

Bridges, Jeff, 231

Bridges, Lloyd, 22

Broadbent, Jim, 259

Brolin, Josh, 250

Bronson, Charles, 57

Brooker, Charlie, 298

Brooklyn Nine-Nine (television series), 8

Brooks, Albert, 146

Brooks, Avery, 42–43, 49, 58

Brooks, Randy, 93

Brown, H. Rap, 30

Bruce, Lenny, 127

Bryant, Kobe, 185

Buffy the Vampire Slayer (television series), 138, 172

Bull Durham (movie), 133

Bullock, Sandra, 136

Burnside, Cedric, 204

Burroughs, Baldwin, 34, 35

Burroughs, Edgar Rice, 271

Burrows, Saffron, 160

Burton, Richard, 36, 38, 47

Burton, Tim, 272

Bus 174 (movie), 252

Buscemi, Steve, 135, 137–138

Bush, George W., 251

Busta Rhymes, 163, 172, 268

Caesar, Adolph, 47
Cage, Nicolas, 92, 106, 131–132, 229
Cagney, James, 45, 49, 57
Caine, Michael, 76, 211
Calderón, Paul, 94–95
Camelot (musical), 35
Captain America (comic books), 254
Captain America: The First Avenger (2011), 235–236
Captain America: The Winter Soldier (2014), 253–254, 257
Captain Marvel (2019), 290–291
Carlyle, Robert, 178
Carmichael, Stokely, 30
Carpenter, John, 242
Carpool Karaoke (television series), 283
Carroll, Diahann, 36
Carter, Ken, 194
Carter, Thomas, 194–195
Caruso, David, 131
Cave, Nick, 84
The Caveman's Valentine (2001), *157*, 166–167, 265
Cell (2016), 270–271
Central High School, Little Rock, Arkansas, 5–6
Changing Lanes (2002), 175–176, 190
Cheadle, Don, 146, 191, 211
Cheney, Dick, 201, 251
Chiba, Sonny, 238
Chicago Hope (television series), 169
Chiles, Lois, 37
The Chinese Connection (movie), 153
Chi-Raq (2015), 210, *243*, 259–260
Chopped (television show), 210
Christensen, Hayden, 176, 177, 218
Christie, Agatha, 261
Christopher, Bostin, 289
Civil Rights Act (1964), 18
Clark, Kimberly Adair, 187
Clark, Spencer Treat, 289
Clark, William Paul, 185
Cleaner (2008), 220–221

Clinton, Bill, 110, 191
Clinton, George, 8
Clooney, George, 146–147
Close Encounters of the Third Kind (movie), 146
Clueless (movie), 258
Coach Carter (2005), 194–195
Cobb, Lee J., 80
Cochrane, Rory, 103
Cohen, Rob, 178
Cole, Nat King, 81
Coleman, Dabney, 106
The Color Purple, 59, 82
colorblind casting, 122–123
Coltrane, John, 79
Coming to America (1988), 50, 62–63
Commodores, 34
Community (television series), 8
Con Air (movie), 132
Concerned Students, 28–29, 34
Conway, Kellyanne, 298
cool, meaning and usage, 1–9
Cool Hand Luke (movie), 236
Cooley High (movie), 37
Cooper, Albert, 36–37, 50
Cooper, Chris, 136
Cooper, Dominic, 251–252
Corbucci, Sergio, 261
Cosby, Bill, 26, 49, 60, 172–173
The Cosby Show (television series), 49, 173
Costner, Kevin, 121
Country of My Skull (Krog), 184
Cousteau, Jacques, 22
Crank: High Voltage (movie), 277
Creature from the Black Lagoon (movie), 14
Crichton, Michael, 92, 108, 145
The Crimson Pirate (movie), 14
Crocodile Dundee II (movie), 51
Cronenberg, David, 77
Cross Creek (movie), 50
Croudins, Peter P., 251

Culp, Robert, 26
Curtis, Christopher Paul, 210
Cusack, Joan, 292
Cusack, John, 205, 270

Dafoe, Willem, 100, 195
Dangerous Minds (movie), 123
Daniels, Anthony, 221
Daniels, Jeff, 57, 219
Danza, Tony, 86
Davidson, Tommy, 85
Davis, Bette, 36
Davis, Geena, 123, 138
Davis, Judy, 114
Davis, Miles, 5, 6
Davis, Ossie, 37, 66, 70, 74, 84
Davis, Sammy, Jr., 81
Davis, Viola, 146
Dazed and Confused (movie), 144
De Niro, Robert, 78, 81, 124–125,
     143, 290
Dead and Alive: The Race for Gus Farace
     (1991), 86
Dead Man Out (1989), 73
Death to 2020 (2020), 298
Death Wish (movie), 57
Dee, Ruby, 36, 70–71, 74, 84
Deep Blue Sea (1999), 150, 160–161,
     220, 267
Def by Temptation (1990), 76–77
Dern, Bruce, 242
Dern, Laura, 108
Destiny's Child, 155
DeVito, Danny, 94
DiCaprio, Leonardo, 240, 248
DiCillo, Tom, 84
Dickerson, Ernest, 99
Die Hard (movie), 60
Die Hard with a Vengeance (1995),
     121–122, 124, 132–133, 164
Diesel, Vin, 177–178, 195, 273
Diggs, Taye, 180
directors, types of, 154–155

Dirty Harry (movies), 57
Disend, Michael, 103
The Displaced Person (1977), 55
Distant Fires (Heelan), 119
District Line (Walker), 45
Ditko, Steve, 224, 235
Django Unchained (2012), 239–241,
     247–248, 283
Do the Right Thing (1989), *64*, 65,
     74–75, 79, 260
Doctorow, E. L., 57
Dogtown and Z-Boys (movie), 274
Dolemite Is My Name (movie), 293
Donaldson, Roger, 100
Donovan, Martin, 232
Douglass, Frederick, 264
Dowling, Peter A., 251
Downey, Robert, Jr., 113, 219, 230
Drescher, Fran, 57
Driver, Adam, 295
Driving Miss Daisy (movie), 74
Drunken Master (movie), 169
Dutton, Charles S., 50–52, 136
Dylan, Bob, 278

Eastwood, Clint, 57
Easy Rider (movie), 182
Eckstine, Billy, 6
Ed Wood (movie), 120
Eddie Murphy Raw (1987), 60–61
Edson, Richard, 74
Edwards, Stacks, 81
Ehle, Jennifer, 252
Eisenhower, Dwight, 5
Eisley, India, 255
Eisner, Will, 224–225
Ellington, Duke, 5
Ellis, Aunjanue, 166
Ellis, David R., 255
Enslaved (documentary), 285
Epps, Omar, 99
ER (television series), 169
Ermey, R. Lee, 180

Esposito, Giancarlo, 65, 74, 106, 114, 226–227
Estevez, Emilio, 92, 105
Estrada, Erik, 105
Eve's Bayou (1997), 142–143, 166, *288*
Ewing, Patrick, 80
Excalibur (movie), 266
The Exorcist (movie), 80
Exorcist II: The Heretic (movie), 80
The Exorcist III (1990), 79–80
The Exterminator (1980), 56–57

Fabio, 79, 80
Falco, Edie, 198
Fallon, Jimmy, 281
Farce of the Penguins (2007), 202–203
Farina, Dennis, 146
Farrell, Colin, 181
Fassbender, Michael, 228
The Fast and the Furious (movies), 177, 178, 273
Fathers and Sons (1992), 103–104
Favreau, Jon, 215
Feige, Kevin, 215, 219
Feore, Colm, 166
Ferrell, Will, 232
50 Cent, 202, 268
The 51st State. See Formula 51
The Fighting Temptations (movie), 210
"Fire and Rain" (Taylor), 33
Fishburne, Laurence, 44, 50, 62, 65, 69, 92, 94, 121, 211, 298
  Jackson mistaken for, 91, 95, 190, 286
Fisher, Chris, 245
Five Deadly Venoms (movie), 44
Five Easy Pieces (movie), 182
Flemyng, Jason, 160
Flipper, Henry O., 56
"Flowers on the Wall" (Statler Brothers), 133
Floyd, George, 298
Fluke (1995), 133–134

Fogelman, Dan, 278
Fonda, Bridget, 124
Fonda, Peter, 296
Foner, Naomi, 130
Foote, Horton, 55
For Colored Girls Who Have Considered Suicide/When the Rainbow Is Enuf (Shange), 41, 42
Ford, Harrison, 91, 101
Forman, Milos, 45
Formula 51 (2002), 178–179, *188*, 190, 265
Forrest Gump (movie), 120
Forster, Robert, 124, 143
1408 (2007), 2, *193*, 205, 270
Foxcatcher (movie), 106
Foxx, Jamie, 133, 240, 248
Francis the Talking Mule (movie), 14
Frankenheimer, John, 111
Frannie's Turn (television series), 91–92, 172
Freedom Riders, 30
Freedomland (2006), 190, 198–199, 204, 297
Freeman, Morgan, 44, 45, 49–50, 90, 202–203, 211, 286, 300
Fresh (1994), 94–95, *98*, 113–114
Friedkin, William, 162
Frye, Max, 105
Full House (television series), 202
Full Metal Jacket (movie), 180
Fuller, Charles, 46
Funny or Die (website), 283

Gaghan, Stephen, 162
Gandolfini, James, 109
Ganja & Hess (1973), 76
Garber, Victor, 259
Garcia, Andy, 183
García, Rodrigo, 230
Garrett, Bernard, 297
Gates, Bill, 256
Gellar, Sarah Michelle, 212

George, Nelson, 68, 85, 122

Get Rich or Die Tryin' (movie), 268

The Getaway (movie), 122

Getz, Stan, 57

Giamatti, Paul, 148, 249

Gibson, Mel, 105

Giddins, Gary, 7

Gillespie, Dizzy, 6, 7, 8

Gilliard, Larry, Jr., 137

Ginty, Robert, 56

Girard, François, 160

Girl 6 (movie), 127

Gladstein, Richard, 95, 240

Glass (2019), 289–290

Gleeson, Brendan, 185

Glover, Danny, 73, 90, 105, 227

Go the Fuck to Sleep (book), 282

The Godfather Part II (movie), 78

Goetz, Bernhard, 57

Goggins, Walton, 242

Goldberg, Whoopi, 105, 203

Goldblum, Jeff, 103–104, 108, 133, 249

Gondry, Michel, 292

Gone in Sixty Seconds (movie), 132

Gone with the Wind (movie), 292

Good, Meagan, 143

Goodfellas (1990), 72, 80–81, 124, 202

Gooding, Cuba, Jr., 210

Goodman, John, 75, 274

Gospel Hill (2009), 226–227

Gossett, Louis, Jr., 180

Gould, Steven, 218

Grace Under Fire (television series), 92

Grant, Cary, 5

Grant, Hugh, 298

Gray, F. Gary, 147

The Great White Hype (1996), 134–135, 264

Greener, Richard, 110

Grier, Pam, 124, 143–144

Grisham, John, 124, 136

Guinness, Alec, 216, 295

Guzmán, Luis, 102, 146, 220, 249

Gyllenhaal, Jake, 130, 294

Gyllenhaal, Maggie, 130

Gyllenhaal, Stephen, 130

Hackman, Gene, 245

Hail Caesar (1994), 112–113

Haley, Alex, 38

Hall, Anthony Michael, 112

Hall, Arsenio, 62

Hall, Katori, 282

Hall, Philip Baker, 140

Halloween II (movie), 277

Hamill, Mark, 212, 295

Hamlet (movie), 264

Hammett, Dashiell, 182

Hanks, Tom, 2, 101

Hard Boiled (movie), 169

Hard Eight (1997), 2, 139–140

Hardison, Kadeem, 77

Harlin, Renny, 123, 160–161, 220

Harriet (movie), 142

Harris, Ed, 220, 296

Harry and the Butler (movie), 211

Hart, Kevin, 211

Hartman, Phil, 105

Hartnett, Josh, 206

Harvey-Salaam, Dyane, 43

Hasselhoff, David, 214

"Hate Whitey Theater," 34

The Hateful Eight (2015), 2, *237*, 238, 241–242, 260–262, 272

Hathaway, Anne, 210, 283

Hayek, Salma, 276, 300

Hayes, Isaac, 153, 239

Hedaya, Dan, 163

Heelan, Kevin, 119

Helander, Jalmari, 259, 281

Hemingway, Ernest, 3

Henderson, Fletcher, 5

Hendra, Tony, 133

Henson, Josiah, 58

Himes, Chester, 282

Hitch, Bryan, 215

The Hitman's Bodyguard (2017), 53, 275–276

The Hitman's Wife's Bodyguard (2021), 300

Hoffman, Dustin, 126, 145

Hoffman, Philip Seymour, 139–140

Holiday, Billie, 2, 3

Home of the Brave (2006), 201–202

Hooks, Robert, 56

Hopkins, Anthony, 234

Hopper, Dennis, 109, 121, 182

Hot Action Cop, 181

Hotel Rwanda (movie), 211

"The House in Turk Street" (Hammett), 182

Houseman, John, 55

Houston, Whitney, 155

Howard, Toni, 285

Howitt, Peter, 251

Hudlin, Reginald, 133, 264

Hudson, Jennifer, 260

Huffman, Felicity, 259

Hughes, Albert and Allen, 107, 126–128

Hulce, Tom, 218

Hunt, Helen, 131

Hurt, William, 292, 296

I Am Not Your Negro (movie), 282

I Spy (television series), 26

Ice Cube, 195–196, 268, 273

The Iceman Cometh (O'Neill), 242

Imperioli, Michael, 103

In My Country (2004), 184–185, 266

The Incredibles (2004), *174*, 186–187

Incredibles 2 (2018), 277–278

Inglourious Basterds (2009), 227–228, 239, 247

The Irishman (movie), 290

Iron Man (2008), 215, 219

Iron Man 2 (2010), 205, 230–231

Irons, Jeremy, 132

Isaac, Oscar, 278

Jackie Brown (1997), 124, 126, 128, 143–145, 146, 155, 239, *263*, 265

Jackson, Elizabeth Harriett Montgomery (mother), 11, 15–16, 21

Jackson, LaTanya Richardson (wife). *See* Richardson, LaTanya

Jackson, Mahalia, 26

Jackson, Michael, 8, 60–61, 155–156

Jackson, Roy Henry (father), 11, 47–48

Jackson, Samuel L.
  Academy Awards, 116, 120, 283, 293
  achievements, 2, 281–287, 303
  acting philosophy, 264–268
  Atlanta career, 33–39
  Best Supporting Actor award at Cannes, 89
  charitable donations, 210
  childhood, 6, 7, 11–19
  Chinese Theater hands/feet print, 283
  clothing choices, 16, 37, 284
  comic books and, 13, 164, 214–215
  commencement speech, 209–210
  daughter born, 47
  death scenes, 302
  drug rehab, 69–71, 88, 171
  drug use, 6–7, 24–25, 33, 35, 52, 68–70
  family roots, 285–286
  first movie, 37–38
  first Great Britain trip, 45
  as golfer, 189–192, 284
  Hollywood Walk of Fame star, 283
  "King of Cool" moniker, 9
  Krystal commercial, 38
  in Los Angeles, 91–97, 169–173
  love life, 33, 35
  marriage, 44–45
  never-happened projects, 211–214
  in New York, 38–39, 41–52
  New York subway incident, 66–67, 79, 89, 120–121

Jackson, Samuel L. *(continued)*
  political activism, 30–31
  as a producer, 142, 178, 285
  as role model, 172–173, 194–195
  roles, choosing, 150–156
  school, 14, 17, 18–19
    (*see also* Morehouse College)
  Screen Actors Guild, 38
  segregation and, 6, 12–13, 16–19
  self-image, 9, 287
  shoe fetish, 283–284
  as stutterer, 15, 303
  theater productions, 42–52, 282–283
Jackson, Zoe (daughter), 47, 170,
    171–172, 209–210, 283
Jane, Thomas, 267
Janssen, Famke, 103
Jarmusch, Jim, 84
Jaws (movie), 160, 239, 298
Jewison, Norman, 47
Jobs, Steve, 256
Johansson, Scarlett, 225
John Goldfarb, Please Come Home!
    (movie), 25
Johnny Suede (1991), 61, 84–85, 93
Johnson, Dwayne "The Rock," 232
Johnson, Magic and Cookie, 209
Johnson, Rian, 295
Jones, Angela, 116
Jones, James Earl, 15, 62, 212
Jones, LeRoi. *See* Baraka, Amiri
Jones, Leslie, 298
Jones, Robert Earl, 55
Jones, Tommy Lee, 162, 233–234
Jordan, Michael, 191
Jovovich, Milla, 182
Judd, Ashley, 136, 183, 211
Judge Judy. See Sheindlin, Judith
Juice (1992), 99–100
Julia (television series), 36
Jumper (2008), 218
Jumpin at the Boneyard (1992), 88,
    93, 102–103

Jungle Fever (1991), 70–71, 83–84,
    89–90, 250, 302
Jurassic Park (1993), 1, 92, 107–108,
    124, *301*, 302
Just an Old Sweet Song (movie), 56, 264
Just Us Theater Company, 37

Kahn, Madeline, 77
Kaling, Mindy, 275
Kang, Sung, 273
Kasdan, Lawrence, 88
Kass, Sam Henry, 135
Kaufman, Philip, 183
Keach, Stacy, 270
Keaton, Michael, 124, 146, 252
Keener, Catherine, 84, 146
Keitel, Harvey, 92
Kennedy, Robert F., 111
Kenny G, 191
Kerouac, Jack, 5
Kesey, Ken, 24
Kill Bill: Vol. 2 (2004), 185–186, 239
King, Don, 264
King, Martin Luther, Jr., 21, 25–26,
    28, 282
King, Martin Luther, Sr., 29
King, Stephen, 205, 270
King Kong (movie), 274
Kingsman: The Secret Service (2015),
    255–256, *280*, 281
Kirby, Jack, 214, 235
Kirby, Luke, 246
Kiss of Death (1995), 121,
    131–132, 198
Kiss the Girls (movie), 211
Kite (2014), 254–255
Kitsch, Taylor, 227
Kleist, Heinrich von, 57
Kloor, Harry, 211–213
Knight, Wayne, 108
Kong: Skull Island (2017), *269*,
    274–275, 281, 292
Kotto, Yaphet, 239

Kranz, George, 59
Krog, Antjie, 184
Krystal commercial, 38
Kudrow, Lisa, 298
Kurtz, Swoosie, 76

LaBute, Neil, 222
Ladd, Diane, 296
Lakeview Terrace (2008), 222
LaMarr, Phil, 96–97, 214
Lancaster, Burt, 14
Landau, Martin, 120
Lange, Jessica, 130, 274
Lao Tzu, 224
LaPaglia, Anthony, 78
Larson, Brie, 275, 283, 290, 291–292
LaRue, Lash, 14
The Last Dragon (movie), 37
The Last Full Measure (2020), 296
Lathan, Stan, 59
Latifah, Queen, 145, 268
Laurie, Hugh, 5
Lawrence, Martin, 74
Lear, Norman, 282
Leary, Denis, 105
Lee, Bruce, 153
Lee, Christopher, 221
Lee, Joie, 78, 103
Lee, Malcolm D., 223
Lee, Spike
  Chi-Raq, 259–260
  Coming to America, 62–63
  Dickerson and, 99
  Do the Right Thing, 64, 65, 74–75, 79, 260
  Ganja & Hess, 76
  Jackson and, 47, 90, 127, 210, 281
  Jungle Fever, 70–71, 83–84, 89–90, 250
  Malcolm X, 90
  Mo' Better Blues, 78–79
  Oldboy, 250–251
  School Daze, 50, 61–62

"Summer Film Camp," 65
  use of "nigger," 126–127
Lee, Stan, 235
Legend, John, 224
The Legend of Tarzan (2016), 271–272
Leigh, Jennifer Jason, 242
Lemmons, Kasi, 142–143, 154, 166–167
Leonard, Elmore, 143, 146
Les Misérables (movie), 283
Lethal Weapon (movies), 73, 104–105
Levin, Gerald, 123
Levinson, Barry, 125–126, 145
Levy, Eugene, 197–198
Lewis, John, 3, 30
Lewis Lee, Tonya, 210
Life Itself (2018), 278–279
Liman, Doug, 218
Liotta, Ray, 81
Little, Cleavon, 37
Little Rock Nine, 5–6
Liu, Lucy, 226
"Living for the City" (Wonder), 83–84
LL Cool J, 160–161, 181, 268
Lloyd, Christopher, 177
Long, Nia, 227
The Long Kiss Goodnight (1996), *118*, 123, 138–139, 220, 252, 291
Loop, Jonah, 236
Lopez, Jennifer, 146
Lorre, Chuck, 92
Losing Isaiah (1995), 130–131
"Love Me Tender" (song), 186
A Love Supreme (Coltrane), 79
Lucas, George
  Christensen and, 218
  Jackson and, 151–152
  Star Wars: Episode I—The Phantom Menace (1999), 158–159, 176
  Star Wars: Episode II—Attack of the Clones (2002), 176–177
  Star Wars: Episode III—Revenge of the Sith (2005), 197

Lumet, Sidney, 172
lunch counter protest, 17–18
Lynch, David, 84

M*A*S*H (television series), 77
Ma Rainey's Black Bottom (Wilson), 50
Mac, Bernie, 223–224, 282
Mackie, Anthony, 297
MacLachlan, Kyle, 111
MacLaine, Shirley, 25
Madonna, 8
Madsen, Michael, 93, 94, 122, 261
Magic Sticks (1987), 59–60
Magnuson, Ann, 167
Mailer, Norman, 57
Malcolm X (movie), 90, 127
Malthus, Thomas, 277
The Man (2005), 197–198, 297
Man That Rocks the Cradle (proposed
    movie), 211
The Manchurian Candidate
    (movie), 111
Mandela, Nelson, 184
Manheim, Camryn, 183
Marathon Man (movie), 264
March of the Penguins (movie),
    202–203
Margolyes, Miriam, 91
Margulies, Julianna, 201
Marshall, E. G., 38
Martin, Strother, 236
Mastai, Elan, 246
Master of the Flying Guillotine
    (movie), 44
Mastrantonio, Mary Elizabeth, 100
The Matrix (movies), 211, 286
Mayfield, Curtis, 82, 186
McAvoy, James, 289
McCain, Franklin, 17
McCallany, Holt, 136
McCarthy, Cormac, 233
McConaughey, Matthew, 124, 136
McDiarmid, Ian, 196, 295

McGovern, Elizabeth, 57, 76
McGregor, Ewan, 158, 176, 177, 295
McIntyre, Samantha, 292
McKay, Adam, 233
McKellar, Don, 160
McTiernan, John, 132, 180
Mean Girls (movie), 258
Meara, Anne, 135
Meat Loaf, 178
Medeiros, Maria de, 116
Meeting Evil (2012), 245–246
Menace II Society (1993), 106–107, 128
Mendes, Eva, 220, 225
Merkerson, S. Epatha, 204
Merrill, Charles, 29
Michael Kohlhaas (Kleist), 57
Michell, Roger, 175, 190
The Mighty Gents (Wesley), 44
Mike D, 3
Millar, Mark, 215–216
Miller, Frank, 224–225
Minnelli, Liza, 155
Miss Peregrine's Home for Peculiar
    Children (2016), 272–273
Mnuchin, Steven, 272
Mo' Better Blues (1990), 67, 78–79
Mo' Money (movie), 119
Mob Justice (1991). See Dead and Alive:
    The Race for Gus Farace
The Mod Squad (television series), 28
Modine, Matthew, 133
Moehringer, J. R., 207
Mo'Nique, 203
Monkees, 182
Monner, Alex, 278–279
Montgomery, Edgar (grandfather),
    11–12, 16, 17, 21, 254
Montgomery, Edna (aunt), 14, 15,
    17, 34
Montgomery, Frances (aunt), 11
Montgomery, Pearl (grandmother),
    11–12, 16, 21, 26–27
Moonraker (movie), 37

Moore, Julianne, 198–199
Moore, Lucene, 35
Moore, Rudy Ray, 260
Moore, Sam, 282
Morehouse College
  admission to, 21
  Advisory Committee, 29–30
  block boys and, 21–23
  Concerned Students, 28–29, 34
  drug use, 24–25, 35
  expulsion from, 30
  graduation, 36
  Harkness Hall lock-in, 29
  King, Martin Luther, Jr., 21,
    26, 28
  majors, 22, 24, 28, 34
  readmission to, 33–34
  theater production, 27–28, 34–35
  Vietnam veterans, 23–24
Morehouse Spelman Players, 34
Morgan, Debbi, 142
Morgan, Tracy, 203
Morse, David, 148
Moss, Carrie-Anne, 232
Mother and Child (2010), 229–230
Mother Courage (Brecht), 45, 297, 300
motherfucker, Jackson's use of, 7–8,
    27, 191, 267
The Mountaintop (Hall), 282
Mulligan, Gerry, 5
Murphy, Eddie, 50, 60–61, 62–63
Murray, Bill, 2
My Cousin Vinny (movie), 88
My Father Is a Hero (movie), 170
Mya, 155

The Naked Gun (movies), 104
NASA, 211–212
National Lampoon's Loaded Weapon 1
    (1993), 92, 104–105
Neeson, Liam, 158–159, 295
Negga, Ruth, 247
The Negotiator (1998), 146, 147–148

Negro Ensemble Company, 36, 45,
    46, 51
Nelson, Ricky, 84
Nelson, Sean, 114
Nesbit, Evelyn, 57
Neville, Morgan, 282
The New Age (1994), 114–115
New Federal Theater, 42
New Heritage Repertory Theatre, 42
New Lafayette Theater, 42
"Newfangled Preacher Man"
    (song), 37
Nicholson, Jack, 182
Nick Fury: Agent of S.H.I.E.L.D.
    (television movie), 214–216, 219
Nielsen, Connie, 180
"nigger," use and impact of, 6, 12,
    19, 126–128
"Night Before Battle" (Hemingway), 3
Nimoy, Leonard, 249
"911 Is a Joke" (Public Enemy), 67–68
Nixon, Richard, 254
No Good Deed (2003), 182
"Nobody Gets Out Alive"
    (Jackson), 276
Nunn, Bill, 37, 50, 65, 74
Nutcracker Suite, 14
NYPD Blue (television series), 170

Obama, Barack and Michelle, 74
O'Connor, Flannery, 55
The Office (television series), 275
An Officer and a Gentleman (movie), 180
O'Hara, Catherine, 77
Ohio Tip-Off (Yoshimura), 45
Okun, Jeff, 161
Oldboy (2013), 210, 250–251
Oldman, Gary, 109, 252, 276
Olgiati, P. R. "Rudy," 18
Olivier, Laurence, 264
Olsen, Elizabeth, 250
On the Road (Kerouac), 5
One-Armed Swordsman (movie), 44

One Eight Seven (1997), 123,
140–142, 152
One Flew Over the Cuckoo's Nest
(Kesey), 24, 45
O'Neal, Ron, 82
100 Centre Street (television series), 172
Original Kings of Comedy (movie), 223
Oscar Awards (Academy Awards),
116, 120, 283, 293
The Other Guys (2010), 232–233
O'Toole, Peter, 46
Out of Sight (1998), 146–147
Oz, Frank, 176, 295

Pacific Flight 121. See Snakes on a Plane
Pacino, Al, 75
Padilha, José, 252
Page, Geraldine, 36
Paltrow, Gwyneth, 140, 219
The Paper Chase (television series), 56
Papp, Joseph, 38, 41, 42
Paquin, Anna, 120
Park, Ray, 158
Parker, Charlie "Bird," 6
Parris, Teyonah, 260
Party of Five (television series), 170
Patinkin, Mandy, 57, 278
Patriot Games (1992), 91, 101–102
Patton (movie), 260
Paulson, Sarah, 289
Pearce, Guy, 162
Peck, Gregory, 275
Peet, Amanda, 212
Pee-wee's Playhouse (television
series), 286
Peña, Michael, 249
People's Survival Theater, 37
Perez, Rosie, 74
Pesci, Joe, 77–78, 81, 191
Pfeiffer, Michelle, 123, 293
Phillips, Joseph C., 85
The Piano Lesson (Wilson), 50–51,
96, 283

Pine, Chris, 212
Pitsenbarger, William H., 296
Pitt, Brad, 84, 109, 228
The Pittsburgh Cycle (plays), 50
The Player (movie), 114
Plummer, Amanda, 3, 116
Plummer, Christopher, 296
Point Blank (movie), 266
Poitier, Sidney, 16, 46, 90, 190
Police Academy (movies), 104
Pollack, Sidney, 175–176
Pomeranc, Max, 133
Portman, Natalie, 177
The Poseidon Adventure (movie), 200
Powell, Colin, 215
The Practice (television series), 135
Presley, Brian, 202
Price, Richard, 75, 152, 153–154
Pride and Prejudice and Zombies
(Grahame-Smith), 270
The Protégé (movie), 54
Pryor, Richard, 4, 37
Public Theater, New York City, 38,
41, 42, 45
Pulp Fiction (1994), 3–4, 9, *87*, 94–96,
115–117, 119–120, 124, 126,
164, 179, 214, 238–239
references to in other movies, 135,
229, 235, 254, 278, 299
Purdee, Nathan, 82
Purlie (musical), 37
Purlie Victorious (Davis), 37

Quantum Quest: A Cassini Space Odyssey
(movie), 211–214
Questlove, 4, 285
Quinn, Anthony, 89
Quintano, Gene, 104

racism
in movie business, 66, 90, 116,
123–124, 136–137, 153–154,
167, 256

instituted as segregation in
    Chattanooga, 6, 12–13, 16–19, 189
in Los Angeles, 91, 119, 286
as overt theme in movies, 55, 56,
    57–59, 62, 74–75, 81, 83–84,
    105–106, 109, 110, 132–133, 136,
    180–181, 184, 222, 247–248,
    261–262, 271, 297, 298
in theater, 42, 43, 44, 46
Rafelson, Bob, 182
A Rage in Harlem (Himes), 282
Ragtime (1981), 45, 57–58
Rahman, Aishah, 41
A Raisin in the Sun (Hansberry), 210
Rand, Ayn, 187, 224
Rapaport, Michael, 160
Rare Exports (movie), 259
Rashad, Ahmad, 191
Rashad, Phylicia, 58–59
Rashomon (movie), 180
"Raspberry Beret" (Prince), 283
Ratzenberger, John, 57
Reasonable Doubt (2014), 251–252
The Red Violin (1999), 159–160, *168*, 252
Redford, Robert, 253, 254
Redstone, Sumner, 209
Reilly, John C., 140, 274
"Rescue Me" (Bass), 79
Reservoir Dogs (movie), 92, 93
Respect Yourself (documentary), 282
Resurrecting the Champ (2007),
    206–207, 265
The Return of Superfly (1990), 82
Reynolds, Kevin, 123
Reynolds, Ryan, 249, 275–276
Rhames, Ving, 116, 131, 146
Ribisi, Giovanni, 180
Ricci, Christina, 203–204
Richards, Denise, 105
Richards, Lloyd, 266
Richardson, LaTanya
    Atlanta performances, 35–36
    The Best Man, 38

biographical information,
    35, 44–45
Chinese Theater shoes, 283
as director, 283
The Fighting Temptations, 210
Frannie's Turn, 91–92
Freedomland, 199
Harkness Hall lock-in, 29
as Jackson's love interest, 35
on Jackson's personality, 125
Juice, 99
in Los Angeles, 91, 169–173,
    209–216
Losing Isaiah, 130–131
Mother and Child, 230
movie critique, 206
in New York, 41, 42
A Raisin in the Sun, 210
Richardson Jackson name
    usage, 283
Sam's drug rehab, 69
sanitation workers strike, 28
at Spelman College, 22–23,
    26–29, 34
The Talented Tenth, 68
The Watsons Go to Birmingham, 210
Ridley, Daisy, 295
The Right Stuff (movie), 202
Ringwald, Molly, 77–78
Rio (movie), 249
Rio Bravo (movie), 144
Ritchie, Guy, 179
Roach, Max, 5
Robbie, Margot, 271
Robinson, Jackie, 16
Robinson, Todd, 296
RoboCop (2014), 252–253, 286
Rock, Chris, 299
Rockefeller, Nelson, 112
Rockwell, Sam, 85, 135
Rocky (movies), 133, 202
Rodriguez, Michelle, 181, 249
Rodriguez, Robert, 224–225

Rogers, Roy, 14
Rollins, Howard E., Jr., 57
Root, Stephen, 232
Roots (television miniseries), 38
Roseanne (television series), 92
Ross, Diana, 46
Roth, Joe, 190, 198–199
Roth, Tim, 3, 89, 92–93, 102, 116, 120, 241, 260–262
Roundtree, Richard, 152, 163, 294
Rourke, Mickey, 90, 100, 231
Rowan, Kelly, 141
The Royal Tenenbaums (movie), 245
Rubin, Sam, 286
Rucker, Darius, 191
Rudin, Scott, 152, 153–154, 162, 283
Rudolph, Maya, 249
Rules of Engagement (2000), 150, 162–163, 190, 234
Rum Punch (Leonard), 143
Russell, Kurt, 261
RZA, 225, 227

Saget, Bob, 202–203
Salerno, Shane, 153
The Samaritan (2012), 246–247
sanitation workers strike, Memphis, 26
Santiago-Hudson, Ruben, 69
Sartre, Jean-Paul, 57
Satterfield, Bob, 206
Save the Cat! (Snyder), 197
Saw (movie), 205
Scacchi, Greta, 160
Schindler's List (movie), 107
School Daze (1988), 50, 61–62, 65, 75, 286
Schreiber, Liev, 145
Schroeder, Barbet, 131
Schultz, Michael, 37
Schumacher, Joel, 136
Sciorra, Annabella, 83
Scorsese, Martin, 81

Scott, George C., 79, 260
Scott, Gordon, 271
Scott, Tony, 94, 109
Scream Blacula Scream (1973), 76
Screen Actors Guild, 38
Sea Hunt (television series), 22
Sea of Love (1989), 66, 75, 198
The Search for One-Eye Jimmy (1996), 135–136
segregation, 6, 12–13, 16–19
Seinfeld (television series), 135
Sellers, Peter, 150
Sergeant Preston of the Yukon (radio series), 13
Sevigny, Chloë, 138
Sex, Lies and Videotape (movie), 93
Sgt. Fury and His Howling Commandos (comic book), 214
The Shadow (radio series), 13
Shaft (2000), 152–153, 163
Shaft (2019), 293–294
Shaft (movies), 152–153, 197, 198, 255
Shakespeare in the Park, 38
Shakur, Tupac, 99, 195
Shange, Ntozake, 41, 42, 45
Sharknado (movies), 200
Shatner, William, 212
Shaw, Robert, 161, 239
Sheedy, Ally, 78
Sheen, Charlie, 105
Sheen, Michael, 232
Sheindlin, Judith, 284–285
Shelton, Ron, 133
A Shock to the System (1990), 76
Shocklee, Hank, 99
Shore, Sig, 82
Showgirls (movie), 252
Shyamalan, M. Night, 164–165, 289
Sim, Dave, 224
Simon, Joe, 235
Simon Says (screenplay), 121
Sin City (movie), 224–225

Singleton, John, 152–154
Sirico, Tony, 135
Sisqó, 218
The Sixth Sense (movie), 164, 289
Skarsgård, Alexander, 271
Skarsgård, Stellan, 182
Skylanders (video game), 213
Slater, Christian, 109, 212
SLJ Factor, defined, 54
Smith, Liz, 90
Smith, Will, 240
Smollett, Jurnee, 142
Snakes on a Plane (2006), *32*,
    200–201, 204, 255
Snipes, Wesley, 44, 83, 89, 169, 283
Snoop Dogg, 249
So Fine (movie), 59
Soderbergh, Steven, 93, 146
A Soldier's Play (Fuller), 46–47, 51, 69
A Soldier's Story (movie), 47
"Something in a Box"
    (improvisation), 36
Something Wild (movie), 106
The Sopranos (television series),
    86, 135
"Soul Man" (Sam & Dave), 282
Soul Men (2008), 223–224, 282
Spacey, Kevin, 136, 147–148
Spell #7 (Shange), 42, 43
Spelling, Aaron, 181
Spelman College, 22–23, 26–29, 34
Spencer, Octavia, 181
Spenser: For Hire (television series), 49
Sphere (1998), 125–126, *129*, 145–146
Spider-Man: Far from Home (2019),
    216, 294–295
Spielberg, Steven, 59, 92, 107–108
Spiral: From the Book of Saw
    (2021), 299
The Spirit (2008), 224–225
Split (movie), 289–290
St. Elsewhere (television series), 50
St. Pierre, Daniel, 212–214

Stallone, Sylvester, 148
Stamp, Terence, 159
Stan, Sebastian, 296
Stanton, Harry Dean, 111
Star Trek: Deep Space Nine (television
    series), 42
Star Trek: Voyager (television
    series), 211
Star Wars: The Clone Wars (2008), 221
*Star Wars: Episode I—The Phantom
    Menace* (1999), 158–159, 176
*Star Wars: Episode II—Attack of the
    Clones* (2002), *149*, 176–177
*Star Wars: Episode III—Revenge of the
    Sith* (2005), 196–197
*Star Wars: Episode IV—A New
    Hope*, 151
*Star Wars: Episode IX—The Rise of
    Skywalker* (2019), 295–296
Star Wars (movies), 151–152, 218,
    265, 295
Starship Troopers (movie), 252
Statler Brothers, 133
Steinfeld, Hailee, 257
Steranko, Jim, 214, 215
Stevenson, Robert Louis, 264
Stewart, Kristen, 218
Stiles, Julia, 227
Stoltz, Eric, 133
Stone, Sharon, 126, 145
Stowe, Harriet Beecher, 58
Stranger Than Paradise (movie), 84
Strathairn, David, 183
Streep, Meryl, 283
The Street Fighter (movie), 238
Strictly Business (1991), 85
Student Nonviolent Coordinating
    Committee (SNCC), 18, 30
Sturges, Preston, 105
Styles, Harry, 4
Sugar Hill (movie), 76
Sullivan's Travels (movie), 105
Sundance Film Festival, 93

The Sunset Limited (2011), 233–234
Super Fly (movie), 82, 265
Super Fly T.N.T. (movie), 82
Sutherland, Donald, 136
Svenson, Bo, 186
S.W.A.T. (2003), 180–181
S.W.A.T. (television series), 181
Sweet Sweetback's Baadasssss Song
(movie), 293

Tales of Manhattan (movie), 159
Tarantino, Quentin
childhood, 238
Django Unchained, 247–248
The Hateful Eight, 260–262
Inglourious Basterds, 227–228
Jackie Brown, 143–145
Jackson and, 124, 125, 126, 225,
238–242, 273
Kill Bill: Vol. 2, 185–186
personality, 126–127
Pulp Fiction, 115–117, 119–120,
179–180
Reservoir Dogs, 92, 93–96
True Romance, 109
Tatum, Channing, 195
Taylor, Elizabeth, 36, 38, 47, 155
Taylor, James, 33
The Texas Chainsaw Massacre
(movie), 150
Thaw, Harry, 57
Theron, Charlize, 184
The Thing (movie), 242
This Is Spinal Tap (movie), 133
This Is Us (television show), 278
Thomas, Rufus, 186
Thompson, Kenan, 201
Thompson, Robert Farris, 4–5
"Thong Song" (Sisqó), 218
Thor (2011), 234–235
Thor: Ragnarok (movie), 234
Thornhill, Claude, 5
Thornley, Wayne, 249

Three Days of the Condor (movie), 254
The Threepenny Opera (musical), 27
Thurman, Uma, 116, 185
Tierney, Maura, 100
Timberlake, Justin, 191, 204
Time Out of Mind (Dylan), 278
A Time to Kill (1996), 124,
136–137, 147
Tin Cup (movie), 133
"To Be a Black Man" (George), 122
Today Show (television series), 169
Together for Days (movie), 37–38
Tolkin, Michael, 114
Tom, Lauren, 60
Tomei, Marisa, 292
Tommila, Onni, 259
Top Secret! (movie), 104
Total Recall (movie), 252
The Towering Inferno (movie), 200
Trainspotting (movie), 179
Travis, Nancy, 133
Travolta, John, 94, 96, 116, 120, 124,
179–180, 212
Trees Lounge (1996), 137–138
The Trial of the Moke (1978), 43,
56, 110
Troma Films, 77
Truck 44 (proposed movie), 211
Truck Turner (movie), 239
True Romance (1993), 94, 109
Trump, Donald, 84, 163, 272,
286–287
Trump, Eric, 163
Tubman, Harriet, 142
Tucci, Stanley, 131
Tucker, Chris, 128, 144
Tucker, Samuel J., 29–30
Turbo (2013), 247, 249–250
Turner, Ike, 92
Turner, Tina, 8
Turturro, Aida, 160
Turturro, John, 74, 78, 88, 135
Turturro, Nicholas, 78

Twain, Mark, 112
Twenty Bucks (movie), 159
20,000 Leagues Under the Sea (Verne), 22, 145
Twilight (movie), 218
The Twilight Zone (television series), 169
Twisted (2004), 183
Two and a Half Men (television series), 92
Two Trains Running (Wilson), 69, 91
2001: A Space Odyssey (movie), 145
Tyson, Cicely, 36, 37
Tyson, Mike, 256

The Umbrella Academy (comic books and television series), 272
Unbreakable (2000), *20*, 164–165, 264, 289–290
Uncle Tom's Cabin (1987), 58–59
Unfinished Women Cry in No Man's Land While a Bird Dies in a Gilded Cage (Rahman), 41
Unforgivable Blackness (movie), 282
Unicorn Store (2019), 291–292
University Homes (Atlanta), 21–23
Unthinkable (2010), 231–232
Urich, Robert, 49
Usher, 155
Usher, Jessie, 293
Ustinov, Peter, 25
The Usual Suspects (movie), 147

Valentino, Venessia, 126
Van Peebles, Melvin, 36, 293
Vance, Danitra, 102
Vaughn, Matthew, 256
Vega, Paz, 225
VelJohnson, Reginald, 60
Verhoeven, Paul, 252
Verne, Jules, 22
Vidal, Gore, 38
Videodrome (movie), 77
Vietnam War, 23–24, 33

Wahlberg, Mark, 232
Waititi, Taika, 162, 234
Walken, Christopher, 109
Walker, Alice, 59
The Walking Dead (television series), 270
Walsh, J. T., 148
Walsh, M. Emmet, 101
Waltz, Christoph, 228, 248
Ward, Douglas Turner, 51, 266
Washington, Denzel, 44, 46–47, 50, 90, 121, 170, 209, 210
Washington, Kerry, 222, 230, 248
Washington, Pauletta, 170, 209
Waterston, Sam, 110
Waterworld (movie), 121, 123
The Watsons Go to Birmingham (television movie), 210
Watts, Naomi, 230
Wayans, Damon, 119, 133
Wayne, John, 150
Weaver, David, 246
Webb, James, 162
Weekend at Bernie's (movie), 59
Weinstein, Bob, 95
Weinstein, Harvey, 95, 185
Weissmuller, Johnny, 271
Weller, Peter, 114
Wesley, Richard, 68
West Side Story (musical and movie), 99
Whaley, Frank, 96
What's Love Got to Do with It (movie), 92
Whedon, Joss, 244, 257
Whitaker, Forest, 121
Whitcraft, Elizabeth, 81
White, Stanford, 57
White Sands (1992), 90–91, 100–101, 123, 127
The White Shadow (television series), 194
Whitford, Bradley, 292

Whittaker, Johnson, 56, 110

Wilcox, Larry, 105

Wilde, Olivia, 278–279

Williams, Billy Dee, 272

Williams, Clarence, III, 28

Williams, Cynda, 78

Williams, George Washington, 271

Williams, Michael K., 252

Williams, Vanessa, 163

Willis, Bruce, 15, 60, 105, 116, 124, 132–133, 164–165, 289

Wilson, August, 50, 51, 69, 91, 239, 283

Wilson, Flip, 291

Wilson, Luke, 245–246

Wilson, Patrick, 222

Wilson, Rebel, 292

Winkler, Henry, 4

Winkler, Irwin, 202

The Wire (television series), 198

Witney, William, 238

Wolfe, George C., 211

Wonder, Stevie, 83–84, 89, 285

Woodard, Alfre, 44, 50, 56

Woodard, Charlayne, 289

Woods, Tiger, 191–192, 256

Woolworth's, Greensboro, North Carolina, 17–18

World War Z (movie), 270

Worth, Irene, 55

Wright, Jeffrey, 89, 102, 163

Wright, Robin, 165

Wyatt Earp (movie), 94

Wyler, William, 201

XXX (2002), 177–178

XXX: Return of Xander Cage (2017), 273–274

XXX: State of the Union (2005), 195–196, 302

Yakin, Boaz, 113

The Yellow Rolls-Royce (movie), 159

Yen, Donnie, 274

Young, Burt, 78

Young, Lester, 2–3, 5

Yu, Ronny, 179

Zahn, Steve, 146

Zeller, Steve, 46

Ziman, Ralph, 255

Zootopia (movie), 249